W9-BVO-301

CLÉOMÈDE
TIBULLE
MUSA
NICOLAS DAMASCÈNE
TROGUE POMPÉE
POLLION
ALBINOVANUS
VIRGILE
LABEO
MÉCÈNE
HORACE
HYGIN
HILLEL LE SAINT
PROPERCE
STRABON
PHILON-LE-JUIF
DENIS D'ALICARNASSE
VERRIUS FLACCUS
OVIDE
TITE-LIVE
GERMANICUS
DENYS DE CHARAX
SENEQUE LE TRAGIQUE
ONOSANDER
PHEDRE
ONKELOS
COLUMELLE
PERSE
ST MATTHIEU
PALÆMON
P. MELA
ASCONIUS
CORNELIUS SEVERUS
PUBLIUS SYRUS
MANILIUS
VALERE-MAXIME
V. PATERCULUS
CELSE
LUCAIN
PETRONE
ST PAUL

HENRI LABROUSTE

HENRI LABROUSTE

STRUCTURE BROUGHT TO LIGHT

Corinne BÉLIER, Barry BERGDOLL, and Marc LE CŒUR

With essays by Martin Bressani, Marc Grignon,
Marie-Hélène de La Mure, Neil Levine,
Bertrand Lemoine, Sigrid de Jong,
David Van Zanten, and Gérard Uniack

The Museum of Modern Art, New York

In association with the Cité de l'architecture et du patrimoine and the Bibliothèque nationale de France,
with the special participation of the Académie d'architecture and the Bibliothèque Sainte-Geneviève.

HENRI LABROUSTE

STRUCTURE BROUGHT TO LIGHT

AN EXHIBITION ORGANIZED BY THE MUSEUM OF MODERN ART, THE CITÉ DE L'ARCHITECTURE & DU PATRIMOINE, AND THE BIBLIOTHÈQUE NATIONALE DE FRANCE.

With the generous participation of the Académie d'Architecture and the Bibliothèque Sainte-Geneviève.

• Glenn D. Lowry, *Director, The Museum of Modern Art*

• Luc Lièvre, *Managing Director and interim President, Cité de l'Architecture & du Patrimoine*

• Bruno Racine, *President of the Bibliothèque Nationale de France*

CURATORS

• Barry Bergdoll, *The Philip Johnson Chief Curator of Architecture and Design, The Museum of Modern Art*

• Corinne Bélier, *Chief Curator, Musée des Monuments Français, Cité de l'Architecture & du Patrimoine*

• Marc Le Cœur, *Art Historian, Research Associate, Architecture Collections of the Department of Prints and Photography, Bibliothèque Nationale de France*

• *With the collaboration of* Emilie Regnault, *Assistant Curator, Cité de l'Architecture & du Patrimoine*

ASSISTANTS

• Margot Weller, *Curatorial Assistant, The Museum of Modern Art*
• Stéphanie Guilmeau-Shala, *Cité de l'Architecture & du Patrimoine*

THE MUSEUM OF MODERN ART

- Glenn D. Lowry, *Director*
- Kathy Halbreich, *Associate Director*
- Klaus Biesenbach, *Director of MoMA PS1*
- Jan Postma, *Chief Financial Officer*
- James Gara, *Chief Operating Officer*
- Patty Lipshutz, *General Counsel and Secretary to the Board of Trustees*
- Nancy Adelson, *Deputy General Counsel*
- Ramona Bannayan, *Senior Deputy Director, Exhibitions and Collections*
- Peter Reed, *Senior Deputy Director, Curatorial Affairs*
- Erika Mosier, *Conservator, Conservation Department*
- Todd Bishop, *Senior Deputy Director, External Affairs*
- Heidi Speckhart, *Officer, Development Office*
- Lauren Stakias, *Associate Director, Exhibition and International Fundraising*
- Rebecca Stokes, *Director, Digital Marketing Communications*
- Jason Persse, *Editorial Manager, Marketing*
- Jennifer Wolfe, *Associate Registrar, Collections Management*
- Jeri Moxley, *Manager, Collection and Exhibition Technology*
- David Hart, *Associate Media Producer, Audiovisual Support*
- Tunji Adeniji, *Director, Facilities and Safety Department*

EXHIBITION ADMINISTRATION DEPARTMENT

- Maria DeMarco Beardsley, *Coordinator of Exhibitions*
- Carlos Yepes, *Associate Coordinator of Exhibitions*

EXHIBITION DESIGN AND PRODUCTION DEPARTMENT

- Jerome Neuner, *Director*
- David Hollely, *Production Manager*

EXHIBITION DESIGN AND PRODUCTION TEAM

- Peter Perez, *Foreman, Frame Shop*

DEPARTMENT OF PUBLICATIONS

- Christopher Hudson, *Publisher*
- Charles Kim, *Associate Publisher*
- David Frankel, *Editorial Director*
- Marc Sapir, *Production Director*
- Hannah Kim, *Marketing Coordinator*
- Rebecca Roberts, *Associate Editor*

GRAPHIC DESIGN DEPARTMENT

- Julia Hoffmann, *Creative Director, Advertising and Graphic Design*
- Samuel Sherman, *Design Manager, Graphic Design*

DIGITAL MEDIA DEPARTMENT

- Allegra Burnette, *Creative Director*
- David Hart, *Associate Media Producer*
- Maggie Lederer, *Senior Producer*

COLLECTION MANAGEMENT AND EXHIBITION REGISTRATION

- Stefanii Ruta Atkins, *Head Registrar*
- Jennifer Wolfe, *Associate Registrar*
- Rob Jung, *Manager, Art Handling and Preparation*
- Sarah Wood, *Assistant Manager, Art Handling and Preparation*

COMMUNICATIONS DEPARTMENT

- Kim Mitchell, *Chief Communications Officer*
- Margaret Doyle, *Director of Communications*
- Paul Jackson, *Senior Publicist*

INFORMATION TECHNOLOGY DEPARTMENT

- Aaron Louis, *Audio Visual Director*
- Charlie Kalinowski, *Audio Visual Manager*
- Howard Deitch, Mike Gibbons, Lucas Gonzalez, and Bjorn Quenemoen, *Technicians*

EDUCATION DEPARTMENT

- Wendy Woon, *Deputy Director for Education*
- Pablo Helguera, *Director, Adult and Academic Education*
- Sara Bodinson, *Director, Interpretation and Research*
- Laura Beiles Coppola, *Assistant Director, Adult Programs*
- Stephanie Pau, *Associate Educator*

ARCHITECTURE AND DESIGN DEPARTMENT

- Colin Hartness, *Assistant to Chief Curator*
- Emma Presler, *Department Manager*
- Margot Weller, *Curatorial Assistant*
- Patricio del Real, *Curatorial Assistant*
- Camille Bédard, Esra Eczacibasi, Lily Wong, and Marissa Zhong, *Interns*

CITÉ DE L'ARCHITECTURE & DU PATRIMOINE

- Luc Lièvre, *Managing Director and Interim President*
- Laurence de Finance, *Director of the Musée des Monuments Français*

PRODUCTION AND COORDINATION (MUSÉE DES MONUMENTS FRANÇAIS)

- Estelle Tessier, *Production Manager*
- Maëlle Viard, *Production Manager*

PRODUCTION CONSULTANT

- Myriam Feuchot (IFA), *Production Department Director*

COLLECTIONS MANAGEMENT

- Hélène Perrel, *Collections Management Director*
- Laetitia Antonini, *Deputy Collections Manager*
- Aélys Josseran, *Collections Management Assistant*

TWENTIETH CENTURY ARCHITECTURE ARCHIVES

- David Peycéré, *Head Curator, Archives Center Director*

IMAGE RESEARCH

- Marielle Blanc, *Image Researcher*

AUDIO VISUAL SUPPORT

- Aude Mathé, *Audiovisual and Photography Project Manager*
- Julien Borel, *Audiovisual Project Manager*

MULTIMEDIA SUPPORT

- Philippe Rivière, *Information Systems Director*
- Jérôme Richard, *Web and Multimedia Project Manager*

MULTIMEDIA PRODUCTION

- Opixido and Mazedia

TRANSLATORS AND PROOFREADING

- Florence Allorent, *Assistant Curator, Proofreading*
- Edith Ochs, *Translator*
- Eileen Powis, *Translator*

MODELS

- Sylvain le Stum, *Architect*
- Angel Garcia, *Model Maker*
- Thierry Martin, *Model Maker*

COMMUNICATIONS DEPARTMENT

- David Madec, *Director*

DEVELOPMENT AND SPONSORSHIP DEPARTMENT

- Guillaume de la Broïse, *Director*

BIBLIOTHÈQUE NATIONALE DE FRANCE

- Bruno Racine, *President*
- Jacqueline Sanson, *Managing Director*

COLLECTIONS DIRECTOR

- Denis Bruckmann, *Collections Director*

DEPARTMENT OF PRINTS AND PHOTOGRAPHY

- Sylvie Aubenas, *Director*
- Corinne Le Bitouzé, *Assistant to the Director*
- Loïc Le Bail, *Head of the Preservation Department*
- Marie-Hélène Petitfour, *Curator in Charge of Loans*
- Caroline Bruyant-Martin, *Framing Director*
- Jude Talbot, *Digitization*

AUDIOVISUAL DEPARTMENT

- Isabelle Giannattasio, *Director*
- Alain Carou, *Image Department Director*
- Anne-Claire Rebours, *Audiovisual Department Lawyer*

CULTURAL AWARENESS GROUP

- Thierry Grillet, *Director*

EXHIBITION DEPARTMENT

- Ariane James-Sarazin, *Department Director*
- Cécile Pocheau-Lesteven, *Curator, Director of External Exhibition Projects*
- Brigitte Robin-Loiseau, Cyrielle Martin, Béatrice Tisserand, and Chiara Pagliettini, *Department of Loans for External Exhibitions*

COMMUNICATIONS DEPARTMENT

- Marc Rassat, *Director*
- Françoise Guillermo, *Assistant Director*
- Claudine Hermabessière, *Assistant Director Press and Media Partnerships Department Director*
- Isabelle Kermet, *Coordinator of Filming*

SERVICES AND NETWORKS MANAGEMENT, PRESERVATION DEPARTMENT

- Annie Bonnaud, *Director of the Centre Joël-Le-Theule (Sablé-sur-Sarthe) and its staff*

ARCHIVES

- Aurélien Conraux, *Head of the Mission to Manage Document Production and Archives*

CATALOGUE

Book published by Éditions Nicolas Chaudun in coproduction with the Cité de l'Architecture & du Patrimoine, The Museum of Modern Art, and the Bibliothèque Nationale de France

EDITIONS NICOLAS CHAUDUN

- Nicolas Chaudun, *Director*
- Aurore de Neuville, *Editor*

THE MUSEUM OF MODERN ART

- Christopher Hudson, *Publisher*
- Charles Kim, *Associate Publisher*
- David Frankel, *Editorial Director*
- Marc Sapir, *Production Director*

EDITOR OF ENGLISH EDITION

- Ron Broadhurst

TRANSLATION

- Sharon Bowman

CITÉ DE L'ARCHITECTURE & DU PATRIMOINE

- Laurence de Finance, *Director of the Musée des Monuments Français*
- Emilie Regnault, *Assistant Curator, Project Coordinator for the French edition*
- Florence Allorent, *Assistant Curator, Proofreading*
- Stéphanie Guilmeau-Shala, *Editorial Assistant*
- Marielle Blanc, *Image Researcher*

BIBLIOTHÈQUE NATIONALE DE FRANCE

- Jocelyn Rigault, *Editorial and Sales Department Director*
- Pierrette Crouzet-Daurat, *Publications Department Director*
- Christophe Stoop, *Sales Department Director*
- Caterina D'Agostino, *Image Researcher*

The Cité de l'Architecture & du Patrimoine, The Museum of Modern Art, and the

Bibliothèque Nationale de France would like to thank the following institutions for their loans:

ACADÉMIE D'ARCHITECTURE, PARIS

- Thierry Van de Wyngaert, *President*
- Paul Quintrand, *Curator-Archivist*
- Marilena Kourniati, *Archive Manager*

ACADÉMIE DE FRANCE, ROME

- Eric de Chassey, *Director*

ARCHIVES NATIONALES, PARIS

- Agnès Magnien, *Director*
- Nadine Gastaldi, *Chief Curator, Maps, Drawings, and Photographs Department*
- Jean-Charles Cappronnier, *Archivist, Maps, Drawings, and Photographs Department*

AVERY ARCHITECTURAL & FINE ARTS LIBRARY, COLUMBIA UNIVERSITY, NEW YORK

- Carole Ann Fabian, *Director*
- Janet Parks, *Curator of Drawings and Archives*
- Carolyn Yerkes, *Curator of Avery Classics*

BIBLIOTHÈQUE SAINTE-GENEVIÈVE, PARIS

- Yves Peyré, *Director*
- Florence Leleu, *Assistant to the Director*
- Marie-Hélène de La Mure, *Curator of Rare Books and Manuscripts*
- Priscille Leroy, *Public Relations and Affairs*

ÉCOLE NATIONALE SUPÉRIEURE DES BEAUX-ARTS, PARIS

- Nicolas Bourriaud, *Director*
- Bruno Girveau, *Head of the Department of Research and Cultural Development*
- Marie-Hélène Colas-Adler, *Architectural Drawings Collections Manager*

MÉDIATHÈQUE DE L'ARCHITECTURE ET DU PATRIMOINE, CHARENTON-LE-PONT

- Jean-Daniel Pariset, *Director*
- Robert Haroutinian, *Map Librarian*

MUSÉE CARNAVALET, PARIS

- Jean-Marc Léri, *Director*
- Françoise Reynaud, *Curator of the Photograph Collections*

MUSÉE DES ARTS ET MÉTIERS CNAM, PARIS

- Serge Chambaud, *Director of the Musée des Arts et Métiers*
- Pierre-Yves Gagnier, *Head of the Heritage and Preservation Department*
- Olivier Delarozière, *Curator, Architecture and Construction Collection*

MUSÉE D'ORSAY, PARIS

- Guy Cogeval, *President*
- Caroline Mathieu, *Chief Curator, Architecture*
- Alice Thomine-Berrada, *Curator, Architecture*

MUSÉUM NATIONAL D'HISTOIRE NATURELLE, PARIS

- Thomas Grenon, *Managing Director*
- Michelle Lenoir, *Libraries and Documentation Director*
- Alice Lemaire, *Curator*

NATIONAL GALLERY OF ART, WASHINGTON, D.C.

- Earl A. Powell III, *Director*
- Andrew Robison, *A.W. Mellon Senior Curator of Prints and Drawings*
- Margaret Morgan Grasselli, *Curator of Old Master Drawings*

INSTITUT NATIONAL D'HISTOIRE DE L'ART, PARIS

- Antoinette Le Normand-Romain, *Managing Director*
- Martine Poulain, *Library and Documentation Department Director*

NEDERLANDS ARCHITECTUURINSTITUUT, ROTTERDAM, NETHERLANDS

• Ole Bouman, *Director*

RIJKSDIENST VOOR HET CULTUREEL ERFGOED (CULTURAL HERITAGE AGENCY), AMERSFOORT, NETHERLANDS

• Cees van 't Veen, *Director*
• Peter Don, *Curator of Photographs, Prints and Drawings*

The organizers would also like to thank, for photographs and films:

La Commission du Vieux Paris (Paris), The New York Public Library (NewYork), Library of Congress (Washington, D.C.), Jean-Christophe Ballot, David Paul Carr, Georges Fessy, Candida Höfer, Alain Le Toquin, Bérangère Lomont, Jean-Claude N'Diaye, Michel Nguyen, Le Conseil Economique, Social et Environnemental; Richard Copans and Stan Neumann, directors of the Collection "Architectures" (Les Films d'Ici); Alain Esméry, Production Director at the Forum des Images; Sylvie Lerat, Communications Director at the Opérateur du Patrimoine et des Projets Immobiliers de la Culture (OPPIC); Jean-François Roudot, filmmaker

The curators would like to give special thanks to those who helped them in designing and preparing the exhibition and catalogue:

Joseph Abram, Claire Alonso, Mathieu Angebault, Patrick Berger, François Boursin, Barbara Brejon de Lavergnée, Martin Bressani, David Descatoire, Fabienne Doulat, Patrick Droulers, Jean-Philippe Garric, Sébastien Gaudelus, Françoise Hamon, Anne-Sophie Haquin, Edward Houle, Claude Jean, Sigrid de Jong, Suzanne Labrouste, Patrick Lamotte, Marie-Hélène de La Mure, Marie de Laubier, Bertrand Lemoine, Séverine Lepape, Neil Levine, Olivier Liardet, Isabelle Loutrel, François Loyer, Robin Middleton, Dominique Perrault, Andrée Rigaux, Philippe Rouillard, Luis Sazatornil Ruiz, Jean-Michel Scharr, Barbara Shapiro Comte, Françoise Simon, Guillemette Simon, Valérie Sueur-Hermel, Marie-Claude Thompson, Gérard Uniack, John Wienk, and David Van Zanten

And for their welcoming reception on the BNF worksite and generous availability:

François Autier, Project Manager at the Opérateur du Patrimoine et des Projets Immobiliers de la Culture (OPPIC); Bruno Gaudin and Virginie Brégal, architects; Jean-François Lagneau, Heritage Architect; and Patrice Girard, architect

Finally, the curators would like to express their most special thanks to Alice Thomine-Berrada and Monique Malcotte.

DROIT
DROIT

CATALOGUE GENERAL
HISTOIRE GENERALE

FOREWORD

This exhibition, the first the Cité de l'Architecture et du Patrimoine has devoted to a nineteenth-century architect, is part of a larger series of monographs dedicated to renowned architects, from Jacques Androuet du Cerceau to Claude Parent and Christian de Portzamparc.

Presenting Henri Labrouste at the Cité de l'Architecture et du Patrimoine carries with it its very own significance, given that his name and ideas crossed paths with our institution's history, and his works are a testament to the values he defended. In 1858, he even sketched out a plan for reconstructing the Ecole Polytechnique on Chaillot hill, though it would never be followed through. He is one of the fathers of a rationalist culture that would long permeate French architecture, from the classics to the moderns, of which the Musée de Sculpture Comparée was one of the bastions. That museum, founded by Viollet-le-Duc, who never hid his admiration for Labrouste, is the source of the collection of casts held by the Cité de l'Architecture et du Patrimoine. It was also there that one of Labrouste's students, Anatole de Baudot, would in 1887 create the first chair of the History of Architecture of the Middle Ages and Renaissance, now known by the name Ecole de Chaillot.

Labrouste deeply marked French architecture. He is one of those creators whose thought and built works fed the critical debate necessary to any evolution. His fourth-year submission, the restoration of Paestum, shook up academic dogma and opened a new field of references from which to draw. The Romantic architects, of which Labrouste was one of the leaders, would make history and context essential components in an architectural project, an approach that is still relevant today. Labrouste's two libraries offer a completely new vision of architecture, of its language and construction, echoing the aspirations of his day. The structure and light of their inner spaces make those buildings not simple shelters but true worlds into which library-goers are plunged. They remind us just how much places of culture and learning have a particular force and how much their architecture is a reflection of shared values. More than a simple precursor to modernity, Labrouste was an ingenious figure of his times, and the exhibition's curators have aimed to show the full richness and complexity of his art.

Here, I would like to give special thanks to the Museum of Modern Art in New York, as well as to the Bibliothèque Nationale de France, for a fruitful collaboration in working on this exhibition and catalogue. I would also like to thank the Académie d'Architecture and the Bibliothèque Sainte-Geneviève for their support and loans, without which this exhibition could not have met its goals, and lastly, thanks to the Compagnie de Saint-Gobain, which has supported this project.

François de Mazières
President of the Cité de l'Architecture et du Patrimoine
Paris, July 2, 2012

Since its foundation eighty years ago, MoMA's Department of Architecture (today the Department of Architecture and Design) has shared the Museum's linked missions of showcasing cutting-edge artistic work in all media and exploring the longer prehistory of the artistic present. In 1932, for instance, no sooner had Philip Johnson, Henry-Russell Hitchcock, and Alfred H. Barr, Jr., installed the Department's legendary inaugural show, *Modern Architecture: International Exhibition*, than plans were afoot for a show the following year on the commercial architecture of late-nineteenth-century Chicago, intended as the first in a series of shows tracing key episodes in the development of modern architecture over the previous two centuries. Henri Labrouste's two seminal Paris libraries were of keen interest to Hitchcock in particular, not least for the way their frank expression of new materials—iron, and gas for light—created unprecedented urban and communal spaces. These two great reading rooms have been continuously admired since they opened, in 1850 and 1868 respectively, but it would not be until 1975, exactly a century after Labrouste's death, that his architecture would be displayed at The Museum of Modern Art, and then at a time when the modern movement itself was increasingly being challenged. If many were bewildered, even scandalized, by Arthur Drexler's puzzling manifesto exhibition *The Architecture of the Ecole des Beaux-Arts*, in 1977, the accompanying book's scholarship marked a major renewal of the study of nineteenth-century French architecture, and of one of that period's most original and uncompromising creators. As the curators of the present exhibition note, Labrouste's work and reputation were launched in the very ambience in which the concept of the artistic avant-garde itself was formed. Nothing could be more appropriate, either in Paris or at New York's Museum of Modern Art, than to take a fresh look at this figure, who began his career by reinterpreting the very fundamentals of then current architectural practice.

Henri Labrouste: Structure Brought to Light is the condensed result of several years of research, initially involving the participation of many in Paris and now brought to fruition under the expert guidance of Barry Bergdoll, MoMA's Philip Johnson Chief Curator of Architecture and Design, and his colleagues Corinne Bélier, of the Cité de l'Architecture et du Patrimoine, and Marc Le Cœur, of the Bibliothèque Nationale de France. I extend to them my appreciation for the quality of their scholarship and the originality of their interpretation of Labrouste's legacy, both historiographically and in contemporary terms. At the Museum we extend thanks also to Margot Weller and Patricio del Real, Curatorial Assistants in the Department of Architecture and Design, and Ron Broadhurst, the editor of the English-language edition of this book. We are especially pleased to be associated in this project with the Cité de l'Architecture et du Patrimoine, which has staged the show in Paris and is a natural ally for us in our shared dedication to both shedding fresh light on history and examining the stakes of the architecture of our own complex time.

Glenn D. Lowry
Director, The Museum of Modern Art

"Henri Labrouste is without a doubt the mid-nineteenth-century architect whose work was the most important for the future."

—Sigfried Giedion, 1941

To house its collections, the Bibliothèque Nationale de France is fortunate enough to possess a set of buildings that illustrate the history of French architecture from the seventeenth to the twentieth century. Between François Mansart and Dominique Perrault, Henri Labrouste's position is first in a line of eminent builders. As Julien Cain put it, his name "is indissolubly linked to the history of the Bibliothèque Nationale" to such an extent that it is now common practice to designate by his name the famous reading room he erected at the heart of the quadrilateral on the Rue de Richelieu—an emblematic space which many library users regretfully left in 1998, when the collections in its former Printed Matter Department were transferred to the new François Mitterrand site.

In 1902, the Bibliothèque Nationale had placed a bust of Labrouste at the entrance to that mythic room. Later, in 1953, it would organize the first exhibition entirely devoted to his work. Nearly sixty years later, we are pleased to be a part of this new and worthy tribute, in collaboration with Paris's Cité de l'Architecture et du Patrimoine and the Museum of Modern Art in New York.

It is important to underscore the generosity of Yvonne Labrouste, Geneviève-Caroline Labrouste, and Monique Malcotte, who successively donated many of their ancestor's archives. Those inestimable documents, of which many are presented in this book, have enriched the important collection of architects' drawings held by the Prints and Photography Department. In preparation for the exhibition, they were categorized, catalogued, restored, and digitized so that they could be viewed online.

The buildings raised by Labrouste for the Bibliothèque Nationale are themselves currently undergoing renovation, a process overseen by architect Bruno Gaudin and the head architect at Les Monuments Historiques, Jean-François Lagneau. The "Labrouste room," soon to be used by the library of the Institut National d'Histoire de l'Art (INHA), will once again open its doors in 2014 after regaining its original luster and clarity. As for the central stacks—so innovative in their day—they will be made accessible to library users themselves for the very first time. Until then, this exhibition is an invitation to rediscover the work of Labrouste, an extraordinary combination of Greco-Roman-imbued classical tradition and industrial modernity.

Bruno Racine

President of the Bibliothèque Nationale de France

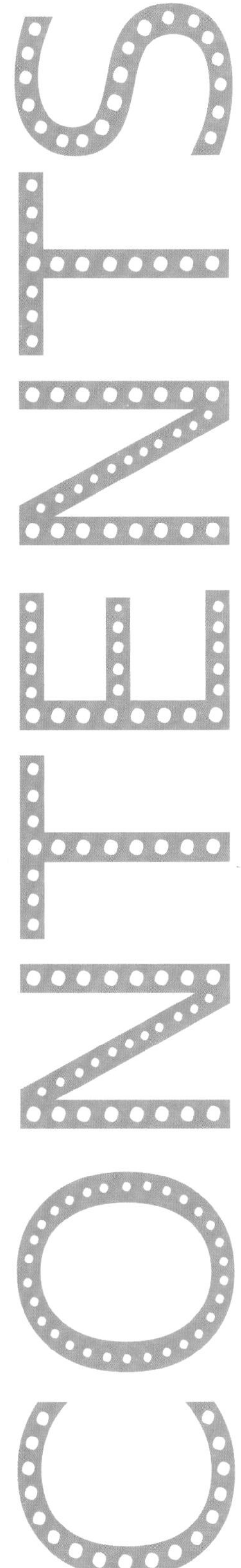
CONTENTS

Generations of writers and eminent intellectuals have worked beneath the domes of the Bibliothèque Nationale; generations of students have succeeded each other beneath the barrel vaults of the Bibliothèque Sainte-Geneviève. Those two reading rooms, which are among the most beautiful spaces in Paris, are the source of Henri Labrouste's fame as an architect. Their powerful expressiveness, the rational solutions that the architect implemented in response to the complex programs entrusted to him, the haunting and strange refinement of their ornaments, and, above all, the importance given to new materials—particularly cast iron, magnified by a subtle play with light—have from the beginning provoked universal admiration and inspired many photographers, from Durandelle in the nineteenth century to Candida Höfer today. While the former buildings of the Bibliothèque Nationale are undergoing an unprecedented renovation campaign, it seemed to us a good time to reevaluate the approach of one of the most uncommon and demanding artists of the nineteenth century, a contemporary of Eugène Delacroix and Victor Hugo, and also to show how important his works and undertakings were in their time and how they have remained so ever since.

Like the masters of the Renaissance or the great architects of the twentieth century—Le Corbusier, Mies van der Rohe, Alvar Aalto—Labrouste created a very personal architectural language and means of conception, combining a deeply classical culture and sentiment with a strong inclination for boldness and innovation. Labrouste is one of the rare nineteenth-century architects whose works have always been a benchmark, both in France and abroad. Since the 1970s and the pioneering work of Neil Levine, we have known that part of Labrouste's originality was first and foremost due to his awareness of the ties between artistic styles and the social history of peoples, then in his search in turn for an architectural expression suited to the mores and spirit of his era. The controversy between Labrouste and the Académie des Beaux-Arts over his restoration of the Greek temples at Paestum was less about strictly archaeological details than about the very issue of models in architecture: at the age of twenty-seven, refuting the ideal and fixed image of Antiquity upheld by the neoclassicists, the young architect wanted to believe there could be a flexibility of style under specific conditions or circumstances. Later, his decision to use iron and cast iron forced him to reconsider the structure of buildings, their distribution and ornamentation. He took traditional masonry, although he refined the expression and thickness of its varied stone courses, and combined it with an architecture of assemblage. In his two libraries, he set large metal frameworks within a stone enclosure and gave those frameworks proportions that fit their properties. Attenuated supports, detailed as columns, skillfully relate human and monumental scale and play a decisive part in the perception of space. Labrouste thus inaugurated a new building practice and heralded the fruitful research that architects would devote for the next century and a half to shaping industrial materials, particularly composite materials such as reinforced concrete.

OTHECA·A·REGIBUS·CONDITA·NAPOLEO II·IMP

By individualizing each element of the construction and demonstrating that such a heterogeneous whole could create a strong sense of harmony, he thus paved the way for the great rationalist trend in European and American architecture at the end of the nineteenth century, which made a distinction between supporting structure and infill, expressively playing with materials and color. That architectural language would exert international influence, up to and including the commercial architecture and office buildings in the United States in the late nineteenth century, among them, the proto-skyscrapers of Louis Sullivan.

Labrouste's work is as poetic as it is rational. Decoration, which arises from the construction and underscores it, has an essential part to play. Ornamentation, which carries a symbolic discourse (inscriptions on the facade, sculpted torches and pedestals, fictive gardens, etc.), follows the sequences of cleverly composed spaces in which shadow and light, thickness and transparency, power and lightness intersect. His reading rooms are magical spaces. At the Bibliothèque Sainte-Geneviève, Labrouste was one of the first to introduce gas lighting into an architectural composition, using it to produce artistic, sensory effects. At the Bibliothèque Nationale, the natural zenithal lighting—soft and diffuse—and the view of simulated trees help give the reading room, despite its size, a strikingly peaceful atmosphere, perfect for study. The two libraries are a testament to the importance Labrouste gave to the general ambience, and to his influence on the work of library-goers. His approach is strikingly contemporary for architects and artists engaged in creating immersive environments today. One need only visit the remarkable Rolex Learning Center (2007–9), built by the architectural firm SANAA, at the Ecole Polytechnique Fédérale in Lausanne, to see just how much a university building, a place meant to spread knowledge, can be the paradigm for a new approach to social relations.

Labrouste's libraries also express shared values. Their respective reading rooms, which are so suited to individual work, were also designed to help a community of researchers: solitary study cannot be separated from the progress of knowledge within society as a whole. Built at a time when modern library science was developing and the first great bibliographic catalogues were being compiled, they are a testament to the nineteenth century's knowledge revolution and as such are important markers for a history we have inherited, in our own digital age.

Bibliothèque Nationale, reading room vaults' springing, near the hemicycle. Photograph: Alain Le Toquin

Over time, everyone who has traced the history of modern architecture has underscored the prominent position of Labrouste and his two libraries, although each time they have been ascribed a different meaning to his work. In 1975, he was one of the great figures of the nineteenth century, with Charles Garnier, singled out by the "manifesto" exhibition *The Architecture of the Ecole des Beaux-Arts* at The Museum of

Modern Art, while in 1976 he was the subject of an important monograph presented by the historian Pierre Saddy at the Caisse Nationale des Monuments Historiques et des Sites (at the Hôtel de Sully). The interpretations we are now presenting in turn are no less of our time: they include such key themes as assembly and hybridization, light and immersive environments. We are not interested in considering Labrouste as a simple precursor to modernity, as did Sigfried Giedion, who looked for forerunners of twentieth-century constructions in the productions of the nineteenth century and saw Labrouste as a misunderstood genius. It seems to us that the issues he raised and the answers he provided were very meaningful in their time, and that they have never ceased to be since, and that it is precisely for this reason that his work has enthralled generations of architects and historians.

Preparing this exhibition gave us a sense of the devotion Labrouste's work instills in those who work within it. At the Bibliothèque Nationale de France, at the Bibliothèque Sainte-Geneviève, and at the Académie d'Architecture, we found enthusiastic collaborators. We are deeply grateful to them and to the lenders to this exhibition for their support and ideas. We hope that those who discover, or rediscover, the work of Labrouste through this exhibition and its catalogue will share the same interest, pleasure, and emotions.

Corinne Bélier, Barry Bergdoll, and Marc Le Cœur

BARRY BERGDOLL
The Museum of
Modern Art

HISTORIOGRAPHY

We are so accustomed to thinking of "avant-garde" as an artistic stance of experimental art and architecture during the opening decades of the twentieth century—when a full-scale attack on academic and historicist attitudes of the nineteenth century was often the battle cry—that it opens to question our larger understanding of modern architecture culture and practice to consider that the term "avant-garde" first left military parlance to describe a new role for artistic practice in the theory of the utopian socialist Saint-Simonians in Paris in the years around 1830.[1] This was contemporary then with the unusually contentious debate over Labrouste's restoration study of Paestum (discussed here by Martin Bressani), a debate that pitted Labrouste against his teachers and against the stalwart *secrétaire perpétuel* of the Académie des Beaux-Arts, Quatremère de Quincy. At stake were nothing less than the fundamental doctrines of the ideal, of imitation, and of the role of architectural practice in relation to society.[2] Such was the vigor of the debate that a half century later in 1877, when Labrouste's drawings of ancient Paestum were engraved and published under the auspices of the Academy, Gothic Revival architect Eugène-Emmanuel Viollet-le-Duc, himself a veteran of standoffs with academic verities, recalled it as "quite simply a revolution on a few elephant folio sheets of paper."[3]

A century later, Peter Smithson—a leading voice in Team X, itself a group that criticized orthodoxy—found the very same drawing the most revelatory moment in a controversial exhibition: "I'd never heard of the Labrouste drawings of Paestum until I went to the Museum of Modern Art's Beaux-Arts exhibition,"[4] Smithson told an audience at London's Architectural Association in 1978. "[T]he rendered shadow of the feathers of the arrows and the shadows of the shields lashed to the columns are drawn so lightly that it's almost impossible to believe it was done by human hand. It's the best rendered drawing I've ever seen. In one long touch of the two hair sable brush the drawing reveals two languages at work: the language of the permanent fabric and the language of its attachments—that which continues

1. See Nicos Hadjinicolaou, "Sur l'idéologie de l'avant-gardisme," *Histoire et critique des arts* (July 1978): 49–76. Here the key text is Emile Barrault, *Aux Artistes: Du passé et de l'avenir des Beaux-Arts* (1830). Barrault had been a classmate of Labrouste at the Collège Sainte-Barbe.
2. See Levine 1977:325–416.
3. Viollet-le-Duc, March 21, 1877:1–2.
4. *The Architecture of the Ecole des Beaux-Arts*, The Museum of Modern Art, October 29, 1975, to January 4, 1976.

1. Gustaf Dahl, Royal Library of Sweden in Stockholm (1871–77), view of the reading room. Photograph: Åke E:son Lindman

5. Peter Smithson, "Once a Joly Swagman: Some Thoughts after Seeing Labrouste's Drawing of Paestum," *AD Profiles 17: The Beaux-Arts*, ed. Robin Middleton (London: Academy, 1978), 34.
6. Louis Sullivan, "The Tall Office Building Artistically Considered," first published in *Lippincott's Magazine* 57 (March 1896): 403–9; reprinted in Leland Roth, *America Builds: Source Documents in American Architecture and Planning* (New York: Harper & Row, 1983), 340.
7. Victor Calliat, *Encyclopédie d'architecture* (Paris: Bauce Editeur, 1856), col. 123.
8. "Henri Labrouste," *Deutsche Bauzeitung* 9 (1875): 280.
9. F. P. Cockerell, "Biographical Notices of Deceased Foreign Members," in *Sessional Papers Read at the Royal Institute of British Architects 1875–1876* (London: Royal Institute of British Architects), 218.
10. See Barry Bergdoll, "The Circulation of Images: Nineteenth-Century French Books and the Avery Library," in *Avery's Choice: Five Centuries of Great Architectural Books, One Hundred Years of an Architectural Library, 1890–1900*, ed. Angela Giral (New York: G.K.Hall; London: Prentice Hall International, 1997), 185–86.
11. Lucien Magne, *L'Architecture française du siècle* (Paris: Firmin Didot, 1889), 53.
12. Ibid., 34.
13. Van Brunt, 1893: 87.
14. Albert E. Richardson, "The Style Néo-Grec," *The Architectural Review* 30 (July 1911): 28.

the idea of architecture and that which is the responsibility of those who use it."[5] In short, Labrouste's work continued to reverberate long after the context of its making was forgotten. Maxims about the relation of form to a building's function, materials, and program recur in appreciations of Labrouste and of his pedagogy already during the architect's lifetime, long before Louis Sullivan was to declare that in searching for the form of tall office building "form ever follows function."[6] When Labrouste closed his studio in 1856, the *Encyclopédie d'architecture* noted that "he set out as a principle the idea that in the design of buildings form should also be suitable and subordinated to function and that decoration should be born of construction expressed with artistry."[7] Even if Labrouste insisted on no speeches at his funeral, obituaries consolidated his reputation as a pioneer of a rationalist position still seeking to assert itself as a doctrine, as much outside France as within. He was celebrated not as an individual talent but as a founding figure of modern architecture, from the *Deutsche Bauzeitung* in Berlin[8] to the Royal Institute of British Architects, which noted of this illustrious foreign member "the vigour and vitality which has given birth to and guided the growth of the highly original art which marks the French school of the second quarter of this century."[9] The 1890s would find not only the Bibliothèque Sainte-Geneviève's facade paraphrased in Charles McKim's 1887 design for the Boston Public Library but also the name of Labrouste—who had transformed a library into an expressive form for exhibiting knowledge by inscribing the names of 810 thinkers and writers on it—as part of the decorative iconography of the reading room of the Avery Architectural and Fine Arts Library (opened in 1897 and also designed by McKim) within Low Library on the new Columbia University campus in New York. There Labrouste's name figures among those which decorate the girders of the reading room, next to Duban, Viollet-le-Duc, Ruskin, Semper, and a host of others destined over the course of the next few decades to be progressively dissociated from the context of their own time, when they were lionized increasingly as prophets of the twentieth century.[10]

Already by the 1890s, then, Labrouste had become a touchstone for a rationalism based in a matrix of classical and Renaissance forms, his work an inspiration for figures from Louis-Jules André to Julien Guadet, even while many of his own pupils developed his lessons in the context of the Gothic Revival. The origins of the analysis of Labrouste not as a talented member of the generation of 1830—i.e., one of the group of Romantics—but as a singular figure who initiated modern architecture was consolidated by the publication of the first *history* of modern and contemporary architecture in French, Lucien Magne's *L'Architecture française du siècle*, published for the 1889 Exposition Universelle—the fair where the monumental cast- and wrought-iron Eiffel Tower marked the modernity of France born of the 1789 Revolution. Magne speaks already of an "art nouveau," in the 1830s. "No one more than Labrouste seemed to have been designated to realize the needed evolution from the academic school to the modern school."[11] The tradition of viewing Labrouste as not only a pioneer but a historically designated actor between Christian and Hegelian history was launched. In Magne's history, juxtaposed with a plate of the Bibliothèque Sainte-Geneviève, one reads "at this period began truly a new art (un art nouveau)."[12]

Labrouste's reputation began to be instrumentalized outside the complex landscape of French professional positions, lineages, and debates. In the Anglo-American debate over the extent to which a Beaux-Arts inheritance—imported into both countries as formal university programs of architecture were being established—might sponsor a new architectural synthesis rather than another revivalist practice in an eclectic and competitive field, Labrouste was a key reference point. Much of this would go under the name "néo-Grec," a confusing term because of the vast discrepancy with which it was used in different times and different places. In Paris at mid-century it designated an approach to etching a severe abstracted floral ornament and treating moldings as though they were cut almost in section, a language that spread quickly from such exemplary public buildings as Constant-Dufeux's facade for the Ecole de Dessin in the Rue Racine, Labrouste's two libraries, and Louis Duc's work at the Palais de Justice in Paris. By the 1870s when foreigners began to frequent the ateliers of the Ecole des Beaux-Arts, it was an established fashion among the architects of speculative apartment blocks filling the avenues of modernizing Paris. What "néo-Grec" meant in the American and British architectural discourse in the late nineteenth and early twentieth centuries was something else entirely. The Boston architect Henry Van Brunt, who had studied under Richard Morris Hunt, the first American to attend the Ecole des Beaux-Arts, celebrated Labrouste in an article published in *The Atlantic Monthly* in 1861 and reprinted in a book, *Greek Lines*, published in time for the World's Columbian Exhibition in 1893, in which he speaks of "néo-Grec practitioners not as masters of a style" but as teachers of a progressive attitude toward tradition and historical sources.[13] In Edwardian London a similar argument was put forth to attack the eclectic landscape of British practice by Albert E. Richardson, a classicist eager to assert the Greco-Roman heritage as a modern language of flexibility. Richardson traced a devotion to an evolutionary modernism back to a small group of mid-nineteenth-century "néo-grecs" including Labrouste: "The néo-Grec style is the epitome of design; its interest is a reflection of the tireless mind of the designer, who, having obtained a great many ideas on his subject, melts these very ideas in the crucible of his imagination, refining them again and again until the minted metal gleams refulgent," wrote Richardson. "By these means, and these alone, is original design possible."[14]

But it was in the 1920s that Labrouste's name began to be bandied about by opposing parties in an increasingly vociferous dispute. "In the Modernist battle Labrouste was used as a banner, becoming a myth," Renzo Dubbini noted recently. It was a myth "loaded with ideological meanings, so that even his extraordinary architectural talent ran the risk of remaining obscured."[15] For the first time positions were advanced not only in the professional press but in exhibitions and general-interest publications.

15. Renzo Dubbini, "Un'architettura per il proprio tempio," in *Henry Labrouste 1801–1875*, ed. Renzo Dubbini (Milan: Electa, 2002), 15; translation by Karen Bowie in the context of a review of the volume in *Journal of the Society of Architectural Historians* 62:1 (March 2003): 140.

1843

Fig. 10. Henri LABROUSTE: LA RÉSERVE
(Ground floor of the library of Sainte-Geneviève.) Cast-iron columns lead freely and boldly through the space as a part of the iron skeleton sunk into the building.

He demonstrated that although students of the academy produced beautiful drawings of antique details, they completely missed the inner organism of the building. He learned to recognize "that the best buildings from an artistic standpoint were precisely those constructed by the simplest, most truthful, and most rational methods."[24]
For the first time, he expressed an expanded MEANING of CONSTRUCTION, yielded by the new possibilities:[25] The essence of construction is found not in the isolated study of the mason's or locksmith's handcrafted details but in the interpenetration of every part of a building.
Labrouste belongs to the generation of 1830 that, as noted in a completely different connection, was guided by a single grand current, by the demand for renewal of social, moral, and intellectual life.[26]
By the time he was assigned the library, Labrouste was regarded by everyone as the purest incarnation of the *esprit nouveau*.[27] For twelve years he had roamed Paris without being entrusted with even a single building. Labrouste was past forty when he received the library commission.

24) Eugène Millet, "Henri Labrouste," Extrait du *Bulletin de la Société centrale des architectes*, Exercice 1879–80, p. 5.
25) This is one of the rare personal statements of the architect H. Labrouste: "*la construction consiste dans la combinaison de toutes les parties architecturales*" [construction consists of the combination of all the architectural parts] "Travaux des élèves de l'école d'architecture de Paris pendant l'année 1839," *Revue gén. de l'arch.*, 1840, p. 59.
26) Willy Spühler, *Der Saint-Simonismus* (Zurich, 1926), p. 22.
27) Delaborde, p. 13.

106

1926

Fig. 11. LE CORBUSIER: COOK HOUSE
It took approximately eighty years before one dared to show uninhibitedly the freedom of Labrouste: an uninterrupted construction (column) even in a living space.

Science and industry gave him very little assistance. Nevertheless, with the library of Sainte-Geneviève he attempted for the first time to insert an iron skeleton into a building, from the foundation to the roof. Sainte-Geneviève is at the same time the first pure library building in France. Labrouste was more sensitive to the possibilities of iron than his architectural contemporaries. The material corresponded with his intention: to condense the meaning of all things![28]
Labrouste inserts the iron frame into the building like the works into a clock:
The massive masonry core encasing the building still remains unaffected, but within this masonry core, from the ground floor to the ridge of the roof, is placed an iron system: columns, ceilings, vaults, girders, roof construction.
In individual rooms of the ground floor (*la réserve*), cast-iron columns without visible beams are connected to the upper story. These slender cast-iron tubes run down the middle of the room, attached to the ceiling only by a narrow flange. Sleek function, no beam with the hint of support and load, no ornament, no capital. These are things that today are dared only by a Corbusier or a Mart Stam. Fig. 10 Fig. 11
The upper story, a double-aisle reading room (84 meters long, 21 meters wide), forms a single structural skeleton with the roof. The semicircular trusses are supported by cast-iron columns and—along the walls—consoles. If the plans are correct, Labrouste already split these semicircular ceiling trusses into three segments so as not to make them totally rigid, in order to allow for expansion. As we know, it was more Figs. 13, 14 [12, 13]

28) Delaborde, p. 13.

107

2. Sigfried Giedion, *Bauen in Frankreich. Bauen in Eisen. Bauen in Eisenbeton* (Leipzig: Klinkhardt & Biermann, 1928), pp. 106–7; English translation: *Building in France, Building in Iron, Building in Ferroconcrete* (Santa Monica, Calif.: Getty Center for the History of Art and the Humanities, 1995)

By the time the Swiss historian Sigfried Giedion lionized Labrouste as the "most prominent figure in the field of architecture at the beginning of industrial development," and juxtaposed images of Labrouste's work with that of fellow Swiss Le Corbusier, a counter argument had already been well established that sought to debunk the tendency to isolate not only Labrouste from his context but also parts of his buildings from the larger whole. The French historian Louis Hautecœur argued at once for Labrouste's genius but insisted on him as a great renewer of classicism rather than a precursor of something that only recently gained acceptance, "the purest incarnation of the *esprit nouveau*," as Giedion claimed in juxtaposing the Bibliothèque Sainte-Geneviève and Le Corbusier's recently completed Maison Cook (fig. 2).[16] The trend seems to have been launched by Jean Badovici, the founder of the avant-garde organ *L'Architecture vivante*, who already in 1926 surveyed nineteenth-century developments, largely negative and retrogressive, singling out the Bibliothèque Sainte-Geneviève as the singly most noble building of the whole century, and claiming Labrouste as the father of "une architecture vivante."
Walter Benjamin would develop this perception into an entire theory of the historical unconscious, even determining that the iron constructions of the arcades, on which

Labrouste drew for his two libraries, were the dream images of the century, projecting forward in his literary analysis what Giedion saw only as a historical archaeology.[17] "The task of the historian," Giedion had written, "is to recognize the seeds and to indicate—across all layers of debris—the continuity of development. The historian, unfortunately, has used the perspective of his occupation to give eternal legitimation to the past and thereby to kill the future, or at least to obstruct its development. Today the historian's task appears to be the opposite: to extract from the vast complexity of the past those elements that will be the point of departure for the future."[18]

Labrouste was not to be elevated singularly.[19] Georges Gromort,[20] a product of the very rationalist strain that traced its origins to Labrouste, having been formed in the atelier of André, which he took over, asserted that Labrouste along with Jacques Ignace Hittorff were at once of, and yet towering above, their generation. For Gromort the Bibliothèque Sainte-Geneviève was a masterpiece of syncretic thinking, but one that has been fundamentally made into a caricature by its champions, insisting on only aspects of the work, like a few elements of exposed iron, rather than on the overall work. "Since when ... do we become preoccupied in crossing the threshold of a great building by the type of joists which are used in the construction of the floors ... I protest only the way in which the critics have seized upon the most insignificant parts of his work and have been wary of insisting on the essential qualities which make this work especially remarkable." The library "is one of the most noble constructions of the nineteenth century; it can hold its own with buildings of the finest periods ... because here we have a truly classic work, and the classic is timeless."[21]

By the late 1920s, Labrouste's reputation had bifurcated. For Hautecoeur and Gromort he was a milestone in the history of French classicism, for Giedion a forerunner of *l'esprit nouveau,* an argument expanded to the wider modern movement two years later when Giedion exhibited his own photographs of Labrouste's two libraries in Vienna in the exhibition *Film und Foto* (interiors exclusively, which he described as similar to the works inside a Swiss watch, so perfectly did their metal armatures fit inside their traditionalist casing), even captioning a view of the reading room of the Bibliothèque Nationale as "Neues Bauen im Jahre 1868 (Bibliothek in Paris)."[22] Just as Moholy-Nagy had transformed the image of Marseille's *pont transbordeur* by radical camera angles and cropping, so Giedion framed views to emphasize the interpenetration of light and material in the Bibliothèque Nationale's stacks.

A hybrid of these opposing views appeared in America, where in 1929 the young historian Henry-Russell Hitchcock published a history of modern architecture since 1850, in which Labrouste is singled out as "the finest architect of the mid-century,"[23] framing there arguments taken up three years later in the catalogue and wall texts of the Museum of Modern Art's first architecture exhibition, *Modern Architecture: International Exhibition*, with its famous designation of the "International Style" as the new style of the age. While Hitchcock's history contains clear paraphrases of Gromort, it hews closer to

16. Giedion 1928 (English-language edition 1995):86.
17. Jean-Louis Déotte, "Walter Benjamin et l'inconscient constructif de Sigfried Giedion," *Images Re-vues* 2 (2010): document 6.
18. Giedion 1928 (English-language edition 1995):86.
19. Louis Hautecœur, "Avant-propos," in *Châteaux, jardins, églises aux XVIIe et XVIIIe siècles,* catalogue of an exhbition organized by the the Service des Monuments Historiques (Vendôme: Launay et fils, 1923), 6. See also Antonio Brucculeri, *Du dessein historique à l'action publique: Louis Hautecoeur et l'architecture classique en France* (Paris: Picard, 2007).
20. Georges Gromort, *Architecture et la Sculpture en France de la Révolution à nos Jours* (Paris: Librairie de France, 1925).
21. Ibid., 60.
22. *Film und Foto: Wanderausstellung des Deutschen Werkbundes* (Vienna: Oesterreiches Museum, 1930), 164. See Werner Oechslin and Gregor Harbusch, eds., *Sigfried Giedion und die Fotografie, Bildinszenierung der Moderne* (Zurich: GTA Verlag, 2010), 68. See also Giedion's article following up on *Bauen in Frankreich,* "Lumière et construction: Réflexion à propos des ateliers de chemins de fer de Freyssinet," *Cahiers de l'art* 4:6 (1929): 275–81.
23. Henry-Russell Hitchcock, *Modern Architecture: Romanticism and Reintegration* (New York: Payson & Clarke, 1929), 31.

24. Ibid., 35.
25. Ibid., 39.
26. Ibid., 123.
27. Walter Curt Behrendt, *Modern Building: Its Nature, Problems, and Forms* (New York: Harcourt, Brace, 1939), 41–42.
28. Giedion 1941:216.
29. Ibid., 218.
30. Ibid., 224.
31. Ibid., 224.
32. Peter Collins, *Concrete: The Vision of a New Architecture* (London: Faber and Faber, 1959). Here quoted from the second edition (Montreal: McGill-Queen's University Press, 2004), 159.

the line of Giedion's recently published *Bauen in Frankreich* in celebrating engineering as the true line of modern evolution in the nineteenth century. Like Giedion, who would soon develop a concept of "constituent" and "transitory" historical facts, Hitchcock was intent on separating the wheat of future prospects from the chaff of momentary importance. Most of nineteenth-century architecture for him, as for Giedion, was to be relegated to the past. "The influence of Paris after the day of Labrouste and Hittorff was, on the whole, repressive and literally reactionary,"[24] he noted, while "Engineering fortunately could go its own way. Thus it was able to produce in the mid-century the only constructions whose quality is worthy of comparison with the libraries of Labrouste ... in which, moreover, it had already been incorporated."[25] Repeating the assumption that it was the interior of the libraries which contained the true seeds of the future, Hitchcock celebrates the metal trusses within Berlage's great Beurs at Amsterdam, concluding, "Thus engineering became again a part of architecture in the way that Labrouste in particular had anticipated half a century earlier ..."[26]

By 1929, then, exactly a century after the disputes in the French Academy over Labrouste's interpretation of Paestum and its consequence for contemporary practice, Labrouste himself was the subject of a battle between modernists and traditionalists. While traditionalists admired the sobriety of the envelope of his two libraries, even the ways they functioned within the harmonious fabric of nineteenth-century Paris, modernists seized upon the notion of rupture and turned their lens almost exclusively on the interiors. This was a view taken up by the German émigré historian Walter Curt Behrendt in his textbook *Modern Building*, published in 1937. If Behrendt largely lionizes Karl Friedrich Schinkel as the forerunner of modernism, he also celebrates Labrouste's use of iron, neatly dismissing the exterior to find a hidden source of modernism within: "Iron construction was first used on a large scale when Henri Labrouste, architect-engineer, built the Bibliothèque Sainte-Geneviève ... As a true representative of that new spirit which thinks first of the organism of each structure, the architect set up within the large reading room ... an iron skeleton ... the exterior of the building does not suggest the nature of the construction so frankly revealed in the interior. Here it seems as though the architect were still afraid of accepting the consequences involved in his courageous design."[27] This view—in which Labrouste is now even called an engineer though he had no such training—was consecrated when Giedion was invited by Walter Gropius to deliver the Norton Lectures at Harvard University. Published in 1941 as *Space, Time and Architecture*, it would go through some seven editions in continual revision for the next three decades, would influence several generations of architects and historians, and would establish Labrouste's libraries, and in particular the stacks of the Bibliothèque Nationale, as the expression of the deep subconscious of modernity embedded in a building that can "pass" in the street. He juxtaposes photographs of the glass wall separating the reading room from the stacks with his own photographs of the great curtain wall of Albert Laprade's Garage

Marbeuf (1928–29; p. 37, fig. 4). Well into his history of engineering, English mills, and early Parisian iron markets, Giedion turns for the first time to French architecture: "Until now we have had to dissect practically anonymous constructions, to find the first signs of the new developments which life, almost unconsciously, was bringing about. Toward the middle of the 19th century, we encounter for the first time in this period a man who unites the abilities of both the engineer and the architect: the architect-constructor Henri Labrouste."[28] The labeling of Labrouste as an engineer is only the first of the myths presented in Giedion's history, along with the image of Labrouste as the tortured genius, shunned for having dared to oppose the academy: "The Academy waged a bitter war against the so-called 'rationalistic school' which Labrouste headed ... [he] ... had to wait more than twelve years for a chance to show his talents in an executed work of importance. It was not until he was past forty that Labrouste was commissioned to build ... in Paris (1843–50)."[29] Despite the fact that his career followed a path quite similar to many returning laureates of the *Grand Prix*, progressing through on-site supervision work under other architects before being trusted with his own commission, Labrouste the misunderstood genius was a perfect type of the embattled visionary of the modern movement. As Giedion proceeds to describe the stack room of the library, "Labrouste's masterpiece," the allusions to Le Corbusier's polemical strategies become more and more overt. The open iron grates of the stacks are said to have been first used "in the engine rooms of steamships,"[30] citing one of Le Corbusier's favored metaphors in the photomontage of *Vers une architecture*.[31] Giedion returned again to Labrouste in a popular volume published in 1959, *Les Architectes célèbres*, organized by Pierre Francastel, who had already taken up Giedion's line of lionizing Labrouste as a pioneer in the darkness of the nineteenth century in his seminal *Art et technique aux 19e et 20e siècles* of 1956.

The first hint of a reaction against the willful separation of Labrouste from the context of his time came in a passing remark in the very same year about Auguste Perret's training in *Concrete: The Vision of New Architecture*, by the Canadian architectural historian Peter Collins: "Henri Labrouste's revolutionary and brilliant contribution towards creating a new architecture is well known, but there is a tendency, which may perhaps be deliberate, to overlook the fact that he was essentially a product of the Ecole des Beaux-Arts."[32] But this had little immediate effect on histories. Hitchcock's *Architecture: Nineteenth and Twentieth Centuries*, published as part of the great project of Nikolaus Pevsner's *Pelican History of Art* series in 1958, for instance, discusses Labrouste's work in the chapter on "Building with Iron and Glass: 1790–1855" along with train stations and exhibition buildings, including the Crystal Palace, while works of the architects with whom he made common cause, Duban and Vaudoyer, occupy an entirely different chapter on architectural developments. A dramatic shift came in the 1970s, when the emergent postmodern critique of modernist orthodoxy and a wave of revisionist evaluations of nineteenth-century architecture developed in Europe and North America

with moments of significant synergy. Here the key date was 1975, when almost simultaneously exhibition projects were launched in Paris and New York. In that year the Caisse Nationale des Monuments Historiques devoted a special issue of its magazine *Monuments Historiques* to a radical reevaluation of Labrouste's work and legacy in the wake of a major ministerial effort to create lists of nineteenth-century buildings for monument protection as well as in preparation for a planned monographic show to take place at the Hôtel de Sully in 1976. And the Museum of Modern Art in New York opened its controversial *Architecture of the Ecole des Beaux-Arts* exhibition in which Labrouste's drawings of Paestum and for his Bibliothèque Sainte-Geneviève were given pride of place. In both cases the exhibitions were at once responses to turbulent debates over the demolition or threat to two major monuments of nineteenth- and early–twentieth-century architecture, Victor Baltard's Les Halles in Paris and Grand Central Terminal in New York, as well as implicit critiques—oddly enough—of modernist orthodoxy.

In Paris a struggle of ownership and interpretation was again launched for Labrouste, but now inverted from the bifurcation in the 1920s since the established architectural profession wanted to maintain the notion of Labrouste as a protomodern, while the nascent postmodernist critique wanted to recontextualize him within the nineteenth century, itself enjoying a great revival of interest which would culminate with the founding of the Musée d'Orsay at the end of the decade.[33] Bruno Foucart—emerging as the great champion of nineteenth-century architecture and soon of the contextualist urbanism of Maurice Culot, Leon Krier, and others—penned the first of the period's critiques of Giedion (whom Foucart incorrectly calls Samuel Giedion) and of Francastel, arguing, "We have finally to let Labrouste get out from under the peremptory claims of theoricians and from his over simplified reputation as a functionalist and user of metal."[34] One year later, when Pierre Saddy mounted the exhibition at the Hôtel de Sully, presenting all Labrouste's works side by side without isolating the libraries from the evidently historicist *hôtels particuliers* for instance, Labrouste was also claimed by practicing modernist architects. Also in 1976 Paul Chemetov and Bernard Marrey organized an exhibition on iron in French architecture since 1848—a date chosen for its socialist pedigree—mounted in the populist setting of the Bon Marché department store, itself a great glass and iron structure. Here Labrouste's libraries took their place next to neighbors that Giedion and Hitchcock had long ago chosen for them: "If his private buildings use signifiers the banality of which is appropriate for their function, the libraries of Sainte-Geneviève and the National place him at the origins of modern architecture."[35]

Arthur Drexler's exhibition of student drawings from the Ecole des Beaux-Arts—along with full-scale gallery presentations of Labrouste's Bibliothèque Sainte-Geneviève and Charles Garnier's Paris Opera—at New York's Museum of Modern Art was immediately perceived as a thinly veiled critique of the modern movement, even though its subject

33. *Histoire de l'art du XIXe siècle (1848–1914): bilans et perspectives* (Paris: Musée d'Orsay, École du Louvre Colloque, 2012).
34. Bruno Foucart,"Labrouste et ses contemporains," *Les Monuments Historiques de la France* 6 (1975): 7.
35. Paul Chemetov and Bernard Marrey, *Architectures: 1848–1914* (Paris: Dunod, 1980).
36. Robin Middleton, ed., *AD Profiles 17:The Beaux-Arts* (London: Academy, 1978). This account draws on my earlier publication, "Complexities and Contradictions of Post-Modern Classicism: Notes on the Museum of Modern Art's 1975 Exhbition *The Architecture of the Ecole des Beaux-Arts*," in *The Persistence of the Classical: Essays on Architecture Presented to David Watkin*, ed. Frank Salmon (London: Philip Wilson Publishers, 2008), 202–17.
37. Jürgen Habermas, "La Modernité un projet inachevé, "*La Modernité, un projet inachevé: 40 architectes*, ed. Paul Chemetov (Paris: Editions du Moniteur, 1982).

was ostensibly the academic tradition in nineteenth-century French architecture and in French and American civic architecture of the late nineteenth and early twentieth centuries. That, of course, was the very architecture tradition that the Museum had set out to curtail from the founding of its Department of Architecture in 1932 with a clear mandate to transform architectural taste and ideology in America and to create a beachhead for international modernism. Forty-three years later, the controversial and puzzling exhibition of the dazzling watercolors of the student competitions was seen as an equally seminal event; indeed it was seen by some even as a bookend that bracketed the episode of modernism in America. Drexler's exhibition and book helped usher in a type of postmodernism which one can only imagine was far from his conscious intent. After decades of missionary zeal, it seemed as if the flagship of modernism was changing the colors on its mast, a position confirmed two years later when the museum's monumental publication on the subject appeared—with Drexler's polemical forward followed by three major historical essays by the young architectural historians Neil Levine, David Van Zanten, and Richard Chaffee. Their collective historical focus would not be the great Gothic Revivalist architect and theoretician Viollet-le-Duc, who had long-established laurels as a protomodernist, but rather the Ecole des Beaux-Arts itself, that bastion of the classical tradition and for many decades the *nec plus ultra* of credentials in the American architectural profession, at least until the late 1930s when Gropius arrived with the legacy of the Bauhaus at Harvard. Even though an international tour of the exhibition was planned, in the end the event was to play itself out in a very American discursive field, one only briefly extended to Britain when Robin Middleton organized, in 1978, a follow-up event at the Architectural Association.[36] Mystery still veils the cancelation of the planned exhibition at Paris's Musée des Arts Décoratifs, and even more so the decision not to print the French translation of Drexler's book in 1980, for which Foucart had penned a now lost preface. The Beaux-Arts show in Paris would have been a significant prelude to the debate over modernism and postmodernism staged a few years later, in 1981, in competing exhibitions on current French architecture, with the presentation of the modernists in an exhibition curated by Chemetov called *La Modernité, un projet inachevé*, a title evocative of Jürgen Habermas,[37] meant to counter the postmodern view that was infiltrating the historiography of architecture since the Revolution as well as the practice of architecture.

Prior to the show's opening in New York, Drexler summarized its importance in a press release: "A more detached view of architecture as it was understood in the Nineteenth century might also provoke a more rigorous critique of philosophical assumptions underlying the architecture of our own time. Now that modern experience so often contradicts modern faith, we would be well advised to re-examine our architectural pieties ... Two central concerns which merit reexamination today, according to the Museum, are the recognition of the importance of a building's system of internal

Previous pages:
3. Frank Lloyd Wright (1867–1959), headquarters of the Johnson Wax Company in Racine, Wisconsin (1936–39), view of the main work room. Photograph: anonymous, 1956

38. Drexler, memo. no. 34, draft press release, April 30, 1975, Museum of Modern Art Archives.
39. Levine 1977:332.
40. Levine 1982:138–73.

circulation in determining it's architectural form, and the use of drawing as a flexible means of visualizing architectural form."[38] The critique was at least two-fold: modern architecture had become diagrammatic, and at the same time students were taught to think of architecture models as ends in themselves. The lost art of Beaux-Arts rendering would reveal the extent to which students in the French academic tradition had been taught to understand the refinements of details and surface treatment, making the very construction of a building into an act of both civic responsibility and artistic investment. What Drexler shared at this point with his young authors, Levine in particular, was a sense that Louis Kahn—and along with him the whole so-called Yale-Philadelphia axis that was recalibrating American architecture around geometric formality, processional progressions, and a material articulation of masonry walls—represented at once a new primitivism in modernism and a synthesis of the old Beaux-Arts/modernist rift that was particularly American.

No less were Levine and Van Zanten directly connected to this recalibration of American architecture away from the Miesian heritage of Skidmore, Owings & Merrill toward the work of Kahn and the latest experiments in meaning and symbolism represented by his Philadelphia colleague Robert Venturi, the single most important American figure in architecture's linguistic turn around 1970. Most polemically intoned was Levine's interpretation of Labrouste. Levine's frame of reference grew directly from the inspirational teaching of one of Kahn's greatest supporters, Vincent Scully. Levine, following Scully's lead, engaged with a wholly different set of issues more aligned with the period's interest in the semiotics of architecture and in Scully's dual interests in Kahn's powerful space making and in Venturi's reevaluation of surface, ornament, and legibility. Levine's essay "The Romantic Idea of Architectural Legibility: Henri Labrouste and the Néo-Grec" was the tour-de-force intellectual exercise of Drexler's book. Self-consciously struggling to deconstruct Giedion's view of Labrouste as a protomodernist engineer-architect, Levine at once resituated Labrouste's undertaking in the complex cultural moment of French Romanticism of the 1830s and made a case for "legibility" as the chief characteristic of that Romanticism. Legibility was of course the preoccupation of the Yale-Philadelphia axis's search for meaning in architecture, nowhere more than at Yale's Department of the History of Art, where a local brand of the period's fascination with semiology and meaning structures was conjugated in relationship to Scully's championing of Venturi, Scott Brown, and Izenour, whose *Learning from Las Vegas*, published in 1972, had been first taught as a Yale architectural studio during Levine's years in residence in New Haven. Venturi's idea of the decorated shed as a building that embraces a disjunctive separation of a working structure from a great sign professing its meaning is not hard to detect in Levine's insistence that precisely such a cleavage was pioneered by Labrouste's Bibliothèque Sainte-Geneviève, which, he wrote, "can only be understood if one accepts the fact that the neo-Grec meant the replacement of classicism by a new way of thinking about architectural

127. HENRI LABROUSTE. Bibliothèque Nationale, Paris, 1858–68. *Glass wall between the stacks (magasin central) and reading room. Early use of large areas of glass in the interior of a permanent public building. The heavy velvet drapery suggests that Labrouste was somewhat alarmed by his own daring.*

128. Glass wall of the Garage Rue Marbœuf, Paris, 1929. *After Labrouste's early recognition of the possibilities of glass, it came increasingly into use throughout the century, ending in immense panes like these whose framework has to be suspended from overhead bridge girders.*

But it was in his methods, in the way he analyzed and executed a task in building, that he stood far in advance of his times and of his colleagues. In spite of this, no studies of this architect have appeared since his death. We have no precise knowledge of the wearisome struggle with the Académie in which he was involved after 1830, or of the resistance he encountered that made a full realization of his ideas impossible. Perhaps the details still lie buried in the archives of the Académie. Some years ago I tried to learn more about the planning and development of Labrouste's most important work, the Bibliothèque Nationale. A search of the Building Department of the Bibliothèque Nationale itself disclosed that Labrouste's plans had been lost.

226

NEW BUILDING PROBLEMS — NEW SOLUTIONS

In the nineteenth century, buildings which owe nothing to the past begin to appear. Their new lines originate in the new demands presented by big towns, multiplied means of communication, and an ever-expanding industry. All these buildings have one thing in common: they are intended solely for a periodic use that involves rapid distribution of large volumes of merchandise. It is no accident that this type of construction should embody the solutions to the main architectural problems of the century. Because these unpretentious buildings contain the seeds of so much that followed, we must treat them at considerable length.

Market Halls

Hall of the Madeleine, Paris, 1824

One of the new problems that were arising first finds a solution in the great public markets, three examples of which will be given. The earliest of such structures to require discussion here was the market hall of the Madeleine, built in Paris in 1824 (*fig.* **129**). The grace of its slender cast-iron columns is reminiscent of Pompeian mural paintings. The lightness of the construction is unbroken by any purely decorative additions. This is one of the earliest examples of the attempts nineteenth-century engineers were making to develop methods of construction which would combine elegance with economy of material.

Hungerford Fish Market, London, 1835

The market which was built in London in 1835 to replace the old Hungerford Fish Market represents a somewhat greater advance, so far as construction alone is concerned. A detailed description of the new Hungerford Fish Market (*fig.* **130**) appeared in the *Transactions* of the Institute of British Architects in 1836.[1] On sanitary grounds, the use of lumber in this building had been forbidden. The cast-iron construction dictated by this provision is particularly noteworthy for the wide roof span of thirty-two feet, with its straight line. It has all the elegance of a much later period. "The chief particularity in the construction," according to the report of 1836, "is

[1] I (1836), 44–46.

227

form and content." Neo-Grec architects "were the first to make the radical distinction between structural principle and decorative form"[39] This rather willful reading of the envelope of Labrouste's library, which is everywhere detailed in relation to static forces and interior program, was meant to underscore an elaborate "literary expression" in the building, something that Levine went on to develop—for Middleton's follow-up conference at London's Architectural Association in 1978—in a breathtaking reading of the building in relationship to Victor Hugo's prescription that the book had killed the building, where the formerly rationalist monument of Labrouste's library was shown to be the frame for an elaborate iconographic program which grounded the whole in literary allusion and mythological iconography, precisely the themes that were increasingly being embraced by the period's postmodernist theorists and practitioners.[40] Nowhere was this connection with emerging postmodern theory and practice more overtly underscored than in an article Van Zanten wrote toward the end of the exhibition's run hoping to counter what he thought were false appraisals of the whole undertaking. "The more we—like the show itself—concentrate on these French ideas, the more we realize that we are doing so in order to understand the architecture being produced around us ... the Modern show is retrospective, not because the subject

4. Sigfried Giedion, *Space, Time, and Architecture: The Growth of a New Tradition* (Cambridge, Mass.: Harvard University Press; London: Cambridge University Press, 1941), pp. 226–27

matter was 19th century drawings, but because it was really about Kahn, Venturi and Moore, Mies and Johnson."[41] The theme was returned to by the recently appointed architecture critic of the *New York Times*, Scully protégé Paul Goldberger, who noted that "Labrouste's work is subtle, rich in meaning and invention, and in a certain sense can be said to have paved the way for the work of such current architects of historical allusion as Charles Moore and Venturi & Rauch."[42]

In the years following the publication of Levine's revelatory and wide-reaching essays on Labrouste, the historical grounding of Labrouste in the complex culture of French Romanticism, as well as in the realities of French state professional practice, has been deepened with fundamental historical research by David Van Zanten, Robin Middleton, Jean-Michel Leniaud, and, more recently, Martin Bressani. All of these seem at some remove from architectural practice and current debates, as was the case during the wane of the postmodern moment in the 1970s and 1980s: architectural practice and architectural history have often moved along independent paths. Still a kind of correction to some middle ground between Giedion's interpretation—which could only account for Labrouste's iron framework—and Levine's—which seemed largely invested in the envelope and its writing on the wall—has begun to emerge in which the tectonic language of Labrouste is found precisely in the relationship between the two. This is an interpretation developed at once by such practitioners as the Dutch architect Herman Hertzberger and by one of Hertzberger's chief champions, the historian Kenneth Frampton. Where Levine rehearses anew the lineage from Labrouste to Kahn in an attempt to write a history of modern architecture concerned primarily with the issue of representation, Frampton proposes a new lineage in which Labrouste's ability to achieve a dialogue between a lightweight columnar armature and a masonry encasement created a symbiotic tectonic expression, which Frampton then traces to a set of practices ranging from Franco Albini in postwar Italy to Enrique Miralles in 1990s Spain. "Labrouste," Frampton notes in *Studies in Tectonic Culture*, "demonstrated a model and a method that Viollet-le-Duc would turn to a few years later, namely the insertion of a prefabricated, fireproof iron armature into a masonry shell tectonically prepared for is reception."[43] With the interpretations of Hertzberger, Frampton, and, more recently, Edward Ford in America and Jacques Lucan in Europe, Labrouste has once again entered the architectural curriculum, and for the first time in a series of analyses in which the rethinking of both container and contained are brought into a search for architectural meaning out of architectural elements rather than overlaid symbols.[44]

Just as Labrouste and his fellow Romantics of the generation that came of age around the time of France's second great political and social revolution, that of July 1830, jettisoned notions of timeless ideals in favor of a view of architecture as a continual record of change and adaption, so Labrouste's own critical fortune is a veritable palimpsest of the architectural debate in the long history of modern architecture, a cipher of changing and even conflicting agendas like almost no other architect of the nineteenth

41. David Van Zanten, "Remarks on the Museum of Modern Art Exhibition: The Architecture of the Ecole des Beaux-Arts," *Journal of the Los Angeles Institute of Contemporary Art* (May 1976).
42. Paul Goldberger, "Beaux-Arts Architecture at the Modern," *New York Times*, October 29, 1975, p. 46. See also Goldberger's follow up article, "Debate Lingers after Beaux-Arts Show," *New York Times*, January 6, 1976, p. 30.
43. Kenneth Frampton, *Studies in Tectonic Culture: The Poetics of Construction in Nineteenth and Twentieth Century Architecture* (Cambridge, Mass.: MIT Press, 1995); Levine 2009.
44. Herman Hertzberger, "Henri Labrouste, la réalisation en art," *Technique et architecture* 375 (1987–88); Jacques Lucan, *Composition, Non-Composition: Architecture and Theory in the Nineteenth and Twentieth Centuries* (New York: Routledge/EPFL Press, 2012).

century. He has been a vital component of the constitution of notions of rationalist architecture, of the heritage of modernism in the "engineer's architecture" of the nineteenth century, and of the genealogy of an architecture of signs and signification in the articulation of post-modernism. This very history is a sign of the brilliance of his architectural works, which continue to engender ideas not only by the books they contain but by the very architectural possibilities they suggest, proof in the end that Labrouste may well have triumphed over Victor Hugo's prediction that "ceci tuera cela": the book will kill the building.

Previous pages:
5. Pier Luigi Nervi, Palazzo del Lavoro in Turin (1960–61), interior view. Photograph: G. Dagli Orti

MARC LE CŒUR
Bibliothèque Nationale
de France

AN ARCHITECT OF SILENCE

His contemporaries spoke of Henri Labrouste's rectitude, his "damning modesty," and his "proud shyness,"[1] yet they also acknowledged his "unshakeable convictions" and his "independent opinions."[2] According to Eugène-Emmanuel Viollet-le-Duc, he "did not look like much; he was prideful and shy, and aware of his worth."[3] Labrouste was also a melancholy man, beset by professional as well as familial obstacles which had to be overcome. Though at the end of his life he lamented the fact that he had not had a more prosperous career, he nonetheless found designing studious and commemorative spaces to be worthy of his temperament and aspirations.

His parents were both from families that had long been involved in maritime trade. A native of Tonnay-Charente, near Rochefort, Dominique Gourg (1764–1851) was the daughter and granddaughter of Cognac merchants who dealt mainly with Northern Europe, and her three brothers, setting out on their own journeys, had been all over the world. As for her husband, the Bordeaux-born Alexandre Labrouste (1762–1835) was the son of a chief of provisions for the king's armies, the grandson of a royal navy broker, and great-grandson of a ship captain. At the start of the Revolution, the collapse of the former royal navy put an end to that tradition, but the country's administrative reorganization offered new opportunities. When he was still a young lawyer, Alexandre Labrouste was named a superior officer in the Garde Nationale (1790), then administrator of the Directoire for the Gironde department (1791). Banished under the Terror (1793–94), he was imprisoned after hiding for several months behind a fake wall in his house and only escaped death through the providential intervention of one of Robespierre's intimates, who was on a mission in Bordeaux. In the end, he finally recovered his administrative duties and was named a representative for his fellow

1. Trélat [1875]:22, 24.
2. Delaborde 1878:7.
3. Viollet-le-Duc, March 5, 1877:1. Yet he specified, "Note that I say proud and not vain; we should make a distinction: pride can lead to noble actions, whereas vanity only breeds petty ones."

1. Bibliothèque Sainte-Geneviève, view of the intrados of the reading room windows. Photograph: Jean-Claude N'Diaye

4. Trélat [1875]:9.
5. Bailly 1876:22.
6. Charles Lucas, "Inauguration du monument de Félix Duban," *La Construction moderne* (November 10, 1894): 62.
7. [Laure Labrouste]1928:90.
8. Ibid.
9. Henri Delaborde, "Notice sur la vie et les ouvrages de M. Duc," *Institut de France. Académie des Beaux-Arts. Séance publique annuelle du samedi 18 octobre 1879 présidée par M. J. Thomas* (Paris: Firmin-Didot, 1879), 42.

citizens at the new legislative assembly: the Council of Five Hundred (1795). This is when he left Bordeaux for good, with his wife and their eldest son, and came to live in Paris. Four more children would be born there. Henri Labrouste was the youngest. Born on May 11, 1801, the future architect grew up on the quiet Rue de l'Université, not far from the Palais Bourbon, where his father sat on the parliamentary council. He never knew his ancestors or his maternal uncles, but it is clear that their distant travels, as his parents recalled them, earned his admiration. At the Ecole des Beaux-Arts, after all, he devised plans for a "monument to honor the sailors of the city of Bordeaux." If such adventures did not instill in him any personal desire to travel, they certainly fed his imagination and aroused a taste for exploration. His father's fate, which had been so intertwined with political upheavals, also taught him about the march of history. Ten years after escaping the Terror, Alexandre Labrouste was decorated with the Legion of Honor by Napoleon himself during the very first bestowing of medals in the Invalides church (July 15, 1804), was named administrator of the debt repayment fund (August 14, 1807), and made a Knight of the Empire (September 29, 1809). He set an example, with his mix of integrity, civic-mindedness, and bravura, and demonstrated that one should never forego one's convictions at the whim of present circumstances.

At the age of eight, Henri Labrouste joined his three brothers at the highly regarded Collège Sainte-Barbe, in the Latin Quarter. The brothers, who would later play an important part in the history of the school, also developed a strong social network during these studies. That was where Henri and his brother Théodore made the acquaintance of Léon Vaudoyer (1803–1872), the son of a renowned architect; and that meeting determined their career. Unlike their older brothers Pierre and Alexandre, who had chosen to follow in their father's footsteps and were studying law, the two opted for architecture and, in turn, each joined the studio overseen by Antoine-Laurent-Thomas Vaudoyer and his nephew Hippolyte Lebas, where they were reunited with their former schoolmate from Sainte-Barbe.

Vaudoyer *père* presented Labrouste for admission to the Ecole des Beaux-Arts, and the young man was admitted in November 1818, first in the painting and sculpture department, then, the following July, in the architecture department. After that, his precocious talent was matched only by his academic triumphs: he was promoted to the first, or upper, class in May 1820; in September 1821, he won second Grand Prix de Rome ("A Courthouse"); then in October 1823, the grand medal for emulation; and finally, in September 1824, the crowning achievement of his studies came in the form of first Grand Prix de Rome ("A Court of Appeals"). He was only twenty-three.

The years he spent at the Villa Medici were among the most glorious in the history of the Académie de France in Rome for the high quality of the young architects in residence there and the fruits their interactions bore. Félix Duban (1798–1870) was there a year before Labrouste; Louis Duc (1802–1879) and Léon Vaudoyer arrived, respectively, one and two years later. His brother Théodore, who also won the

Grand Prix de Rome, joined them in 1828. Labrouste (fig. 2) held a distinctive position among the group, one that was both marginal and central. In Rome, he was silent and "inclined to solitary studies,"[4] as in Paris, where he had liked to do his thinking in the Luxembourg Gardens; yet he was nevertheless, according to Antoine-Nicolas Bailly, "almost the master of his brilliant schoolmates and friends, who all took pleasure in recognizing his superiority."[5] Around 1830, Duban indeed agreed that he had "immense talent"[6]; in 1867, Duc would recall "those good and happy years when I took lessons from you in Rome,"[7] and Vaudoyer would say that his childhood friend had "guided [him], so to speak, in taking [his] first steps."[8]

During their stay in Rome, Labrouste and his friends would record innumerable monuments throughout Italy, either to add to their own learning or to prepare works they were required to send each year to the Académie des Beaux-Arts in order to demonstrate their progress (p. 85, fig. 31). The approach they adopted together marked a shift from prior practices: they were no longer "sticking to ready-made admiration and conventional interpretations; they were instead examining everything anew, mastering every detail and demanding proof of ancient genius from certain neglected or unrecognized details as attentively as they did from the order and forms of the whole."[9] They wanted to "study everything without any intermediary and ... pass no judgment that was not the

2. Charles-Philippe Larivière, *Portrait of Henri Labrouste*, 1825, oil on canvas, 47 × 37 cm, Académie de France, Rome, AFR-P61

3. Henri Labrouste with the engraver Sauvage, "Etruscan tomb in Corneto," J. Marquet de Norvins et al., *Italie pittoresque* (Paris: Amable Costes, [1834–36]), n.p.
4. Théodore Labrouste, *Imaginary View of an Etruscan Tomb*, 1881, 16 × 30.2 cm, private collection

fruit of their own observation."[10] That type of analysis, founded on experience and reason, produced a number of works which, when they were shown in Paris, frequently drew attention for the quality and intelligence of the renderings as well as for the number of drawings, which was often greater than required.

His methodical spirit had inspired Labrouste to base his first submissions on three types of antique edifices, classifying them in a way that was not even imagined by the set rules: "the first year [1825], temples; the second [1826], honorific monuments; the third [1827], public monuments."[11] In 1828, his work started to become much more personal, without forgoing its analytical nature, and now echoed the seafaring tales that had nourished his childhood. After imagining a reconstruction of the port of Antium

(p. 70, fig. 18), for his fourth-year submission he studied the three temples at Paestum, a site founded by Greek colonizers and considered to be protected by Poseidon, or Neptune, the god of the oceans and seas (see pp. 89–93). And in 1829, he decided to devote his final submission to plans for a cenotaph dedicated to the memory of the sailor Jean-François de La Pérouse and his crew, whom Louis XVI had asked to undertake an expedition around the world in 1785, and whose shipwreck had finally been located after forty years of speculation (p. 72, figs. 20 and 21). The discovery had reawakened the young architect's family memories, particularly that of a naval battle in the American War of Independence in which his uncle Jean Georges Gourg had fought alongside La Pérouse in 1781. Thus he intended not only to honor the victims of the fateful expedition: his monument, which was to be raised on a "sea wall of granitic rocks" jutting into the sea, perhaps near Brest, where La Pérouse had embarked, was also meant to "offer French sailors heading off for distant undertakings the last proof of France's acknowledgment and respect." In so doing, Labrouste was echoing the ancients' taste for "all that which reminds citizens of the virtues of their ancestors and inspires a desire to imitate them," as he had written earlier in the essay accompanying his drawings of Paestum.[12]

His project was finished in December 1829, when residents at the Villa Medici received the report the Académie des Beaux-Arts had devoted to their submissions from the year before. Labrouste discovered only then the serious, unfair reproaches his work on Paestum had garnered. Reading one of the critiques of Duban's last submission was also a source of upset: "As a construction, Mr. Duban offers few details ... The Académie feels it must remind pensionnaires that, in their fifth-year project, they must make use of construction studies they have previously made of ancient and modern monuments."[13] The warning was an advance condemnation of his own cenotaph plans. So he chose not to submit them and, in order to hew to the straight and narrow of the Académie's requirements, he resolved to send in their place a design which he would finish the following April (pp. 74–75, figs. 22 and 23). Like the La Pérouse cenotaph, his border bridge was to be erected at the edge of the country; it similarly expressed an idea of travel, but instead of magnifying the moment of departure, it symbolized the return, specifically his own return to Paris after five and a half years abroad.

Like Duban, who had returned a year earlier, Labrouste first found teaching to be a means for spreading his ideas and fighting his battles. On August 1, 1830, just after the revolution that overthrew the Bourbons and put Louis-Philippe on the throne, he founded an atelier at the request of eight dissident students of his former masters Vaudoyer and Lebas, an atelier that would soon produce, in his words, "the first protest against official teaching, which has become exclusive, blind and fatal"[14] (see pp. 193–99). Young artists and writers had already begun to defy academic dogma: just as Labrouste was winning the Prix de Rome, the 1824 Salon had provoked a new quarrel of the Ancients and the Moderns among painters, and when he came back from Italy, the stormy performances of Victor Hugo's *Hernani* were lastingly breaking with

10. Trélat [1875]:10.
11. Bailly 1876:6.
12. Labrouste would have the name of La Pérouse engraved on the facade of the Bibliothèque Sainte-Geneviève, not far from those of other great sailors: the British James Cook and the French Louis-Antoine de Bougainville.
13. "Rapport fait par la section d'architecture sur les ouvrages des pensionnaires pendant l'année 1828," in Leniaud 2005:275–76.
14. Millet 1879–80:214.

15. "Discours prononcé au nom de l'Académie des Beaux-Arts par M. [Léon] Vaudoyer," in *Funérailles de Félix Duban* (Paris: Ducher, 1871), 18.
16. Ibid.
17. [Gustave Bourdin], *L'Autographe au Salon et dans les ateliers*, 2nd year, no. 8, June 17, 1865, p. 63.
18. Bibliothèque Nationale de France, Engravings, VZ-1030 (3)-FOL, MFILM P-64641.
19. F. Mazois, *Les Ruines de Pompéi*, vol. 1 (Paris: Firmin Didot, 1824), 24.

the traditional codes of French theater. But unlike the Romantics, with whom they were soon identified, Duban and he had retained "the greatest respect and the most utter admiration for the classical masterpieces,"[15] of which only servile imitations seemed to them blameworthy. Nonetheless, "by studying them from a new point of view, [they aimed] to draw broader learning from them."[16] As one of Labrouste's former students had rightly written, "Victor Hugo was the head poet, Delacroix was the painters' flag: Mr. Henri Labrouste brought architects the revelation of true antiquity."[17]

In 1832, Labrouste was named Duban's inspector on the worksite for the new Ecole des Beaux-Arts buildings, but he despaired for quite some time of ever obtaining a public commission himself. In the meantime, he continued to produce what were essentially works on paper. He first made several drawings for illustrated publications. The most popular represented ancient vestiges that had recently been uncovered in Pompeii, Segni, and especially Corneto (the current Tarquinia), where he had visited Etruscan tombs in 1829 with Duc, Vaudoyer, and his brother Théodore. His drawing of the Tomb of the Mercareccia, published in 1836 in one of the installments of *Italie pittoresque* (fig. 3), inspired his brother in 1881 to produce an imaginary view as well, revealing the tenacity of emotions felt over a half-century earlier upon exploring the tombs (fig. 4).

Well accustomed to student competitions since the start of his studies, Labrouste also took part in several public competitions in France and abroad. They brought him several notable prizes but still no commission. His choice of competitions was a testament to his penchant for places of contemplation and meditation (plans for the church of Saint-Paul in Nîmes, 1835, and of Saint-Aubin in Toulouse, 1844), as well as his desire to help the most outcast of his contemporaries return to mainstream society (Hospice Cantonal des Aliénés in Lausanne, 1836–37, and prison in Alessandria, Piedmont, 1839–40).

On July 28, 1835, at noon, during the celebrations for the fifth anniversary of the July Revolution, history once again wrought havoc on Labrouste's destiny: Alexandre Labrouste, who had come to watch the Garde Nationale's parade, in which his sons Théodore and Henri were marching, was mortally wounded in an assassination attempt by Giuseppe Marco Fieschi as Louis-Philippe was passing by. On August 5, he was buried with the thirteen other victims of the assassination attempt in the Invalides church, that is, the very place where Napoleon had bestowed on him the Legion of Honor. As fate would have it, too, the emperor's coffin, brought back from the island of St. Helena, was later transferred to rest beneath the Invalides dome on December 15, 1840. The architects responsible for designing that event were Louis Visconti … and Henri Labrouste, whose first son was born on that very same day. The child, whose given name was Charles-François-Napoléon, died soon thereafter on January 7; on January 19, Labrouste was decorated with the Legion of Honor. This series of events, by turns glorious and tragic, mixing the fate of three generations of one family with those of two sovereigns, would find its epilogue in the competition for Napoleon's tomb in 1841. Labrouste, with his

REVUE GÉNÉRALE
DE
L'ARCHITECTURE
ET DES
TRAVAUX PUBLICS
JOURNAL
DES ARCHITECTES DES INGÉNIEURS
DES ARCHÉOLOGUES DES INDUSTRIELS ET DES PROPRIÉTAIRES
SOUS LA DIRECTION DE M CÉSAR DALY ARCHITECTE
SCIENCE ET ART
GÉOLOGIE STÉRÉOTOMIE MACHINES
TERRASSEMENT
MAÇONNERIE CHARPENTE COUVERTURE
PONTS ROUTES CANAUX ÉDIFICES PUBLICS
CONSTRUCTIONS PARTICULIÈRES
PEINTURE SCULPTURE
DÉCORATION AMEUBLEMENT
BATIMENTS RURAUX JARDINS &
SALUBRITÉ
LÉGISLATION JURISPRUDENCE
HISTOIRE
RUE MONSIEUR-LE-PRINCE N° 60 A PARIS
H. LABROUSTE DEL.
ANDREW BEST LELOIR SC.

5. Henri Labrouste with the engravers J. Andrew, A.-J. Best, and I. Leloir, title page from *Revue générale de l'architecture et des travaux publics*, 1840, Bibliothèque nationale de France, Paris, Prints, HZ-465 (1)-PET

Next page:
6. Henri Labrouste with the engraver A. Thiebault, introductory frontispiece for *Revue générale de l'architecture et des travaux publics*, 1840
7. Henri Labrouste, *Caryatids Preserved at the Museum of Studies in Naples*, 1826, 26 × 21.7 cm, Bibliothèque nationale de France, Paris, Prints, VZ-1030 (3)-FOL

marked interest in funerary and commemorative architecture, presented a monument that was as remarkable for its uniqueness as it was for its evocative power. His plan, like the La Pérouse cenotaph before it, was imbued with very personal fixations. The memory of his father, who now lay in rest a few yards from Napoleon, and that of his late son would never be separated from that of the imperial figure.

For the *Revue générale de l'architecture et des travaux publics*, which had just been founded by César Daly, a former student of Duban's, he composed two images in 1840 that illustrated his work methods. On the title page (fig. 5), presented in trompe-l'oeil, he simulated a stele decorated with bas-relief or chiseled patterns of which some details (the sepia tone and frieze of small characters standing out against a row of Corinthian pilasters) seemed to have been inspired by his rendering of the monumental door of the Castel Nuovo in Naples[18]; for the introductory frontispiece (fig. 6), he transposed a Greek high-relief that François Mazois had published in 1824[19] and which he himself

ART
HISTOIRE
SCIENCE
REVUE GENERALE DE
L'ARCHITECTURE
ET DES TRAVAUX PUBLICS

ΤΗ ΒΑΛΑΛΙ ΤΟ ΤΡΟΠΑΙΟΝ ΕΣΤΑΘΗ

had sketched two years later (fig. 7). The hundreds of drawings he had done in Italy thus formed an iconographic catalogue that would continue to feed his work, but the subjects he drew from it were never reproduced literally: as he preferred an architecture of the senses to an architecture of the mind, Labrouste used details chosen for their symbolic or simple decorative value, then he tweaked them and made them part of a novel overall composition. The four eagles holding heavy garlands found at the corners of Trajan's column (p. 7, fig. 4) and the Vendôme column, one of the most emblematic Paris monuments of the First Empire, thus signified Napoleon's presence on the bier ship and funeral wagon for the Return of the Ashes (p. 80, fig. 27). They also appeared beneath the great shield from the 1841 competition (pp. 82–83, fig. 29). A collection of sculpted tools on a Roman cippus[20] would influence, similarly, the tomb of woodworker Antoine Albouse (1852).[21]

20. Bibliothèque Nationale de France, Engravings, VZ-1030 (7)-FOL, MFLM P-66502.
21. Labrouste 1853: pl. 6.

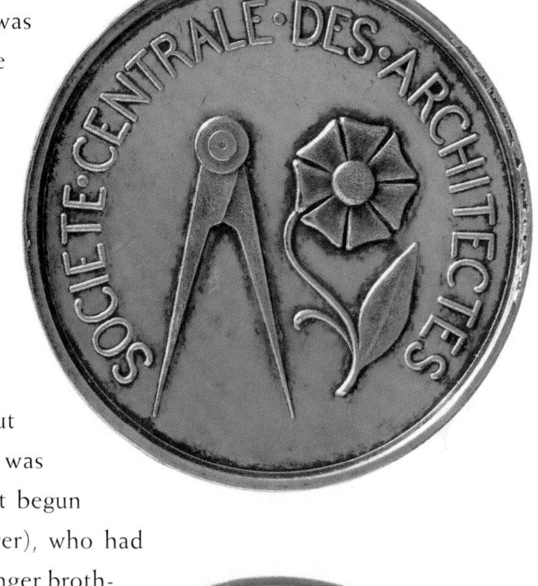

8. Henri Labrouste, with the medalmaker E.-A. Oudiné, attendance token for the Société centrale des architectes, 1846–47, front and back, Paris, Bibliothèque nationale de France, Paris, Prints, RESERVE MUSEE OBJ-239 (2, 3)

Labrouste left the Ecole des Beaux-Arts worksite in 1838, when he was commissioned to oversee upkeep for the Pont de la Concorde, the Dépôt des Marbres on the Rue de l'Université, and the Bibliothèque Sainte-Geneviève, which was still within the royal Collège (now Lycée) Henri-IV, but which was already planned to be moved; at the same time, the administration made him responsible for several historic monuments in the Paris region, particularly the Tour de Montlhéry. These different duties allowed him to wait until his plan for the Bibliothèque Sainte-Geneviève was definitively adopted. In the summer of 1843, Labrouste began construction on his first major project. Stone and iron had at last won out over pencils. He was forty-two (see pp. 95–123). The final location was near the Collège Sainte-Barbe, on which reconstruction had just begun in very fraternal circumstances: Alexandre Labrouste (the younger), who had been head of the school since 1838, had indeed given his two younger brothers the commission to create new plans for the establishment. Théodore oversaw their implementation alone until 1852, then, after the library was finished, Henri took over from him. The two structures, though administratively independent, thus formed a very homogeneous whole: on the Place du Panthéon their respective facades echoed one another, and in the back they seemed to be interconnected.
His career took off after the Revolution of February 1848: when the Second Republic began, the government asked him to sit on several committees; on July 6, he organized, with Duc, the funerals for the victims of the June Days uprising; on July 17, he was named a member of the Historic Monuments Commission; and on December 17, he was elected vice president of the Société Centrale des Architectes, of which he was one of the founding members and for

which he had designed, two years earlier, a remarkable members' token (fig. 8). On a very small surface (3.3 centimeters in diameter), he managed to express what he felt was the essence of architecture: on the one hand, a marriage of science and art, "of precision and liberty," symbolized on the back by a compass and a flower; on the other, a creation of the mind, combining reason and imagination, expressed on the front by a woman's head, half-Cybele, half-Athena, from which monuments of all kinds and from all eras sprang. This figure was similar to the La Pérouse cenotaph plan, in which the architect had wanted it to look like the structure was emerging from the rocks.

The new Bibliothèque Sainte-Geneviève attracted marked interest from the French and foreign press; it contributed to Labrouste's reputation and earned him the rank of officer of the Legion of Honor (January 22, 1852). Shortly thereafter, his students gave him a portrait of himself by Ingres (fig. 9). The drawing, which was done at the artist's home on May 25, 1852, contained a curious detail: Labrouste was wearing a wedding ring, though he was still officially unmarried. He had met his fiancée Clémence Dassys (1804–1898), the daughter of a modest woodworker in Fontainebleau, in the 1830s, but his own mother, doubtlessly, had opposed their marriage. The architect, though he was so dedicated to the truth, had resolved to lead a second, secret life and hide from those close to him his relationship with the young woman, as well as the children they had together: in addition to the

9. Jean-Auguste-Dominique Ingres, *Portrait of Henri Labrouste*, 1852, pencil on paper, 31 × 23.5 cm, National Gallery of Art, Washington, D.C., 1995.47.52

10. J.-N. Truchelut, *Henri Labrouste*, c. 1870, photograph, 11.3 × 8.5 cm, Bibliothèque nationale de France, Paris, Prints, HZ-465-PET FOL

previously mentioned son, there was Marie (1838–1925), Emile (1843–1890), Léon (1846–1907), and Laure (1848–1938). The death of his mother in April 1851 freed him from his secret: after a year of mourning, he finally married Clémence (June 12, 1852) and legitimized his children.

Duban's election to the Académie des Beaux-Arts (March 18, 1854) marked a change of era, as did a showing of some of the most remarkable submissions from Rome for the fourth year of the Salon in 1855, which won Duban a gold medal (1828 submission: the Porticus Octaviae in Rome) and Labrouste a first-class medal (1829: Temple of Neptune in Paestum). The debates the two had aroused at the start of their careers were over, and after a long period of neglect by the administration, Labrouste was now being given all kinds of official functions. He was named a member of the Conseil Général des Bâtiments Civils (January 1, 1854), then general inspector of diocesan buildings (December 5, 1857). In 1854, importantly, he became the architect for the Bibliothèque Impériale, which was slated to be restored and enlarged, and of the diocese of Rennes, where there were plans to build a new seminary. In March 1856, he also received his first major private commission: building a sweeping mansion for the banker and collector Louis Fould, the brother of the minister of state. Labrouste then stopped running his atelier, in which for over a quarter of a century he had trained over four hundred students.

The following years, which were dominated by his work on the Bibliothèque Impériale and the Rennes seminary, were punctuated with tomb projects and construction for private clients. He thus produced a plan to build new quarters for the Ecole Polytechnique on Chaillot Hill (1858–59; not carried out) and built the headquarters for the French railway company PLM (1860–63). In 1865, while the first articles on the Bibliothèque Impériale's new reading room were coming out (it would be open to the public three years later), many awards and honors crowned his career. Labrouste was first elected a corresponding member of several foreign architecture associations, then, in December 1873, president of the Société Centrale des Architectes (fig. 10). On November 23, 1867, he also entered the Académie des Beaux-Arts, where he joined Duban and Duc; the following year, Vaudoyer joined them, in turn, and the four friends from the Villa Medici were reunited beneath the Institut's dome.

Labrouste's last work was a monument dedicated to the fifteenth-century typographer Ulrich Gering, raised at the end of the vestibule in the Bibliothèque Sainte-Geneviève. On the bust's pedestal, he had the first book printed in France sculpted, presented open, like one final invitation to study. Labrouste himself died at his worktable on June 24, 1875, in his wife's childhood home in Fontainebleau. Sitting in one of the armchairs he had designed for the Bibliothèque Impériale, he was writing the program for a competition for the students at the Ecole des Beaux-Arts: the "tomb of a talented architect who was poor all his life and died still young." This striking, almost premonitory moment recalled his finest successes: teaching, building libraries, and commemorative architecture. The Société Centrale des Architectes' token, which his son Léon had reproduced on his tomb (fig. 8), could itself stand in for what Labrouste had always fought for: the triumph of reason.

BARRY BERGDOLL
The Museum of
Modern Art

LABROUSTE AND ITALY

Both the disposition and the tools for breaking with the architectural conventions of early-nineteenth-century Neoclassicism that led Henri Labrouste to be recognized—as Eugène-Emmanuel Viollet-le-Duc recalled a half century later[1]—as the initiator of a veritable revolution in architecture were first honed in the least expected of places: amidst the ruins of classical antiquity. Labrouste was one of the youngest architectural students ever to win the Grand Prix—he was but twenty-three when his design for a *Cour de cassation*, a masterfully composed Doric-temple-fronted design for a majestic courthouse, was singled out by the jury, allowing him to join the sculptor, engraver, painter, and musician also awarded residency that year at the French Academy in Rome in the Villa Medici. Within months of arriving in Rome, however, Labrouste began to develop an entirely new perspective on the lessons of Rome and even the very nature of contemporary architecture and society. The five years in Italy were intended for study and enrichment, filling portfolios with studies after buildings that could be reference points both for a working office and for a teaching atelier, the veritable graphic cogs of a self-reproducing machine aimed at perfecting an architectural ideal and providing standards for the public buildings required in post-Revolutionary French society. An annual submission was required of highly finished and detailed measured drawings after the finest ancient structures, gradated to guide progress, almost like the study of a language, from the mastery of the components of classical buildings through the comparative study of buildings of a similar functional or symbolic type to, in the fourth year, the complete restoration of a major building in carefully studied and exquisitely rendered detail, accompanied by a text explaining the rational for restoration. In the fifth year, shortly before the *pensionnaire* headed home, an original composition was to mark the transition from the study of antiquities to the creation of architecture imbued with all that had been learned. In 1825, Labrouste submitted a study of the elements

1. Viollet-le-Duc, March 5, 13, and 21, 1877:1–2.

1. Henri Labrouste, Imaginary Reconstitution of an Ancient City, undated, 65.6 × 46.1 cm, Académie d'architecture, Paris, 255.1

of the Temple of Antonin and Faustina in the Forum, and especially its great portico, useful for the work underway back in Paris by one of his teachers, Hippolyte Lebas: the church of Notre-Dame-de-Lorette, with its great Corinthian portico. The next year, he sent seven large sheets of Trajan's Column as well as renderings of triumphal arches, including the Arch of Titus in Rome and that of Trajan at Benevento. In the third year, he worked on a comparison of two great monuments of ancient Rome, the Flavian amphitheater (Colosseum) and the Theater of Marcellus, the very building that had been the subject of his teacher A.L.T. Vaudoyer's study almost a half century earlier; both were canonic buildings for studying the use of the orders on multistory-buildings and were as applicable to great works of arcaded engineering as they were as examples of the visual ordering of a facade of windows (as they had been in the development of the Renaissance palazzo). The turn to Paestum—as Martin Bressani studies in this volume—was not to move to a complete temple, after studying monumental columns, triumphal arches, and arenas, but rather to move to the study of an entire city, to take on the urban morphology of which the acropolis was the most impressive remaining part of a complex that could provide a portrait of an ancient site and its changes over time, a place that could reveal a micro-history for studying the very relationship between formal change in architecture and the underlying beliefs and social and political organization of a society.

Over the course of the 1820s, then, the mandate so carefully put in place by the generation of Labrouste's teachers was fundamentally transformed by the young architects who arrived at the Villa Medici in successive years and began to broaden the range of

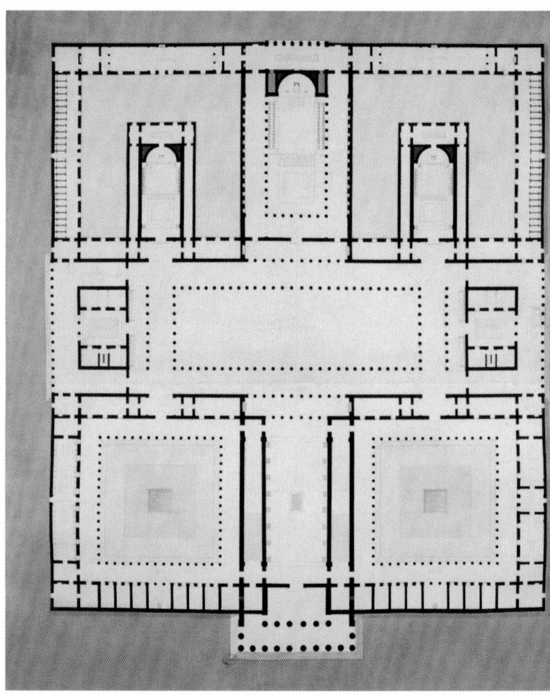

historical periods to be studied, bringing new criteria to bear on what type of lessons even the most frequently studied monuments had to offer. Labrouste was not the first. He had been preceded a year earlier by Félix Duban, and some would argue by Abel Blouet (Grand Prix, 1821) and Emile Gilbert (Grand Prix, 1822), who would later be prime advocates of an austere rationalism in which truth to materials and to structure predominated as generators of architectural form and expression. But for decades to come, Duban and Labrouste would be seen as the fathers of what was briefly called "architectural romanticism" by the 1830s, two very different sensibilities who each in their own way translated into architecture new experiments in the literary and visual arts, associated with the turn to historical rather than mythological material in painting, and the sense of historical detail in literature. By the time Labrouste was at work on his ambitious study of Paestum, he and Duban had been joined by Louis Duc (Grand Prix, 1825), Léon Vaudoyer (Grand Prix, 1826), and Labrouste's brother Théodore (Grand Prix, 1827). They would be seen for the rest of their lives and beyond as comrades in arms. They began to see their work as a shared research project, not only traveling together but also sharing drawings so that each could make a personal copy and to explore

2. Henri Labrouste, Trajan's Column in Rome, details of the bas-reliefs, [1825–30], 25.4 × 43 cm, Bibliothèque nationale de France, Paris, Prints, VZ-1030 (7)-FOL
3. Henri Labrouste, Plan for a Court of Appeals, overall plan, Grand Prix de Rome for architecture, 1824, 113 × 97 cm, École nationale supérieure des beaux-arts, Paris, PRA 178-1

4. Henri Labrouste, Trajan's Column in Rome, elevation of the pedestal, second-year submission from Rome, 1826, 97.4 × 65.8 cm, Académie d'architecture, Paris, 251.1

5. Henri Labrouste, Flavian Amphitheater, known as the Colosseum, in Rome, details of the construction of its vaults, third-year *envoi* from Rome, 1827, 41.6 × 51.5 cm, Académie d'architecture, Paris, 257.4

6. Henri Labrouste, Flavian Amphitheater, known as the Colosseum, in Rome, plan and cross section, third-year *envoi* from Rome, 1827, 102.5 × 68.5 cm, Académie d'architecture, Paris, 257.1

7. Henri Labrouste, Pantheon in Rome, lateral elevation of the portico and profile of a pilaster, [1825–30], 41.1 × 46.9 cm, Académie d'architecture, Paris, 268.7

new historical thinking through architectural observation, coordinating their *envois* so that the exhibition in Rome and then back in Paris would make a larger statement. By 1828, they became intrigued by the utopian socialist followers of Saint-Simon in Paris, a group whose vision of the artist as the leader of social progress began to color their thinking about the very role of the architect, and indeed of the artist in general, as belonging to an avant-garde.

Rather than isolating a classical high point of poised perfection in the arts, the group began to look at monuments as records of civilizations in evolution, legible traces of the process of change. They cultivated a new way of looking at architecture and even landscapes as the encounter between the material realities of mankind as builders and technical innovators and architecture as the embodiment of the potential of communal poetry. To a certain extent they were following the lead of important teachers at the Ecole des Beaux-Arts, notably Charles Percier, who had already become fascinated with the range of expressions, both regional and personal, in the Italian Renaissance (long considered the most relevant updating of the classical legacy), and the inspiring historical lectures of Jean-Nicolas Huyot, who had encouraged an examination of the multiple origins of ancient societies in earlier cultures. Labrouste and his colleagues gravitated not only to the classical sites of eighteenth-century antiquarian tourism—the sites of the Roman fora, the Colosseum (figs. 5, 6), the Basilica of Constantine, the Pantheon (fig. 7), or the Temple of Vesta—they also followed with great excitement the latest excavations and the interests of the archaeologists, antiquarians, and historians of the period who were excavating in Pompeii, discovering Etruscan cities and tomb sites of Etruria, Tuscany, and beyond (fig. 9), and following up on the stylistic diversity of architecture in Sicily—a terrain explored by Percier's student Jacques Ignace Hittorff from 1822 to 1825 and which yielded hybrid architectures from the Greek colonial sites of Agrigento and Selinunte to the Norman-Saracenic sites of Palermo, Céfalu, and Messina, all sites of hybrid mixtures. The techniques of stratigraphy gradually introduced by archaeologists for more careful dating and possible historical reconstruction became for these young archaeologist-architects not simply an approach to digging through layers in order to sift the evidence for recomposing a timeless ideal—the idea of platonic imitation that the powerful theorist and somewhat doctrinaire *secrétaire perpétuel* of the Academy, Quatremère de Quincy, defended in his treatise *De l'imitation* in 1823—but also evidence of the encounter in architecture between the demands of structure and materials and the poetic expression of larger societal beliefs. Developing a new method of rendering architecture—one that depended in part on the use of the *camera lucida* for close observation—Labrouste and his friends paid as much attention to depicting the details of materials and constructions as proportions, underscoring the relationship between form and its material support. The Colosseum, for instance, was studied not simply as an embodiment of the refined Roman solution for the superimposition of the orders, a guide then to modern construction using the proportional matrix of ancient classicism, but also as an engineering feat of great prowess, its vaulted forms intimately related to a careful

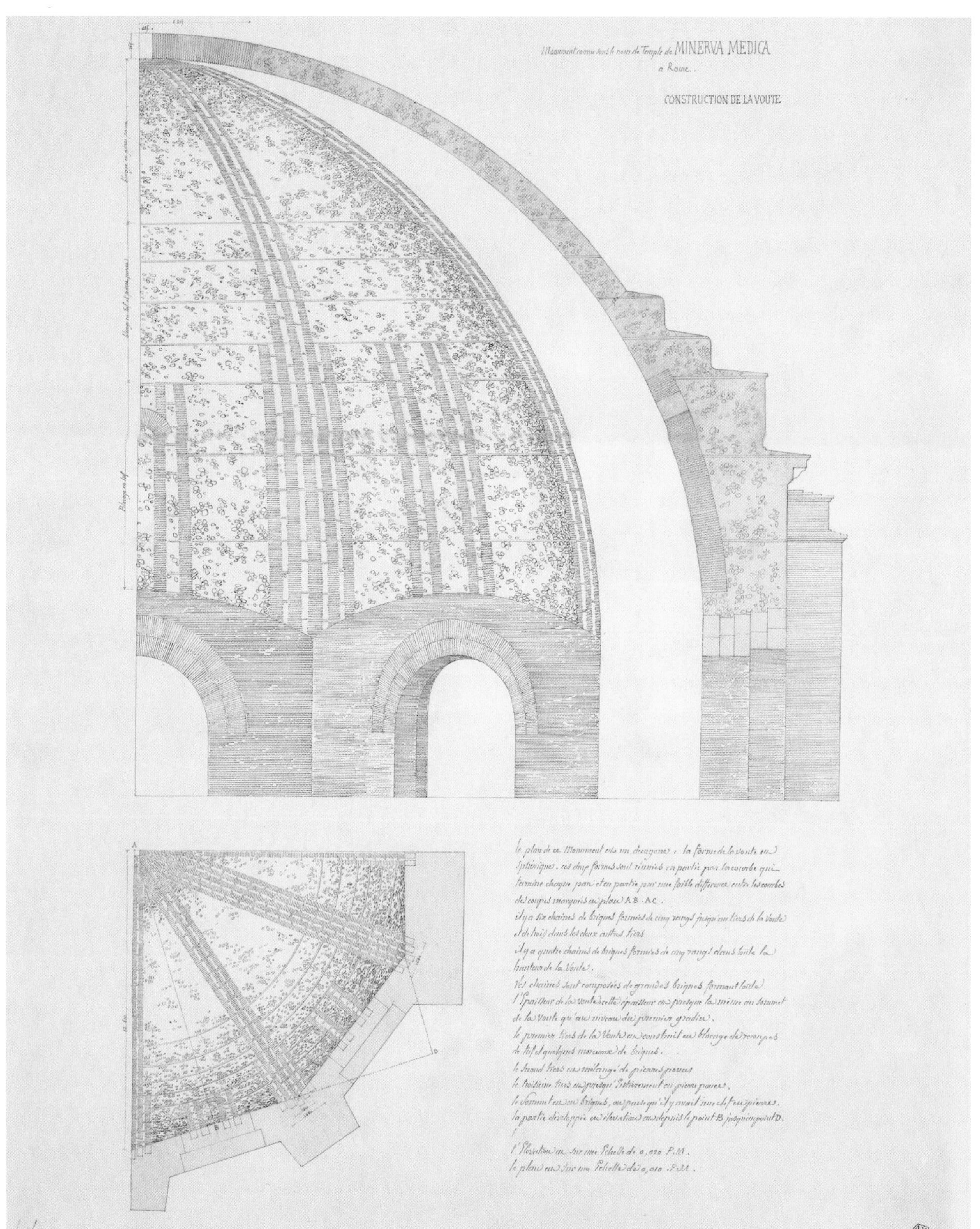
Monument connu sous le nom de Temple de MINERVA MEDICA
a Rome.
CONSTRUCTION DE LA VOUTE
le plan de ce Monument est un decagone. la forme de la voute est
sphérique. ces deux formes sont réunies en partie par la courbe qui
termine chaque pan et en partie par une faible difference entre les courbes
des coupes marqués en plan AB. AC.
il y a six chaines de briques formées de cinq rangs jusqu'au tiers de la voute
et de trois dans les deux autres tiers
il y a quatre chaines de briques formées de cinq rangs dans toute la
hauteur de la voute.
les chaines sont composées de grandes briques formant toute
l'épaisseur de la voute cette épaisseur est presque la même au sommet
de la voute qu'au niveau du premier gradin.
le premier tiers de la voute est construit en blocage de recoupes
de tuf et quelques morceaux de briques.
le second tiers est mélangé de pierres ponces
le troisième tiers est presque entièrement en pierre ponce.
le sommet est en briques, on pense qu'il y avait une clef en pierres.
la partie développée en élévation est depuis le point B jusqu'au point D.
l'élévation est sur une échelle de 0,020 P.M.
le plan est sur une échelle de 0,010 P.M.

selection and deployment of different types of stones, soft and hard, that created a language of form derived from material considerations. The domed vault of the so-called Temple of Minerva Medica (fig. 8), a late Roman (fourth century) nymphaeum, was of interest for its hybrid and experimental mixture of brick and coarse Roman concrete, a system made all the easier to study once part of the dome collapsed in 1828; and Labrouste prepared carefully observed and annotated studies. These studies announced two major themes of all his Roman studies: the collage of materials in both structuring and cladding of buildings that created a veritable language of architecture from an ever broadening palette of materials, as well as a fascination with monuments whose historical dating placed them at the crossroads between cultures, styles, and places. Such drawings would come in great use not only for teaching but for his own articulation of both the arcades and the meeting of different types of stone, brick, and iron in the Bibliothèque Sainte-Geneviève over a decade later.

In the late 1820s, the group led the way toward conceiving of Italy as a veritable laboratory of historicism, the philosophy that all cultural manifestations are the products of their relative place in an ordered progression of historical development, whose laws and dynamics could be perceived in all societal forms. Their approach to site visits and observations translated into architectural thinking some of the new philosophy of history that had been introduced by the so-called romantic historians François Guizot, Augustin Thierry, and Jules Michelet in these years. Their writings were tinged with a political critique of the present and the belief that the transitional nature of post-Revolutionary French society could find parallels in the structure of historical evolution in general, as well as with a radical recognition of the subjective aspects of historical knowledge. "The past changes along with the present," wrote Guizot in 1820 as the future romantic architects were studying architecture under the guidance of the examples set by Neoclassical masters. "Le spectacle est demeuré le même; mais c'est un autre spectateur qui occupe une autre place" (The spectacle remains the same, but the spectator is new and in a different place).[2] Through comparative method these writers sought to understand parallels between different phases of history, detecting patterns of development and even thinking of historical research, according to historian Lionel Gossman, as an act of decipherment.[3] Labrouste and his friends set out to explore the remains of Italy more broadly than earlier generations, and they followed eagerly new discoveries, notably of Etruscan tombs replete with vibrant mural paintings that revealed as much about Etruscan life as about artistic practice. Rather than weeding away the evidence of various periods to get to a moment of essential truth, Labrouste began to find the evidence of transition, of cultural interaction, and even of hybridity in the completeness of the landscape. As César Daly later recalled, a fascination both with the evidence of Greek colonization at Paestum and in Sicily—where Labrouste traveled twice in1828—and with things Etruscan seized this generation: "It was an outburst of the primitive genius of old Greece which came to envelope our whole Rome School

2. F. Guizot, *Discours prononcé pour l'ouverture du cours d'histoire moderne* (Paris: Ladvocat, 1820), 2, 4.
3. Lionel Gossman, "History as Decipherment: Romantic Historiography and the Discovery of the Other," *New Literary History* 18, no. 1 (Autumn 1986): 23–57.

8. Henri Labrouste, Temple of Minerva Medica in Rome, cross section and partial plan of the dome, 1828, 52 × 41.5 cm, Académie d'architecture, Paris, 266

Next pages:
9. Henri Labrouste, Etruscan tomb, known as Del Mare, in Corneto, longitudinal and transverse cross sections, plan, and details of the decoration, 1829, 26.3 × 41.8 cm, Bibliothèque nationale de France, Paris, Prints, VZ-1030 (9)-FOL

1400
2770
390
225
530
1690
750

4. Daly 1862: col. 5.
5. Ibid., col. 6.

and to incite them to study it. The oldest temples, city gates, and theaters on Italian soil, tombs older that Rome itself, were excavated, measured, and drawn by our *grand prix* winners; they understood, no doubt, that the more they looked back to the primitive sources of art the greater would be their chances of encountering pure form, a form free of all corrupting contacts with the fancies and fashions of advanced periods of civilization. Studied in their original simplicity, it seemed to them easier to grasp the true spirit of art forms, to recognize better their raison d'être, and to appreciate more reasonably the sentiment or generative force which had given birth to them."[4] Etruscan tombs then were, as Daly said, paradoxically a cradle for a new art. "Never has one drawn architecture better than at that time, and with less charlatanism in color and more conscientious respect for the forms of the art."[5]

10. Henri Labrouste, Etruscan tomb, known as Della Mercareccia, in Corneto, longitudinal section, plan, and details, 1829, 26.5 × 41.5 cm, Bibliothèque nationale de France, Paris, Prints, VZ-1030 (9)-FOL

11. Henri Labrouste, Etruscan tomb, known as Delle Bighe, in Corneto, plan of the ceiling and elevation of the back wall, 1829, 42 × 26.5 cm, Bibliothèque nationale de France, Paris, Prints, VZ-1030 (9)-FOL

The romantic historians became fascinated by the ways in which modern cultures were equally the products of mixtures and confrontations between cultures in the past—in France, for instance, as the product of native Celtic elements transformed by the arrival of the Romans. Stylistic diversity was itself a mirror of cultural change, and the language of Roman classical architecture was itself a relative value, a language that had evolved and might be used with full understanding of that historical resonance. The *pensionnaires* were drawn especially to architectures of transition rather than ones that represented a period of supposed poise and perfection. Already en route for Rome, Labrouste had been struck by the transition from the medieval to the early Renaissance in the banded architectures of Tuscany, as well as the dome of Florence's cathedral, Santa Maria del Fiore. He arrived at Christmas 1824, just as the city had erected a monument to Brunelleschi, looking up from the public square to his great achievement of the dome, a monument Labrouste sketched. A pendant was planned, to be sculpted by Luigi Pampaloni (erected 1830), at the same time as a new appreciation

12. Henri Labrouste, Altar of the Temple of Mercury in Pompeii, preserved in the Museum of Studies in Naples, general elevation and details, 1826, 25.8 × 21 cm, Bibliothèque nationale de France, Paris, Prints, VZ-1030 (3)-FOL
13. Henri Labrouste, Pompeii paintings preserved in the Museum of Studies in Naples, 1826, 25.5 × 20.4 cm, Bibliothèque nationale de France, Paris, Prints, VZ-1030 (3)-FOL

14. Henri Labrouste, Imaginary Reconstitution of an Ancient City, undated, 26.1 × 44 cm, Académie d'architecture, Paris, 255.2

for Arnolfo di Cambio, the medieval predecessor of Brunelleschi, sparked debates over the relationship between the Middle Ages and the Renaissance. Santa Maria del Fiore was to become the veritable symbol for the Romantics of the complex progression toward the Renaissance, a story not of the overthrow of medieval taste by a return to a correct neo-antique but rather the assimilation of classical ordering systems into the technologically progressive experimentation of the medieval. In a little-known design of 1844 for the competition for a new church of Saint-Aubin in Toulouse,[6] Labrouste was even to propose the ways in which he might extend the experiment of historical updating launched in Florence into a new type of a domed French church design set inside a walled cemetery, a prelude to the project for synthesizing the series of transitional thresholds in architecture that his friend Vaudoyer would soon incorporate in both a historical account of the evolution of architecture in France—in the Saint-Simonian *Magasin Pittoresque*, with the pronouncement that "the real aim of the Renaissance should have been the introduction of an antique spirit into the art of the middle ages in order to lead that art towards the rational construction which it was lacking"[7]—and in his project for Marseille Cathedral in the early 1850s.[8] But as the Renaissance moved from the experiments of Arnolfo and of Brunelleschi to canonized

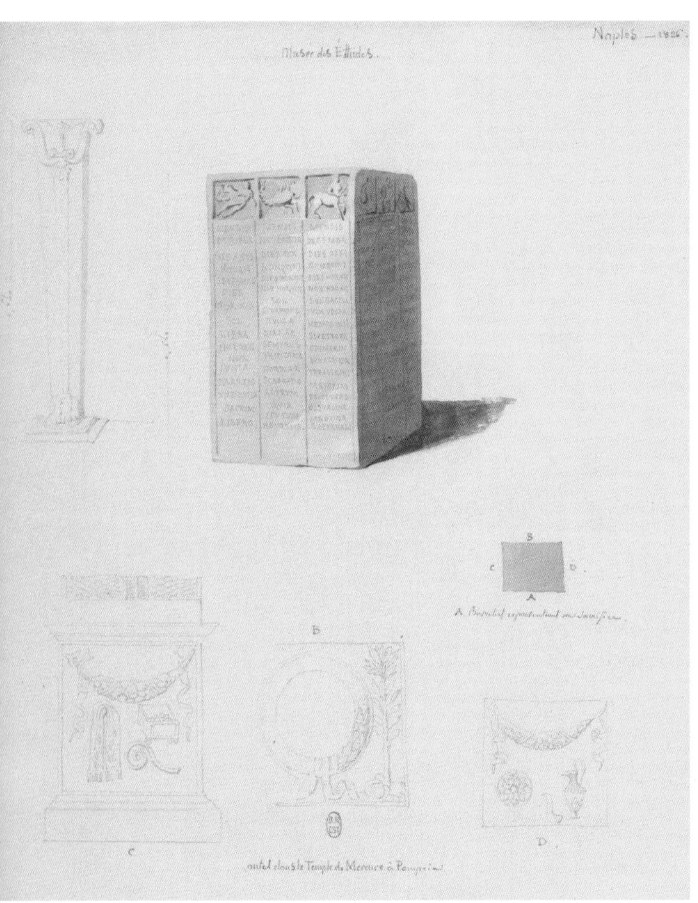

principles of imitation, it enchained architectural progress rather than advancing it. Historical study would move from the search for eternal truths to the understanding of unfinished and even derailed projects in historical progress. In 1826, Labrouste advised Duc, en route for the Academy, to draw all he could—a sheet filled with technical details of the construction drawn by Duc is indeed among Labrouste's drawings preserved at the Bibliothèque Nationale—and later Duc would take inspiration from it for a project for a new cathedral in Birmingham, England, submitted in a competition of 1851. "As far as Florence Cathedral is concerned, I share your opinion, it is, I think, the most beautiful monument of modern architecture, and I would happily trade my 15,000 sketches for a well done study on this monument."[9]

The underground chambers of Etruscan tombs at Corneto, represented in both relief carving and mural painting, in which a simulacrum of quotidian life is prepared for the deceased, seemed to bring yet another complex society into physical contact with the present, much the way the ongoing excavations of Pompeii gave a view of later Roman daily life. Both encounters would color Labrouste's architectural sensibility for the rest of his life, not only in the precise lessons for architectural design, but in the desire to capture the evocative sense of being surrounded by an ambience, a world of evocations. Many years later, both an architect and a painter, Emile Trélat and Henri Delaborde, would look back on this period in which Labrouste's drawings played a major role in changing architectural rendering and historical study and describe it not only as rational but as evincing a whole new approach to architecture as an "organism." Like so many artists of the 1820s, the Romantic architects were fascinated by the studies into comparative anatomy and into evolution at Paris's Muséum d'Histoire Naturelle as well as the debates there between Georges Cuvier and Geoffroy Saint-Hilaire over the relationship of form and function. For Labrouste

6. Louis Peyrusse, "Un projet d'Henri Labrouste pour l'Eglise St. Aubin de Toulouse (1844)," in *Mémoires de la Société Archéologique du Midi de la France* (Toulouse: Société Archéologique du Midi de la France, 2002), 205–15.
7. [Albert Lenoir and Léon Vaudoyer], "Etudes d'architecture en France, ou notions relatives à l'âge et au style des monuments élevés à différentes époques de notre histoire", *Le Magasin Pittoresque* 10, no. 25 (June 1842): 195.
8. Barry Bergdoll, "*Léon Vaudoyer: Historicism in the Age of Industry* (New York: Architectural History Foundation, 1994).
9. Letter from Labrouste to Duc, July 7, 1827 (Los Angeles: Getty Research Institute).

it referred doubly to architecture's nature as a complete organism, in which structure, materials, and configuration all led to a completeness whereby outer form was the expression of both physical and social determinants, but also to the idea of the organic as it was being formulated by Saint-Simonian thinkers, namely an architecture that was at one with its society, a reflection of its belief systems, its habits, its political organization. As he moved from studying Pompeii to Paestum, he saw not three temples sitting in a grassy plane but rather the center of an urban civilization, gates and city walls equally records of the progress of a society of Greek colonists who slowly adapted forms to a new place; in his report he speaks of the "architecture of Posidonia," referring to the original Greek name of the colony as a first reference to an architecture of local rather than universal characteristics and validity.

Equally novel was his particular attention to evidence of the architectural imagination in other arts. In Pompeii, as in Rome, he made studies, not simply on site but also in the museum, of the whole range of artistic materials that might traditionally be used as evidence by an archaeologist. But he also exploited the full range of imagery by which the architectural imagination of a society could be captured: buildings as depicted in mosaics, on coins and medals, on bas reliefs in the illusionistic wall painting found still in many of the houses and preserved in the Naples museum. Social life of the ancients was a prelude to thinking of an architecture that might serve the social needs of the present. Labrouste's drawings, as Trélat would note, "amazed everyone ... one discovered there things that had no authorized place in documents drawn following the Academy's rules. In his studies after buildings, he overlooked nothing, he noted down everything, he describes down to the level of the *mortar joints* and he takes them up in his written descriptions. Here one reads fluently the organism of the structure."[10]

His sketchbooks began to fill with images of contemporary daily life observed in the villages, including festivals and temporary decorations, as well as sketches that imagine ancient rituals, rituals of agriculture, activities that might have given rise to the ornamental vocabulary of architecture, studies that ultimately creep into his official restoration study in the perspective sketch of Temple C, which he argues was a civic basilica (what Labrouste calls a *portique*) because of its unusual plan with a central spine of columns bisecting the space. He imagines the space shortly after a ceremony, decked with shields and other weapons that have been put down in victory. He is as attentive to graffiti on the walls as he is to the evidence of construction details—like the metal joints in the stonework of the pavement—when he peels away the facade to allow a perspective view into a complete building to better record the organic life of its society.

Around 1828, Labrouste began to create for himself a whole new type of composite drawing in which he imagined cities composed of historical strata, depicting them in colorful scenes that captured the interaction between the rituals of civic life and the language of architectural expression (fig. 1). At the same time as he recorded the antique

10. Trélat 1875:14.

15. Henri Labrouste, Basilica of Saint Francis in Assisi, details of frescoes by Giotto, c. 1825, 26 × 41.8 cm, Bibliothèque nationale de France, Paris, Prints, VZ-1030 (5)-FOL

16. Henri Labrouste, House of the Tragic Poet in Pompeii, a perspective view from the atrium, [1825–30], 21 × 26 cm, Bibliothèque nationale de France, Paris, Prints, VZ-1030 (4)-FOL

monuments of the acropolis at Agrigento, for instance, during his 1828 trip around Sicily with Duc, he also did sketches of the upper town with its remaining city walls. It would be the matrix in which he imagined, in quick sketches and finished watercolors, a city of a highly polychromatic architecture in which both the infrastructure of city walls and defensive tower and the monumental temples and tombs within the dense urban fabric are covered with an expressive, colorful skin, in various states of cracking and repair. Applied color, as well as material variety and signs of the passage of time, were evidence of life in architecture. The polygonal stone work of the access road to the town pays homage to the type of "Cyclopean wall" that now fascinated a whole generation as evidence of the earliest structural engineering, while the city gate—the place of honor to visitors or soldiers arriving home—breaks pattern to introduce finely cut ashlar and an affirmative arch. Above are hung shields and spears as though a victorious armed expedition has just returned to celebrate its victories. The drawing, possibly not completed until his return to Paris, in fact comprises elements from a broad range of sources—the Etruscan gateway at Volterra, for instance (fig. 17)—evidence of how a whole might be constituted from both surviving remains and from a few fragments, with the methods of both Romantic comparative history and of comparative anatomy. At the same time as he studied the way a hill town might be formed of successive strata—in which the natural formations of the rock and the human formations of the wall seem literally to build on one another—Labrouste worked repeatedly on what might be a pendant study, trying to reconstitute an imagined port city based on modern-day Anzio (fig. 18), which he visited on a trip to the central Italian regions of Latium and Marche in summer 1828 with Vaudoyer, a trip focused on a quest for

17. Henri Labrouste, Etruscan portico, known as Porta dell'Arco, in Volterra, perspective view and detail of a capital, 1825, 25.6 × 20.5 cm, Bibliothèque nationale de France, Paris, Prints, VZ-1030 (6)-FOL

18. Henri Labrouste, "Three Altars and a Port," 1828, drawing in the album presented to Pierre Guérin, Columbia University, Avery Architectural & Fine Arts Library

19. Henri Labrouste, altars found in the port of Antium and preserved in the Capitoline Museums in Rome, profile and elevations, 1830, 21.5 × 25.8 cm, Bibliothèque nationale de France, Paris, Prints, VZ-1030 (7)-FOL

evidence of remains of Vitruvius's basilica at Fano. The completed watercolor was offered in homage to the director of the academy, the painter Pierre Guérin, in an *album amicorum* prepared for his departure after six years as director to return to Paris. While each *pensionnaire* offered an image, the architects adopted a singular approach to this album: Duban, Labrouste, Duc, and Vaudoyer each selected a different setting in which to compose a series of fragments that would animate a space in a rich dialogue between the arts but also between architecture and the artifacts of daily life. All were staged as though someone had just left the scene—a frequent attribute of Guérin's own paintings—beginning with Duban's image of the interior of an Etruscan tomb lit by the hole that an imagined explorer has just created in the stone ceiling; Vaudoyer brought together the artifacts of Pompeii now in the museum of Naples and staged them in the ruins of an atrium-peristyle house, Vesuvius smoking in the distance; and Duc put fragments as objects of study in his own studio in the Villa Medici. But the most suggestive display of the relationship between artifacts and the historical imagination was Labrouste's view of the port of ancient Antium, re-created by combining the

ICI
SONT
DEPOSES
LES
DEBRIS
DV
NAVFRAGE
DE
LAPEROVSE
LEXPEDITION DE LAPEROVSE PARTIE LE 1 AOVT MDCCLXXXV SOVS

RECIT DE LEXPEDITION DE LAPEROVSE

evidence of three rostral altars he had drawn in Rome's Capitoline Museum (fig. 19) and the evidence of the studies he had made after the micro-architectures that populated ancient Roman fresco painting and ancient coins, which he seems never to have missed the chance of sketching for a growing catalogue of the concentrated urban vistas contained on ancient coins, the means by which architecture traveled literally from place to place throughout the far-flung Roman Empire. The preparatory sketches are to be found in Labrouste's sketchbook no. 325, concerned very largely with urban morphology and growth and labeled "Compositions" on the title page. From the evidence of these three great cylindrical stones in the museum, Labrouste allowed his imagination to restore the missing architectural setting and the lost cityscape of Antium's great harbor with its towering lighthouse (which he moved freely as he studied the overall pictorial composition in a series of sketch versions), colonnaded stoa, and Diocletian windowed warehouses. Reconstituting a whole city from a few significant fragments established a remarkable parallel with the claims of the natural scientists such as Cuvier, who asserted that he might be able to recover the whole organizational physiognomy of a dinosaur from a single key surviving skeletal fragment.

Casting about for a subject for his final year's *envoi*, which required the design of an original building for the uses of modern France, Labrouste studied two subjects, each of which would also be testing grounds for the conviction that as much as an ancient architecture could embody the spirit of the gods of the sea, for instance, in a cityscape, a modern architecture could express at once its time and place and embody specific ideas. He considered the idea of a monument to the great lost eighteenth-century explorer the Comte de La Pérouse, appointed by Louis XV to undertake a voyage around the world in the wake of the discoveries of Captain Cook, a voyage that ended in tragedy when his ship, the *Astrolabe*, vanished in 1788. News of the discovery of elements from the wreckage precisely forty years later off the coral atoll of Vanikoro in the Santa Cruz chain of islands in the South Seas fired the public imagination. Labrouste, who spent part of the previous year exploring Etruscan tombs at Corneto—one of which, though lost today, is even named for him—could not fail to be struck by the parallels. He set out to design a modern monument which could have some of the same relationship to the historical record and to the mystery of understanding a whole social context from artifacts left behind. His imagined coastline is at once powerful and ambiguous: Are we looking at a geological formation of boulders or at sculpted cyclopean retaining walls that are gradually peeled back to provide fine stone work, much as one finds in many ancient Etruscan tumuli, which are both of the earth and on it? The astrolabe itself becomes a sort of rostral altar before the tomb, which takes its features essentially from the Etruscan temple at Cori, which Labrouste's brother Théodore had just begun to study for his own fourth-year *envoi*, and which one year earlier Labrouste had incorporated on the obverse of an

20. Henri Labrouste, Plan for a Cenotaph Commemorating La Pérouse, main elevation, 1829, 64 × 98.4 cm, Académie d'architecture, Paris, 282.1

21. Henri Labrouste, Plan for a Cenotaph Commemorating La Pérouse, longitudinal section, 1829, 63.5 × 97.9 cm, Académie d'architecture, Paris, 282.3

22. Henri Labrouste, Plan for a Border Bridge between France and Italy, lateral elevation, fifth-year *envoi* from Rome, 1829–30, Musée d'Orsay, Paris, gift of Madame Léon Malcotte, 2009, ARO 2009 50

23. Henri Labrouste, Plan for a Border Bridge between France and Italy, perspective, fifth-year *envoi* from Rome, 1829–30, 65 × 97.5 cm, Musée d'Orsay, Paris, gift of Madame Léon Malcotte, 2009, ARO 2009 51

imaginary antique coin he designed as his contribution to the album assembled by the *pensionnaires* for the visiting painter Pierre-Jean David. Here the tomb is clearly related as well to the portico above an ancient port, subtitled with the well wishes "A l'Heureux Retour" for David as he set off for Paris.[11] For the La Pérouse monument, Labrouste, having studied the fine lettering of Roman incised inscriptions, makes for the first time an architecture which is as much about incising information in stone as it is about representing an ordering system in its surface, combining the two- and three-dimensional features he admired in Etruscan tombs as well as in his own studies of both monuments and their representations in murals, mosaics, and on coins. Inside the tomb above the rock is an interpretation of a sequence of Etruscan tombs, creating a vestibule and then a room with lateral light where the artifacts are arranged in the type of evocative piling of the sort found in newly opened tombs. The deeply personal identification with the experience of the Etruscan tomb, and all that it unlocked—not only of the historical project of a more complex view of the evolution of Roman civilization but also the extent to which it occasioned debates among the young architects who made common cause over the nature of architectural meaning—is commemorated over and over again, in the imaginary Etruscan tombs that Duban gave as homages, beginning with Guérin, then in pendants created for

Vaudoyer and Duc, and finally in the unrealized project for a modern Etruscan tomb that Labrouste designed in 1871–72 for his friend Duban (fig. 26).

But in the end it was not a funeral architecture that Labrouste conceived for his final project but rather something extremely forward looking, a design for a frontier bridge over a ravine separating Italy and France, or more accurately Savoy and France, as depicted here (figs. 22, 23). His choice of a modest bridge across a ravine was anything but a straightforward piece of engineering—despite the disappointments of his teachers, notably Vaudoyer who encouraged his own son Léon to do something with some spatial complexity, something "with a little architecture" to it, "un peu d'architecture," rather than a simple utilitarian structure.[12] Labrouste indeed was interested in how the simplest of forms—a burial mound, an urban marker, a rostral column, a rural bridge—could convey a world of ideas, the significance of a site in human history. Almost like someone cleaning their way out of the house, he literally redesigned the very bridge by which he had entered Italy at Beauvoisin five years earlier.[13] His daughter, trained as an architect but writing under the pseudonym Léon Dassy, perhaps described it best many years later: "A monumental bridge which serves as the border between two friendly countries ... Here we find, in the thinking that imagined it, a desire to endow his creation with a very precise usage, an original expression, like an individuality all its own; and even more this bridge, even while being a French monument, was also a link between France and the host country from which the young architect was bringing back his fruitful studies."[14] Again the monument emerges like an organism from the rock which it gradually tames, moving from rocks that seem to take their cues from geology to recall the so-called cyclopean walls of the Etruscans, gradually refined into the stereotomy of Roman construction. The bridge itself is composed of the markers

11. Le Normand-Romain, Fossier, and Korchane 2005: ill. 9k.

12. A. L. T. Vaudoyer to Léon Vaudoyer. Letter in the library of the Institut National d'Histoire de l'Art; forthcoming in a publication to be prepared by Barry Bergdoll.

13. L'Abbé H.-J. Perrin, *Histoire du Pont-de-Beauvoisin* (Paris: Picard, 1897).

14. Dassy [Laure Labrouste] 1879:7.

of space that delineate that most human of constructs: a border. Here something that unites also marks a division: words differentiate while the ancient Roman arches over the road celebrate the linking of the two sides of the ravine, the two nations, and finally the center is marked by one of the cippi or tumuli that fascinated this whole generation briefly known as "Etrusques," taking on the name of the period that had fascinated them and that they felt exemplified their architectural values.

Labrouste returned from Italy, then, not simply with a stock of images and the study material that would make it easy for him to respond to the unexpected demand by a group of students in his own former atelier—that of A.L.T. Vaudoyer and Hippolyte Lebas—to open a teaching studio, but also with a philosophy of both construction and of architecture, of the science and of the art of his profession. It would be eight years before he would be entrusted with the Bibliothèque Sainte-Geneviève, a container not only for a vast library but also, in a sharply synthetic way, for a new philosophy of architecture's relationship to its society and to historical time, even the present. It was a present that felt intensely historical when he returned to Paris only months before the July Revolution of 1830 brought down the reign of the restored Bourbon monarchs and ushered in the constitutional monarchy of Louis-Philippe. And although he would have to wait a time to be entrusted with a major monument—an eight-year stretch which many interpreted as an ostracism of this radical who had been the first to embody the idea of the architectural avant-garde—in fact he would be entrusted with trying to give architecture and urban form to some of the most significant landmarks of a country once again looking to define itself. At first this would be through

24. Henri Labrouste and Th. Labrouste, First Plan for Decoration and Lighting for the Pont de la Concorde in Paris, perspective view and overall plan, 1836, 43.9 × 58.5 cm, Archives Nationales de France, Paris, Maps and Plans, VA/LVI piece 11

25. Henri Labrouste, Final Plan for Lighting for the Pont de la Concorde in Paris, elevations, plan, cross section, and details of a candelabra, 1840, 67.9 × 50.9 cm, Académie d'architecture, Paris, 283

ECLAIRAGE DU PONT DE LA CONCORDE

26. Henri Labrouste, Plan for a Tomb for Félix Duban, perspective view, transverse cross section, and plan, 1871–72, 50 × 33 cm, Académie d'architecture, Paris, 317

ephemeral decorations of the sort that he had so admired in Italy—notably in a sketch of an Italian piazza all decked out in garlands.[15]

Three days after the July Revolution, on August 1, 1830, Labrouste opened his atelier and began almost immediately to formulate a whole new philosophy on the training of architects; in February 1831 he was named to a commission by the Ministry of Fine Arts to reform the architectural instruction at the Ecole des Beaux-Arts; and in July 1832 he joined Duban on the reconstruction of the very buildings of the Ecole des Beaux-Arts, helping then not only to build anew but to do so by the picturesque *mise en scène* of the medieval and Renaissance fragments that had been assembled there as part of Alexandre Lenoir's now dispersed Musée des Monuments Français. Between designing in dialogue with what was called the remains of "notre architecture nationale" (our national architecture) and defining a credo by which to teach, Labrouste was pulling together his work of the previous five years. To his brother Théodore he laid out his ambitions for his atelier: "I want to teach them how to compose with the most simple of means. First of all they need to see clearly the purpose of their design, that they layout the parts following the hierarchy of importance it is reasonable to assign to each. Then I explain to them that firmness of structure comes more from the combination of different materials than from their massiveness, and, as soon as they know the first principles of construction, I tell them that they should derive from the construction itself a rational, expressive form of ornament. I repeat to them often that the arts have the capacity to make all things more beautiful; but I insist that they understand that form in architecture must always be fit to the function it will serve."[16] Eugène Millet, later associated with Viollet-le-Duc and the Gothic Revival, wrote of his passage through the studio that Labrouste made the students study construction from his own drawings, both Italian studies and newly made study sheets, since he did not trust the construction courses of the Ecole. He was literally trying to rebuild the discipline of architecture. "We will review the different masonry methods and bonds of the monuments of the Cyclopians, in order to come to the methods of the most beautiful walls of antiquity or the middle ages."[17] And as Labrouste's daughter later paraphrased her father's credo:"In architecture every form has its rationale and its logical consequences. I insist to my pupils that a work of art has a meaning, that its form is the result of a set of deductions that come in sequence, that it satisfies a need, and that it expresses an idea."[18] But the "idea" was not confined to structural truth; it also derived from the determining role of a program, a program that was not simply a given but that could fulfil the role of a transformative social mission. While this would take a literal form in his projects submitted in 1837 for the Hospice Cantonal des Aliénés of Lausanne, it might also be said to permeate the approach he took to the designs of commemorations and festivals, all of which extended his reflections on the place of ornament in architecture, which he could justify only if it were related to structure and born of a civic purpose. Already in 1831 he worked with Jean-Antoine Alavoine on the décor for the first commemoration of the July Revolution on the Place de la Bastille, literally then designing the materials for a new holiday that could help construct the citizen of the new regime through the transformation of urban space. He would work with Duban on the third edition, in 1833. It is likely that there had been a certain symbiosis between his archaeological observations and his later participation in inventing a language for the civic décor of Paris. Well informed through letters—those between Vaudoyer father and son survive to document this—the *pensionnaires* followed the concerns and projects of the day back in Paris. In 1829, a competition had been held to redesign the Place de la Concorde, articulating its vast open space rendered somewhat amorphous ever since the original moats around the central space, designed by Ange-Jacques Gabriel in the mid-eighteenth century, had been filled in. By the time the project was begun, a revolution had changed the very political system of France. Under

15. Bibliothèque Nationale, Labrouste, Dessins d'Italie, Frame F18514.
16. Letter of November 20, 1830, quoted in [Laure Labrouste] 1928:24.
17. Millet 1879–80:210.
18. [Laure Labrouste] 1928:29.

27. Henri Labrouste, Funeral Wagon Designed for the Return of emperor Napoleon I's remains, lateral and frontal elevations, plan, 1840, 23.5 × 34.3 cm, Institut National d'Histoire de l'Art, Paris, Bibliothèque, Jacques Doucet collections, OC 134

28. Henri Labrouste, Tomb of Caecilia Metella on the Via Appia in Rome, details of the frieze and profile of the entablature, [1825–30], 66 × 98.4 cm, Académie d'architecture, Paris, 253

Next pages:
29. Henri Labrouste, competition entry for the tomb of emperor Napoleon I in Invalides church in Paris, perspective view, plans, cross sections, and elevations, October 1841, 100.7 × 150.5 cm, Musée d'Orsay, Paris, gift of Madame Labrouste, 1889, RF 4198

Louis-Philippe, in the 1830s, Hittorff extended the project into a veritable linking of the spaces of the Champs-Elysées, the Place de la Concorde itself, and the adjacent Tuileries, creating an urban promenading zone and rewriting the Parisian urban fabric through a system of urban lighting, covered benches, and other elements of "street furniture" of a sort known chiefly from ancient Pompeii or the Via Appia but now updated to make a civic monumental language out of cast iron and the new technology of gas lighting. In 1836, Labrouste was entrusted with extending that project to the left bank of the Seine, imagining a whole new treatment of Perronet's Pont de la Concorde (figs. 24, 25). Like Hittorff, Labrouste intended to translate the elements he had studied in the ancient city—columns, pylons, candelabras, and the like—not only into urban markers but also through an innovative use of cast iron, a material he would soon propose for the creation of a great reading room reached itself by ascending a stair weaving under and over a bridge-like structure. In the 1830s, he studied urban infrastructures in Paris and in London, fascinated especially by the use of cast iron in everything from the fountains of the Place Royale (Places des Vosges) to the new iron bridge by the Hôtel-Dieu to the construction of dioramas and railroads in England. In making his own contributions to the period's exploding modern urban transformations, Labrouste began now to explore, with astounding ornamental freedom, the creation of a language for a modern civic furniture that drew on what he had seen of the quest for communal meaning in ancient tombs, specifically in the tumuli and cippi of the Etruscan cities of the dead. At the same time, he sought to create a new iconography for a new technology, the technology of urban lighting. Having redesigned the bridge that linked France and Italy, he now sought to imagine a modern bridge that could transform the very heart of the modernizing French capital. Labrouste worked with his brother Théodore from 1836 to 1841 on this project, studying a series of figures and lighting features in the form of candelabras as well as a series of exedral benches similar to those Baltard created in these years on the Pont Neuf. His work was indeed to serve as a major element in the décor of a political spectacle of high stakes for Louis-Philippe's flagging regime in 1840, when it was decided to stage a dramatic return of Napoleon's ashes for burial in Les Invalides (fig. 27). Louis Visconti and Labrouste now collaborated in extending the linking of urban spaces by architectural markers to create the processional route of the great catafalque that Labrouste designed, a monumental composition of caryatids holding aloft a sarcophagus set atop a giant shield, as Louis-Philippe was eager to underscore Napoleon as a military hero rather than a fallen head of state (fig. 28). This in turn was set atop a great base with huge swags, motifs that Labrouste had studied on the Tomb of Caecilia Metella along the Via Appia, a place where the ancients paid homage to the dead and where the modern Romans enjoyed a shaded *passeggiata*. Similar themes were taken up in the boat that Labrouste designed to carry the emperor's remains on their

PROJET DE TOMBEAU POUR

L'EMPEREUR NAPOLÉON

SOUS LE DOME DES INVALIDES

1. OCTOBRE 1841

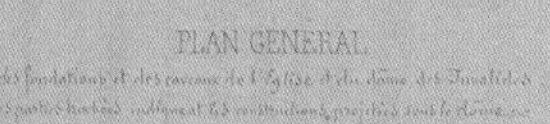

PLAN GENERAL

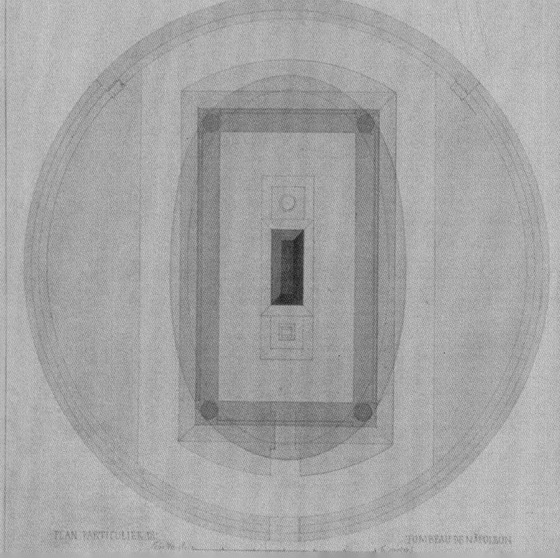

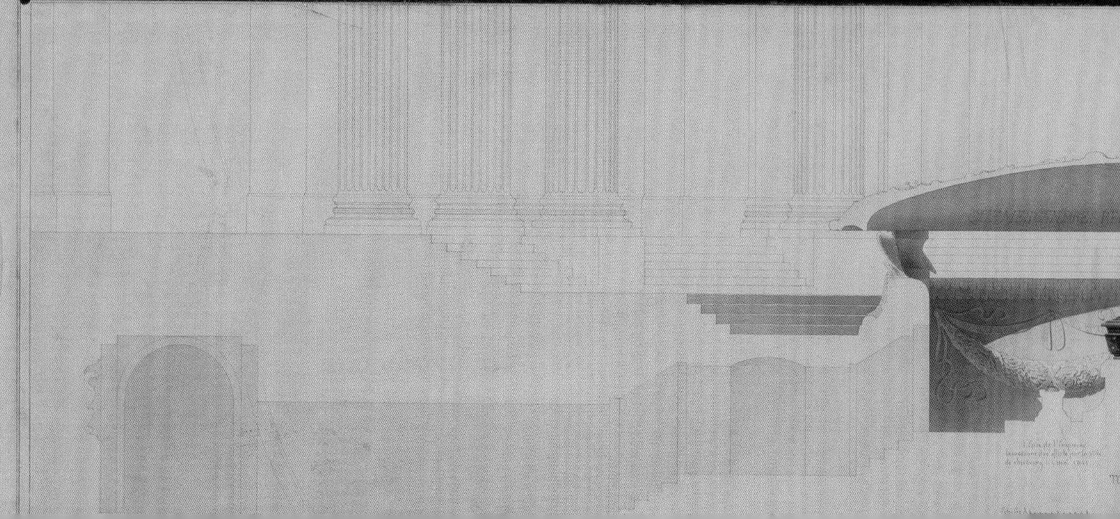

PLACE SOUS LE DOME DES INVALIDES CE TOMBEAU COMMUNIQUERAIT PAR UNE GALERIE SOUTERRAINE
AVEC LES CAVEAUX DU DOME DEJA CONSACRES A D'AUTRES SEPULTURES — IL SERAIT CONSTRUIT EN MARBRE BLANC
DANS CE TOMBEAU SERAIENT DEPOSES LE CORPS DE NAPOLEON, L'EPEE DE L'EMPEREUR, LES DRAPEAUX D'AUSTERLITZ
REMIS AU SENAT PAR L'EMPEREUR, LA COURONNE D'OR OFFERTE PAR LA VILLE DE CHERBOURG ET D'AUTRES OBJETS PRECIEUX
LE TOUT EST RECOUVERT PAR UN BOUCLIER COLOSSAL EN BRONZE DORE PORTE PAR QUATE AIGLES EN MARBRE BLANC
ET SUR LE QUEL SONT INSCRITS DANS DES COURONNES LES NOMS DES VICTOIRES DE NAPOLEON ET SES TITRES A L'AD-
MIRATION DE LA POSTERITE — DEUX BASRELIEFS SONT PLACES AU CENTRE ET REPRESENTENT, L'UN NAPOLEON DANS
UN CHAR DE TRIOMPHE ET COURONNE PAR LA VICTOIRE. AU DESSOUS SONT INSCRITS CES MOTS: MORT EN EXIL LE 5
MAI 1821. L'AUTRE BASRELIEF REPRESENTE LE RETOUR TRIOMPHAL DE NAPOLEON APRES SA MORT: UN VAISSEAU
RAMENE DE Ste HELENE EN FRANCE LES CENDRES DE NAPOLEON. AU DESSOUS SONT INSCRITS CES MOTS: RAMENE
EN FRANCE LE 15 DECEMBRE 1840.

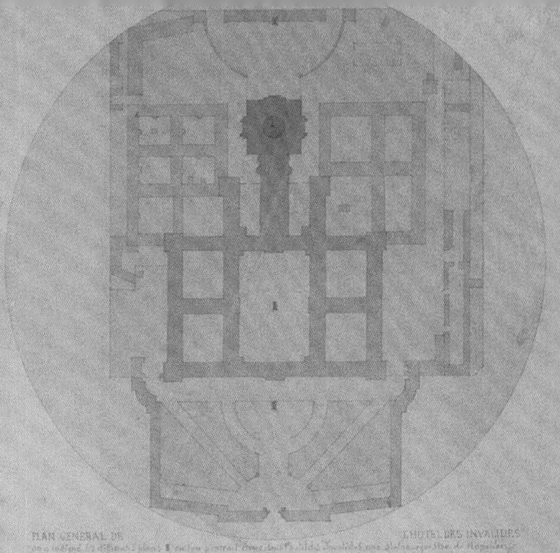

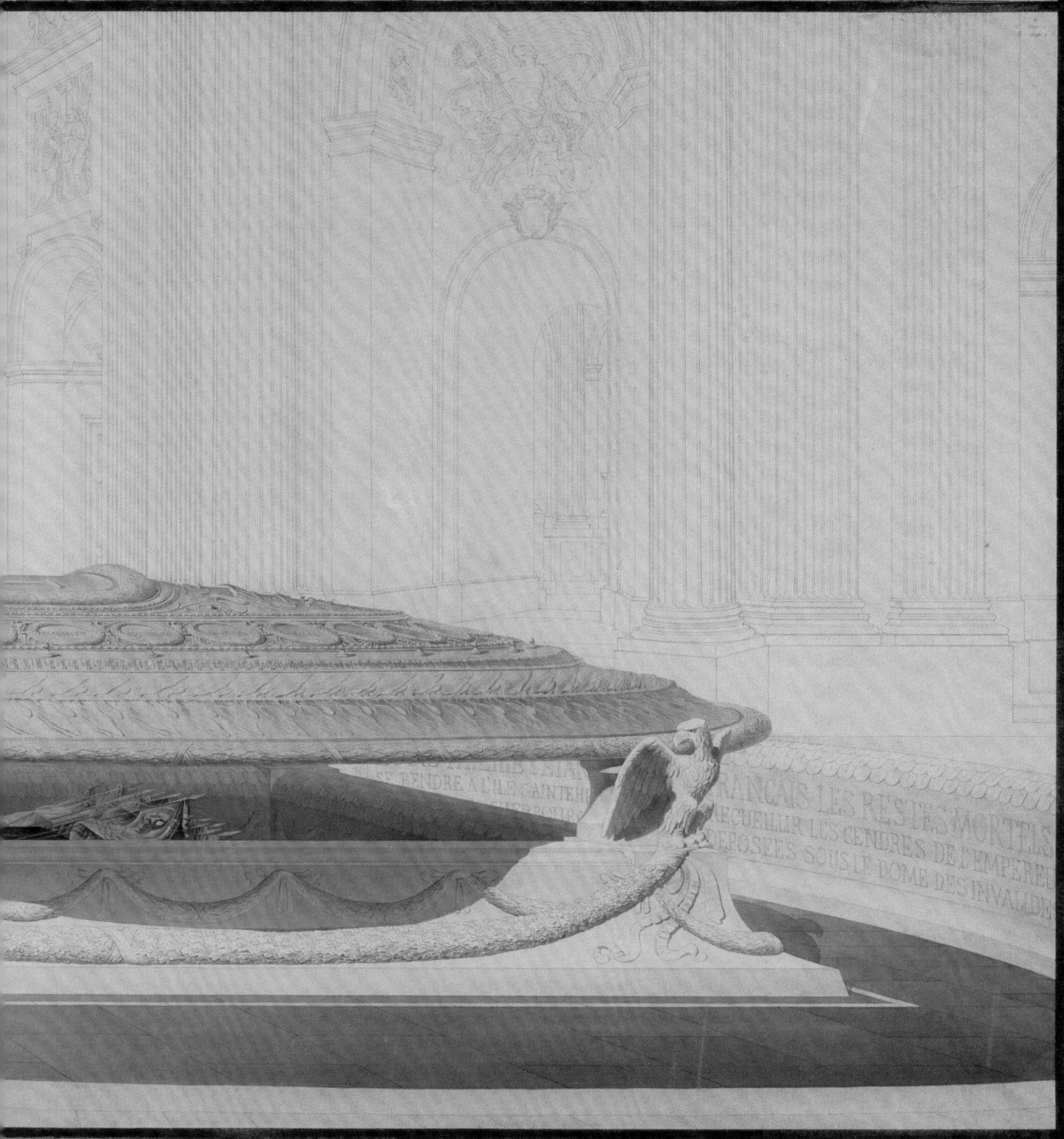

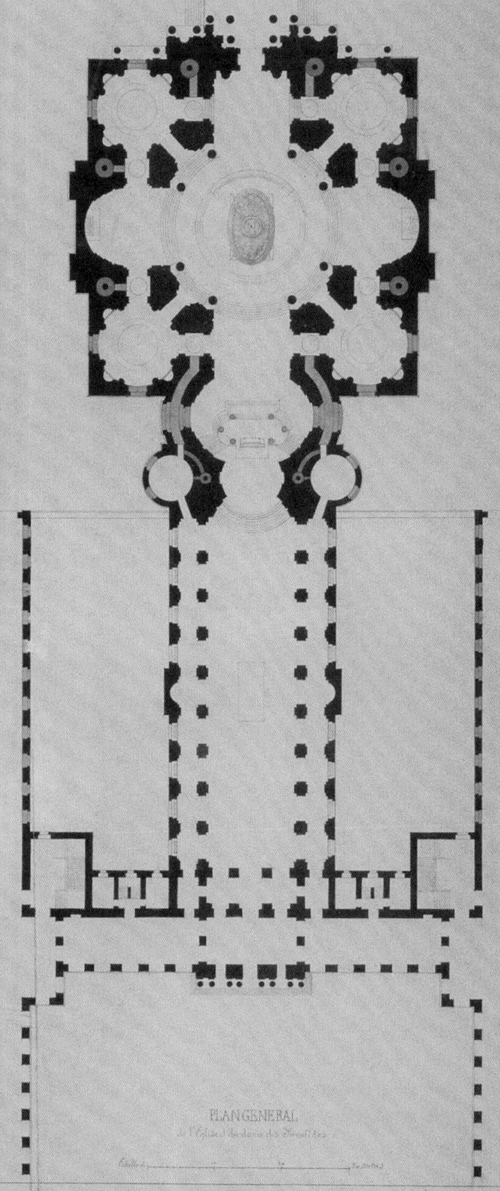

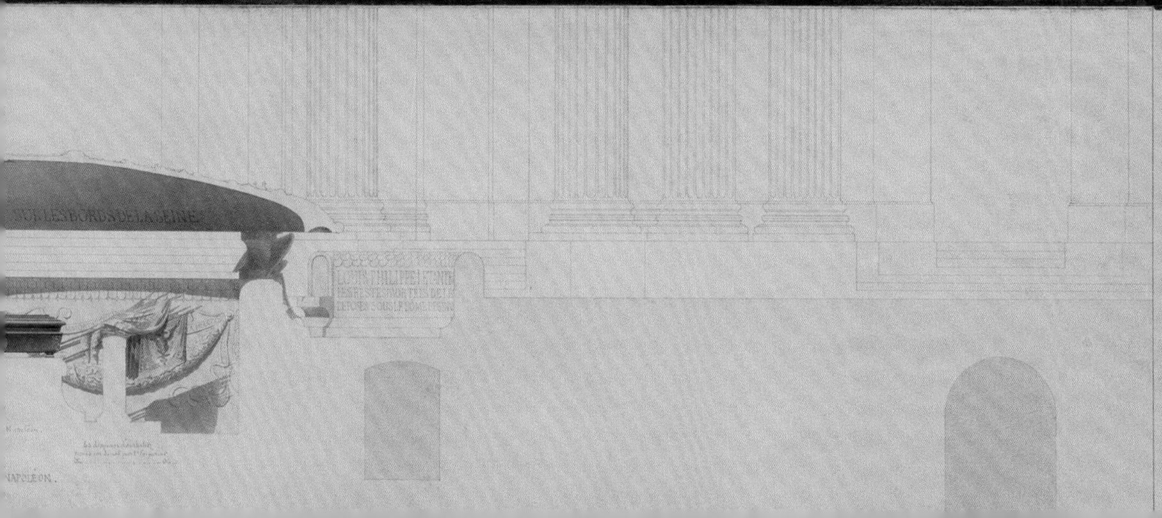

PORTE ANTIQUE,
A PERUGIA
AUGUSTA
PERUSIA

voyage down the Seine from Rouen to Courbevoie, a few miles from Paris, where the sarcophagus was transferred to the funerary carriage and passed under the first of several landmarks Labrouste designed to punctuate the passage.

Many of these motifs would be reconfigured in the brilliant design that Labrouste submitted one year later in the competition launched for the permanent tomb of Napoleon, a project won by Visconti. Labrouste's design (fig. 29) was radical in its minimal intervention into the space of the church. In the crypt he imagined a great garlanded cylinder with the sarcophagus set atop a high pedestal, flags laid diagonally next to it. But, in the upper church, rather than a monumental baldachin of the type Visconti ultimately built, Labrouste decided to create a modernized Etruscan tomb. Like the great circular structures that rise above many Etruscan tombs and indicate subtly the presence of the dead in the landscape, Labrouste imagined a huge elliptical bronze shield, rich in legible iconography, set over the open rectangular crypt of white marble. This was held aloft just enough for a viewer to peer into the gap between the shield and the open crypt, in a line of deep shadow, allowing fragmentary glimpses of the artifacts in the tomb. The whole was of a subtlety that no doubt scarcely served the political capital Louis-Philippe's administration hoped to accrue from the bold but potentially explosive gesture of repatriating Napoleon's remains, even if Labrouste's originality was awarded a gold medal. The project was engraved and celebrated in the *Revue générale de l'architecture et des travaux publics,* founded in 1840 by architect César Daly (a pupil of Duban) and a frequent organ of the Romantic point of view as it was now beginning to manifest itself in designs for the great challenges of the day. As Daly put it, "The fundamental idea of this composition is absolutely new, one can find nothing like it in antiquity or in any other period...," and he concluded that with this new opening, "Art has not yet spoken its last word."[19]

19. Daly, December 1841: col. 613–14.

By the time this competition was announced, work had begun on construction of the Bibliothèque Sainte-Geneviève, a building that would be the vessel for all of Labrouste's research, from his studies of the assemblage of materials that comprised the language of ancient architecture to his studies of the relationship between ceremonies and rituals and the symbolic language of architecture to his notion that architecture could be a tonic for a society. Never inclined to manifestos, or even grand historical narratives, Labrouste left behind a credo not only in masonry and iron but also in iconography, completing the loop by which he had moved between the buildings of ancient societies and the iconography of their architecture in the other arts, and in particular in images that circulated on coins. In 1840 he would undertake two great exercises in architectural iconography for two of the great organs of the profession he was so dedicated to renewing: the frontispiece of Daly's *Revue générale,* whose woodblock engravings would circulate through the postal service to readers even beyond the borders of France; and the design of the medal that was given to each member attending the meetings of the newly formed Société Centrale des Architectes, of which he

30. Henri Labrouste, Gate and Walls of the Alatri Citadel, elevation, 1829, 40.7 × 25.7 cm, Bibliothèque nationale de France, Paris, Prints, VZ-1030 (8) FOL

31. Henri Labrouste, Etruscan arch, known as Porta Augusta, in Perugia, elevation and plan, c. 1825, 66.5 × 97.3 cm, Académie d'architecture, Paris, 278

20. Quoted in Anonymous 1849–50: col. 151.

was a founding member. In both frontispiece and medal, a city comprised of monuments from the most diverse periods of the history of architecture would be viewed above the walls of the *civitas*. In both, medieval monuments were given their full place in the cityscape, just as within a few years many of the leading figures of the Gothic Revival would emerge from Labrouste's atelier. In the frontispiece the city is poised over the caption "History," held aloft by two caryatids identified as "Art" and "Science," the two terms by which all great architecture emerged from a dialectic between material reality and poetic imagination. On one face of the medal, designed by Labrouste and engraved by Eugène-André Oudiné, were paired a flower and a compass, indicative of the organic relationship between imagination and physics, or, as Labrouste explained, emblems of "precision" and of "freedom" ("précision et liberté").[20] On the other face, the city was the crown of a female figure. Having invented the iconography for both the architectural press and for the professional society of architects, Labrouste designed not only the means of modern commemoration, but also the very circulating iconography that would provide echoes and clues of the rich exploration in new materials and new symbols for the nineteenth century that would be the building blocks of his two great libraries, libraries in turn that would collect the artifacts he had just designed.

32. Henri Labrouste, Saint Mark's Basilica in Venice, details of the bronze doors, 1830, 20.4 × 25.3 cm, Bibliothèque nationale de France, Paris, Prints, VZ-1030 (10)-FOL

33. Henri Labrouste, The Apostolic Palace in the Vatican, vaults of the second floor loggias, perspective views and detail, 1830, 41.2 × 25.6 cm, Bibliothèque nationale de France, Paris, Prints, VZ-1030 (8)-FOL

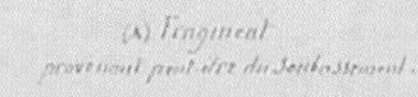
(A) Fragment
provenant peut-être du Soubassement.

MARTIN BRESSANI
McGill University

THE PAESTUM CONTROVERSY

In April 1829, Henri Labrouste, in residence at the Villa Medici, sent his fourth-year submission from Rome to Paris: a set of twenty-three drawings illustrating the current state and a restoration of the three Greek temples in Paestum, Italy. Never had a submission from Rome been as detailed, both in terms of its precision and for the number of drawings included (fig. 1).[1] Despite its exceptional quality, the work was subject to a niggling and rather mean-spirited critique from the Académie des Beaux-Arts. That judgment was the beginning of a famous controversy, fueled by the painter Horace Vernet, head of the Académie de France in Rome. In order to best refute the critiques, Vernet went on an expedition to Paestum himself. In May 1830, he sent a detailed report to Paris, which demonstrated, point by point, how faithful Labrouste's renderings were. When his colleagues at the Académie refused to issue a retraction, Vernet asked Minister of the Interior François Guizot to relieve him of his duties. The minister not only refused to let him step down, but he clearly established, in his official response, that the Académie de France in Rome was administratively independent from the Académie des Beaux-Arts in Paris. Vernet would remain in office until the end of his term in 1834. The affair, which was reported in the press, had a strong impact, making Labrouste the standard-bearer for the Romantic rebellion in architecture.

Despite some historians' hesitations, the ill will in the Académie's report cannot be ignored.[2] Labrouste was the first to complain about it to Vernet. The report signed by permanent secretary Quatremère de Quincy—much longer than any other examination of a fourth-year submission by the Académie—raised a long series of archaeological questions that, at first glance, appear rather finicky. One feels a certain irritation in comments on Labrouste's view as compared to Delagardette's work *Les Ruines de Paestum* (1799), which

Research for this paper was made possible by support from the Social Sciences and Humanities Research Council of Canada.

1. Louis Duc's 1830 submission—a restoration of the Colosseum in Rome—would also include twenty-three drawings, but fourth-year submissions were usually less ample: Duban's (1828) had fourteen drawings, and Gilbert's (1827) and Blouet's (1826) each had ten; Villain's (1825) had eight, and Lesueur's (1824) five.
2. See the reservations expressed by Jean-Michel Leniaud, in Leniaud 2005, and by Pierre Pinon in Pinon and Amprimoz 1988.

1. Henri Labrouste, Paestum, fragments from a single edifice, fourth-year submission from Rome, 1828–29, 66.7 × 98.2 cm, École nationale supérieure des beaux-arts, Paris, Env 22-22

3. Letter from Labrouste to Vernet, July 8, 1830 (Fossier, Chave, and Kuhnmunch 2010:125).
4. Letter from Vernet to Quatremère de Quincy, May 29, 1830 (Fossier, Chave, and Kuhnmunch 2010:111).
5. Trélat 1875; Delaborde 1878; on the other hand, the engineer Alexandre Corréard reproaches Labrouste for not taking into account the materials used and the means of construction, *Journal du génie civil, des sciences et des arts* 7 (1830): 413, note 1.
6. Benjamin Constant, "Réflexions sur la tragédie," *Revue de Paris* 7 (1829): 135.
7. The three temples are respectively known today as the Temple of Hera II, the Temple of Hera I, and the Temple of Athena.
8. Henri Labrouste, "Mémoire explicatif de la restauration des Temples de Paestum," École des Beaux-Arts, ms. 240.II, f. 31 and 32 and its draft, ibid., PC 77832-7-200. The essay and the plates would be published after Labrouste's death, with some important changes: Labrouste 1877.

2. Henri Labrouste, Paestum, plan for the restoration of the Temple of Neptune, longitudinal cross-section, current state, fourth-year submission from Rome, 1828–29, 66.5 × 190.9 cm, École nationale supérieure des beaux-arts, Paris, Env 22-10
3. Henri Labrouste, Paestum, plan for the restoration of the Temple of Neptune, longitudinal cross section, restored state, fourth-year submission from Rome, 1828–29, 66.4 × 189.5 cm, École nationale supérieure des beaux-arts, Paris, Env 22-11

had been the authoritative take on the subject—but nothing points to the notion that Quatremère de Quincy had picked up an unfortunate Romantic bent in the work of the young resident in Rome.

In 1829, the Académie sought above all to invalidate the accuracy of his reproductions. The following year, it shifted its attention to the restoration's more easily debatable aspects. Labrouste quickly pointed out that slippage. Back in Paris, he wrote to Vernet, "I went to see Quatremère de Quincy, who began by changing the subject. He told me that I could not fight my masters' critiques of my restoration without being guilty myself. He refused to understand that my qualm was not about the critiques of my restoration, but about the questioning of the accuracy of my recording of the current state."[3] Labrouste insists that the accuracy of his measured drawings be acknowledged (fig. 2). Rather than "quick sketches made on site to create preestablished systems,"[4] to use the terms in which Vernet impugned Delagardette's method, Labrouste based his approach on a rigorous examination of the material facts during his two expeditions to Paestum. Striving for the truth is the foundation of his anti-academic attitude. Historians have written a great deal about the "rationalism" of his restoration project—that is, his insistence on the constructive aspect,[5] but the young architect did not so much seek to establish a constructive logic *in abstracto* as to reestablish a historical truth. Like Romantic drama, which aims to escape the "false and purely conventional genre" of classical theater by evoking the charm of "local color,"[6] Labrouste wanted to dispel the conventional view of antiquity conveyed by academic doctrine by stressing the specificity of Paestum's architecture. His fascination with history, moreover, led him to study three buildings rather than a single monument, as was customary practice. As they were built over a period of more than one hundred years, the temples at Paestum allowed him to reconstruct a long-term evolution.

One of the most notable aspects of his work is indeed the issue of chronology. Delagardette saw the Temple of Neptune as the last built of the three monuments, as its form came closest to the classical Greek temple (fig. 3). The "basilica" (or "portico," as Labrouste termed it) and the Temple of Ceres, whose forms were comparatively more primitive, were judged the oldest.[7] Labrouste, in contrast, supposed that the Temple of Neptune's Greek purity indicated that it had been erected first, while the two other structures were the fruit of a process of adaption to the new colonial environment. He sums it up in his explanatory essay:

> These observations lead me to consider the Temple of Neptune as being Greek Architecture, and built at a time in which the Trezenians native to the Peloponese [sic], founders of Posidonia [sic], had not yet forgotten the architectural principles that they had brought with them from Greece. And to consider the portico and the Temple of Ceres to be subsequent to the Temple of Neptune and built at a time when the Posidonians [sic], having grown more powerful, wished to create *a new architecture* [our emphasis]. These two monuments alone present *the Typical architecture of Posidonia*.[8]

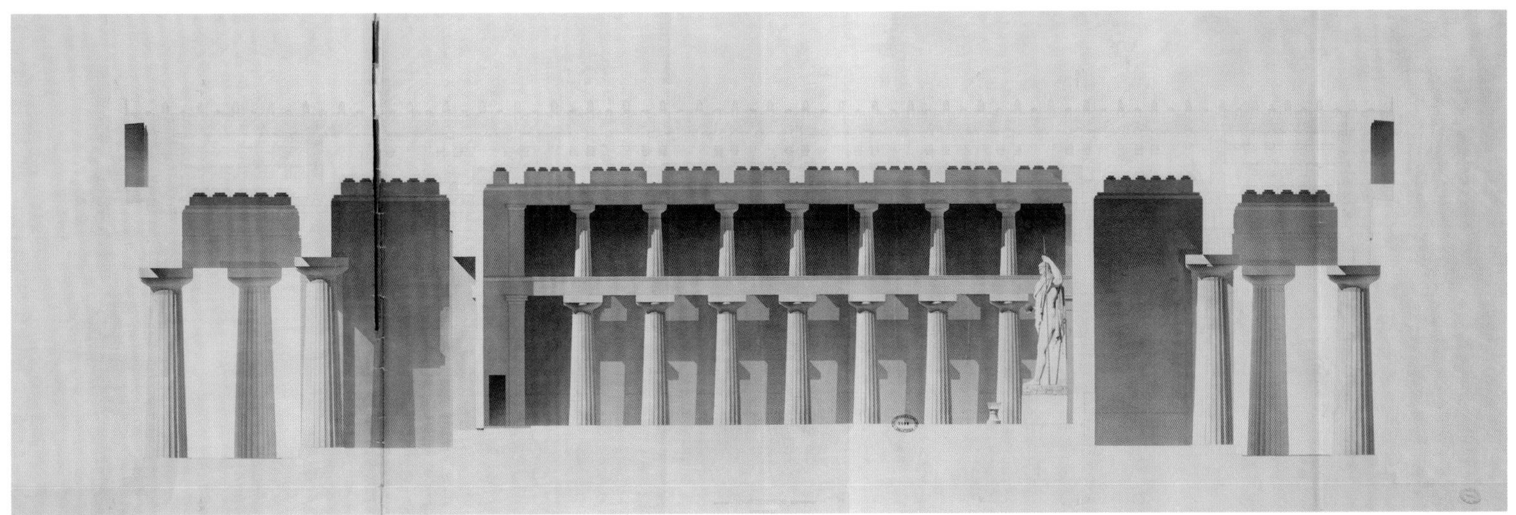

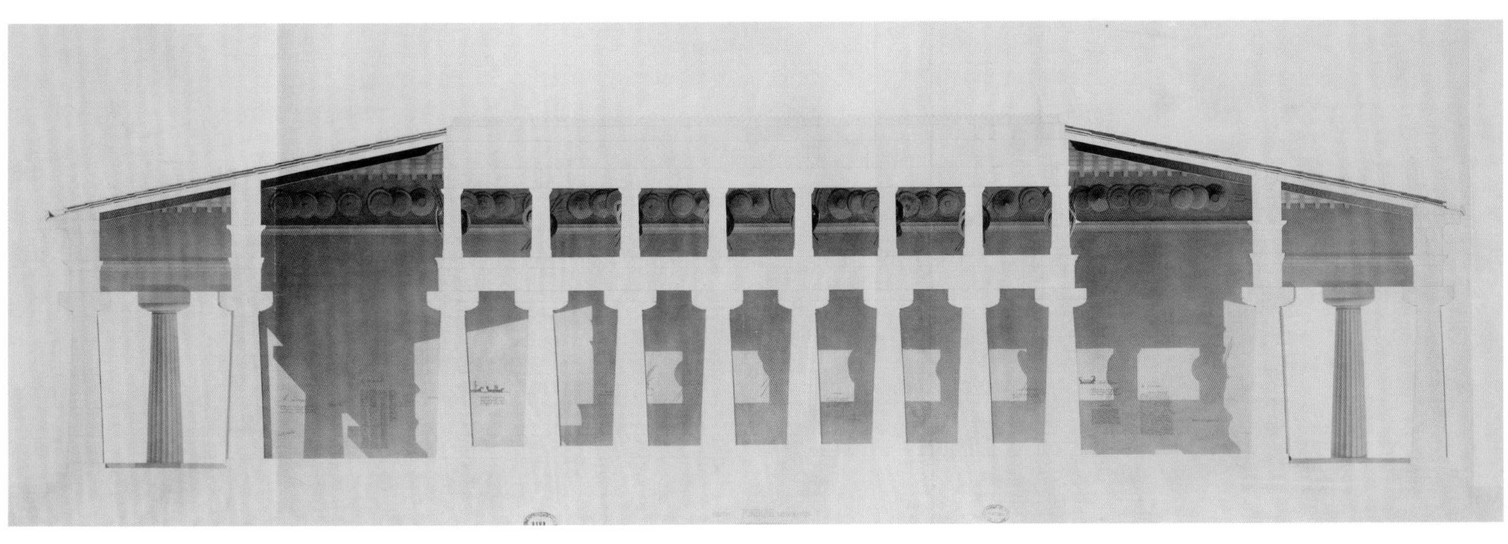

9. Ernest Beulé, "L'architecture au siècle de Pisistrate. Les temples de Paestum," *Revue générale de l'architecture et des travaux publics* 16 (1858): col. 15; Dassy 1879.
10. Levine 1975:792.
11. Fossier, Chave, and Kuhnmunch 2010:379.
12. P. Morey, "Temple dit de la Paix, à Paestum," *Nouvelles Annales publiées par la section française de l'Institut archéologique* 2 (1838): 98–106.
13. Mariano Vasi, *An Instructive Itinerary from Rome to Naples* (Rome: Poggioli, 1827), 278–86.
14. Labrouste, "Mémoire explicatif ... ," loc. cit., f. 29.

Previous page:
4. Henri Labrouste, Paestum, plan for the restoration of the Temple of Neptune, longitudinal cross section, restored state, fourth-year submission from Rome, 1828–29, 66.1 × 190.2 cm, École nationale supérieure des beaux-arts, Paris, Env 22-20

5. Henri Labrouste, Paestum, walls of the city and cross section of a tomb, fourth-year submission from Rome, 1828–29, 66.7 × 98.2 cm, École nationale supérieure des beaux-arts, Paris, Env 22-23

In its report, the Académie did not single out this chronological reversal, but other commentators of the time were quick to note its provocative nature.[9] By documenting the formation of "a new architecture" typical of Poseidonia (the former name of Paestum), Labrouste was defending the right of architectural creation: each region and each era must be free to express their own characteristics. As historian Neil Levine summed up, "by this specificity, Labrouste offered a radical reinterpretation of Greek architecture as Greek and thus called into question the fundamental quality of classicism—that eternal reappearance of supposedly similar forms in certain chosen civilizations."[10] In its reports on the work of the architecture students written in the following years, the Académie would indeed repeatedly express its worry about their neglect of the canonic repertoire. In 1831, it thus criticized "the system used for some time now by the architect residents" for introducing into their submissions "profiles, ornaments and a taste for certain imperfect works from those eras, in which the arts, still in their infancy, had not yet attained the degree of perfection that characterizes the edifices of the proud ages of Pericles and Augustus."[11]

In Labrouste's case, a taste for "imperfect works" could be seen in the Etruscan influence he noted at Paestum. In the introduction to his explanatory essay, Labrouste firmly denied that the temples of Paestum had been built by the Etruscans, as a group of Italian archaeologists had claimed in the eighteenth century. But he did not deny that the Greek colony of Poseidonia had been subjected to their influence. The first plate of his restoration reproduces, outside the city walls, several tombs that look like the Etruscan graves at Corneto (fig. 5). The last plate reproduces the capitals of the Temple of Peace, which Pierre Morey would identify several years later as Etruscan[12] (fig. 1). Even more significant, his chronology of the temples and his designation of the "basilica" as a "portico" with a civic purpose are borrowed from a book that defends the Etruscan influence in Paestum: *An Instructive Itinerary from Rome to Naples* by the archaeologist Mariano Vasi, a guide for travelers often reprinted during the first half of the nineteenth century.[13]

The Etruscan presence indeed seeped into his restoration of the temples. To decorate the interior of the Temple of Ceres (fig. 6), he was inspired by the tombs at Corneto. He supposed that the entryway columns in the *cella* were Ionic, a type of order specifically associated with the Etruscans. In his description of the "portico" as a civil meeting place, he supposes that Poseidonian society was a mix of two cultures. He quotes Cicero, who describes native and conquering citizens fighting over the use of one such portico in Pompeii.[14] The layout, longitudinally divided by a colonnade, seems like the perfect image of a society divided into two classes (figs. 3, 4). Other details, such as the two types of stone used in the construction of the portico and the Temple of Ceres, also show, according to him, the culturally mixed nature of the architecture. Rather than tracing a conventional evolution toward the pure form of the Temple of Neptune, Labrouste enjoys documenting a regression into eclecticism.[15]

This sort of architectural hybridization would obviously have shocked the Académie des Beaux-Arts, particularly as they would have recognized therein one of the Romantic rebellion's favorite themes. In his famous preface to *Cromwell* in 1827, Victor Hugo wrote in praise of mixed genres, in which he sees the main characteristic of modern drama. According to the poet, Romantic literature must show man as a combination of two beings, one flesh and the other immortal. And the stage sets of a drama should give the impression of life, with historical and geographical color imbuing the backdrop. Labrouste's restoration project perfectly illustrates this delight in expressiveness: the Temple of Ceres's mix of Doric and Ionic orders; the dynamic ambulatory space of the portico, decorated with a picturesque concatenation of weapons, shields, and inscriptions.

The Paestum temples' evolution as described by Labrouste also illustrates a Romantic conception of the progress of history. The Saint-Simonians, for example, saw history as a cycle in which short organic periods of cultural unification alternated with long "critical" ages, which were a kind of interregnum characterized by a mix of ideas and cultures.[16] The philosopher Pierre-Simon Ballanche, one of the sources of Saint-Simonian historical doctrine, puts the emphasis on these eras of transition—ages of "social palingenesis," as he elegantly puts it. These periods, which undergo "frequent colonization, conquests, a mixing of the races, and diverse modifications of the original institution" hold, according to Ballanche, the keys to history's secrets.[17] The history of the three temples as told by Labrouste conforms to this analysis. From the Temple of Neptune's stylistic unity to the hybrid constructions of the portico and the Temple of Ceres, we can see a shift from an organic period to an age of social palingenesis. Perhaps the Poseidonians wanted, as Labrouste writes, "to create a new architecture for themselves," but they only succeeded in building something heterogeneous. "The typical Poseidonian architecture" is thus a hybrid form, as would be the architecture of the nineteenth century.

15. Bressani 2007.
16. This theory was propagated by Émile Barrault in his *Aux artistes. Du passé et de l'avenir des beaux-arts (Doctrine de Saint-Simon)* (Paris: Alexandre Mesnier, 1830).
17. [Pierre-Henri Ballanche], *Essais de palingénésie sociale*, vol. 1 (Paris: Jules Didot aîné, 1827), 86.

6. Henri Labrouste, Paestum, plan for the restoration of the Temple of Ceres, lateral and main elevations, plan and cross sections, restored state, fourth-year submission from Rome, 1828–29, 65.9 × 190.6 cm, École nationale supérieure des beaux-arts, Paris, Env 22-16

BUFFON
VOLTAIRE
MASSILLON

MARTIN BRESSANI
McGill University

MARC GRIGNON
Université Laval

THE BIBLIOTHÈQUE SAINTE-GENEVIÈVE AND "HEALING" ARCHITECTURE

Henri Labrouste's masterwork, the Bibliothèque Sainte-Geneviève, was one of the July Monarchy's most prominent projects. Built to house the collections of manuscripts and printed matter from the former Abbaye Sainte-Geneviève—the largest collections in France after the Bibliothèque Royale's—it had a vaulted iron reading room which, when it opened to the public in February 1851, was "one of the most sizable in Paris, and ... certainly the most imposing and the most beautiful"[1] (fig. 2).

The building was one of the key elements in restructuring the Place du Panthéon, a place with a strong symbolic dimension relating to the July Monarchy. The project began in the late 1830s and was completed after the Revolution of 1848. In a note written in 1852 to his friend César Daly, the editor of the *Revue générale de l'architecture et des travaux publics*, Labrouste took pleasure in listing the ministers who had successively been in office since he had been commissioned with the project. "In all, eleven ministers," he concluded, "but there was only one architect."[2] His work was the product of a single vision that transcended political tribulations.

It has often been noted that Labrouste had to wait a long period after returning from the Villa Medici before obtaining his first important commission—years of waiting which some explain as the aftereffect of the scandal caused by his Paestum restoration project. In fact, Labrouste followed the normal trajectory for Rome's prizewinners; they could never predict when they would have a chance to obtain a prestigious commission from the government. The 1830s were for him a time of intellectual growth, which led him to reflect on the social influence of architecture.

Research for this paper was made possible by support from the Social Sciences and Humanities Research Council of Canada.

1. Calonne 1853:463.
2. Labrouste 1852: col. 384.

1. Bibliothèque Sainte-Geneviève, view of the busts and paintings decorating the vestibule. Photograph: J.-Cl. N'Diaye

THE INFLUENCE OF THE ARTS ON HEALTH

Before we look into the famous building on the Place du Panthéon, we should follow the trajectory that would lead him to consider architecture as a means for social regeneration. His study of the monuments at Paestum had already revealed his knowledge of Romantic theories on the development of societies. When Labrouste returned from Italy, fiery debates were taking place between utopian thinkers in search of a formula for the future that could regenerate France. Neo-Catholics, Saint-Simonians, and later Fourierists bent the Romantic movement toward a social and political end. The artist or writer had to become "humanity's tutor," in the words of the Saint-Simonian Émile Barrault.[3] The young Labrouste, in a letter written in 1832 to his friend Louis Duc, also considered the artist to have an almost apostolic role in society:

> The more I see this sick world, the more I feel the time coming when this world will throw itself into the doctor's arms, and that doctor is the artist. The artist is the only one in our day who can heal humanity of an ailment which has been unknown until now; the artist is the only one who can give the heart its heat back, and the heart is what is sick today, and the soul is dry.[4]

Reacting to the pessimism of the early days of the July Monarchy—a feeling intensified by the cholera epidemic that was ravaging Paris when he wrote the letter—Labrouste underscored his affinity with essayist Charles Magnin, who was "one of those people who believe that in some furrow of this greatly tilled earth has been planted the seed of a new tree of life that must give humanity rest and shade."[5] His letter to Duc continues in a more concrete vein, evoking the case of the very outdated Hôtel-Dieu hospital:

> I have been told that a doctor has just published a book whose title is *De l'influence des arts sur la santé* [On the Influence of the Arts on Health]. You see that the doctor is also counting on us to remedy, either physically or morally, human infirmities ... As regards the facade of the Hôtel-Dieu, I was speaking to my students of the character of hospitals. I told them: I do not know anything more misguided than the idea for such a monument. They wanted to make it serious, and they made it woeful. It must seem to all those poor sick people that when they enter the hospital, they will never come back out ... If I were to make a hospital, I would put paintings in all the rooms. I think paintings, with their different colors and especially the subjects portrayed, would do something to help sick people heal ... In the end, I am one of those people who believe, like that doctor, that the arts have an influence on health.[6]

It is the entire doctrine of character in architecture, as understood by the academic tradition, that Labrouste is denouncing here. To him, a hospital building should be

3. Émile Barrault, *Aux artistes. Du passé et de l'avenir des Beaux-Arts* (Paris: Alexandre Mesnier, 1830), 76.
4. Lucas 1895:268.
5. Ibid. Labrouste does not provide a precise source, but one can clearly recognize remarks made by Magnin in an article published on July 15, 1832, in the *Revue des deux mondes* and reprinted in 1843 in the first volume of his *Causeries et méditations historiques et littéraires*: "De la statue de la reine Nantechild et des révolutions de l'art en France au moyen âge." Magnin was a former student at the Collège Sainte-Barbe and a member of the association of its friends, as was Labrouste.
6. Lucas 1895:268.
7. Michel Foucault, *La Naissance de la clinique. Une archéologie du regard médical* (Paris: Presses universitaires de France, 1963); English translation: *The Birth of the Clinic: An Archaeology of Medical Perception*, trans. A. M. Sheridan Smith (New York: Vintage Books, 1994). Michel Foucault et al., *Les Machines à guérir* (Paris: Institut de l'environnement, 1976).
8. Étienne Esquirol, *Des maladies mentales considérées sous les rapports médical, hygiénique et médico-légal*, vol. 2 (Paris: Baillière, 1838), 581.

2. Charles Lansiaux, Bibliothèque Sainte-Geneviève, general view of the reading room, 1917, photograph, 17.1 × 23 cm, Musée Carnavalet, Paris, 546

contributing to the patient's healing process rather than simply expressing its functionality in a conventional way. By taking an interest in "the influence of the arts on health," the architect takes part in the medical discourse which at the turn of the century had made hospitals "healing machines." From such reflections arose a new conception of space as a medium that could exert a beneficial influence over people. The need for rationality and efficiency led to a new instrumentality, as Michel Foucault would later explain,[7] but the new conception cannot be reduced to the implementation of systems for surveillance and classification, such as "panopticism": the movement was also part of the development of a new environmental sensitivity. The famous alienists Philippe Pinel and Jean-Étienne Dominique Esquirol had indeed established a relationship between the physical and the moral by identifying the "moral means" for treating the insane. It was by placing patients in a specific psychological setting that the doctor felt he could influence their emotional impulses. In his asylum in Charenton, Esquirol performed experiments with music in treating the sick. He would abandon that course of treatment not because it was ineffective, but, quite the reverse, because the patients were too shaken up by it.[8]

"HEALING" ARCHITECTURE

Pinel and Esquirol's ideas are especially relevant to the development of Labrouste's thought in the 1830s because, in the first period of his career, he took part in competitions for building asylums and prisons. The architect won first prize in both the 1836–37

3. Bibliothèque Sainte-Geneviève, library monogram in the reading room. Photograph: Jean-Claude N'Diaye

competition for a cantonal asylum for the insane in Lausanne and the 1839 competition for a central prison in Alessandria, near Turin. In those remarkable projects, which were never built, he worked to create a setting with soothing qualities, thus showing a new awareness of the role of atmosphere, something which would find its chief expression in the Bibliothèque Sainte-Geneviève. Labrouste sent his plans for an asylum for 120 insane people to the canton of Vaud's Council of State on June 24, 1837. His submission included no fewer than eight drawings, of which only two remain today (figs. 4, 5).[9] During the long preparatory phase, Labrouste visited several similar establishments, including Dr. Esquirol's clinic in Ivry. After winning the competition, he began discussions with the canton of Vaud for the choice of a site, an exchange which would continue from July 1837 to January 1839.

His proposed project, with its panoptical dimension, contrasted with the proposals from other competitors.[10] Rather than a classical composition made up of a series of orthogonal courtyards, Labrouste adopted a fan-shaped plan, which would allow for better surveillance. But he did not see the project only from that angle. The plan, he tells us, "must lead to the well-being and soothing of the sick people residing in or treated at this asylum."[11] Judging that the insane are particularly sensitive to their physical surroundings, Labrouste, following in Esquirol's footsteps, examines a series of environmental factors affecting their well-being: a pleasant view of the countryside, a good amount of sunlight, continuous circulation of air, protection from noise, and the presence of gardens or greenery in each of the quarters. He even foresees a rudimentary sort of air conditioning, something that was still rare at the time, which has "cold air circulate during the summer through conduits made to carry heat during the winter, and thus cool the rooms and cells, which would be soothing to the insane."[12]

His prison project testifies to similar preoccupations (fig. 6).[13] After discussions with Charles Lucas, the inspector general of prisons and author of the influential book *De la réforme des prisons ou de la théorie de l'enfermement* (On Prison Reform, or the Theory of Incarceration; 1836–38), Labrouste sought to "contribute ... to the moral regeneration of condemned men."[14] He thus proposed solitary confinement at night and group work during the day, in order to help inmates' improvement and reeducation. As far as the actual architecture goes, he developed several inventive solutions that soften the prison atmosphere, such as large

9. See Saddy 1976; Saddy 1977:27–29; Leniaud 1983; Fussinger and Tevaearai 1998:31–35; Renzo Dubbini, "Pragmatismo architettonico e programmi di utilità pubblica Losanna, Alessandria, Rennes," in Dubbini 2002:100–120.
10. Fussinger and Tevaearai 1998:33–35.
11. Henri Labrouste, copy of the essay accompanying his proposed project for the insane asylum in Lausanne, Bibliothèque Nationale de France, Estampes, HZ-465 (1) – PET FOL, folder 9, f. 2–5.
12. Ibid.
13. See Saddy 1977:33–36; Dubbini, op. cit.
14. Henri Labrouste, copy of the essay accompanying his proposed prison project, October 1839, Bibliothèque Nationale de France, Estampes, HZ-465 (1) – PET FOL, folder 12.

vertical windows surrounding the cell building, without bars or grates, because they were set more than two meters off the ground. The chapel, at the center of the workshops, "must be simple in decoration like the rest of the establishment, but nevertheless should retain a feel of severity and even nobility which may also, following our stated goal, be effective on a population that is deprived of emotions and for that reason hungers for them." Slipping from the space's character to its psychological effect, he concludes with the idea that "art, even in that sorry abode, could contribute to the moral betterment of the inmates."[15]

FOURIERIST ATTRACTION

Thus architecture takes on a "healing" power, through the effects of a specific physical and psychological "climate," notably based on the precepts of Esquirol, for whom "atmospheric vicissitudes [modify] man's physical and moral state."[16] Following a Romantic trend, Labrouste was also interested in what was then called "animal magnetism" or "magnetic somnambulism"—that is, hypnosis. The doctor Pierre Foissac, a practitioner of magnetism, described in 1837 how "the physical agents that surround us alter, perfect, or deteriorate our bodily forms," as well as "the cerebral organ" and the "faculties that spring from it."[17] In his sketchbooks, Labrouste mentions a book by Alfred Fillassier, *Quelques faits et considérations pour servir à l'histoire du magnétisme animal* (Several Facts and Considerations in Furtherance of a History of Animal Magnetism; 1832),[18] a sizeable medical thesis described at the time as "the boldest apology that has yet been composed in support of animal magnetism."[19]

15. Ibid.
16. Étienne Esquirol, *Des passions, considérées comme causes, symptômes et moyens curatifs de l'aliénation mentale* (Paris: Didot Jeune, 1805), 15.
17. P. Foissac, *De l'influence des climats sur l'homme* (Paris: Baillière, 1837), 404.
18. Académie d'Architecture, Fonds Labrouste, sketchbook no. 331.
19. J. Bouillaud, "Magnétisme animal," *Encyclographie des sciences médicales*, vol. 18 (Brussels: Établissement Encyclographique, 1838), 266.

4. Henri Labrouste, Competition Entry for the Construction of a Cantonal Asylum for the Insane in Lausanne, outbuilding and building, 1837, 45.2 × 61.8 cm, Bibliothèque nationale de France, Paris, Prints, HD-1176 (1)-BOITE FOL

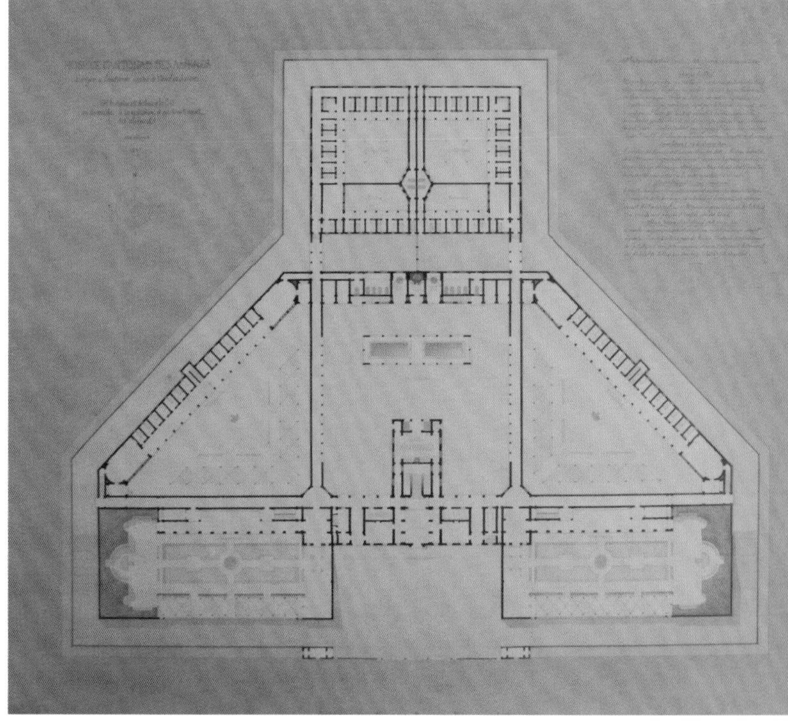

PLANS D'UN PROJET D'UNE PRISON CENTRALE POUR ALEXANDRIE.

It is easy to understand the reason for his interest in such theories. If physical atmosphere is able to transmit magnetic energies, architecture can make an even better claim to possess therapeutic powers.

His attention to Charles Fourier's utopian socialism allowed him to deepen such a conception. According to Fourier's grandiose theory, God directs the material world through "passionate attraction," which is also humanity's true motor. The term, which is vaguely rooted in mesmerism and magnetism, designates the mechanism of desires that determine our actions. Fourier's utopia was to free such a mechanism from social hindrances. In the 1830s, the Ecole Sociétaire that formed around Fourier spread his ideas through different publications, including *La Phalange*. Though he was not a Fourierist, Labrouste read that journal and was in contact with several eminent members of the Ecole Sociétaire, particularly those who were involved with the arts: the architect César Daly and Gabriel-Désiré Laverdant, the most important Fourierist art critic along with Eugène d'Izalguier. Fourier himself had never developed an aesthetic doctrine, but his disciples recognized art and architecture as powerful means for reestablishing a balance between the passions. For Laverdant, "sensual work arises from the affections themselves. Touch [that is, the only one of the five senses that is present in the whole body] creates architectural art [which] embraces the other arts in its arms, and holds them within its breast."[20] It was by developing a special form of tactility that the architect "worked for the good of humanity,"[21] helping reestablish a balance between the body and desires. The "phalanstère," Fourierist utopia's fundamental architectural unit, was thus to be conceived as a total environment with therapeutic virtues that could affect society as a whole. Its spatial organization created a "climate" that was favorable to harmonious human relations. Moreover, the phalanstère was imagined within a heavenly landscape. Fourier went even so far as to dream of a planetary transformation of the environment and climate.[22] Humanity in its entirety could thus wear the "atmospheric clothing" appropriate to each person's needs.

THE BIBLIOTHÈQUE SAINTE-GENEVIÈVE, A REFUGE IN THE LATIN QUARTER

The work by Labrouste that comes closest to Fourierist ideals is the agricultural colony for orphans and foundlings in Le Mesnil-Saint-Firmin, which he expanded between 1845 and 1848, at the most intense moment of the construction of the Bibliothèque Sainte-Geneviève (fig. 8).[23] The establishment, which was supported by the Société d'Adoption des Enfants Abandonnés and overseen by the Frères Agronomes de Saint-Vincent de Paul, was not, strictly speaking, a Fourierist undertaking, but the movement for agricultural colonies was taken up from the start by the disciples of Fourier, who often commented in *La Phalange* on the latest experiences of what they sometimes called "phalansterions." So it is not surprising that, in preparing his plans for Le Mesnil-Saint-Firmin, Labrouste consulted the Fourierist newspaper *La Démocratie pacifique*.[24] But the agenda and

20. Gabriel-Désiré Laverdant, "De la mission de l'art et du rôle des artistes," *La Phalange*, 14th year, 1st series, vol. 1 (1st semester 1845): 258.
21. Ibid.
22. Charles Fourier, *Traité de l'association domestique-agricole*, vol. 1 (Paris: Bossange, 1822), 370.
23. See Watteville 1845; anonymous 1847; Saddy 1977:61–64.
24. See Saddy 1977:61.

5. Henri Labrouste, Competition Entry for the Construction of a Cantonal Asylum for the Insane in Lausanne, overall plan, 1837, 46 × 60 cm, Bibliothèque nationale de France, Paris, Prints, HD-1176 (1)-BOITE FOL

6. Henri Labrouste, Competition Entry for the Construction of a Central Prison in Alessandria (Piedmont), overall plan, perspective view of the cross-shaped building, and a cross section of the chapel, 1839, 103.3 x 67.5 cm, Académie d'architecture, Paris, 285.1

Next pages:
7. Place du Panthéon and Bibliothèque Sainte-Geneviève, Artedia collection

AUX GRANDS HOM

25. Levine 1975; Levine 1982 (2); see also Van Zanten 1987, and Bressani and Grignon 2005.
26. Bougy 1847:150.
27. *Journal général de l'instruction publique* 7 (May 16, 1838): 531.

8. Henri Labrouste, Expansion of the Mesnil-Saint-Fermin Agricultural Colony in Merle, elevation and plan of the colonists' building, plans of the site, and overall view, 1846, 51.8 × 67.7 cm, Bibliothèque nationale de France, Paris, Prints, HD-1018-FT 6

9. Louis-Auguste and Auguste-Rosalie Bisson, known as the Bisson brothers, Bibliothèque Sainte-Geneviève, overall view of the main facade, 1853, photograph, 21 × 33.5 cm, Académie d'architecture, Paris, 492

means were so modest, limited to renovating and expanding a few farm buildings, that it is hard to see in them any attempt to create the new tactility described by Laverdant. Surprisingly, it was at the Bibliothèque Sainte-Geneviève that Labrouste could concretize his Fourierist ambitions, though that masterpiece of the "rationalist school" cannot be reduced solely to that label (figs. 1, 9). The austere building reflects many preoccupations, both architectural and social. Historian Neil Levine has already shown how Labrouste profoundly calls into question the Académie's doctrine, founded on types drawn from a canonical repertoire.[25] But the building's social dimension has rarely been singled out. Though its purpose was considerably different from that of hospitals, prisons, or agricultural colonies, the Bibliothèque was also thought to have "healing" properties because of the way it could influence its users, mainly college students. The only place for study in Paris that remained open after nightfall, thanks to its gas lighting and central heating, the Bibliothèque helped maintain order in a Latin Quarter peopled with students who, when they could not stay at home in the evening "for lack of fire and light," were liable to give in "to dissipation and debauchery."[26] Nighttime openings were instituted by the minister Salvandy in 1838, when the Bibliothèque was still housed beneath the rooftops of the former abbey, which later became the Collège Henri-IV. For the *Journal général de l'instruction publique*, that innovation signaled "progress for our civilization; it is a gain for our studious youth that no one would dare to question."[27] The *Revue générale de l'architecture* went one step farther: "When one thinks about what those six or seven hundred students would do in the evening in the past; when one considers … how much wild spending was the consequence of their idleness,

28. Anonymous 1842: col. 333.
29. Henri Labrouste, "Bibliothèque Sainte-Geneviève. Projet d'un bâtiment à ériger sur l'emplacement de l'ancienne prison de Montaigu et destiné à recevoir la Bibliothèque de Sainte-Geneviève" (AN, F 21 1362).
30. Ibid.
31. Ibid.

Previous page:
10. "Bibliothèque Sainte-Geneviève, a Perspective View of the Main Facade," Daly, 1853, pl. 31.

11. Henri Labrouste, Bibliothèque Sainte-Geneviève, elevation and cross section of the southwest angle of the facade, late 1850, 99 × 66 cm, Bibliothèque Sainte-Geneviève, Paris, Ms. 4273 (33).

one cannot applaud enough the idea of opening to young people in the evenings the only library in which they may truly study fruitfully."[28] In his presentation of his plan for the new building, Labrouste himself underscored the fact that the students in the Latin Quarter "now come to use the library during the long winter evenings which were once lost to little theaters, bars, and fencing halls."[29] He also notes that it was during the nighttime hours that the Bibliothèque attracted the most users: "each evening, 7 to 800 people [come] to benefit from the long hours that are best for in-depth study."[30] These were "the conditions," Labrouste sums up, "that became the program for the new building to be built."[31]

That central heating and gas lighting had been installed beneath the rooftops of the Collège Henri-IV, above students' dormitories, also justified the move, as the dilapidated nature of the historic buildings was reason to fear the risk of fire. The decision to transfer the venerable collection into a new construction nevertheless drew forth protestations from several readers nostalgic for the former space. The choice of a new site was also subject to controversy. Architect Alphonse de Gisors, Labrouste's predecessor, had chosen the location of the former Collège de Montaigu, which had become a military prison during the Empire, on the north side of the Place du Panthéon. But for economic reasons, other voices recommended instead appropriating an already existing building: the Palais du Luxembourg

or the Théâtre de l'Odéon, for instance. Labrouste, who took over from Gisors in June 1838, was categorical: "It is ... between the Ecole de Droit, the Ecole de Médecine, the Ecole Normale, the Collège de France, and the Sorbonne that the Bibliothèque Sainte-Geneviève must remain located. That is, on the Place du Panthéon as it is today ... the real and graphic center ... of the student quarter."[32]

The location was a "real and graphic center" not only because it was situated at the heart of the Latin Quarter, but also because of its relationship to the neighboring Panthéon. The future Bibliothèque was part of a major plan for redesigning the square, which notably presupposed that all the old buildings on the north side would be demolished (fig. 13). Labrouste, who could thus determine the precise location of his library, decided to align its central axis with the threshold of the Panthéon (fig. 7).

The geometrical and symbolic relationship is easy to understand. We know how Soufflot's Neoclassical monument changed uses with political vicissitudes. Built as the Eglise Sainte-Geneviève, then transformed into the Panthéon during the Revolution, it was given back to the Catholic church under the Restoration (April 1816) and once again became the Panthéon during the early days of the July Monarchy.

The famous inscription "Aux grands hommes la patrie reconnaissante" (To Great Men from the Grateful Nation) was then restored to its facade and the sculptor David d'Angers was commissioned to create a new pediment, which was inaugurated in 1837, only a few months before Labrouste began his first studies for the library. On each end of the pediment, d'Angers presented a group of young students hard at work, expressing the future of the nation; the one on the left (the side of the future library) showed "university students" (fig. 7). The iconography is immediately echoed in Labrouste's building, where "real" students assemble.

32. Henri Labrouste, report addressed to the Minister of Public Works, March 6, 1843 (AN, F 21 1362).

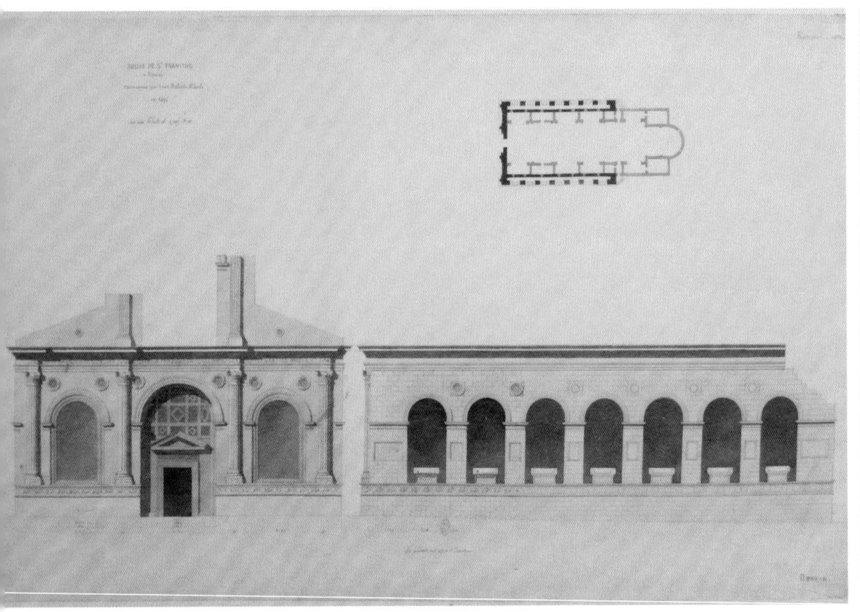

12. Henri Labrouste, Malatesta Temple or church of Saint Francis in Rimini, elevation of the main façade, lateral elevation and plan, 1830, 35.4 × 41 cm, Paris, Bibliothèque nationale de France, Prints, VZ-1030 (2)-FOL

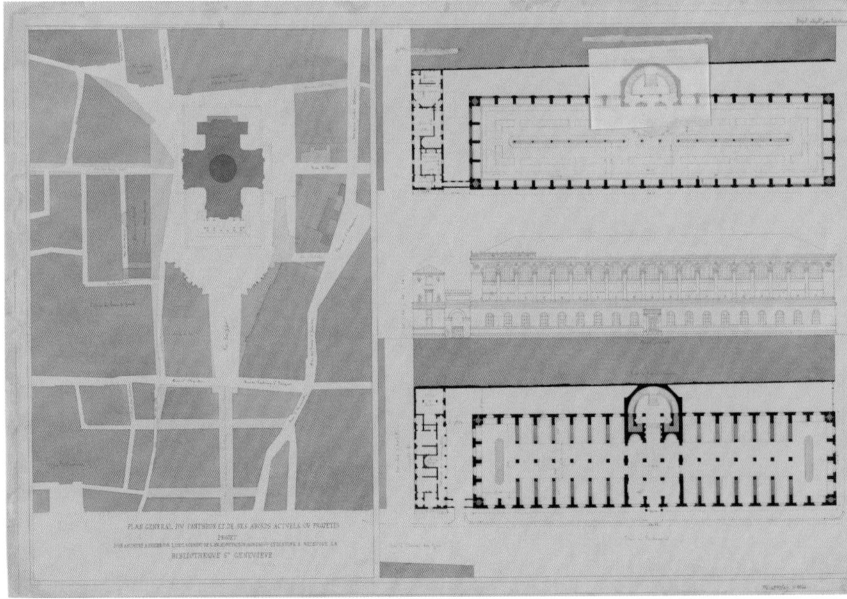

13. Henri Labrouste, General Plan of the Panthéon and Its Surrounding Area, Current and Projected States, c. 1842, 66.5 × 102 cm, Bibliothèque Sainte-Geneviève, Paris, Ms. 4273 (1)

Next pages:
14. Bibliothèque Sainte-Geneviève, overall view of the reading room. Photograph: Michel Nguyen

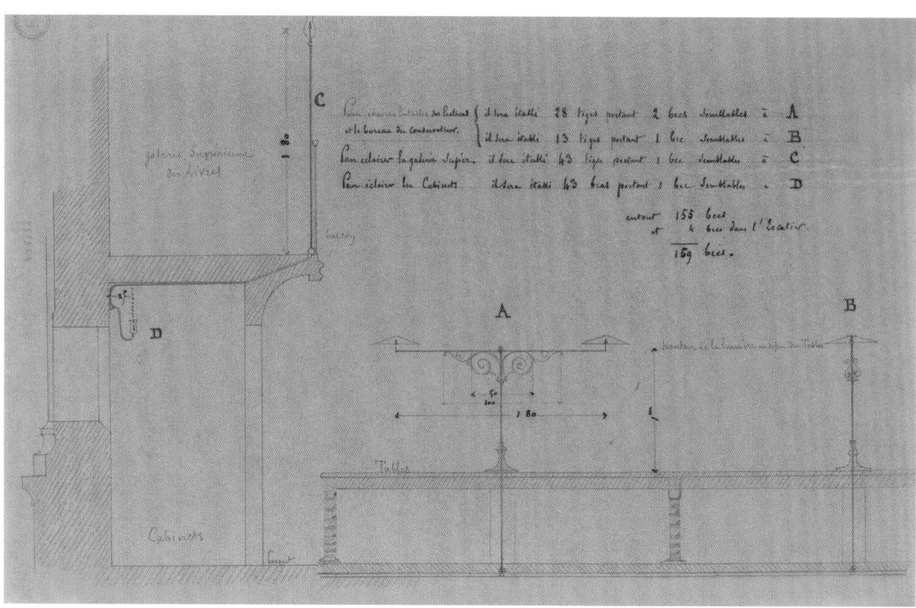

15. Henri Labrouste, Bibliothèque Sainte-Geneviève, detail of the installation of gas lights on the tables and shelves of the reading room, August 1850, Paris, BSG, Ms. 4273 (124)

His decision to engrave the names of great authors on the facade of the Bibliothèque strengthened ties to the Panthéon even more (fig. 11). At the time, it was said that the building's exterior was "slightly bizarre in style and ornamentation."[33] Indeed, the austere, monotonous facade did not respect the rules of classical composition, which would have required a play of volumes, for example a projection in the middle and at the ends, however discreet. Labrouste also hid the roof space behind a cornice, which underscores even more the "rigidity [of the] long entablature."[34] But the architect wanted such sobriety, a reflection of the "severe and serious nature that behooves the institution."[35] "With its blank walls covered with inscriptions," Anatole France would write in 1922, the Bibliothèque Sainte-Geneviève resembles "less an edifice devoted to studies than a gigantic mausoleum imitated from the antique."[36] The continuous garland wrapping around the building and the lists of names engraved on the second-floor infill panels are indeed part of the repertoire used by Labrouste in his funeral monuments. In designing the arcade, he drew inspiration from the side arches of the Malatesta Temple built in Rimini by Alberti, which housed the tombs of the Malatesta family (fig. 12). Facing the Panthéon, his Bibliothèque thus became a kind of commemorative monument enclosing the books in which the thoughts of "great men" lay at rest.

33. Duchatelet, "Bibliothèque Sainte-Geneviève," *Le Siècle*, December 17, 1850, [p. 3].
34. Calonne 1853:466.
35. Labrouste, "Bibliothèque Sainte-Geneviève. Projet d'un bâtiment … ," loc. cit.
36. Anatole France, *La Vie en fleur* (Paris: Calmann-Lévy, 1922), 181–82.

ATMOSPHERIC DRESS

Behind the stern and vaguely funerary exterior a very curious atmosphere was deployed. Despite the relative sobriety of its interior, the Bibliothèque Sainte-Geneviève offers an early example of a total environment to which all the different industries and French decorative trades contributed. Labrouste brought together cast iron, laminated iron, wrought iron, and bronze, as well as canvas painting and porcelain, wax-varnished fresco, ceramics, tapestry, stucco, and terra-cotta.

The remarkable decorative ensemble was coupled with a precise mastery of climate using new technologies for lighting, heat, and ventilation. In the 1830s, hydrogen gas lighting was rapidly developing, and Labrouste took a great deal of interest in it, envisioning various solutions.[37] Bathed with light in the daytime by the giant windows surrounding it, the reading room was lit in the evening by over 150 gas jets, set on the reading tables and along the lateral bookshelves (figs. 15, 16). Use of that type of lighting

37. Bressani and Grignon 2011.

16. Henri Labrouste, Bibliothèque Sainte-Geneviève, study of iron shelves for the reading room (not as built), 1848, 68.1 × 51 cm, Bibliothèque Sainte-Geneviève, Paris, Ms. 4273 (63)

in a public building of this size was still experimental, and the first system, installed in 1850, had to be replaced in 1858 by a more stable one, less prone to fumes.[38]

The alternation between day and night became Labrouste's main iconographic theme. On the outside, he framed the entryway with two bas-relief candelabras, which were meant "to recall the introduction of evening sessions … by Mr. de Salvandy"[39] (p. 128, fig. 3). Inside, sculpted herms of men and women, set on either side of the pedestal of some of the reading room's columns, represent day and night, depending on whether they face east or west[40] (fig. 25). Higher up, the design of the iron arches evokes the sun and the moon (p. 190, fig. 6), and at the room's exit a tapestry represents *Study Surprised by Night*, in which two cupids figure as Morning and Evening (figs. 17, 18). Last, the medal struck in 1844 to commemorate the laying of the first stone shows two female allegories symbolizing daytime study, with a cockerel, and nighttime study, with an owl. Much has been said about the great amount of light in the daytime, but Labrouste considered the evening ambience just as important. The essential role of night is magnificently represented on a plan for the reading room, which Labrouste surrounded with a black wash representing darkness.

The 1840s were a watershed period for research on central heating in France, with heat often considered a "fluid" not unlike light. The "heating committee" created in 1849 for the library recommended the builder Léon Duvoir-Leblanc's solution, a hybrid system in which gigantic furnaces located in the cellars brought hot water to stoves hidden under the floors to heat air, which was then spread into the room through a series of grates.

38. Christine Vendredi-Auzanneau, "Chronologie de la construction de la Bibliothèque Sainte-Geneviève," in Leniaud 2002:150.
39. Trianon 1851:30.
40. Levine 1982 (2):170.

17. Charles Lansiaux, Bibliothèque Sainte-Geneviève, view of the reading room facing the entrance, 1917, photograph, 17.1 × 23.1 cm, Musée Carnavalet, Paris, 548
18. Bibliothèque Sainte-Geneviève, view of the revolving door at the entrance to the reading room. Photograph: Jean-Claude N'Diaye

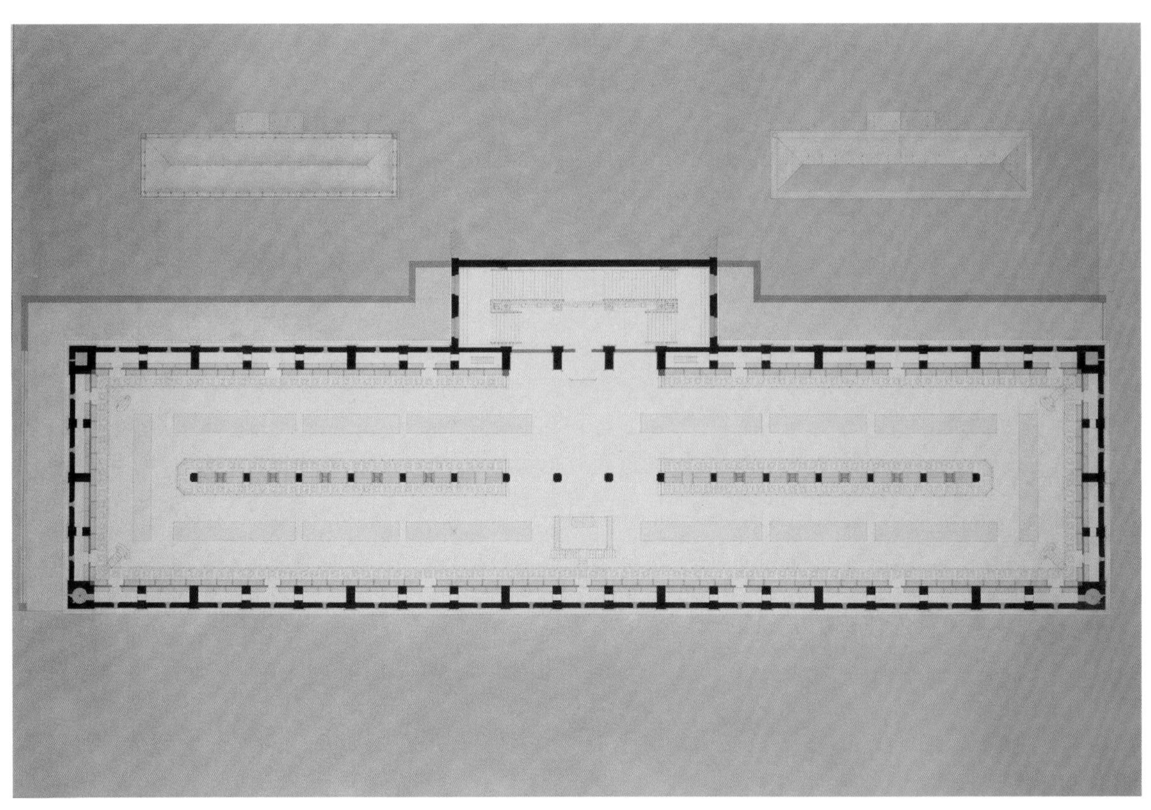

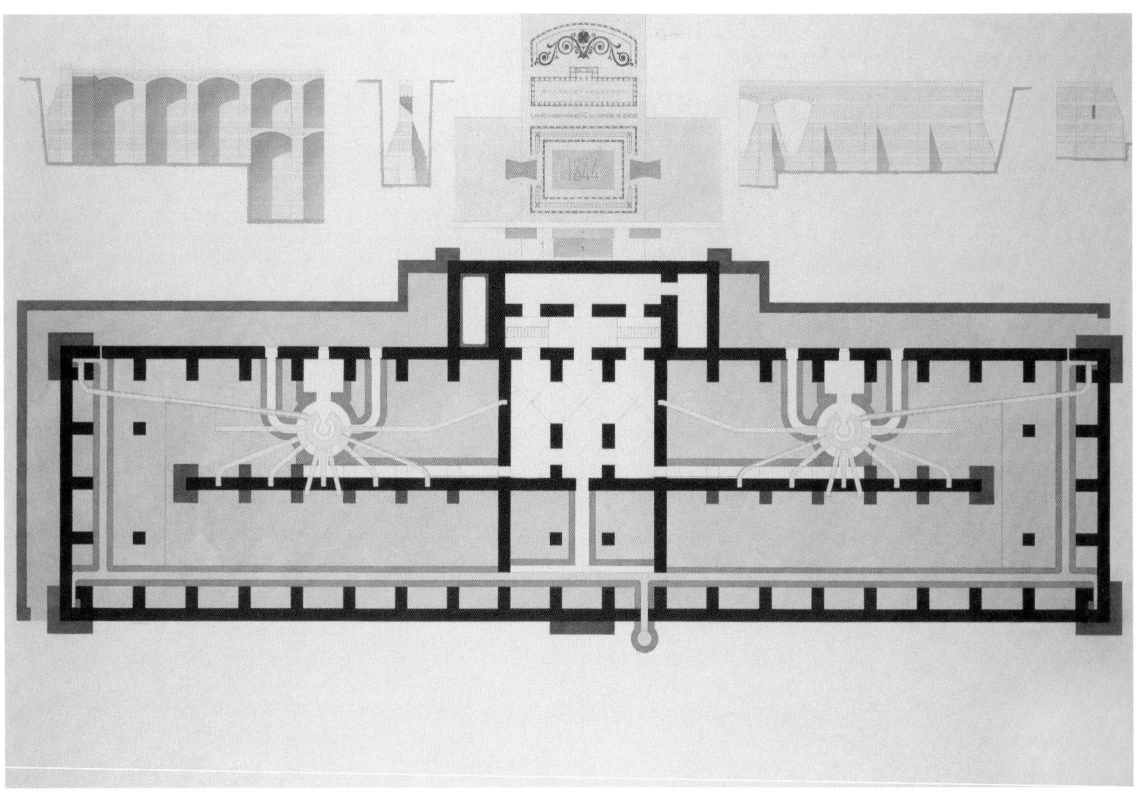
1844

The system is spectacularly illustrated by Labrouste in the basement plans (fig. 20). The system aims to fulfill all the conditions required for good thermal comfort—always maintaining a temperature of 16° to 18°C (61° to 65°F) even during the worst cold spells—and abundant ventilation.[41] The reading room as a whole behaves like a ventilation chamber, with hot air rising from grates at the foot of the bookcases in the central spine and circulating up to the roof trusses. Circulation allowed for 10,000 cubic meters of air to be renewed per hour, which was required, among other reasons, to protect against the pollution caused by gas leaking from the lighting system, inevitable at the time.

41. See the report from the Minister of Public Works recommending Léon Duvoir-Leblanc's submission, June 15, 1849 (AN, F 21 751).
42. Labrouste 1852: col. 382.
43. Calonne 1853:463.

THE FERTILE GROUND OF THE IMAGINATION

The decorative and technical elements mobilized by Labrouste were not a simple affirmation of modernity; they were coordinated to create a controlled environment, the sort of "atmospheric dress" Fourier described. The desired effect on the reader is progressive, and works both through a forward movement in space as well as through the passing hours, from day into night. The essential correlation between the spatial and temporal dimensions determines the work's sense of unity, thus offering a powerful metaphor for the paths of knowledge, leading to utopian thought.

The path begins at the Place du Panthéon, where, as we have already noted, an atmosphere of commemoration reigns. But when the threshold of the library is crossed, the reader enters a space suited to meditation and contemplation.[42] The vestibule's thick, fluted pillars, aligned in the dim like those of an Egyptian tomb, lead to the back stairway, which seems to rise "in a diorama-like light"[43] (fig. 22). The strangeness of that effect is even stronger when night falls. The vestibule had no lighting of its own, but Labrouste

19. Henri Labrouste, Bibliothèque Sainte-Geneviève, plans of the upper level, the rafters, and the roof, October 1850, 67 × 103 cm, Bibliothèque Sainte-Geneviève, Paris, Ms.4273 (9)
20. Henri Labrouste, Bibliothèque Sainte-Geneviève, plan of the basement, with cross sections, and detail of the cornerstone, late 1850, 65.7 × 97.5 cm, Bibliothèque Sainte-Geneviève, Paris, Ms. 4273 (6)

21. Henri Labrouste, Bibliothèque Sainte-Geneviève, longitudinal cross section of the vestibule, late 1850, 65.5 × 98 cm, Bibliothèque Sainte-Geneviève, Paris, Ms. 4273 (37)

44. Labrouste 1852: col. 382.
45. Ibid.
46. Trianon 1851:29.
47. See, among others, Hermant 1851.
48. We are paraphrasing Alberto Manguel, *La Bibliothèque, la nuit* (Arles: Actes Sud; Montréal: Leméac, 2006), 36–37.

placed six large gas candelabras in the stairway, so that evening visitors would once again be caught by the mysterious light and drawn upstairs, toward the reading room.

Should readers linger in the vestibule—as sometimes there was a wait for seats to free up in the reading room—the sense of having entered an unusual world is all the more intense. On the lateral walls, above two rows of busts of illustrious men, Labrouste had Alexandre Desgoffe, a disciple of Ingres, depict a "painted garden" compensating for the "wide space planted with tall trees" he would have liked to "provide in front of the building"[44] (fig. 21). The fictive vegetation matches each of the busts: "With no care to the climate of Paris, I could, in this fertile ground of the imagination, plant trees from all countries, and place near St. Bernard palm trees from the Orient; near Racine, flowering orange trees; near La Fontaine, an oak tree and a reed; and myrtles and bay trees near Poussin."[45] A striking engraving published in *L'Illustration* showcases the trompe l'oeil effect created by pairing architecture and frescoed painting.[46]

Atop the thick masonry piers, slender cast-iron beams—painted green and standing out against a blue ceiling mimicking the sky—echo the branches of the trees painted by Desgoffe. These elements are of course part of the building's structure, but as metaphoric vegetation they are also part of the imaginary life of the garden of knowledge. Their unusual thinness, appropriate given the strength of iron but in striking contrast to the thickness of the piers—an imbalance that would shock commentators of the day[47]—seems to confirm their half-real, half-fictive nature. The thin, spiderlike metal limbs announce the reading room's cast-iron vault.

THE REFECTION OF THE MEMBERS OF A COMMUNITY

At the top of the stairway, the reader is faced with a gigantic copy of Raphael's *School of Athens*, faithfully rendered by the Balze brothers. The figures of Plato and Aristotle, at the center of the composition, are exactly at the level of the reader standing on the second-floor landing. The relationship between the real world and the fictive world is thus further underscored. And here, too, the nighttime effect is striking: seen in a diffused light during the day, the painting in the evening is caught in the intense halo projected by the four powerful gas lamps facing it.

Finally, leaving the large light well that is the stairway, the evening reader—let us continue to follow him along—enters the relatively dim reading room, the culmination of his journey. The garden in which authors enjoy eternal life, which is only evoked in the vestibule, truly materializes in this room, whose thin cast-iron columns and vaults with ornamental arches look like large trees. The "fertile ground of the imagination" has now been given a third dimension. Here, the reader can dive into the world of great authors and guarantee their books a modicum of immortality, with reading being, in this sense, a ritual of rebirth.[48]

22. Bibliothèque Sainte-Geneviève, view of the vestibule facing the staircase, c. 1880, anonymous, photograph, 27.7 × 21 cm, Bibliothèque nationale de France, Paris, Prints, HZ-465-PET FOL

BIBLIOTHÈQUE SAINTE-GENEVIÈVE
FONDÉE PAR LES GÉNOVÉFAINS EN 1624
DEVENUE PROPRIÉTÉ NATIONALE EN 1790
TRANSFÉRÉE DE L'ANCIENNE
DANS CET ÉDIFICE EN 1850

49. Viollet-le-Duc, *Dictionnaire raisonné de l'architecture française du XIe au XVIe siècle*, vol. 8 (Paris: A. Morel, 1866), 9.
50. Fourier, op. cit., vol. 2, 37, 42.
51. Édouard de Pompery, *Théorie de l'association et de l'unité universelle de C. Fourier; introduction religieuse et philosophique* (Paris: Capelle, 1841), 285.
52. Fourier, op.cit, vol. 2, 40.
53. V. Considérant, *Description du phalanstère et considérations sociales sur l'architectonique*, 2nd ed. (Paris: Librairie sociétaire, 1848), 64.
54. Fourier, op. cit., vol. 2, 19.

The space's dynamic character highlights this phenomenon. First, the iron arabesques, like the painted trees in the vestibule, seem to crystalize the reader's intellectual wanderings (fig. 23). Then, the room, divided into two naves, establishes a circular path, with the vault elegantly curving at both ends to form an uninterrupted circuit. The deambulatory space underscores the "work" of assimilation and interpretation needed to resuscitate the thought of dead authors.

The spatial organization refers to a precise historical model: the refectory in medieval monasteries, and, more specifically, the one in the former priory of Saint-Martin-des-Champs, which had also been transformed into a library during the same period by a close friend of Labrouste's, the architect Léon Vaudoyer. The alignment of the worktables along the axis of the two naves, as in a monastic refectory, leaves no doubt as to its intention. The analogy is a clever one, because we know that the rule of St. Benedict required that monks be read to during meals, the absorption of food helping to assimilate the word of God. In his *Dictionnaire raisonné de l'architecture française*, Viollet-le-Duc defines the refectory as the "room destined for the refection of the members of a community"—thus underscoring the regenerative function of the space, both physically and spiritually.[49]

With its mode of construction and its configuration, the room also evokes the covered, gaslit arcades burgeoning in the capital at that time. If the medieval refectory anchors the great reading room in history, the allusion to Paris's arcades orients it toward a utopian future. That type of light and airy deambulatory space, breaching the thick urban tissue, had been used as a model for the Fourierist palace. The "gallery-street" indeed forms the backbone of the *phalanstère* and galvanizes its inventor's eloquence. It brings all parts of the building into communication and is "one of the most precious charms of the Palace of Harmony," the "room of universal ties" where all of the *phalanstère*'s important activities take place.[50] Like the Bibliothèque Sainte-Geneviève's reading room, Fourier's gallery-street is a technological world, whose climate and atmosphere are paid particular attention: "wide furnaces spread a soft, even temperature everywhere; gas pipes, a luxurious, inexpensive light; networks of large reservoirs distribute ample hot or cold water to every place. In short, here, air, water, heat, and light, intelligently mastered by man, are also abundantly lavished upon him."[51]

This is the perfect "harmonian" social space, where men and women come together. On holidays, the phalansterians eat "at a double row of tables,"[52] as in medieval refectories. This is how the Fourierist Victor Considérant describes the gallery-street in 1834:

> The gallery—which bends along the flanks of the *edifice sociétaire* and takes the form of a long belt around it, connecting all the parts to the whole, and providing connections from the center to the periphery—is the conduit through which life circulates in the great phalansterian body; it is the magisterial artery which, from the heart, carries blood to all veins; it is also, at the same time, the symbol and architectural expression of the greatest social rallying and passionate harmony of the

> *Phalange* within this great unitary construction where each room has a special meaning, where each detail expresses a specific thought, responds to a need, and coordinates itself to the whole, and whose whole reproduces, completes, makes visible, and embodies the Association's supreme law, the integral thought of harmony.[53]

23. Henri Labrouste, Bibliothèque Sainte-Geneviève, perspective view of the reading room, 1842, plans approved by the minister in 1843, 44.5 × 57.5 cm, Musée d'Orsay, Paris, RF 4141

Next pages:
24. Henri Labrouste, Bibliothèque Sainte-Geneviève, transverse cross section of the reading room, late 1850, 66 × 99 cm, Bibliothèque Sainte-Geneviève, Paris, Ms. 4273 (41)

The Bibliothèque Sainte-Geneviève's relationship to the gallery-street is of course on the order of poetic evocation, but there is at least one clue that makes its ties to Fourierist doctrine explicit. There are 810 names engraved on the facades, divided into twenty-seven groups of thirty under the arcades on the upper level, from Moses down through to the Swedish chemist Jöns Jacob Berzelius, who died in 1848. The number is highly symbolic, because Fourier's harmonian theory "sets at 810 the number of distinct characters which make up the entire scale or general keyboard of characters" in humanity.[54] In 1847, the year Labrouste established the list of names in collaboration with the librarians, *La Phalange* printed an unpublished manuscript by Fourier entitled

55. Fourier, "Du clavier puissanciel des caractères," *La Phalange. Revue de la science sociale* 6 (2nd semester, 1847): 5ff.
56. Van Zanten 1987:98.
57. Lorédan Larchey, "Nouveautés anecdotiques," *Le Bibliophile français. Gazette illustrée des amateurs de livres . . .* , vol. 2, no. 3 (January 1869): 199–200.
58. Fourier, *Traité de l'association domestique-agricole*, vol. 1, 106.

"Du clavier puissanciel des caractères" (On the Power-Potential Keyboard of Characters): "After having dealt with the problems inherent in balancing and rallying the passions, we must address a more brilliant riddle, that of the balancing of characters, of their 'power-potential' keyboard, or the symmetrical distribution of the 810 types of souls given by God to the human race that are necessary in composing a social man."[55]

If our interpretation is correct, Labrouste is thus celebrating, in his way, all of the "810 types of souls," making the Bibliothèque a *"clavier puissanciel"* working toward a future regeneration. Here, architecture is "healing" through the suggestive force of its atmosphere. It creates a space of desire in which new alliances can freely form through ages and cultures. It is once again the passage from day to night that best reveals this utopian vector. Historian David Van Zanten has described how the pillars in the perimeter's deep arcades of masonry allow the even diffusion of light, though the main facade is south-facing.[56] That uniform light can be thought analogous to a mastered vision of knowledge. When evening comes, however, shadow and light establish new relationships that call forth another cognitive mode, as is perfectly illustrated by the main figure in *Study Surprised by Night*, who is looking at two books simultaneously, one lighted and the other in darkness (fig. 18). At night, it is the light of the gaslights that determines the atmosphere, making the passage of time imperceptible. The atmosphere is more immersive, with "the combined emanations of the gaslights and the four hundred readers who pile in there each evening."[57] The gas jets give light to the shelving and especially to the tables, where sixty-six lamps are aligned, while the large space beneath the vault remains in relative darkness. Light is thus concentrated around the readers, creating halos in the dark—the very image of Romantic inwardness. Beneath those whispering gaslights, the mind is freed from the yoke of the plausible, which is associated with daylight. This is when utopian thought awakens.

By giving night a new part to play, Labrouste is thus questioning the classical association of knowledge and sunlight. The Bibliothèque composes a Romantic ode to the imagination's power to transfigure daytime reality, in a creative act that finds an echo in some of the curious studies for cast-iron ornamentation for the reading room. The new order that could regenerate the world is hidden and must be revealed by developing a special language. If the revelation takes place during the night, it is only by daylight that it takes shape: nocturnal reverie must be fertilized by diurnal substance, as is suggested by the juxtaposition of the male (day) and female (night) figures sculpted on either side of the pedestal of the columns (fig. 25). The world is thus regenerated by this incessant back-and-forth between day and night. For if man is destined to dissolve into the cosmic harmonies, as Fourier wrote, "he must seek the tie that draws them into a whole."[58] It is the force of that "tie" which, according to Romantic faith, is a source of concord and prevents the universe from dispersing into a chaotic multiplicity. The Bibliothèque as a whole expresses the force of that tie, and contains within its powerful masonry the internal dynamism of its deambulatory metallic space. The fragile garland connecting the cast-iron hook to the small masonry column on the top corners of the facade is its enigmatic emblem (fig. 11).

25. Bibliothèque Sainte-Geneviève, reading room, herm personifying night. Photograph: Jean-Claude N'Diaye

ÉLIEN
TERTULLIEN
LES SAMON CUS
MINUTIUS-FÉLIX
CENSORINUS
ORIGÈNE
St CYPRIEN
HÉRODIEN
St DENYS D'ALEXANDRIE
PLOTIN
LONGIN
RABBI JUDA LE SAINT
CALPURNIUS
ANATOLIUS
NÉMÉSIEN
PORPHYRE
S-J. AFRICANUS
DIOPHANTE
ACHILLES-TATIUS
ARNOBE L'ANCIEN
EUMÈNE
SPARTIEN
LACTANCE
VOPISCUS
JAMBLIQUE
ARIUS
EUSÈBE
MAXIME D'ÉPIRE
HILAIRE
VICTORINUS
St ATHANASE
St BASILE
THÉON D'ALEXANDRIE
EUTROPE
St DAMASE
St CYRILLE
St GRÉGOIRE
AMMIEN MARCELLIN
LIBANIUS
THEMISTIUS
AUSONE
VÉGÈCE
DONAT
FIRMICUS
St ANTOINE
F-CL. JULIEN
AURELIUS VICTOR
St AMBROISE
HÉLIODORE
LONGUS
CLAUDIEN
St GRÉGOIRE DE NYSSE
St ÉPIPHANE
PRUDENCE
St JEAN CHRYSOSTOME
RUFIN
HERMOGÈNE
PAUL OROSE
ASSER
THÉODORE
St AUGUSTIN
SYNESIUS
PÉLAGE
SYMMAQUE
St PAULIN
SULPICE-SÉVÈRE
St JÉRÔME
OBSEQUENS

MARIE-HÉLÈNE
DE LA MURE
Bibliothèque
Sainte-Geneviève

FROM FEATHER TO STONE: THE *CONSTRUCTION SITE JOURNAL* AND BUILDING THE BIBLIOTHÈQUE SAINTE-GENEVIÈVE

The Bibliothèque Sainte-Geneviève's rare books department holds a collection of manuscripts which has grown over the centuries since the institution was founded. At the heart of the collection one can find a small rectangular book measuring 230 by180 millimeters which, inside a simple brown metisse binding, holds several school exercise books filled with handwritten recto and verso pages in thick penmanship on which the ink often runs out. A donation of Henri Labrouste's heirs, manuscript 3910 documents the implementation of the architect's first major public commission, between August 1843 and February 1851. It shows the different stages of the building's construction: after the *Construction Site Journal* on the construction of the Bibliothèque Sainte-Geneviève (f. 1–192) comes the *Journal of Transferring the Former Bibliothèque into the New Building*, December 23, 1850–February 4, 1851 (f. 195–98). Bound along with the rest is the draft of a letter addressed to the Minister of Public Instruction in which Labrouste requests compensation for the library employees who have helped in moving the collections (f. 201–201v).

The volume is a treasure for architectural historians: it shows the viewpoint, over time, of the master builder and allows us to follow the daily progress of a construction site in the mid-nineteenth century in its administrative, political, and social context. It thus has a unique place in the typology of sources for the history of architecture and falls

1. Bibliothèque Sainte-Geneviève, main facade, detail of spans. Photograph: Jean-Claude N'Diaye

into the category of "private and personal writings": sources that are both ample and incomplete, where individual history and collective history intersect.

When Labrouste began his first notebook, the preliminaries were finished. The architect had been given a commission, imagined a work, designed and presented a scale project, reworked it as often as the building contractors required until it was finally accepted and approved. From the first page, the tone is set and the action gets underway. It is August 1, 1843. "On July 31, the whole staff was called in to the office for general instructions. We chose a large room in the old buildings for the office, on the Rue des Sept-Voies [now the Rue Valette] and the courtyard. The temporary office for moving the library had been established on the Rue Jean-Hubert [which now no longer exists]. *Start of work.* Demolitions."

The thunder in those concise words is echoed, eight years later, by the satisfaction that underlies the description of the successive stages of validating and concluding the undertaking:

> December 1850 ... The new building was handed over on December 16; there was a statement written up in duplicate, which was sent, with the signatures of those in charge of the project, to the Ministers of Public Works and of Public Instruction. That very same day, I gave Mr. de Lancy all the keys to the building, the heating contract and an inventory of all of the items of furniture contained in the library. That very evening, Mr. de Lancy had the institution's new caretaker sleep in the building. On Sunday, December 29, the Minister of Public Works (Mr. Bineau) visited the worksite, or rather, the building. He was accompanied by Mr. de Noue. He seemed satisfied. At the end of the day, Mr. de Noue came back with Mr. Boulay de la Meurthe, the vice-president of the Republic. He, too, seemed satisfied.

Between those two dates, day by day, for over eight years and without later changes, Henri Labrouste would write over two hundred pages chronicling the construction work.

WHY WRITE, AND FOR WHOM?

In 1843, Henri Labrouste was forty-two years old. Clearly, by becoming his own memorialist, he wanted to provide the great construction project with the solemnity it deserved. The *Journal* was probably useful, too, as notes on an experiment, which could be reused. But could it also, perhaps, have been written for other eyes, as an attentive reading of the text allows us to suppose? The first indication of this is the ubiquitous use of the implicit. For example, the agency is referred to on the first day, but it is not presented as such; the same is true of participants of all kinds, especially administrative ones—Messrs. Dessalle, Prost, Guillemot, Jenvrin, etc.—whose presence punctuates the text yet whose role is never precisely specified. Also implicit are the regulatory requirements by which the architect scrupulously notes, immediately following the revolutionary days of February 1848, the number of workmen from each trade on the construction site. The use of titles in citing their names is also a clue: Labrouste is not addressing a specific reader, but

2. Henri Labrouste, *Journal des travaux de la construction de la Bibliothèque Sainte-Geneviève*, August 12–22, 1844, Bibliothèque Sainte-Geneviève, Paris, Ms. 3910 (f. 28v)

12 Pose de la première pierre. (voir le procès verbal).
13 on reprend les travaux interrompus par la pose de la 1re pierre on fait les murs pour contenir le béton sous le mur de refend dans la grande fouille. le Bureau de Mr Lefame offre à mon bureau et mon Bureau accepte des bouquets. –
14 on continue comme la veille.
15 on continue comme les jours précédents; mais les ouvriers qui avaient demandé à travailler malgré la fête du 15 août sont obligés de quitter le chantier à midi par la pluie.
16. on continue. Mr Vrost est venu pour l'affaire de Ste Barbe.
17 on continue – j'ai vu Mr George que j'avais invité à venir par écrit. il demande à conserver l'escalier seulement de la maison et offre de démolir de suite le reste de la partie en saillie il promet d'y mettre les ouvriers mercredi pour démolir.
18. D. on travaille
19 On continue comme la veille les premières assises de maçonnerie dans les caves sous l'escalier est terminée.
20 on continue. Bouligand demande que le mur de clôture de Ste Barbe soit démoli j'ai remis au lendemain pour m'entendre avec Mr Nomet le Directeur étant à la campagne.
21. Garde à la Mairie on continue je suis venu dans la journée et j'ai vu Mr Nomet de Ste Barbe pour activer la démolition de son mur sur la rue Jean Hubert.
22. on commence la démolition du mur de Ste barbe sur la rue Jean Hubert. Mr Georg a commencé hier la démolition ou la découverture de la maison. aujourd'hui il n'a pas d'ouvriers. Mr Verrot receveur des domaines est venu et m'a remis l'acceptation des congés pour octobre de tous les locataires de la maison rue des cholets 3 à l'exception de Mr Deblds et libraire.

3. Bibliothèque Sainte-Geneviève, entrance on the Place du Panthéon. Photograph: Michel Nguyen

Next pages:
4. Bibliothèque Sainte-Geneviève, view of the lateral bay windows in the reading room. Photograph: Jean-Claude N'Diaye

neither does he exclude the possibility of one day offering his chronicle for perusal by well-informed eyes as part of his professional and pedagogical work.

The perspective is varied: he is rendering an account of the project and showing off his knowledge; illustrating "what construction means," by setting down, day after day, the progress and tribulations of a construction site; offering a peek at the time needed to complete the project: the monotonous series of days ("We continued on," "we continued on, as we had the day before") as well as the breaks, whether planned or unforeseen; attesting to the role of each partner; demonstrating his own scrupulous management of public funds. But we might also think that Labrouste, as implicated as he was in defining and developing the profession he had chosen, also wanted to use his own case to illustrate how ubiquitous the architect was: appointed to the Dépôt des Marbres and the agricultural colony of Mesnil-Saint-Firmin, two projects for the new Commission on Historical Monuments, commissioned to renovate the Hôtel du Tillet, and to serve on different committees and a Salon jury at the Société des Architectes. He noted scrupulously each trip he made for one or another of his duties, in striking contrast to the almost complete absence of any remarks about his private life.

FROM PAGE TO PAGE ...

The Bibliothèque Sainte-Geneviève gradually rises from the page—as we know it, of course, but also as it was for a time, with its cherry laurel seedlings outside, the red-lined names on the busts in the vestibule, the gilded candelabras in the stairhall, the porcelain medallions that punctuated the length of the reading room, the green color of the tables that echoed the curtains and drapes of the doorway.

The construction site progresses and lives before our eyes: receiving materials from the stone yards of the Ile-aux-Cygnes, repeated requests to the Maintenance department for scaffolding, stays, fences for the worksite, the site being taken over by the builder who sets up a *shack* on the asphalt-covered roof, unearthing the medieval remains of Montaigu and the archaeological finds when digging the foundations: coins and medals (turned over to Albert Lenoir, who "did not seem to find any interest in them"), plaster tombs, human bones (which attract "many people who came together for such circumstances"); laying the cornerstone (recalled later, on anniversary dates), an opportunity for a ceremony, a commemorative medal and bouquets given to the agency by the builder; other rituals, such as a tip for the masons after they set the keystone to the arched entrance (fig. 3), as well as after the last masonry block is put in place and the workers decorated it with flags; interruptions for adjudications, accidents and even funerals, conscription of workmen for a task, political events; the problems of weather: bad weather that precluded any outdoor work or weakened fresh cement that was poorly protected by waterproof tarps, the risk of frost which required unfinished masonry to be protected by straw; difficulties involving provisions and transporting materials; delays and defects; "doing and undoing ...": correcting alignment or leveling, discarding poor quality or "*mistreated*" stones, repairing poorly smoothed coatings; repeated theft of wood or lead; technical experimentation.

Over the course of the text, each person has a part to play: first and foremost the institutional partners, the ministers of Public Works and Public Instruction (the worksite was monitored—on site as well as in the offices—by the division and council of Civil Buildings; there were expropriations, arbitration, occupational medicine, meetings at the ministry annually or with each change in personnel); police headquarters and the Préfecture de la Seine (adjudications, alignments, leveling, sidewalks, public safety, etc.); the Bibliothèque Sainte-Geneviève and the Collège Henri-IV; the architect and his collaborators (use of five successive offices, the agency's daily functioning, distribution of tasks, sick leaves, vacations or weddings); the builders and their clerks, whose procrastination, delays, breaches of trust and trickery are sprinkled throughout the chronicle; the workers, all trades taken together; the artisans and artists who worked on the development and décor.

The *Construction Site Journal* shows different times affecting the worksite: seasonal time, first, which, for the outdoor parts, is marked on November 1 by the "closing of summer days, the beginning of winter days," and in early March by a return to outside work and the arrival of masons from the Limoges region; the time of the month, as accented by Saturdays or Sundays, depending on the trade, for payday and the post-"carouse"

day after; the time of the week, punctuated or not by the builder with a day of rest on Sunday, sometimes followed by a "Holy Monday"; the time of day, given its rhythm by bells, from dawn to dusk. And last, he records the time, constrained or festive, in which there was no work. Technical hindrances were the only unavoidable reason; religious or civil holidays were only off at on the contractor or workers' discretion.

In that world, in which family and provincial networks intertwined, in which lean salaries—regularly rounded out with a bonus—led to strikes, in which obtaining a certificate determined what would happen the next day, accidents were a major risk. A worker could fall into the pit or from the top of a wall, or scaffolding could collapse, or there could be a cladding accident, or one could be hit by a falling stone or board, or the building could even fall apart. Labrouste notes for each of the twenty-six occurrences that he is listing the circumstances of the accident, the name and type of wound, the response (bloodletting, transportation home or to the hospital, etc.). If death occurred, everyone would go to the burial and the worksite was closed.

Constant conflict is set against this backdrop. Much of it has the architect or agency fighting with one builder or another: failure to follow orders, cheating on materials or their deposit value, incompetence, insulting behavior, complaints about payment of bills, mistakes in the rendering of the masonry inventory drawings, a careless approach to safety, and failings and defects of all kinds frequently required recourse to arbitration by the higher Administration. Dissention sometimes affected relationships between the builder and his foreman or workmen, or even between two trades manning the "artillery battery." Just outside the fences at the time, other construction work was proceeding to develop the shape of the public square, the Place du Panthéon. The new 12th (now 5th) arrondissement town hall was being built by architect Jacques-Ignace Hittorff, and the Collège Sainte-Barbe was being rebuilt, overseen by Théodore Labrouste. The latter construction site would interfere many times with the library's: confusion in delivering materials, stones from the library that fell on the *collège*'s grounds, accidents on one worksite or the other and recourse to the doctor on hand whoever he was, borrowed material, etc.—not to mention "the exchange between the State and the Société de Sainte-Barbe regarding the plot of land once intended for the librarians' lodgings" (August 25, 1846). The Collège Sainte-Barbe, because of its geographical, familial, and professional proximity, has a strong presence in the text. Further in the background, we can see Paris being built. And the *Journal* lets us see the ties from one construction site to the next. Looking for information on the merits of Silly stone, Labrouste goes, successively, to the worksite for the church of Sainte-Clotilde, where François-Christian Gau is at work, then to the Ministry of Foreign Affairs worksite, overseen by Jacques Lacornée; he speaks to Rousseau, the Palais National's architect, "to find out which builder cleaned and whitewashed the facade of the Théâtre Français." His colleagues also come to the Place du Panthéon, even Thomas Donaldson, the president and founder of the Royal Institute of British Architects, who comes from London and "examines [the] drawings and visits the construction site"

on December 27, 1848. Artists were also part of the network, and they placed their students there and followed their work, as Ingres did with Alexandre Desgoffe.

... AND HISTORY

The political situation only appears in passing throughout the July Monarchy. Labrouste is frequently stationed for guard duty with the Garde Nationale in the Tuileries, at city hall, or at the Louvre; on December 31, 1847, as the agency is getting ready for the customary visit to the minister, "official visits are countermanded following the death of Madame Adélaïde, the king's sister." On the other hand, the *Journal* offers a chronology of the Revolution of 1848 and its aftermath, insofar as it affects work on the construction site: the February events, the July Column (March 4), reception of architects by the temporary government, a protest on the Champ-de-Mars (April 2), the collection of "patriotic donations," general elections and proclamation of the Republic (May 4). During the June Days, after a complete work stoppage for four days, the worksite is "entirely stripped of its fences, and the one around the administration building especially has greatly suffered"; Labrouste, charged with organizing the victims' funerals, must also decide with the Administration what "indemnity to allot the builders after the damage caused"; the inspectors must make replicas of lost plans; the vestibule is requisitioned and, between July and September, shelters the troops stationed at the Place du Panthéon: kitchen smoke blackens the walls as well as the terra-cotta piled upstairs. After the Constitution is declared, public unrest and electoral consultations set the rhythm for public life as well as for life on the construction site: the legislative elections on July 8–10, 1849, and on March 10–11 and April 28–29, 1850, all take place in the new building.

FURTHER

This wealth of information offers many paths for research. The source of the birth of a building, the *Construction Site Journal* is an institutional archive. But beyond that, it documents the history of the architecture of its time and that of the networks—administrative, academic, artistic, social, technical, and industrial—that crossed paths: the political, social, and economic history of Paris; the city and its 12th arrondissement; the people as a building force; the climate; and a man, in the end, whose passionate involvement on his construction site appears through the "stenographic" dryness of his tone.

Manuscript 3910 cannot be understood outside of its context. The Henri Labrouste collection at the Bibliothèque Sainte-Geneviève has, since the national events that in 2001 celebrated the 150th anniversary of the building and the 200th of the birth of its architect, benefited from special attention: all of the texts have been microfilmed, a detailed inventory of the graphic works has been made in the Catalogue of Archives and Manuscripts in Higher Education,[1] and an online critical edition of the *Construction Site Journal* is now part of a "virtual Henri Labrouste library."[2]

1. Calames online catalogue, http://www.calames.abes.fr/pub/ms/Calames-2009224112361401.
2. "Henri Labrouste," Bibliothèque Sainte-Geneviève, http://www-bsg.univ-paris1.fr/bsg/hlabrouste.htm.

ART ET ARCHÉOLOGIE
BE
BF
BG

MARC LE CŒUR
Bibliothèque Nationale
de France

THE BIBLIOTHÈQUE NATIONALE: BETWEEN RATIONALISM AND ILLUSIONISM

If there is a subject that ought to please an architect and also fuel his genius, it is a public library project.
—Etienne-Louis Boullée, *Architecture: Essai sur l'art,* c. 1793

Work on the "restoration and enlargement" of the Bibliothèque Impériale (Nationale after 1870) took up the last twenty years of Labrouste's life and helped, like the Bibliothèque Sainte-Geneviève, to usher him into the pantheon of history's great architects. Like the earlier library, the project was universally admired once it was finished, and has aroused a sense of astonishment ever since. Labrouste's two masterworks nevertheless have notable differences.

When he was called on to replace his colleague Visconti on February 16, 1854, Labrouste was almost fifty-three years old. He was a more patient person who had had many other commissions—particularly that for the new seminary in Rennes (figs. 2, 3). The new assignment brought him face to face with, in his own words, the "most precious monument in the capital after the Louvre"[1] and the "richest scientific depository in the world."[2] The institution had been housed in 1724 in the former Hôtel de Nevers, north of the Palais Royal and along the Rue de Richelieu, which leads from the Louvre to the Grands Boulevards. By 1833, it was extended toward the south and east of the rest of the block, annexing the former palace of Cardinal Mazarin, but

1. Letter from Labrouste to the Minister of State, January 25, 1858, Bibliothèque Nationale de France, Archives, C-328 (2), 1858, no. 12.

2. Labrouste, "Projet de restauration et d'agrandissement des bâtiments de la Bibliothèque Impériale," April 1859 (AN, F 21 1360). At that time, the Bibliothèque was made up of five distinct departments. The Printed Materials department was the largest; the other departments were Manuscripts, Medals, Prints, and Maps and Geographical Collections.

1. Bibliothèque Nationale, view of the reading room. Photograph: Georges Fessy

3. Letter from Prosper Mérimée to Labrouste, February 19, 1858, Bibliothèque Nationale de France, Archives, C-328 (2), 1858, no. 16.
4. "Rapport fait au Conseil [Général des Bâtiments Civils] par M. Duban, Inspecteur Général," April 27, 1859 (AN, F 21 1360).
5. Delaborde 1878:17.
6. Anatole de Baudot, "L'architecture contemporaine," *L'Union des architectes et des artistes industriels* (June 16, 1902): 4.
7. Labrouste 1868:13.

excluding the privately owned properties to the northeast, along the Rue Vivienne (fig. 4). Under the Second Empire, this heterogeneous agglomeration of courtyards and buildings, which did not especially lend themselves to the conservation and consultation of library collections, looked like the "saddening spectacle of the ruins of a palace."[3] Plans for its reconstruction were contemplated beginning in the late eighteenth century. Innumerable proposals were put forth in vain, ranging from simple improvements to the institution's transfer to another site. When Labrouste was named architect for the Bibliothèque, it was no longer a question of moving the library, or even of rebuilding the entire structure. As a result, his own plan had to take into account the buildings to be conserved as well as those that were to be replaced over time, in order to ensure that the institution would never close down entirely. He also had to invent a system of methodical distribution for the collections, just as there were ongoing debates about the ways of organizing a general catalogue. According to his friend Félix Duban, there would be a "new program, one that marks a complete shift from the established ways of thinking to date about the layout and organization of a library."[4]

In order to resolve such complex issues, Labrouste could not rely solely on the solutions he had found for the Bibliothèque Sainte-Geneviève, no more than those of the British Museum library, completed in 1857, which the government had nevertheless asked him to study closely. He finally had to reconcile the sometimes diverging opinions of several decision makers, first among whom was Prosper Mérimée, who in December 1857 was named president of a committee "charged with examining the modifications to include in the organization of the Bibliothèque Impériale," then Jules-Antoine Taschereau,

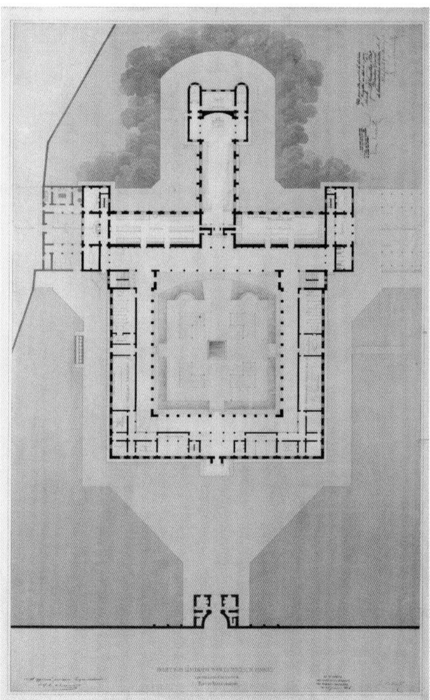

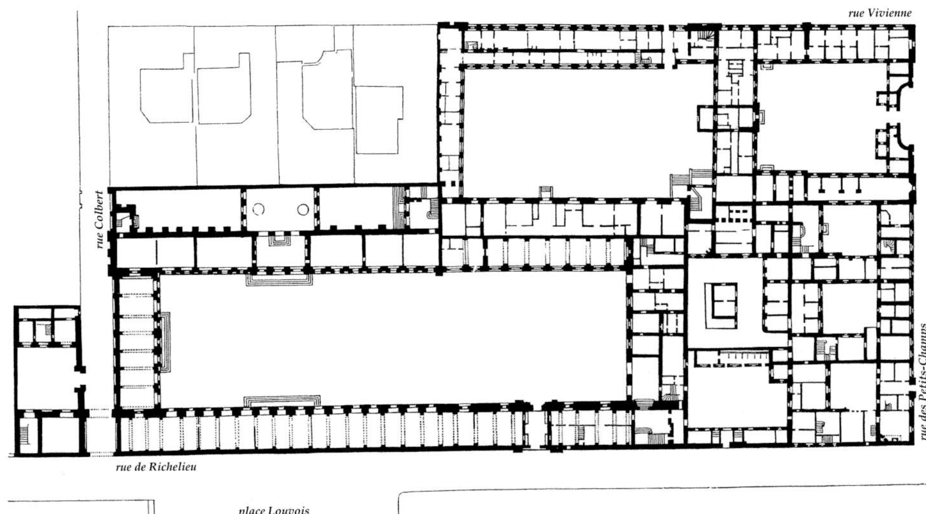

the Bibliothèque's general administrator from July 1858. Despite all the constraints he had to face and the disagreements that constantly set him against the administrator, Labrouste managed to build a truly original, personal work. Raised amid new constructions, the main reading room, more than anything else, is one of the most emblematic spaces in modern architecture. In order to understand its meaning, it is important to describe and analyze the work, which is more discreet but no less remarkable than what was done in the rest of the plan.

OF BRICKS AND STONE

From 1854 to 1858, Labrouste devoted himself to the restoration and renovation of the buildings to be saved on the eastern side of the block: the former mansion of Charles Duret de Chevry (called the "Hôtel Tubeuf"), built in 1635–41 by Jean Thiriot along the Rue des Petits-Champs, and, afterward, the Galerie Mazarine, built on two levels by François Mansart in 1644–45, situated parallel to the Rue Vivienne.

First during his stay in Rome, then in the 1840s, the architect had already worked on projects for restoring ancient or medieval monuments, but he had never encountered French structures from the classical era. Despite his notorious disdain "for the art of modern times, for the architecture of the seventeenth century in particular,"[5] he was more than willing to work with the buildings of Thiriot and Mansart, because they were both built in brick and stone, following the convention of their time. The facades, which emphasized the means of construction by distinguishing frame from infill, corroborated his own teachings. At the same time, Labrouste indeed recommended to his students that they "seek out ... architectonic decoration by combining materials"[6] and later spoke of his preference, where architectural polychromy was concerned, for "using naturally toned materials."[7] The design of the Hôtel Tubeuf and the Galerie Mazarine worked so well for him

2. Henri Labrouste, New Seminary in Rennes, transverse cross section of the *cour d'honneur* and elevation of the main facade, second project, 1856, 68 x 104.8 cm, Bibliothèque nationale de France, Paris, Prints, HD-1018-FT 6.

3. Henri Labrouste, New Seminary in Rennes, plan of the ground floor, second project, 1856, 104.5 × 67.7 cm, Bibliothèque nationale de France, Paris, Prints, HD-1018-FT 6

4. Plan of the Bibliothèque Royale in 1845, after Laborde, December 1845, plate III. The north side is to the left

Next pages:
5. Bibliothèque Nationale, overall view of the reading room. Photograph: Luc Boegly

CONDITA NAPOLEONE III IMP
CONTRÔLE

CONTROLE

that, after agreeing to update the Louis XIII style of the new mansion he was building for Louis Fould from 1856 to 1858, he would use brick in most of his projects and buildings. Labrouste did not simply restore the facades of the Bibliothèque's old buildings nor redesign their interiors; he also razed the buildings of minor importance that hid them from view. On the Rue des Petits-Champs, he only retained the central doorway of the entrance wing, which he flanked with two modern grilles, and he erected another grille along the Rue Vivienne, thus revealing the Galerie Mazarine's facade to the public (fig. 6). According to *L'Illustration*, "opening the view to an overlooked or unnoticed monumental work" was a true "artistic revelation."[8] Labrouste also planted a garden with trees at the foot of the gallery, which he enhanced with a fountain inspired by the one at the Villa Medici; to the north, the neighboring property's unsightly blank wall was covered with a brick and stone décor that echoed the rear facade of the Hôtel Tubeuf, which it faced.

This first phase of work, which was widely praised by the press, shows just how important Labrouste found "unity," which to him was "at all times the essential law, the fundamental condition for architectonic composition."[9] One of his first students, Jean-Baptiste Lassus, wrote in 1845 that "unity of style in architecture is like the exactitude of sounds in music."[10] In this case, Labrouste gave prominence to the most notable and homogeneous buildings and did away with those he found extrinsic, and he made additions that fit in with the general style (grilles, vases, lampposts, fountain, etc.) without falling into any form of pastiche. The search for harmony could already be seen in the Bibliothèque Sainte-Geneviève, where he recoiled from using any element from the original building; and for the new vestibule, in particular, he chose to employ modern

8. Dauban, 1856:37.
9. Delaborde, 1878:19.
10. Lassus, "De l'art et de l'archéologie," *Annales archéologiques*, vol. 2 (Paris: Bureau des Annales Archéologiques, 1845), 77; cited in Foucart 1978:79.
11. Letter from Prosper Mérimée, February 19, 1858, op. cit.

busts rather than the remarkable old ones that the library owned. He would do much the same when enlarging the Bibliothèque Nationale.

"A HOUSE FOR BOOKS"

Labrouste was first given the information about the program to follow some time in 1858, but already in February of that year, Mérimée had shown him that the committee over which he presided wanted "France to show that it is still an artistic nation, one that gives the world models to follow, [and for] France to show, also, that it has become a practical nation. One does not give an artist of your stature advice. The committee will not tell you: use bricks, iron, glass. Build a *true library*, so that all may see from without, as they will feel within, that it is a house for books [la maison des livres]."[11]

After drawing up several different drafts, Labrouste finally sent a definitive proposal to the Conseil Général des Bâtiments Civils, which was officially adopted in April 1859 (fig. 7). The construction site, where there would be successive demolitions and reconstructions,

6. Bibliothèque Impériale from the Rue Vivienne side, with view of the Hôtel Tubeuf, the Galerie Mazarine, and the new garden before the trees were planted. Dauban 1856:37

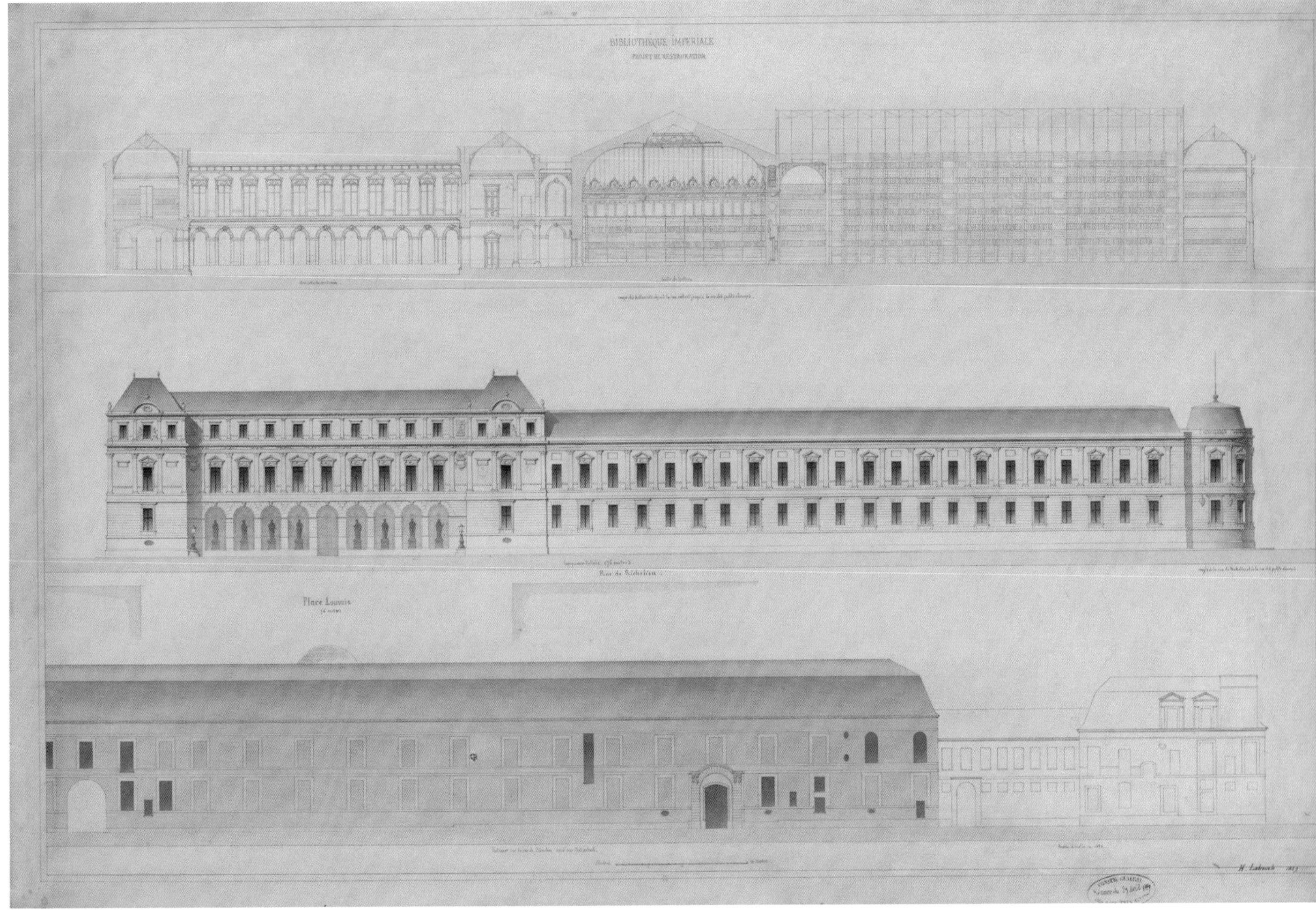

7. Henri Labrouste, Reconstruction Plans for the Bibliothèque Impériale, longitudinal section and elevation of the Rue de Richelieu, with an elevation of the existing building; plans submitted to the Conseil Général des Bâtiments Civils on April 29, 1859, 68 × 102.5 cm, Bibliothèque nationale de France, Paris, Prints, HD-1019 (1)-FT 6

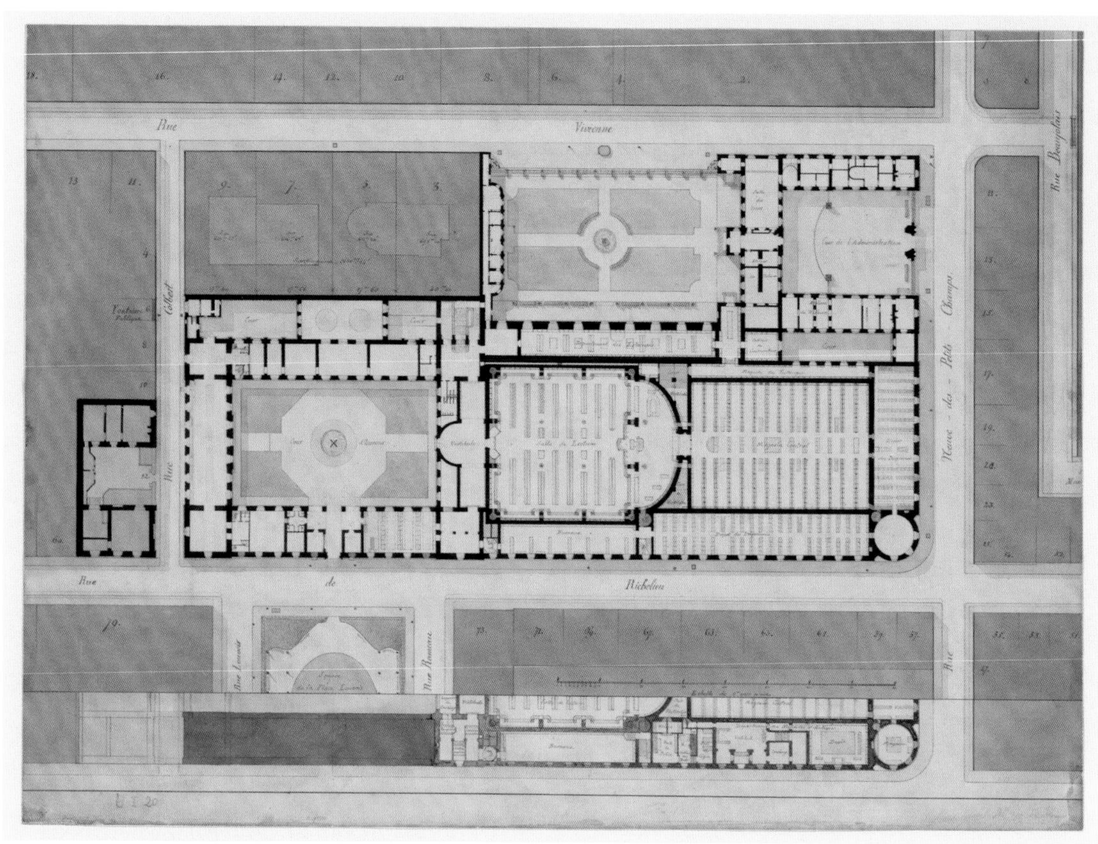
Rue
Vivienne
Rue
de
Richelieu

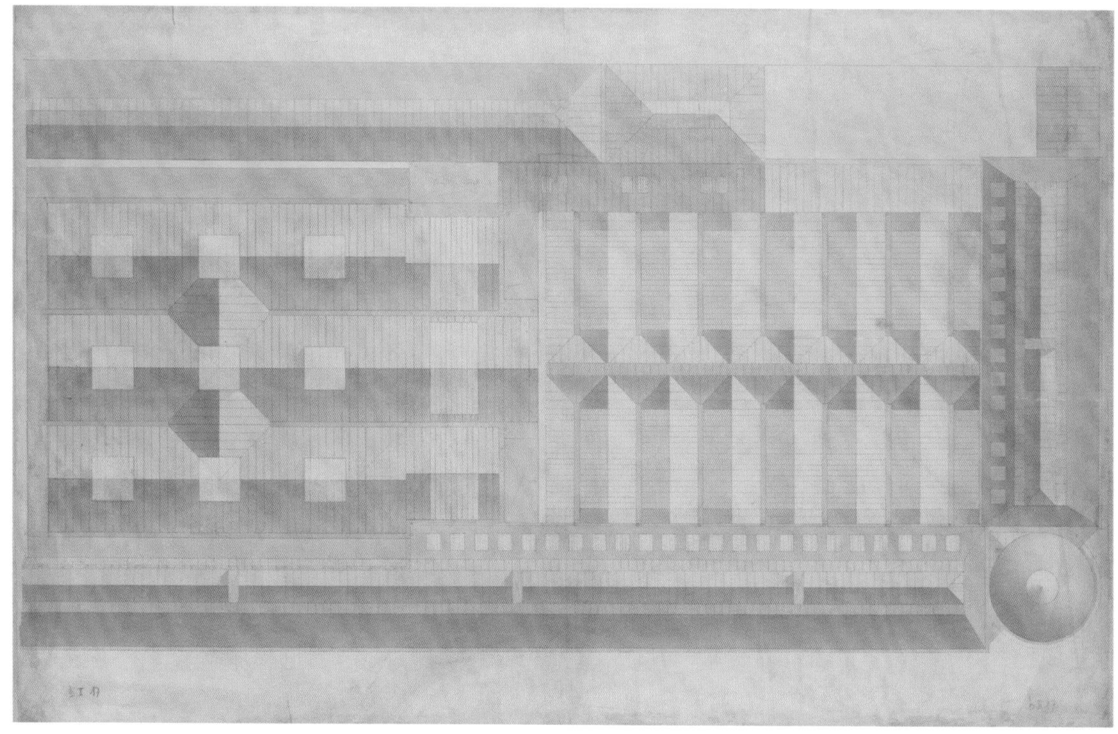

started on the Rue des Petits-Champs on June 1 and progressively stretched to the north in the following years. The reading room opened to the public in June 1868. In 1873, when the last section of the Richelieu wing was being completed, the architect was already considering extending the Bibliothèque to the privately owned properties on the northeast corner of the Rue Vivienne. His death two years later would keep him from completing that final project.

Of the old buildings, Labrouste only spared the two wings erected around 1730–40 by Robert and Jules-Robert de Cotte to the northeast and north of the *cour d'honneur*—that is, the only buildings expressly constructed for the Bibliothèque shortly after it was established at the site. In several years, the Hôtel de Nevers and its annexes (built by Pierre Le Muet from 1646 to 1649), the three adjoining mansions on the Rue des Petits-Champs (by the same architect, 1642–43), and the whole southern half of the large courtyard were replaced by a new reading room and main stacks for printed books, which Labrouste wrapped, on the street side, with long galleries intended to house overstock from the collections (fig. 8). Though they were adjoining, the different areas were independent of each other and the passageways that connected them, because of the risk of fire, were kept to a strict minimum. The whole formed a compact set of autonomous spaces (fig. 9).

However, Labrouste did not want to make the establishment look like a fortress. But after opening up the garden on the Rue Vivienne, to the east, and the Hôtel Tubeuf courtyard, to the south, he came up against the new administrator, Taschereau, who was opposed to having a series of arcades to the west open onto the *cour d'honneur*, which gave onto the street (fig. 7). Taschereau considered that "the Bibliothèque [was] no longer safe if everyone [could] see into its inner buildings."[12] Labrouste, however, aimed to open it up to the city on all sides, as a testament to the accessibility of knowledge. To do so, he also grounded the project in the urban environment.

Thus, as Labrouste wrote, the "point of departure" for his project was moving the Bibliothèque's entrance toward the widest part of the Rue de Richelieu—that is, right in front of the Place Louvois.[13] The Place Louvois was converted into a *square* (public garden) in 1859, very likely at the architect's request. That transformation indeed allowed for "a fitting introduction to a monument devoted to scholarly study" which he had not managed to realize in front of the Bibliothèque Sainte-Geneviève: a "space planted with large trees [preparing readers] for contemplation."[14] It is easy to see how removing any visual obstacle between the public garden and the *cour d'honneur* could highlight the correlation between nature and intellectual work, and better predispose readers to the task at hand. On Taschereau's insistence Labrouste nevertheless had to forego his portico and replace it with a solid wall, which would forever leave the Square Louvois outside the Bibliothèque's doors (fig. 13).

The new buildings were based on the design, proportions, and rhythm of the courtyard-facing facades of the old Hôtel de Nevers, which had already inspired Robert de Cotte and his son. Ever in search of unity, Labrouste thus conformed to classical architectural language, but he adapted its details in his own way. As at the Bibliothèque Sainte-Geneviève, but in a more discreet way, he also managed to represent on the

12. Léon Labrouste, 1885:53.
13. Labrouste "Projet de restauration," op. cit.
14. Labrouste 1852: col. 382.

8. Henri Labrouste, Bibliothèque Impériale, overall plan, 1868, 45.2 × 62.5 cm, Paris, Bibliothèque nationale de France, Prints, HD-1019 (1)-FT 6.
9. Henri Labrouste, Bibliothèque Impériale, plan of the roofs of the reading room, the central storeroom, and lateral storerooms, c. 1862, 67 × 105 cm, Bibliothèque nationale de France, Paris, Prints, HD-1019 (1)-FT 6

Next pages:
10. Bibliothèque Nationale, lateral view of the reading room from the hemicycle. Photograph: Georges Fessy

11. Louis-Emile Durandelle, Bibliothèque Nationale, view of the rotunda from the Rue de Richelieu, c. 1880, photograph, 41.1 × 34.3 cm, Bibliothèque nationale de France, Paris, Prints, HD-1176 (1)-BOITE FOL
12. Louis-Emile Durandelle, Bibliothèque Nationale, view of the main facade, across from the Square Louvois, c. 1880, photograph, 32.8 × 42.7 cm, Bibliothèque nationale de France, Paris, Prints, HD-1176 (1)-BOITE FOL

13. Bibliothèque Nationale, facade of the reading room giving onto the *cour d'honneur*. Photograph: Jean-Christophe Ballot
14. Henri Labrouste, Basilica of Maxentius and Constantine in Rome, plan and perspective view, [1825–30], 98.1 × 66.1 cm, Académie d'architecture, Paris, 267.1

exterior the way the interior was arranged: on the street, the base's uninterrupted stone coursing expresses the length of the book stacks, while the pilasters or engaged columns on the upper level underscore the presence of perpendicularly set shelves between the bays. As for the elegant rotunda's dome, which rises above the intersection of the Rue de Richelieu and the Rue des Petits-Champs—a then infrequent arrangement in Paris that would soon be much copied—it prefigures the cupolas in the reading room (fig. 11). The "series of facades whose calm, uniform look reveals a place of study"[15] connects the very disparate old buildings preserved at both ends of the site. The diachronic unfolding of historical styles, from the Rue Vivienne to the *cour d'honneur*, from Louis XIII to Louis XV, shows the institution's longevity and durability. From the outside, nothing hints at the extraordinary originality of the installations that extend past the walls: Labrouste keeps it a surprise for readers.

"INFILL, OR ALMOST FURNITURE"

The southern side of the *cour d'honneur* forms the frontispiece of a new sequence which runs from north to south and successively includes the Bibliothèque's vestibule, the new reading room, and the main stacks (fig. 13). Here, Labrouste could give his imagination free rein, and if he made the details of the low entrance wing match those of the existing neighboring facades (principle of unity), it was in order to contrast the dissonance in scale with the upper section behind, which was something he liked to do. His models—most certainly ancient—are a mix of the Basilica of Maxentius and

Constantine in Rome (fig. 14) with the Arch of Augustus in Perugia (p. 84, fig. 31). The attic's marble disks in particular recall that Etruscan arch's metopes, much as the string of shields he hung high up in his reconstruction of the "Portico" in Paestum in 1828–29 did (p. 91, fig. 4). That composite assemblage was so unusual in such a setting that a librarian at the Bibliothèque would soon write that "the back of the courtyard [by Jules-Robert de Cotte] is a palace, and the front is a railway station."[16] The remark was meant to be pejorative, but it is true: in its major lines, the "front" does look like the facades of Paris train stations, especially the Gare Montparnasse, which was finished in 1852.

The vestibule was no less disconcerting (fig. 15). The severe, stony space, which daylight only reached through the entryway's fanlight and two skylights, seems to be hewn from rocks like the tombs of Etruria or those of Phoenicia, which had just been studied by Julien Thobois, who at the time was the architect's main assistant after having been his student.[17] On the perimeter, continuous stone drapery, accented by fifty-four marble disks, also evokes ancient civilizations: the bas-relief's trompe-l'oeil motif echoes those of Pompeii and the Etruscans (the "Tapestry" tomb in Corneto, with painted drapery), but its technique is a reference to the Assyrian sculptures exhibited at the Louvre since 1847 (fig. 16). Labrouste

15. "Rapport fait au Conseil," op. cit.

16. Henri Bouchot, "Les derniers travaux de décoration exécutés à la Bibliothèque nationale par M. Pascal, Architecte," *Revue des arts décoratifs* (September–October 1891): 81.

17. In 1861, Thobois left the Bibliothèque Impériale worksite for several months to accompany a mission in Phoenicia overseen by Ernest Renan, and to produce archaeological studies.

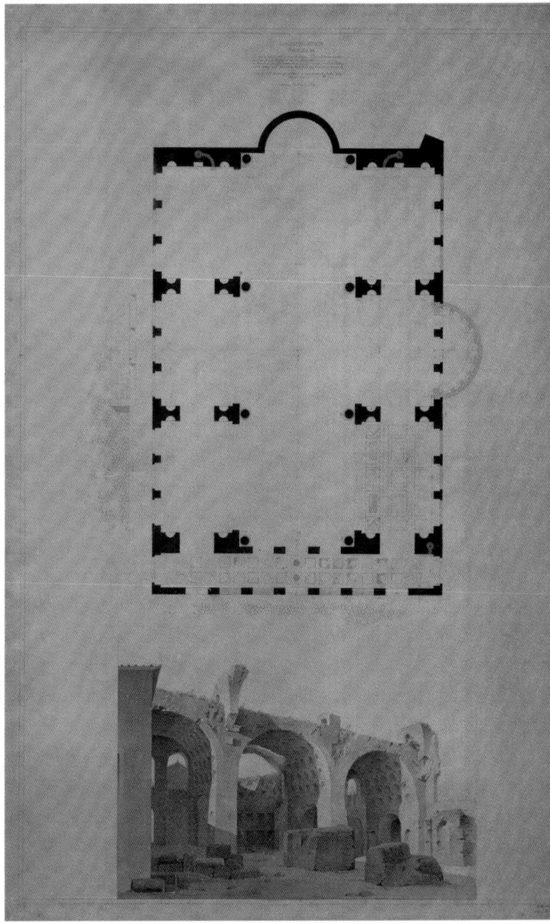

was already familiar with this type of bas-relief sculpture, and he had already made use of it a first time on the stairwell landing at the Bibliothèque Sainte-Geneviève in an almost abstract version. From the mid-1850s, his ornamentation, willingly drawn from the repertory of passementerie and jewelry, took a much more figurative turn. His stone draperies became more realistic, as in the projects for the decorations of the narthex of the chapel at the Rennes seminary (c. 1862), in the tomb of his friend Duban (1871–72; p. 78, fig. 26), and in the realized tomb of Louise Thouret (1872–73). At the Bibliothèque Nationale, a breeze, suggested by the floating ribbons painted on the wall at the far ends of the vestibule, seems to lightly lift the fringes that hem the bottoms of the walls.

A dimly lit wooden vestibule leads to the reading room, a grand square space thirty-five meters on each side, extended on the south side by a hemicycle (figs. 5, 10, 17). Like the one at the Bibliothèque Sainte-Geneviève, the reading room is surrounded by large arches (three on each side) whose piers form inner buttresses. Its location at the center of the site nevertheless required new arrangements: as the three-bay windows opening onto the *cour d'honneur* were unable to provide sufficient light, light had to be introduced from above.[18] Labrouste first planned a faceted glass roof atop an imposing vault (fig. 7), then a coffered ceiling with glass in the center, but such solutions ran the risk of casting shadows onto the readers and the books they were consulting. The approach finally adopted was much more ingenious: nine domes on pendentives with an oculus in the

18. Unlike the Bibliothèque Sainte-Geneviève, the Bibliothèque Nationale had no artificial lighting before electricity was intstalled in 1924. Until that date, it would only receive readers from 10 A.M. to 4 P.M.

15. P. Robert, Bibliothèque Nationale, view of the vestibule, facing the large main staircase, undated, photograph, 23 × 28.4 cm, Bibliothèque nationale de France, Paris, Prints, VA-237 (4)-FOL. Left, the revolving door, the door in the wall, the large vase, and its pedestal date from after Labrouste's death

16. Bibliothèque Nationale, detail of the vestibule's stone wall. Photograph: David Paul Carr

middle of each, so that the circles of light overlapped and produced diffuse, even lighting (fig. 20). As for the hemicycle, it was topped by a vault with a skylight.

The metal structure is entirely autonomous. Even more than at the Bibliothèque Sainte-Geneviève, it is set into the masonry "like the mechanism of a watch in its case."[19] Labrouste plainly showed that the two structural systems were independent of each other. "The walls which close and isolate have a full, solid look ... Inside, on the other hand, is a lightness suitable to infill, or almost furniture."[20] Its sixteen cast-iron columns, detached from the walls, support iron arches on which both the domes and the higher roof beams are set (p. 189, fig. 5). The domes themselves are made up of a framework in which ceramic plaques are set—white, double-curved panels and friezes in concentric relief—whose thinness (only nine millimeters) led the architect to remark that they were only "what the shell is ... to the whole egg."[21] That solution allowed for optimal use of light and paved the way for "a marriage of iron and enamel in modern art."[22] The domes' structure adopted the latticework principle of large cage crinolines (figs. 19, 22), which in the mid-1850s were themselves inspired by progress in metal construction.[23] The surface decoration expresses its reinforcement; it also cleverly underscores the clothing analogy by simulating white petticoats enhanced by a series of colored plaits. For David Van Zanten, the nine domes suggest velaria lifted by a breeze[24]; Robin Middleton, however, sees "obvious echoes" of the hot-air balloons held by poles that Duban had projected for the July festivities in 1834.[25] Given the above, we can also see the domes as the materialization of an image often repeated by caricaturists of the time[26]: the curious spectacle of crinolines billowing, as though carried by the breeze already felt in the vestibule.

"DECORATED CONSTRUCTION"

Subordinating the décor to the structure was essential to Labrouste. From 1830 on, he urged his students to "draw reasoned, expressive ornamentation from the construction itself "[27]; later, according to those who knew him, he affirmed that "architecture is decorated construction,"[28] setting himself apart from his friend Duban, who saw it as "a constructed decoration."[29] The two precepts express a shared desire to highlight structural elements, whether visible or underlying, but they suggest different means, which were adopted one after the other in each of his libraries. In the Bibliothèque Sainte-Geneviève, the malleability of cast iron allowed him to embellish the arches in the reading room (p. 190, fig. 6); ornamentation thus arose from a judicious use of materials. In the Bibliothèque Nationale, on the other hand, he magnified the industrial nature of the iron arches and beams by using painted arabesques; the construction was now marked by added-on ornamentation. The rivet heads, always accented with gold, were thus connected either by intertwining golden wires, like the laces of a corset (fig. 21), or by red and black spirals and foliage (fig. 23). Nevertheless, cast iron remained his preferred material for interior fittings. Since his first plans for the Pont de

19. Giedion 1959:139.
20. Gosset 1889:220.
21. Bailly 1876:20.
22. Alphonse Gosset, "Les Coupoles d'orient & d'occident," *Travaux de l'Académie nationale de Reims* 87 (1891): 354.
23. Philippe Perrot, *Les Dessus et les dessous de la bourgeoisie: Une histoire du vêtement au XIXe siècle* (Paris: Librairie Arthème Fayard, 1981), 194, 222.
24. Van Zanten 1979:62; Van Zanten 1987:241.
25. Middleton 1999:49 (fig. 41), 50.
26. See notably Valérie Sueur-Hermel, ed., *Daumier. L'écriture du lithographe* (Paris: Bibliothèque nationale de France, 2008), 121, fig. 115.
27. Letter from Labrouste to his brother Théodore, November 20, 1830; cited in [Laure Labrouste] 1928:24.
28. Alfred Darcel, "La peinture vitrifiée et l'architecture au Salon de 1864," *Gazette des Beaux-Arts* (July 1, 1864): 86 ; A. Gaspard, "Autour de Sainte-Blandine," *Lyon-Revue* (September 30, 1882): 163–64; Daly 1887.
29. Charles Blanc, "Félix Duban et ses dessins," *Le Siècle*, April 4, 1872, [p. 3] ; A. Gaspard, op. cit.

17. Louis-Emile Durandelle, Bibliothèque Nationale, overall view of the reading room facing the hemicycle, c. 1880, photograph, 34.5 × 42.9 cm, Bibliothèque nationale de France, Paris, Prints, HD-1176 (1)-BOITE FOL

18. Louis-Emile Durandelle, Bibliothèque Nationale, overall view of the central storeroom, c. 1880, photograph, 32.8 × 42.7 cm, Bibliothèque nationale de France, Paris, Prints, HD-1176 (1)-BOITE FOL

la Concorde, he had known how to draw forth powerful artistic effects from it, playing at once on the fullness of forms, the indentation of outlines and the graphic treatment of surfaces. At the Bibliothèque Sainte-Geneviève, the balusters and candelabras had already bent to his creative whim; for the Bibliothèque Nationale, he designed heaters and column bases as true sculptures whose volumes subtly responded to the domes (figs. 24, 25).

Labrouste had more leeway with the decoration of walls. Those of the reading room and the hemicycle were entirely covered with books on the lower part, between the buttresses. To him, books were a library's "most beautiful ornaments."[30] To the north, the bookshelves sat beneath three windows opening onto the *cour d'honneur* (fig. 29), and from east to west beneath paintings representing "simply trees and a sky,"[31] rendered by Alexandre Desgoffe from 1864 to 1868 (figs. 1, 26). The architect had at first rejected the possibility of using "historical subjects" (something that was, in any event, quite far from his usual areas of interest). His original justification for this was the height of the wall,[32] and he later explained that historical subjects "would perhaps have had the disadvantage of distracting readers who had come here to work."[33]

The sight of fictive trees, populated with birds and squirrels, was certainly suggested to him by the example of painted gardens in ancient dwellings he saw in Italy, such as the House of Sallust in Pompeii. The large oak tree hanging over the characters in *Jacob's Struggle with the Angel*, painted by Eugène Delacroix in 1861 in the church of Saint-Sulpice (Labrouste's parish), had perhaps also attracted his attention. In any case, he explicitly based his design on three reasons he shared with the minister[34]: he mentioned the precedent of the Galerie Mazarine, to the rear of the reading room, whose niches

30. Labrouste 1852: col. 383.
31. Letter from Labrouste to the Minister of the Emperor's Household and of the Fine Arts, April 29, 1864, Bibliothèque Nationale de France, Archives, C-328 (2), 1864, no. 24/2.
32. Ibid.
33. Léon Labrouste 1885:66.
34. Letter from Labrouste to the minister, April 29, 1864, op. cit.

19. Bibliothèque Nationale, view of the ceiling domes. Photograph: Karl Johaentges

20. Leturc and Baudet, contractors, Bibliothèque Nationale, plan of the domes in the reading room, undated, 85.5 × 74.8 cm, Musée d'Orsay, Paris, gift of Serge Gosset, 1986, ARO 1986 1116

Bibliothèque Nationale
Salle de Lecture
Plan des Fermes et Coupoles.
CONSTRUCTIONS en FER
LETURC & BAUDET
PARIS
62 & 64 rue du Rocher
31,275
31,24

were decorated with trompe-l'oeil landscapes in the seventeenth century; he also recalled that Desgoffe had already painted trees under his guidance in the vestibule at the Bibliothèque Sainte-Geneviève; and last, he indicated that the new décor "[would echo] the opposite side of the same room, where large openings allowed the trees in the *cour d'honneur* to be seen." In his mind, the paintings were therefore to act as an extension of the real vegetation outside. The development of his interior décor on three sides is very much like certain *spectacles de curiosité,* popular entertainments that had fascinated Parisians since the start of the century.

AN "IMMENSE ARTISTIC MACHINE"

The panorama, invented in 1787 by the English painter Robert Barker, was displayed in a large rotunda whose interior was entirely covered with an uninterrupted painted canvas. Lit from above, it gave spectators, standing on a central platform in the darkness, the feeling of being part of a stage set or a large landscape. In the early 1820s, the painter and decorator Louis Daguerre (later one of the inventors of photography) would perfect the procedure with his diorama: a sequence of changes in light directed onto a monumental diaphanous canvas, painted with the same subject on both sides and stretched at the back of a stage, created varying effects on the painting, including simulating the progression from day to night.[35] Because the public, having no tangible reference point, could not forget the material reality of the painted canvas, the illusion greatly depended in both the panorama and diorama on strategies that hid, on the one hand, the edges of the painting, and, on the other, the sources of light. From 1830, the use of actual objects in the arrangement blurred the line even more between what was a real space and what was fictive.[36] In 1839, the writer Alfred Desessarts would underscore the merits of the two systems and their "immense.... resources, from the point of view of reality":

> There, through a combination of perspective, gradations of tones, the place the spectator occupies, and lastly the staging of the immense artistic machine, one forgets that the objects that strike one's vision were born out of a paintbrush. It is nature herself, it is life itself that one is admiring ... With the Diorama, the effect draws away from you and loses itself in infinite space; with the Panorama, it comes looking for you, it surrounds you, it speaks to you from all sides: to the right, to the left, before, behind, everywhere is painting, or rather, everywhere is a striking reality that dominates you with its power.[37]

35. See Alexis Donnet, *Architectonographie des théâtres de Paris* (Paris: Didot l'Aîné, 1821), 318–23 and pl. XXIII ("Diorama"), 341–45 and pl. XXIV–XXV ("Panorama").
36. F., "Diorama. Vue du Mont-Blanc, Prise de la vallée de Chamouny," *Journal des artistes* (November 20, 1831): 355–57.
37. Alf. Desessarts, "Panorama: Incendie de Moscou," *La France littéraire*, 8th year, vol. 35 (1839), 324. Desessarts was named librarian at the Bibliothèque Sainte-Geneviève in 1846.

21. Bibliothèque Nationale, springing of the reading room's vault. Photograph by the author

22. "Dress and the Lady," *Punch, or the London Charivari*, vol. 31, August 23, 1856, p. 73

Labrouste could not but be attracted by such spectacles which, ingeniously combining architecture, painting, and natural light, held such sway over the public's imagination and soul. Moreover, he himself copied the plan of the diorama in London built in 1823 by Augustus Charles Pugin and James Morgan.[38] As soon as he had the chance, he in turn made use of illusionist tactics. The upper level of the Bibliothèque Sainte-Geneviève, designed precisely when Jacques-Ignace Hittorff was erecting the monumental Panorama on the Champs-Elysées (1838–39, destroyed in 1856; fig. 27), offered on all sides the enveloping spectacle of the Paris sky, against which the imposing dome of the Panthéon stood out to the southwest. Conversely, the vestibule's darkness expressed, in the architect's words, "the shade of the [painted] trees that strike our gaze"[39] and, as a critic noted, "place[d] the stairway ... in a diorama light that does not give a bad impression."[40] But it was at the Bibliothèque Nationale that the artifices imagined earlier by Barker and Daguerre were the most effectively used and combined. Furthermore, they were more fitting for a space built within a larger complex than for an entirely freestanding structure.

In the reading room, the views of the outside—painted and real—and the continuity of the scene from one bay to the next were derived from panoramas, as were doubtlessly the form of the hemicycle and the idea to hide its glass ceiling from readers' eyes. In the attic, the means for "managing the light [of the lanterns] with the most simple system of scrims,"[41] however, employed one of Daguerre's tricks. The décor in

38. Bibliothèque Nationale de France, Prints, HD-1176 (2)-BOITE FOL, MFILM F-18497.
39. Labrouste 1852: col. 382.
40. Calonne 1853:463.
41. Léon Labrouste 1878: col. 151.
42. Lorédan Larchey, "Nouveautés anecdotiques," *Le Bibliophile français: Gazette illustrée des amateurs de livres, d'estampes et de haute curiosité* (January 1869): 199.
43. See Donnet, op. cit.
44. Germain Bapst, *Essai sur l'histoire des panoramas et des dioramas* (Paris: Imprimerie Nationale, 1891): 9.
45. Hermant 1869:225.
46. Ibid., 226.
47. Bailly 1876:20.

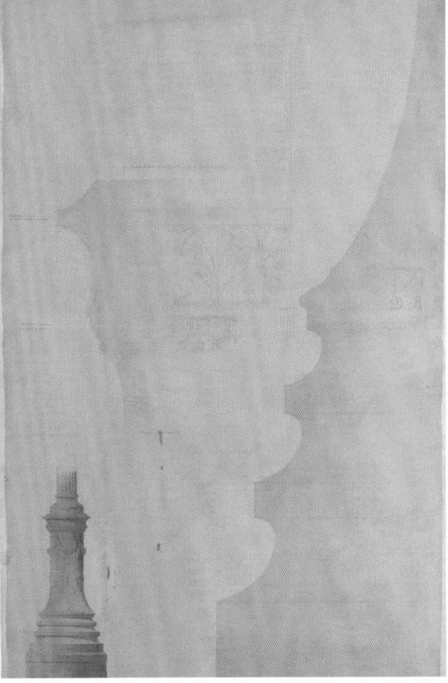

the vestibule, which one critic found to have "a false diorama feel,"[42] seems inspired by the "feigned drapery" decorated with escutcheons that Daguerre had also represented several decades earlier on his diorama's interior wall.[43] Last, and importantly, the vestibule and the doorway into the reading room were like the "dark hallways" the public took to reach a panorama's platform:

> In the course of his trajectory, [the spectator] loses all sense of light and, when he reaches the place he must stand, he moves without transition from darkness to a view of the circular painting displayed in the most direct light. Then all points of the panorama can be seen at once, and a kind of confusion arises. But soon, as the eye gets used to the daylight, the painting imperceptibly has its effect, and the more one gazes at it, the more one is in the presence of reality.[44]

The vestibule of the Bibliothèque Nationale thus takes on its full meaning. Its chiaroscuro, its blank walls, and its interminable stone wainscoting punctuated by marble disks work to disorient and stun readers in order to prepare them for the sensory experience Labrouste created for them.

Like several of his contemporaries, the architect Achille Hermant saw Desgoffe's decorations as an evocation of the Garden of Academus in which the members of the Platonic school gathered.[45] For him, these were "conventional landscapes [which] were the expression, or, if you will, the sensible image of a thought, nothing more."[46] This view did not show an understanding of the objective Labrouste had set for himself, which he described as follows:

> When I was in secondary school, after or before class, I would go study in the Luxembourg Gardens, especially in the plant nursery. There, nothing distracted me, and my gaze as well as my mind could rest happily on the beautiful, luxurious greenery surrounding me. I thought that in a place of study, the representation of what had held so much charm for me would be, first, an unpretentious decoration for the Bibliothèque, as well as a chance for rest for the minds of the readers occupying the reading room.[47]

23. Henri Labrouste, Bibliothèque Impériale, model for the ornamentation of the beams in the lateral storerooms, details of the front and underside highlighting the rivets, undated, 60 × 73 cm, Bibliothèque nationale de France, Paris, Archives, 2011-001-4142

24. Henri Labrouste, Bibliothèque Impériale, model for the heaters in the reading room, overall elevation and detail, undated, 106.5 × 68.1 cm, Bibliothèque nationale de France, Paris, Prints, HD-1019 (5)-FT 6

25. Henri Labrouste, Bibliothèque Impériale, model for the central columns in the reading room, elevation and profiles of the base, details of the frieze, undated, 105 x 67.3 cm, Bibliothèque nationale de France, Paris, Prints, HD-1019 (5)-FT 6

Labrouste therefore did not depict an idealized nature, but rather he restored the atmosphere of the garden of his youth and shared with the library's readers the sensations he himself had once felt, for, as was written in 1866, just before the Pépinière (nursery) was destroyed, "those trees, that shade ... that solitude [are good and healthy] for intellectual workers."[48] Adopting the solutions used in panoramas and dioramas allowed Labrouste to produce the illusion of *really* studying in a forest which extended into the heart of the reading room. The domes continue the cluster of trees in Desgoffe's panels by simulating what one journalist had called, several years earlier, the "crinolines of the trees' foliage at the Luxembourg Gardens."[49] Christian Beutler also pointed out that the arches, as though studded with stars, have alternating male and female busts where they begin, symbolizing the sun and the moon; that the stylized thistles decorate the base of the columns; and that the heaters evoke a topiary effect like the boxwoods that typically decorate French gardens.[50] Birds even seem to have flown straight out of the surrounding landscapes: four owls (symbols of Athena) are perched at the corners of the room, and an eagle with wings outspread (an imperial symbol, eliminated in 1870) presided over the door leading into the main stacks.

48. Alcide Dusolier, *Les Spéculateurs et la mutilation du Luxembourg* (Paris: Librairie du Luxembourg, 1866), 9.
49. Sauveur Galeaz, "Tartelettes," *Le Tintamarre* (November 8, 1857): 5.
50. Beutler 1965:324.
51. Roux-Spitz 1938:30.

OF IRON AND LIGHT

Built as an extension of the reading room, the main stacks were the most mysterious and also most inventive of the new installations. The public could not enter them but can sense their importance by the gigantic size of the glass opening (nine meters high) within the converging walls of the hemicycle and by the sculpted medallions of great authors above the bookshelves all shown in profile facing the stacks. On either side of the door, two imposing caryatids bear a piece of entablature which seems, from a distance, to be a pile of books ready to be handed over to the readers (figs. 30, 31).

The large space, designed to house 900,000 books, occupies some 1,218 square meters—a surface area equal to that of the reading room. There are five levels of shelving (including a basement) perpendicular to a large central aisle (figs. 18, 28). Their height of 2.3 meters is calculated to allow library workers to take any book needed without the use of a ladder. Michel Roux-Spitz, one of Labrouste's successors at the Bibliothèque Nationale, saw in it "as opposed to the spirit of dispersion in the old libraries of the 18th century ... an idea of concentration and absolute centralization of the book storerooms with an attempt to create quick vertical transit."[51]

Expanding on the principle behind the reading room's construction, Labrouste here encased two distinct metal structures in the stone perimeter: the first supports the roof, and the second supports the floor or rather the footbridges between which were fit

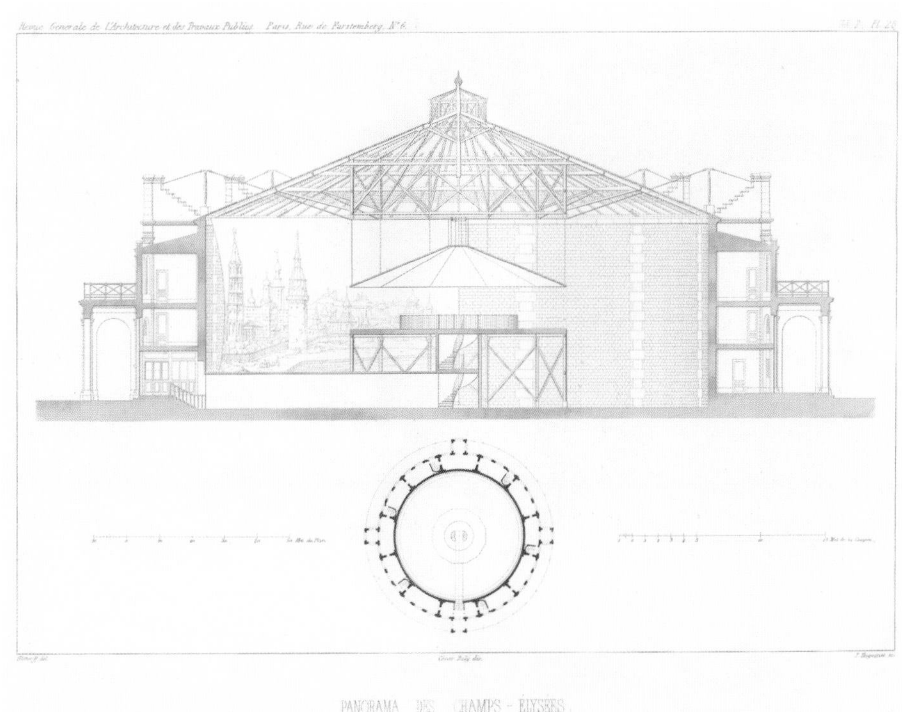

26. Bibliothèque Impériale, reading room, view of an aisle before placement of the books, anonymous, photograph, 1868, 30.5 × 25 cm, Bibliothèque nationale de France, Paris, Prints, HD-1176 (1)-BOITE FOL

27. "Panorama of the Champs-Élysées, Cross-section and Plan," *Revue générale de l'architecture et des travaux publics*, vol. 2, 1841, pl. 28

shelves rising on a single support of over 11.5 meters (p. 184, fig. 3). A contemporary recognized in it "the principle of iron bottle racks."[52]

The issue of lighting was, once again, particularly tricky. In 1859, Labrouste still envisioned a large continuous roof of which we do not know the details (fig. 7). It was only later that he found the most appropriate system to use. As one of his sketchbooks illustrates, the solution was revealed to him in the sheds atop the linen workshops in Saint-Quentin (fig. 32).[53] The merit of saw-toothed roofs, with windows on their short sides, was tacitly underscored later by a German doctor: "The oculist's ideal will certainly be the glass roof. One need only have stepped foot inside a weaver's workshop one time to understand that with such lighting there is no dark patch, even in the most immense room."[54] Labrouste thus covered the two lateral parts of the main stacks with a succession of sheds that he lined underneath with two vast translucent ceilings (fig. 33). And to help bring light all the way down to the basement, he used the idea of open-work cast-iron floors imagined for the library at the British Museum, giving them, however, an unprecedented design. For Henri Béraldi, the "book storeroom [evoked] the machinery of an ocean liner—a gigantic ocean liner: the machinery of a ghost ship."[55]

***

Labrouste's contemporaries were quick to celebrate the boldness and rationality of his solutions, the combination of materials used to further an innovative conception of space, as well as the originality of his decorations and ornamentation. But his overall artistic approach would long remain misunderstood because it had not been clearly

52. Y., "La Bibliothèque impériale. La nouvelle salle de lecture," *Le Figaro*, May 18, 1868, p. 2.
53. See Anonymous, "Inauguration du Chemin de fer de Saint-Quentin," *L'Illustration: Journal universel* (June 8, 1850): 357.
54. Hermann Cohn, "[Hygiène] L'écriture, la typographie et les progrès de la myopie," *La Revue scientifique de la France et de l'étranger* (March 5, 1881): 297.
55. Béraldi 1893:31. Later, Giedion would in turn allude to the "holds in steamboats" (Giedion 1959:139).

28. Bibliothèque Nationale, view of the central storeroom facing the reading room. Photograph: Alain Le Toquin.

29. Louis-Emile Durandelle, Bibliothèque Nationale, view of the north side of the reading room, c. 1880, photograph, 37.6 × 34.5 cm, Bibliothèque nationale de France, Paris, Prints, HD-1176 (1)-BOITE FOL

Previous page:
30. Bibliothèque Nationale, view of the reading room hemicycle. Photograph: Georges Fessy.
31. Bibliothèque Impériale, reading room, view of the door to the central storeroom, anonymous, photograph, before 1870, 34.5 × 25 cm, Bibliothèque nationale de France, Paris, Prints, VA-237 (5)-FOL

32. Henri Labrouste, Workshops in Saint-Quentin, sketchbook, c. 1858, Académie d'architecture, Paris, 341
33. Bibliothèque Nationale, exterior view of the roofs of the central storeroom, anonymous, photograph, July 30,1954, Bibliothèque nationale de France, Paris, Prints, VA-237 (3 bis)-FOL

expressed by him. In 1852, Labrouste confided to César Daly, "You know … that I don't like to write, especially not in order to talk about what I have done … I prefer to concern myself with what is to be done. I prefer to look at what is ahead of me rather than what is behind."[56] Also, several changes were enough to undermine the fragile balance he had created. The panorama effect was quickly altered by the construction of a "temporary" wooden gallery in front of the reading-room windows (1866), then, after his death, by cutting down the last tree in the *cour d'honneur* (1884). As for the vestibule, it quickly lost its sepulchral feel: Labrouste's successor, Jean-Louis Pascal, brought light in through openings made on either side of the entry door, before thinking—unsuccessfully—to decorate it above with a large allegorical frieze (1896). Few valued at its true worth what Alphonse Gosset was one of the first to call "Labrouste's poetry."[57]

In the twentieth century, many historians have attempted to decipher his intentions. Most have pointed out the reading room's religious character. According to Bruno Foucart, it is "a basilica, a Byzantine temple to reading" which once again shows "the original tie between the forest and the cathedral."[58] To him, "libraries are the temples of another religion, that of knowledge. They can benefit from the same aims as buildings dedicated to the service of transcendence."[59] In the same vein, others have seen the hemicycle as an apse[60] or chancel,[61] the vestibule as a narthex,[62] and the domes as an echo of the Seljuk mosques in Turkey.[63] David Van Zanten believes that the references are more to be sought in Pliny the Younger, or even Piranesi.[64] All of these interpretations are well founded, but none is fully correct in and of itself. That is because the immense room, a space that is both sacred and profane, is only made up of "illusions and allusions."[65] Labrouste's originality lay precisely in his ability to synthesize disparate sources with the goal of transmitting an idea and awakening emotions. In order to produce the hoped-for result, he did not overlook any approach, or any contrast. Just as he helped to update brick and stone construction before becoming one of the first to combine iron and ceramics, he brought together shadow and light, the heavy and the ethereal, and felt free to seek his formal inspiration in his own renderings from Italy, from the interiors of panoramas and the Musée du Louvre, from women's wardrobes and even the rooftops of factories. The result is dazzling. After submitting to French classicism around the periphery of the block, starting with the *cour d'honneur* he composed a series of spaces that first evoke the buried nature of primitive tombs, then lead imperceptibly toward the dematerialization of architecture: walls, ceilings, and floors seem to disappear beneath the light that falls on them, while the vegetation on the Rue Vivienne side and in the Square Louvois seems to slip into the heart of the building complex. The tangible reconstitution of a garden, the Bibliothèque Nationale's reading room thus becomes a metaphor for the culture of knowledge whose gardeners are scholars.[66] As Van Zanten wrote, it is certainly "the most full and powerful architectural symbol the 19th century produced."[67]

56. Labrouste 1852: col. 381.
57. Gosset 1889:221.
58. Bruno Foucart, "Henri Labrouste et ses contemporains," in *Monuments historiques* 1975:7.
59. Foucart 1978:84.
60. Saddy 1977:81.
61. Lesage 1998:228.
62. Ibid., 231.
63. Loyer 1996:583.
64. Van Zanten 1979:63–64; Van Zanten 1987:242–44.
65. Van Zanten 1979:64.
66. Beutler 1965:324.
67. Van Zanten 1979:64.

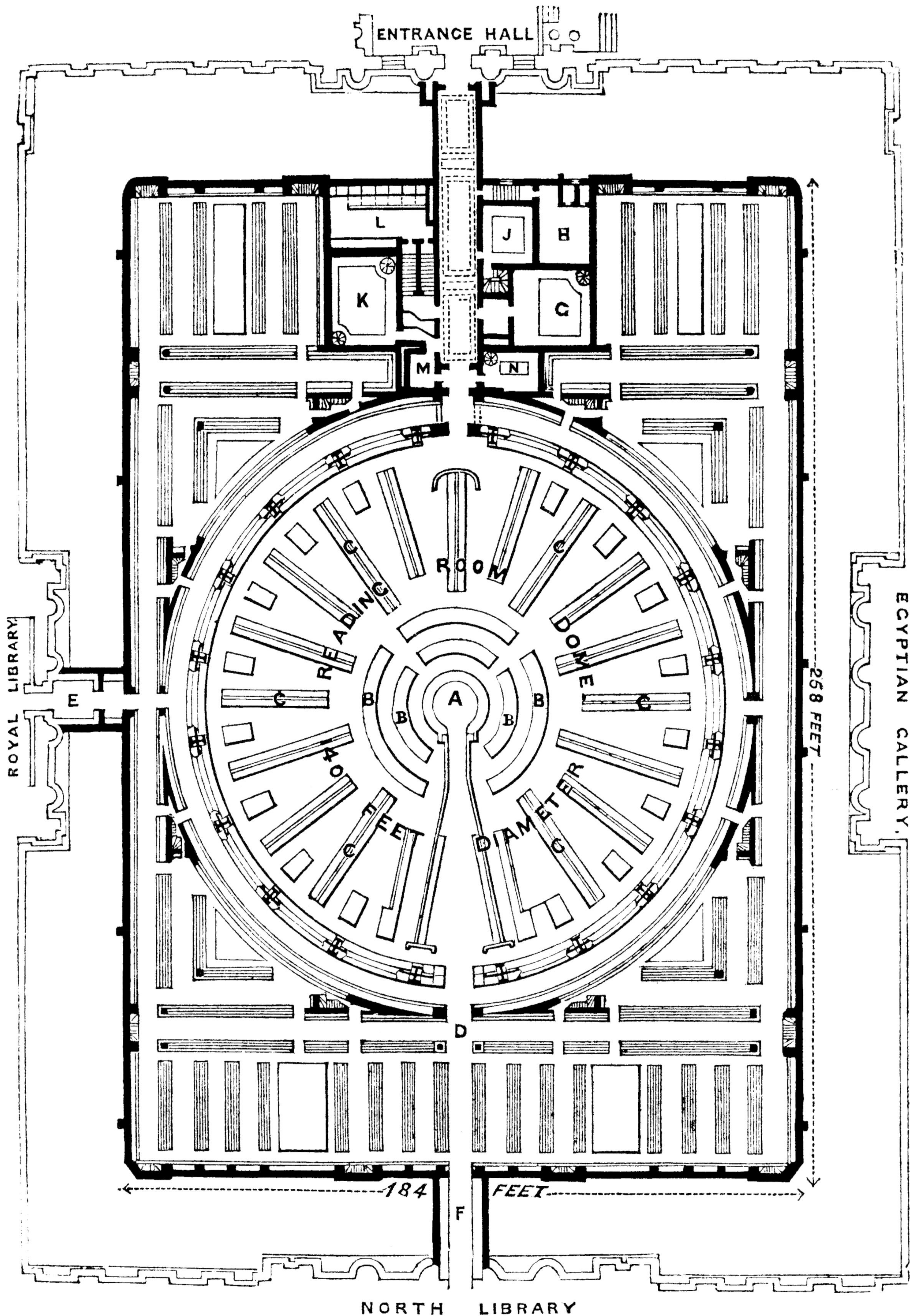
ENTRANCE HALL
L
J
H
K
G
M
N
READING ROOM DOME
140 FEET DIAMETER
A
B
B
B
B
C
C
C
C
C
C
C
C
D
E
F
ROYAL LIBRARY
EGYPTIAN GALLERY.
258 FEET
184 FEET
NORTH LIBRARY

NEIL LEVINE
Harvard University

THE PUBLIC LIBRARY AT THE DAWN OF THE NEW LIBRARY SCIENCE: HENRI LABROUSTE'S TWO MAJOR WORKS AND THEIR TYPOLOGICAL UNDERPINNINGS

Henri Labrouste is best known for two buildings, both libraries. Although the Bibliothèque Sainte-Geneviève (1838–50; fig. 3) and the Bibliothèque Nationale (originally Royale, later Impériale, 1857–68; fig. 4) have generally been conflated as early examples of iron construction, they were designed to fulfill very different programmatic purposes for very different kinds of sites. Their distinct expressive forms and compositional types represent carefully calibrated responses to the varied needs of a new reading public at the moment the public library itself was emerging and being theorized.

1. A. Panizzi and S. Smirke, Library of the British Museum in London, plan (1852–57), British Museum, London, in *New Reading Room and Libraries* (London: John Murray, 1867), n.p.

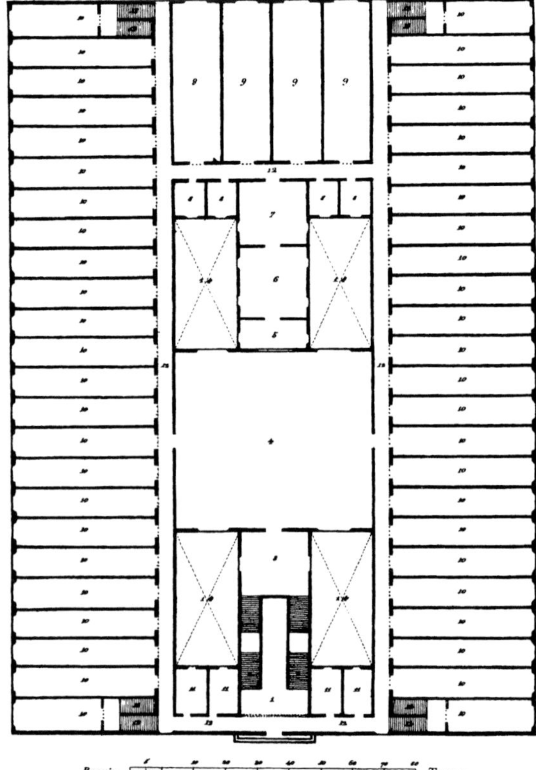

Following the confiscation and nationalization of religious and aristocratic libraries during the French Revolution and in response to the acceleration of book publishing, the period 1815–50 saw the emergence of the new discourse of *bibliothéconomie*, or library science. Most famous of the early tracts on the subject was Leopoldo della Santa's *Della costruzione e del regolamento di una pubblica universale biblioteca* (1816). It stressed the importance of cataloguing, security, and surveillance; clarified the role of the reference librarian in relation to the reading public; called for the elimination of high bookcases necessitating ladders; and proposed, for the first time, a physical separation of reading room from book storage spaces (fig. 2). The theoretical discourse was accompanied by a spurt of books on the subject of library history, the most important of which was Léon de Laborde's *Etude sur la construction des bibliothèques* (1845) in which Labrouste's first library, then in construction, was discussed.[1]

The Bibliothèque Sainte-Geneviève was conceived toward the end of this period of investigation. It is unclear how much Labrouste was aware of the issues brought into play or how much he knew about library history. We do know that he was acquainted with Domenico Fontana's Vatican Library (1587–88), the former Bibliothèque Sainte-Geneviève begun by Claude de Creil (1672–1733; fig. 5), Etienne-Louis Boullée's Bibliothèque Royale project for the Richelieu site (1785), and Jules de Joly's recent Chambre des Députés library (1827–34). These were all well-known examples of the postmedieval gallery-type library that traced its origin back to Juan de Herrera's Escorial Library (1567–84). Characterized by a long, usually vaulted hall lined with closed bookcases reaching to cornice level, such spaces more often than not placed a concern for representation over that for work and study. Prints depicted people strolling through the spaces rather than sitting and reading. The emphasis on the display of precious collections of books aligned the gallery-type library with museum galleries for painting and sculpture.

The unusual program and constricted site of the building designed to replace the seventeenth- and eighteenth-century structure had a major impact on Labrouste's interpretation of the conventional library paradigm. The main reason for leaving the old quarters was the institution of evening hours in 1838. The choice of the Bibliothèque Sainte-Geneviève for this novel experiment arose from the fact that, because of its location in Paris's Latin Quarter, it was designated to serve students rather than more advanced researchers. Book purchases were consequently directed toward these contemporary curricular needs. And the institution changed accordingly—not for the good in the eyes of many—from being one of the four great "public libraries" of Paris to becoming a mere "cabinet de lecture," as Laborde and others put it, akin to commercial subscription libraries where the average person might go to read the newspaper or a novel, or to find refuge from the cold.[2] Labrouste understood this transformation.

1. Laborde, April 1845.
2. Laborde, April 1845:27.

2. "Plan for an Ideal Public Library," Leopoldo della Santa, *Della costruzione e del regolamento di una pubblica universale biblioteca* (Florence: G. Ricci, 1816), n.p. Entryway (1), staircases (2), vestibule (3), reading room (4), catalogue office (5), catalogue room (6), rare books storeroom (9), books storeroom (10)

3. "Bibliothèque Sainte-Geneviève, Reading Room, Interior Perspective," Trianon 1851:29

4. "Inauguration of the New Reading Room at the Bibliothèque Impériale, June 15," Bernard 1868:408

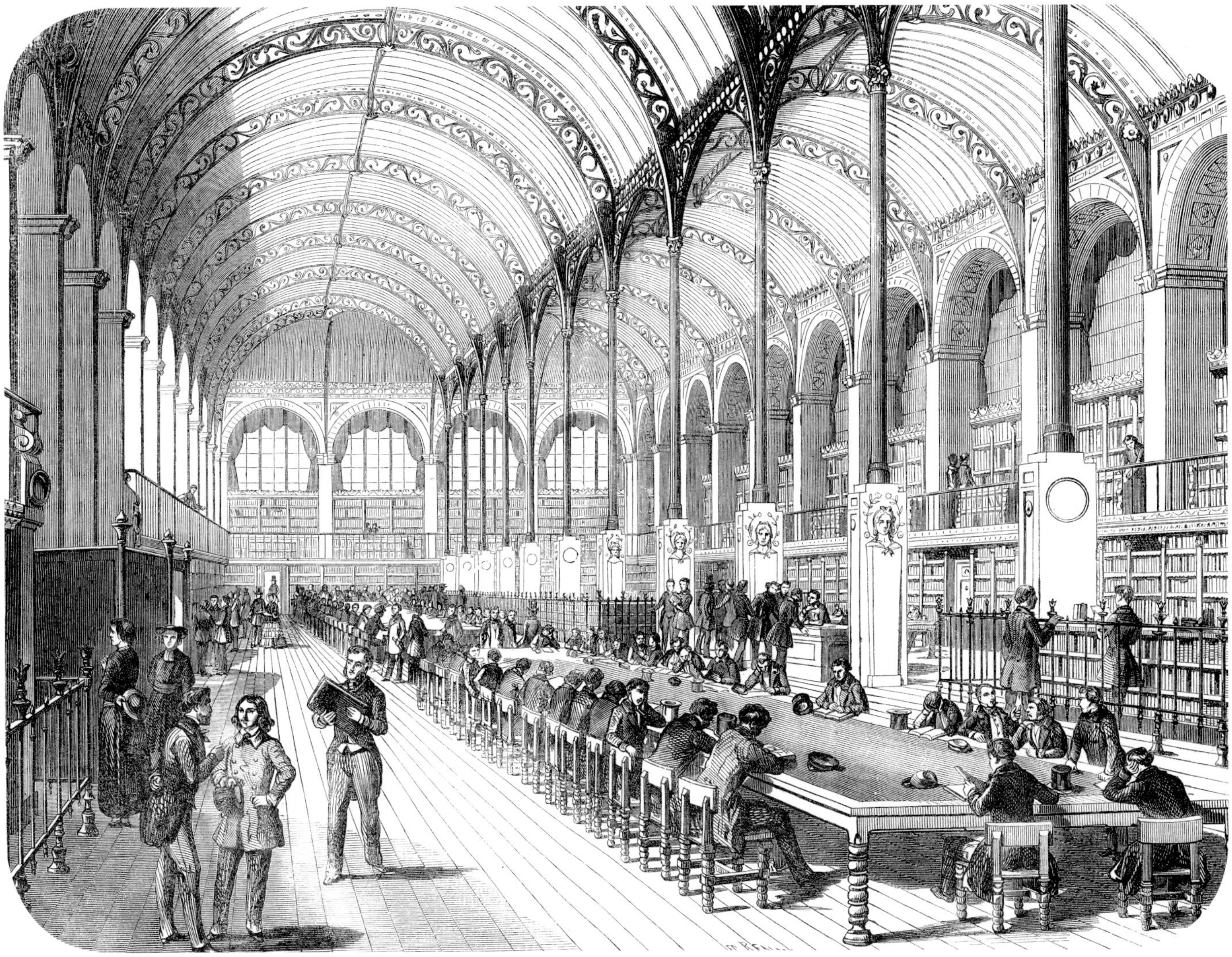

In presenting the project to the government, he described it as a "Library primarily intended for Students" and thus now "a Reference Library [*Bibliothèque d'Etude*]" of "paramount usefulness in the neighborhood inhabited in large part by students."[3] These students, he moralized, can "make use of the library during the long winter evenings that were previously wasted in small theaters, bars, and fencing halls."[4] The evening hours, it was thought, were of particular value to "poor students" whose "lack of money" meant that "their day jobs prevented them" from using the library in the daytime.[5]

The disproportionately long and shallow site facing the monumental Panthéon, the shrine to heroes of the French nation created out of the eighteenth-century church of Sainte-Geneviève, presented other constraints. It precluded the possibility of relying on the compositional type Labrouste learned at the Ecole des Beaux-Arts, wherein multiple book-lined galleries, in discriminately accommodating reading rooms and storage space, were disposed in parallel and crisscrossing patterns around interior courtyards (fig. 6). From the late 1820s through the early 1850s, the various designs by Louis Visconti for the Bibliothèque Royale followed the same pattern, with their multiple courtyards, grand staircase, and long vaulted galleries lined by floor-to-ceiling bookcases (fig. 7).

Given the fact that his original brief called for housing 190,000 books with room for expansion by at least 50 percent, seats for around four hundred readers, and consultation and storage space for a considerable collection of manuscripts, incunabula, prints, and antiquities, Labrouste's choices were limited. No doubt in response to the proximity of the Panthéon, he never considered either a three-story or one-story solution. While he knew Benjamin Delessert's two-and-a-half-story, single-height-interior

3. Henri Labrouste, "Bibliothèque de Ste Geneviève. Projet d'un bâtiment ... destiné à recevoir la bibliothèque de Ste Geneviève," n.d., 1–2, Fasc. 1-Construction, F[21] 1362, Archives Nationales, Paris (hereafter AN).

4. [Labrouste], "Bibliothèque de Ste Geneviève," n.d., Fasc. 1, F[21] 1362, AN.

5. "Des séances du soir dans les Bibliothèques publiques et de l'Etablissement de ces séances à la Bibliothèque de Sainte-Geneviève," n.d., 1, F[17] 3497, AN.

6. The last was a euphemism for the theology classification, the library's largest. Labrouste, "Bibliothèque de Ste Geneviève," 2.

7. Labrouste, "Bibliothèque de Ste Geneviève," 2.

5. "Former Bibliothèque Sainte-Geneviève (1672–1733), begun by Cl. de Creil, Inside Perspective," Claude du Molinet, *Le Cabinet de la Bibliothèque de Sainte Geneviève* (Paris: Antoine Dezallier, 1692)

6. Léon Vaudoyer, Plan for a Public Library, plan, competition at the École des Beaux-Arts, 1821, École nationale supérieure des beaux-arts, Paris, Pj 256-01

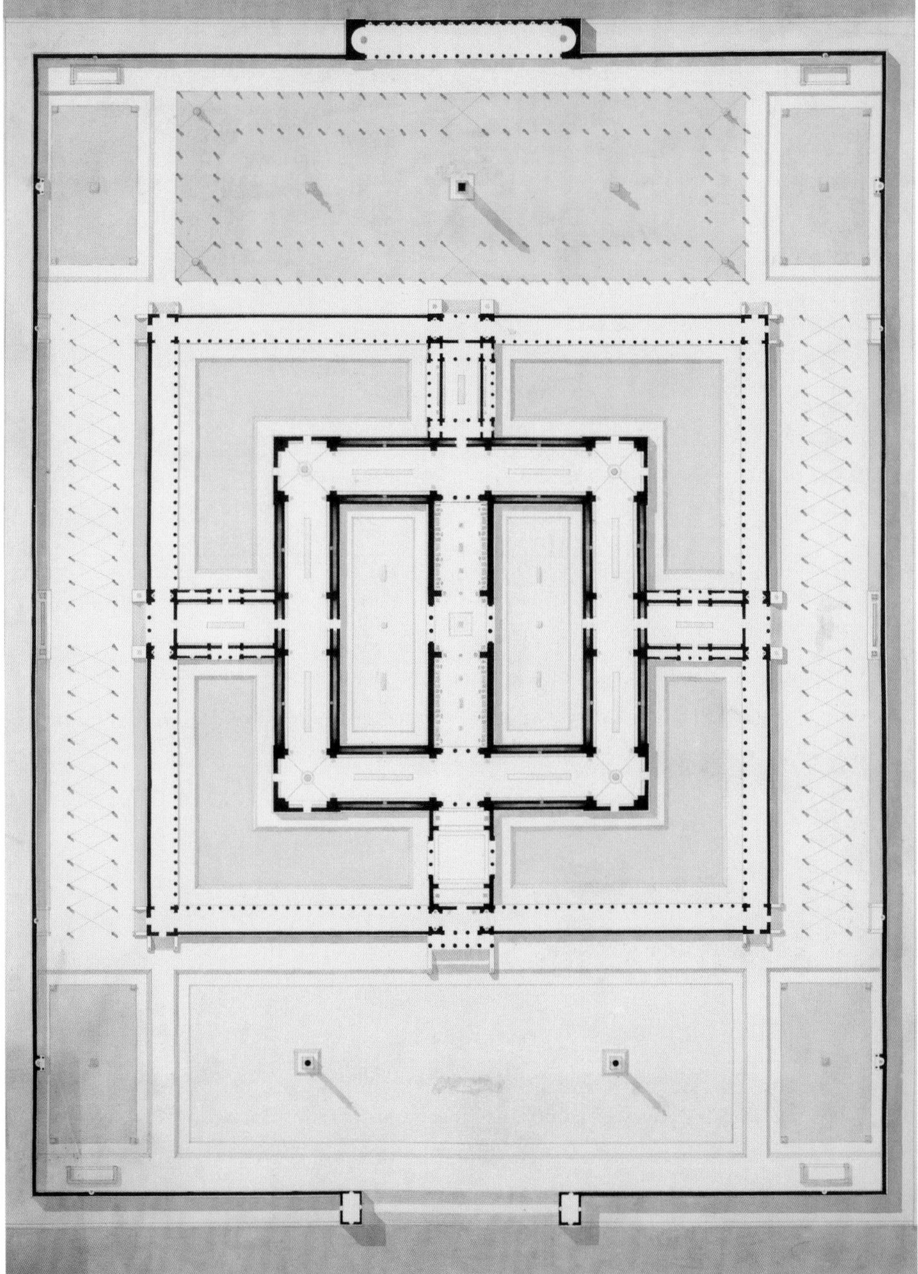

design for the Bibliothèque Royale at the Place Bellechasse (1838) based on the model of Jeremy Bentham's Panopticon (fig. 8), Labrouste would certainly have been put off by its utilitarian, warehouse-like appearance that barely differentiated between spaces for reading and for storage. In Labrouste's two-story structure, a generous, light-filled reading room occupies the entire piano nobile above a base reserved for supplementary functions. One side of the ground floor was to house special collections, the other to be a depository ("dépôt") for duplicate books, out-of-date editions, incomplete series, and, especially, "rarely requested books."[6] The latter was therefore not a *magasin*, or bookstack, as many have suggested, but rather exactly what Labrouste called it—a depository.

The typical student users of the library would have made their way directly upstairs to the space Labrouste designated as a "salle de lecture" or "salle d'étude et de lecture." Labrouste considered the reading room to constitute, both metaphorically and literally, the library as such, "the Library strictly speaking," as he said.[7] It housed the majority of books in the library's collection, especially those used on a daily basis.

8. Labrouste 1852: col. 383.
9. Etienne-Louis Boullée, *Architecture: Essai sur l'art*, ed. Jean-Marie Pérouse de Montclos (Paris: Hermann, 1968), 131, 126. See also the English-language translation in *Boullée's Treatise on Architecture*, ed. Helen Rosenau (London: Tiranti, 1953).
10. Bougy 1847:153.
11. P. L. Jacob [Paul Lacroix], *Réforme de la bibliothèque du roi* (Paris: Alliance des Arts, M. Techner, 1845), 21.
12. Labrouste 1852:383.
13. See, e.g., Gustave Planche, "Le Musée du Louvre," *Portraits d'artistes—peintres et sculpteurs*, vol. 2 (Paris: M. Lévy, 1853), 268; and Théodore de Banville, "Le Quartier Latin et la Bibliothèque Sainte-Geneviève," *Paris Guide par les principaux écrivains et artistes de la France*, pt. 2, *La Vie* (Paris: Librairie Internationale; A. Lacroix, Verboeckhoven, 1867), 1358.

It was lined with easily accessible bookshelves (fig. 3). Those around the perimeter were staggered in height, eliminating the need for ladders; the lower level was set against the arcade piers and supported a gallery on which the upper shelves were placed. Underneath the gallery was an internal service corridor that had an additional range of shelving back-to-back with that facing into the room. More back-to-back shelving was placed between the central columns. None of the shelving was in closed cases typical of gallery-type libraries. Instead, a light, freestanding railing allowed access by the library staff while keeping users at a safe distance.

Although the longitudinal division of the space by the central line of bookshelves made surveillance problematic in Laborde's view, it served a number of expressive purposes. It undercut the totalizing effect of a single vaulted space, as in Boullée's Bibliothèque Royale design, at the same time as it denied the hierarchical character of a nave with side aisles. In the Bibliothèque Sainte-Geneviève, the bipartite partitioning of space literally democratizes it. Seated at long tables between parallel rows of books, students would have felt enclosed by them, as if in a more domestically scaled, individually oriented "cabinet de lecture." The books themselves thus defined the space at the level they were read, while visually receding in perspective to the plane of the shelving under the arcade windows and becoming, as Labrouste wrote, "the most beautiful ornament of the interior."[8]

The Bibliothèque Sainte-Geneviève adopted the model of the postmedieval gallery-type library of display but gave it a new definition and a new meaning in response to the modern social requirements of its program. The traditional library grew out of aristocratic and ecclesiastical conditions demanding a representational form showcasing the uniqueness of a collection. The gallery type implied an ambulatory, admiring visitor. An engraving of the former Bibliothèque Sainte-Geneviève captures the spectatorial aspect perfectly (fig. 5). Boullée's perspective of his library's interior pushed the vicariousness of the experience to an extreme (fig. 11). The "spectacle of books," he stated, is enacted by figures in togas representing "the spirits of those celebrated men" whose books' great "thoughts" they proclaim and share with one another.[9]

The interior perspective of Labrouste's library illustrating an article written by one of its librarians, Henry Trianon, gives an entirely different impression of how the gallery type might be deployed (fig. 3). Instead of images of visiting dignitaries or an ideal intelligentsia, it shows a somewhat motley group of young people either seated and reading or waiting in line at the catalogue desk. The picture is decidedly nonelitist and informal. Except for the books and the figures bent over them, it could be any kind of mid-century public space. No doubt this is why so many observers likened the Bibliothèque Sainte-Geneviève to a "*cabinet de lecture* [commercial lending library] on a large scale."[10] The user base of students and the institution of evening hours led the historian and soon-to-be conservator of the Bibliothèque de l'Arsenal, Paul Lacroix, to rant against the "hostile and pernicious invention" of "evening hours" that serve to "popularize reading and dilapidate libraries" and, most alarmingly, "to lead public libraries into becoming *cabinets de lecture*."[11]

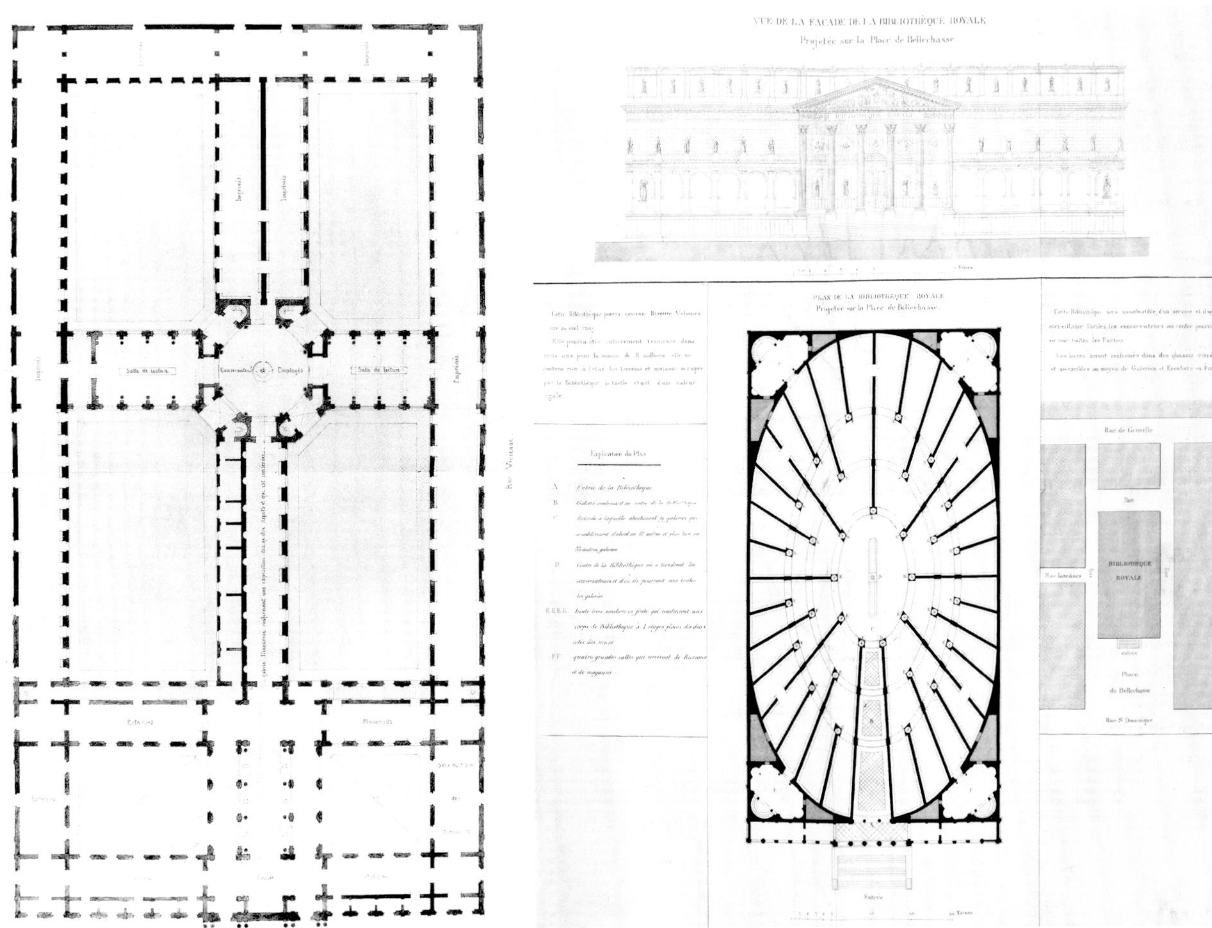

The democratic, quotidian, nonelitist bearing of the Bibliothèque Sainte-Geneviève is exemplified by the prominence of the modern instrument of the catalogue. The multi-volume author-and-subject catalogue was given pride of place in the reading room. Framed by an ambo-like piece of furniture in which the reference librarians would sit, the catalogue desk was located directly opposite the room's entrance (fig. 9). Its prominence made it clear to the user that prior knowledge was no more necessary than the privileged relationship with the librarian often required elsewhere. But even before entering the building, the user would have been apprised of the library's holdings, and of its *mode d'emploi*, by the names of the authors inscribed on the facade directly behind the books themselves. Labrouste called this lapidary list a "catalogue monumental," playing on the adjective's dual suggestion of large scale and publicness.[12] The list of 810 names carried a simple, easily understood meaning, different from the kinds of allegorical and mythological decoration that usually obtained in gallery-type libraries. Labrouste was criticized for the "puerile" and "naive" simplicity of the decoration, which he no doubt saw as a straightforward means of announcing a new kind of public institution in terms anyone could read.[13]

7. Louis Visconti, Plan for a Royal Library, Richelieu site, plan of the upper floor, 1847, dimensions, Paris, AN, Maps and Plans, N III Seine 1138
8. "Plan for a Royal Library, Place Bellechasse, Plan, Elevation and General Site Plan," Benjamin Delessert, *Second Mémoire sur la Bibliothèque royale, sur l'emplacement où elle pourrait être construite et sur la meilleure disposition à donner aux grandes bibliothèques publiques* (Paris: Impr. de A. Gratiot, 1838)

9. Bibliothèque Sainte-Geneviève, information desk. Photograph by the author

Labrouste was appointed architect of the largest and most important library in France, the Bibliothèque Impériale, in 1854, and commissioned for a design to enlarge it three years later. One of the special class of libraries known as national libraries, it was the oldest example of the type. Laborde described it as a "sanctuary of science."[14] It was more a repository of knowledge than a mere place for reading. At the opposite extreme from the Bibliothèque Sainte-Geneviève, it was a research institution whose users had to be accredited to work in its main collections. Prosper Mérimée, who was to be instrumental in writing the program and directing Labrouste's thinking, referred to it as "an essentially literary and scientific establishment."[15]

A debate over how to modernize the institution and whether to renovate the existing buildings or rebuild elsewhere had been going on since the eighteenth century. Designs by Boullée, Visconti, Delessert, Laborde, and others offered different solutions though all accepted the model of the gallery-type display library. In 1845, Hector Horeau explicitly revived the Boullée scheme, magnifying the size of its reading room and multiplying the number of surrounding galleries to create almost a caricature of the type (fig. 10).

Labrouste's design, which was in large part built between 1859 and 1868, when the new *salle de travail*, or reading room, and *magasin central*, or main stacks, were completed (fig. 14), forsook the gallery-type display library in favor of a new prototype, the divided reading room/stack concept, invented by the head librarian of the British Museum, Anthony Panizzi, and realized there between 1852 and 1857 (fig. 1). Labrouste approached the library's design as a research problem rather than a compositional one. In this, he had Mérimée as a guide.

14. Laborde, December 1845:116.
15. P[rosper] Mérimée et al., "Rapport présenté à S. Exc. le ministre de l'instruction et des cultes par M. P. Mérimée, sénateur, au nom de la commission chargé d'examiner les modifications à introduire dans l'organisation de la Bibliothèque impériale," *Journal des débats*, pt. 2, July 23, 1858, 2.

10. Hector Horeau, Plan for a Royal Library, plan, elevation and cross-section, 1845–47, Bibliothèque nationale de France, Paris, Manuscripts, Modern Archives, 122, correspondence

Projet de l'administration
rue vivienne
rue richelieu

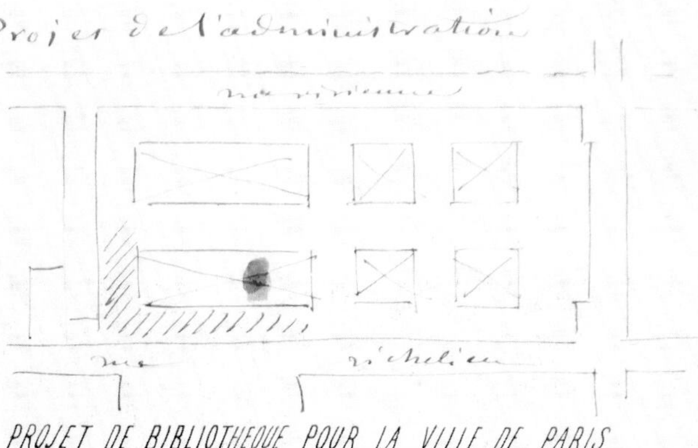

PROJET DE BIBLIOTHEQUE POUR LA VILLE DE PARIS.

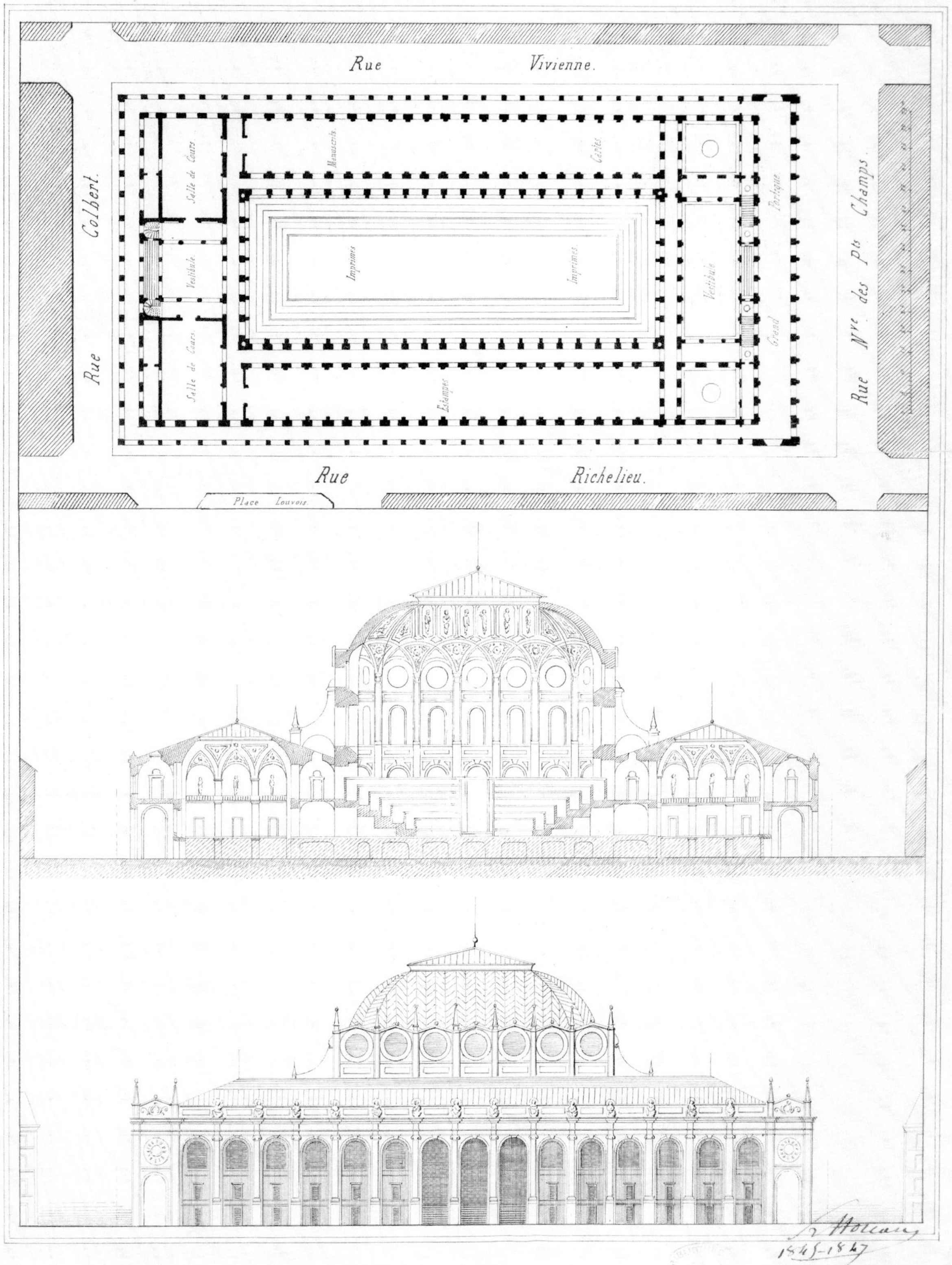

Rue Vivienne.
Rue Colbert.
Rue Nve des Pts Champs.
Rue Richelieu.
Place Louvois.
Salle de Cours
Vestibule.
Salle de Cours.
Manuscrits.
Cartes.
Imprimés.
Imprimés.
Estampes.
Vestibule.
Grand Portique.
Moreau
1845-1847

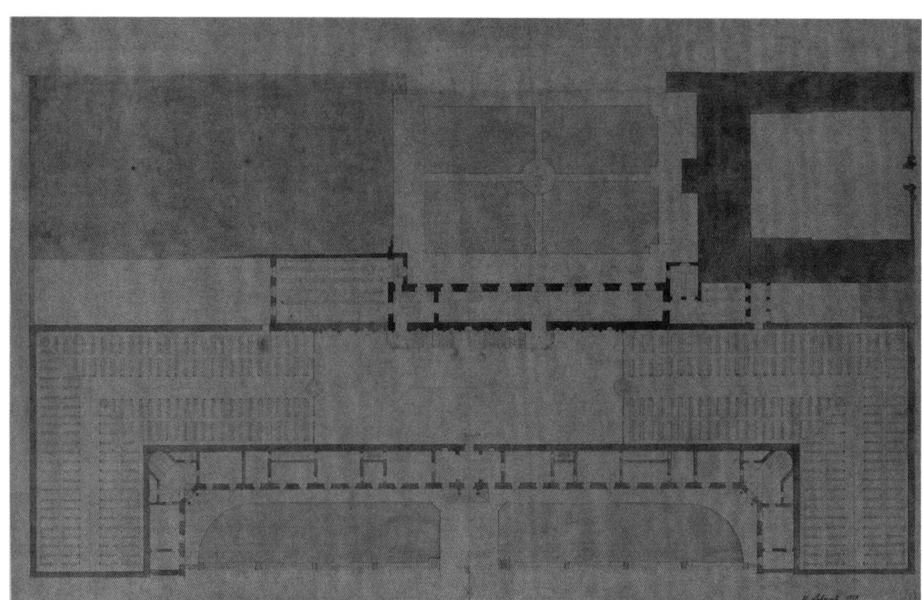

16. Prosper Mérimée, "Nouvelle Salle de Lecture au British Museum," *Le Moniteur universel*, August 26, 1857; reprinted in Mérimée, *Etudes Anglo-Américaines*, ed. Georges Connes (Paris: Librairie Ancienne Honoré Champion, 1930), 141.

Previous pages:
11. Etienne-Louis Boullée, Plan for Reconstructing the Bibliothèque Royale, inside perspective, 1785, 63 × 98 cm, Bibliothèque nationale de France, Paris, Prints, RESERVE, HA-56-FT 7, pl. 36

12. Henri Labrouste, Bibliothèque Impériale, preliminary plan, overall plan, 1858, Bibliothèque nationale de France, Paris, Prints, HD-1019 (1)-FT 6

13. Henri Labrouste, Bibliothèque Impériale, preliminary plan, overall plan, 1858, Bibliothèque nationale de France, Paris, Prints, HD-1019 (1)-FT 6

Mérimée, a close friend of Panizzi, visited the British Museum library shortly after it opened and published a rave review of it, declaring that it was "destined … to serve as a type."[16] On Mérimée's advice, Labrouste toured it and met with Panizzi prior to beginning design of the Bibliothèque Impériale. Labrouste came away impressed by the concept of a top-lit reading space surrounded by multistory stacks, designed as self-supporting iron bookshelves, extruded into building-like structures, entirely skylit, with grated floors allowing light to penetrate throughout.

The preliminary program for the Paris library, drawn up in late 1857 by a government commission headed by Mérimée and including Laborde, called for, among other things, two reading rooms—a *salle de travail* for accredited researchers and a smaller *salle de lecture* for the general public—plus major storage space for the library's book holdings. During the following year Labrouste developed two designs offering alternative visions of how the requirements might be accommodated based on the new Panizzi "type," one razing almost all the existing structures on the site, the other preserving the most significant. The more radical, and destructive, scheme preserved only the sacrosanct Galerie Mazarine, turning its upper floor into the Cabinet des Estampes and its ground floor into the unrestricted, public reading room (fig. 12). The new construction, in the form of a distended shallow U, opened onto the street with an abbreviated forecourt closed by a thin, most likely two-story range of rooms serving various functions. Behind was a taller volume containing a skylit *salle de travail* and L-shaped stacks to either side. The entire U-shaped volume of reading room and stacks was roofed in iron and glass, while the stacks themselves were constructed of an integrated system of adjustable iron shelving and floor grating. The only separation between the three spaces were floor-to-ceiling iron and glass partition walls. As if to call attention to the boldness of this gesture, Labrouste placed a glass-enclosed spiral staircase in the center of each partition wall, half inside the reading room and half inside the stacks. The transparent partitions thus clarify the distinct and specialized realms of reading and storage while at the same time revealing the interpenetration of the two in daily use. A functional unity replaced the earlier unity in display of the gallery-type library.

The less radical scheme presented an analogous differentiation of *salle de travail* from stacks but resolved the connection between the two in a less dramatic way (fig. 13). The *salle de travail* again occupied the middle of the construction but was smaller and square rather than oblong. Both it and the public reading room (located in the north-east corner of the site) were approached from the existing court. The court, the *salle de travail*, and the stacks formed a continuous sequence of spaces. The *salle de travail* was again a top-lit, single-height space; but instead of being book ended by the stacks, it was simply extended to approximately double its length to form the iron and glass *magasin central*. The only separation between *salle de travail* and stacks was a floor-to-ceiling partition wall drawn as glazed except for a central masonry portal. This simple juxtaposition of the spaces for reading and storage created a clear-cut division between the work of research and that of fetching the books, while allowing the reader to witness the latter operation.

As might be expected, the less radical of the two options was preferred, and Labrouste developed the final design for the library in the spring of 1859 based on it. Numerous changes were made during design development and construction (fig. 14). The most important in terms of Labrouste's approach to precedent were (1) the widening of the *salle de travail* relative to the *magasin* and the reduction in length of the latter; (2) the

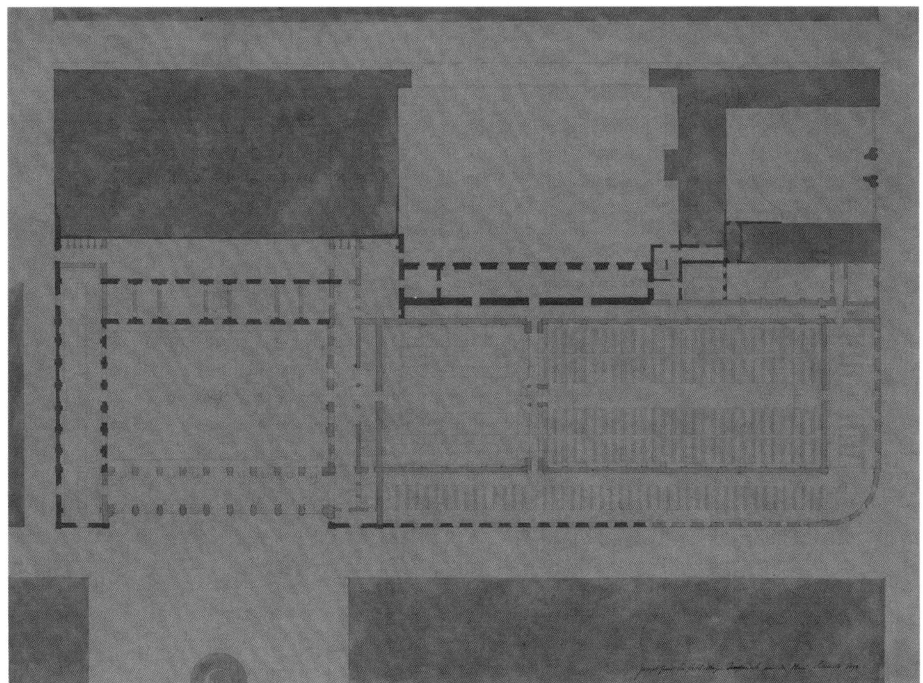

substitution of nine top-lit domes supported by a grid of iron columns for the originally flat, uniform skylit ceiling; and (3) the introduction of a masonry wall between the reading room and stacks in the form of an ellipse, creating an intermediary space called the "hemicycle."

The relative aggrandizement of the *salle de travail* destroyed the close identification between it and the stacks that obtained in both *avant-projets*. The emphasis on the public space led Labrouste to reconsider how to articulate it in relation to its use and users. As in the Bibliothèque Sainte-Geneviève, the introduction of internal supports broke down the scale of the space to give its users a greater sense of their individual place in it (fig. 4). The grid instantiates an omnidirectionality that equalizes all seats in the room. The tables are placed perpendicular to the side walls. This serves to impede the ambulatory sense of movement found in the gallery-type library while directing the attention of those entering the room to the hemicycle, where a curtained portal provides a vignette-like glimpse of the iron and glass stacks. The only books on the walls of the *salle de travail* would be volumes in low demand. Unlike in the Bibliothèque Sainte-Geneviève, they were to serve as a kind of wallpaper of *pure* decoration. Above, within the arches, were paintings of trees meant to complete the calm, nondistracting character of a room devoted to intellectual pursuit. Their non-narrative character contravenes the allegorical and mythological decorative programs characteristic of the gallery-type library.

The hemicycle establishes a clear distinction between the reading public and library staff while creating a monumental space for their interaction. It embraces, as it were,

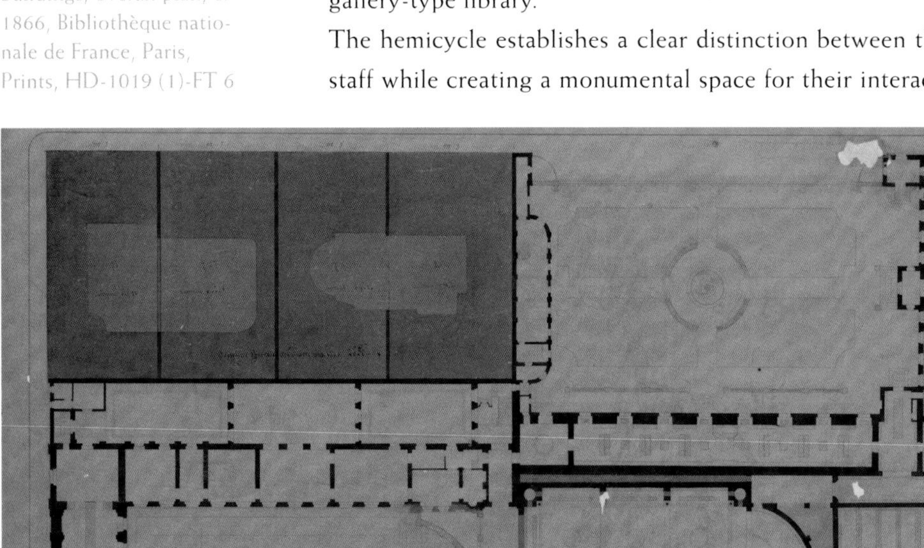

14. Henri Labrouste, Bibliothèque Impériale, preliminary plan of the extension of the new buildings, overall plan, c. 1866, Bibliothèque nationale de France, Paris, Prints, HD-1019 (1)-FT 6

the readers in the space of the reference librarians and catalogue. The reference desk's mediating position follows della Santa's pattern, but its form derives from the ambo-like catalogue desk of the Bibliothèque Sainte-Geneviève. Instead of serving the limited needs of student readers, it has here been expanded into an architectural space to accommodate the more specialized and wide-ranging needs of the privileged users of the national library.

Nothing is allowed to intrude into the space of the *salle de travail*. The hemicycle serves as a buffer. Because of its contained, calming, rather dimly lit space, the *salle de travail* has led many in the twentieth century to think of it as a sacral environment. This seems to have been the farthest thing from Labrouste's mind. As in his earlier library, he sought a secular form of expression, a space for public use, which contemporaries likened to a kind of "*jardin d'Académus*."[17] Everything from the even grid of columns to the "wallpaper" of books and trees serves to describe a human-oriented, nonhierarchical place where individuals, who have serious work to do and serious thoughts to ponder, are free to do just that, as if in their own quiet landscape of the mind.

Despite their similar use of iron, Labrouste's two libraries are fundamentally different in terms of the types they represent and the means by which they transform them. That the main space at the Bibliothèque Impériale was called the *salle de travail* and not the *salle de lecture*, as in the Bibliothèque Sainte-Geneviève, signals their differences in purpose, use, and expression. Each library was based on an established prototype. In each case Labrouste transformed the model in subtle, intelligent, and carefully considered ways so as to modernize and adapt it to the specifics of program and site. Rather than a mere pioneer in the use of iron—the "architect-constructor" portrayed so compellingly by Sigfried Giedion—Labrouste can once again be seen as an architect who gave typological conventions unique and profoundly meaningful forms of expression through the sheer power and clarity of a heightened sense of the medium as an art of shaping space and surface to purpose through design.[18]

17. Y., "La Nouvelle Salle de lecture à la Bibliothèque Impériale," *Moniteur des architectes*, new ser., vol. 3 (1868): 94.
18. Sigfried Giedion, 1941 (4th edition 1962):216–26.

BERTRAND LEMOINE
Académie
d'architecture

LABROUSTE AND IRON

Nothing in Henri Labrouste's education and early career would lead one to predict that he would become one of the pioneers of iron and glass architecture and that he would be the author of two of the most famous buildings to use it. When he won the Grand Prix de Rome in 1824, he had distinguished himself for his extraordinary drafting talent and for his ability to master the codes that this formidable exercise required. His production during the five years he spent in Rome is also a testament to other essential qualities. Indeed, his sketchbooks reveal a great aptitude for capturing the essence of what he was observing. His famous fourth-year submission, the rendering and restoration of the Temples of Paestum, goes beyond the architectural image; it is the very structure of the monument he intends to reveal, as well as the way in which the decorative elements are integrated into it. The frieze of colored shields, which he represents with such virtuosity, shows that ornamentation is not just a decorative component. It is also a way of staging elements, whether tectonic or not, that have their own existence and which fully participate in the structure's organic nature. Labrouste's work in restoring the colors, following in the footsteps of Jacques Ignace Hittorff, nine years his senior, is also worthy of notice. The same curiosity, the same love for the truth would lead Labrouste to an early interest in the new resources that industry could offer construction.

When in 1838 he was commissioned to rebuild the Bibliothèque Sainte-Geneviève, already one of the largest Paris libraries, iron allowed him to respond to the project's requirements: offering the best conditions possible for natural lighting in the reading room and guaranteeing the collection's preservation by protecting it most specifically from the risk of fire, since iron is noncombustible. In the 1830s, the use of

1. Bibliothèque Sainte-Geneviève, view of the reading room. Photograph: Jean-Claude N'Diaye

iron had already been tested on a fairly large number of public buildings, particularly in England, France, and Russia, and commented upon in scholarly publications accompanied by descriptions and figures.[1]

METAL AGAINST FIRE

There had been a great deal of fire damage during the early nineteenth century in buildings with wooden roof structures or floors, storing flammable materials such as: furniture and fabrics, as well as papers or oils. Because of their particular vulnerability (notably due to the many candles burned) and their use as public gathering places, theaters were the first buildings progressively built with metal frameworks. The first to benefit from this improvement was the Grand Théâtre in Bordeaux, built by Victor Louis. Inaugurated in 1780, it included a timber roof structure combined with a hanging iron and "pottery" ceiling—that is, hollow bricks—that isolated the performance space from the attic. Two years later, the Théâtre de l'Odéon in Paris, built by Marie-Joseph Peyre and Charles De Wailly, only had a simple timber roof structure, but the architect Ango offered to create a system of iron reinforcements for the trusses and the floorboards.[2] One of the first metal roofs in Paris was at the Théâtre Français, whose timber roof structure had been partially destroyed by a fire in 1781. Many other of the capital's theaters had met a similar fate, such as the Cirque Olympique in 1826 and the Salle Favart in 1838 (a fire caused by an overheated furnace), so most of the new performance halls were fitted with iron roof structures in the first decades of the nineteenth century, as were some provincial theaters, including the one in Saint-Quentin in 1844. These roof structures, inspired by timber ones, combined wrought-iron bars, sometimes arching, with composite beams, sometimes made from cast iron, to form a complicated lattice of flat bars, struts, ties, and queen posts, with often redundant structural rafters to limit the risk of the bars' buckling.

From the end of the eighteenth century, fires in several textile factories in England had also led to the use of metal frameworks in industrial buildings. Paving the way, two factories built in 1792–93 by William Strutt, in Derby and Milford, combined cast-iron columns, mixed wood and cast-iron beams, and brick jack arches. After that, other factories would adopt completely cast-iron beams: Shrewsbury in 1796, Salford in 1799, Leeds in 1803, Belper in 1803, etc. The span of most of the beams did not exceed 3 meters; if it reached 4.2 meters, it required a fairly dense number of supports. The St. Catherine docks in London, built in 1827, also used that type of structure.

During the Restoration and the July Monarchy, a growing number of buildings were designed with metal roof structures. Along with theaters, one could include the Paris Bourse, completed in 1827 from plans drawn up by Éloi Labarre; the Mint in Nantes (1825); the Palais-Royal chapel by Pierre-François-Léonard Fontaine in 1829; the Chamber of Deputies amphitheater by Jules de Joly in 1833; the Collège de France

1. See Bertrand Lemoine, *L'Architecture du fer. France: XIXe siècle* (Seyssel: Champ Vallon, 1986), and particularly its bibliography, pp. 318–19 ("techniques de construction"), for the specialized literature of the time (treatises by Bury and Hoyau, Jean Rondelet, François Thiollet, Charles Eck, Émile Leconte, and A. Guettier).
2. Published in Jean Rondelet, *Traité théorique et pratique de l'art de bâtir*, vol. 3, 7th ed. (Paris: Firmin Didot, 1834), 310–18.
3. Different solutions were proposed. See Archives de la direction du Patrimoine, Ministère de la Culture et de la Communication, and Charles Louis Gue. Eck, *Traité de l'application du fer, de la fonte et de la tôle* (Paris: Carilian-Gœury and Vor. Dalmont, 1841), 37–38, 28–29.
4. See Emil and Gauthey, *Mémoire sur les ponts en fer*, 8th year (1800), Archives de l'École Nationale des Ponts et Chaussées, manuscript 233, t. 24.

by Paul-Marie Letarouilly in 1842; certain parts of the Louvre, such as the Pavillon Denon; the spire of Rouen Cathedral, etc. In 1833, the spectacular burning of the roof of Chartres Cathedral was the last convincing event needed to prove that fire could threaten even highly prominent buildings. The roof structure was rebuilt three years later from plans by engineer Émile Martin and carried out by the Mignon iron works with the help of cast-iron voussoirs,[3] a technique François Debret would use during the partial reconstruction of the roof of the Basilica of Saint-Denis in 1836–45. The fire at the Court of Auditors, rebuilt in 1845 by Lucien van Cleemputte, also attracted attention to the dangers faced by archives and libraries.

THE FIRST METAL STRUCTURES

The technique of making arches out of cast-iron voussoirs was also widely experimented with at the time. The principle of the metal voussoir, directly inspired by masonry arches, was subject to its first trials in bridges at the end of the eighteenth century in England, notably with the construction of Sunderland Bridge in 1792–96, which had a considerable span of 75 meters. In 1779, Coalbrookdale Bridge had already shown the possibilities iron could offer, but simply transposing the principles of a wooden framework limited its span to 30 meters. The building of iron bridges was swift in England. There were around ten in 1800, thirty some twenty years later. It was much slower in France, though iron was less expensive than masonry as of 1800.[4] After the Pont des Arts, built in 1801–3 by Louis-Alexandre de Cessart and Jacques Dillon with a modest span of 17 meters, the first large metal bridge in France was the Pont d'Austerlitz, inaugurated in 1806. Designed by the engineers Becquey de Beaupré and Corneille Lamandé, it had five arches spanning 32 meters. Like a stone bridge, each was made up of large cast-iron voussoirs 1.6 meters long by 1.3 meters high. As for the Pont des Arts, the cast-iron members came from factories in Conches, in the Eure department. The largest cast-iron bridge built in France, the work was demolished in 1854, after intense traffic had weakened the structure. The other notable work built with cast iron during the first half of the century was the Pont des Saints-Pères in Paris, across from the arcade portals of the Louvre. Completed in 1834, it remained in service for a century. In building it, the engineer Antoine-Rémy Polonceau used a principle of tubular arches connected to the roadway by metal circles.

In 1783, the courtyard of the Halle au Blé, a ring-shaped building constructed fourteen years earlier, was covered with a remarkable wooden roof, destroyed by fire in 1802. The architect François-Joseph Bélanger—who, after travels in England, had already proposed in vain a metal roof structure in 1783—finally managed to convince municipal officials that his solution was viable, notably by stressing the patriotic interest it held: "Finally, it is time to teach educated Europe that we no longer need to borrow from the English our knowledge in the art of building, and that if they were the first

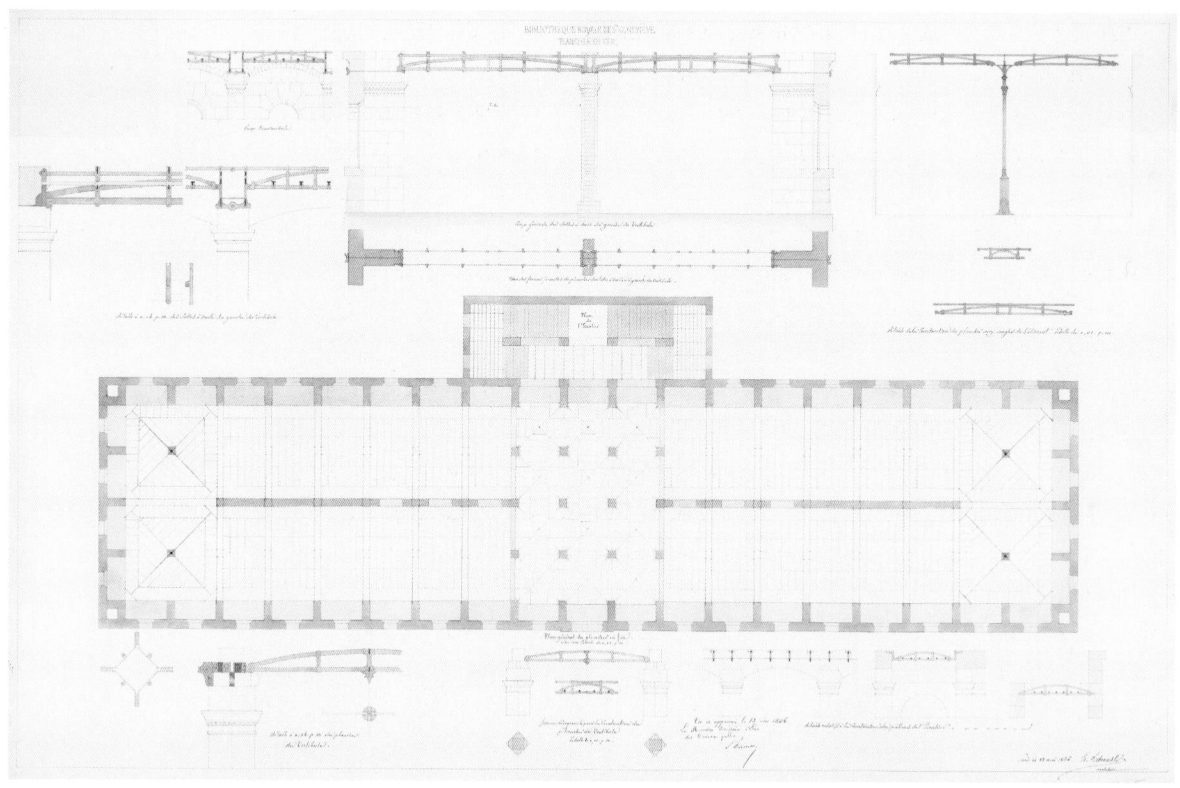

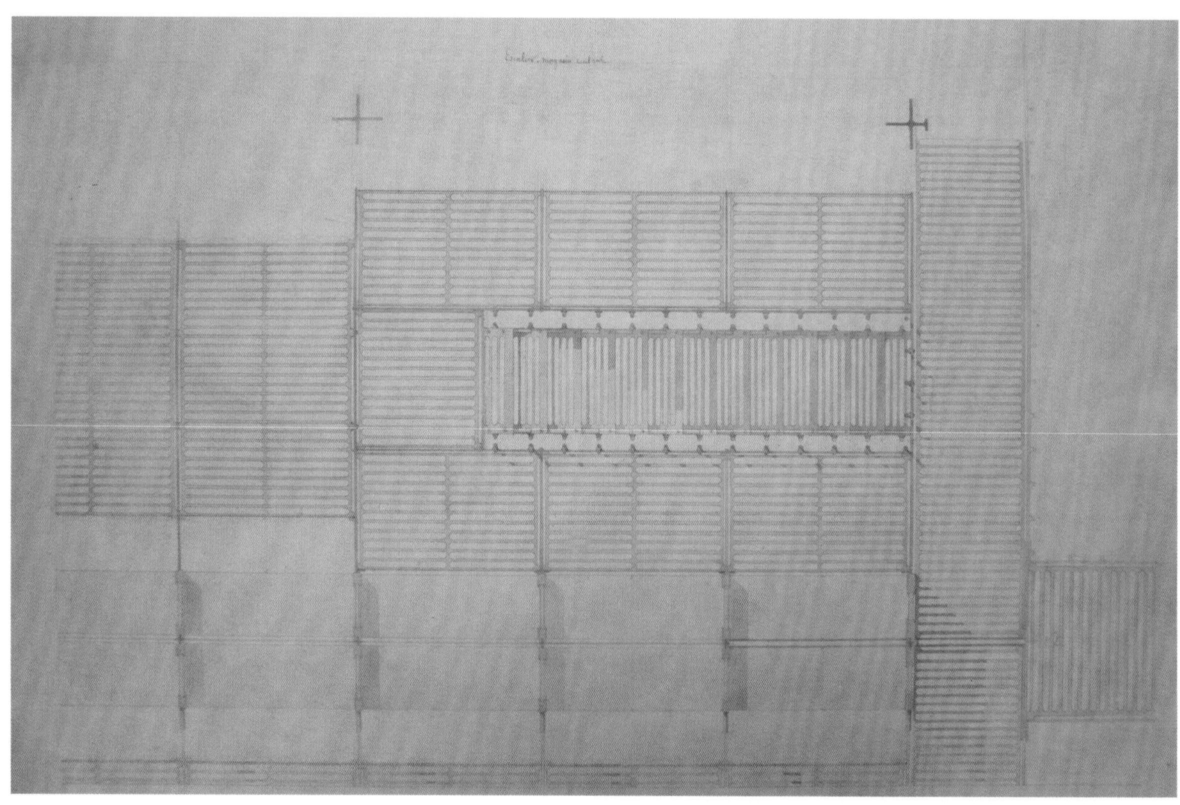

to substitute cast iron for stone and timber in the construction of different beams, it is because they lacked stones and wood, but, long before, we had the very exemplar in France of designs just as daring, that we have even been able to perfect them and carry them out in dimensions they have not yet dared to attempt."[5] Approved in 1808, the plans designed by the engineer François Brunet include fifty-two large quarter-circle cast-iron arches, made with voussoirs bolted together and braced by fifteen ring frames of the same type. The cast-iron elements were supplied by the Le Creusot iron works, one of the main French production sites. Completed in 1813, the new dome left a lasting impression on people. The structure was preserved when the Halle au Blé was transformed into the Bourse du Commerce in 1888 by the architect Henri Blondel, a former student of Labrouste.

The use of iron and cast iron was also motivated by the possibility of reducing the number of panel points and creating glass canopies. This is why composite structures were progressively adopted—combining cast-iron columns, iron roof frameworks, and glass panels—in building covered markets in Paris (the Marché de la Madeleine by Marie-Gabriel Veugny, 1824–38; the metallic roof structure of the Marché des Blancs-Manteaux by Peyre and Louis-Ambroise Dubut, 1837–39). The slaughter houses at the poultry market near Les Halles were also given a metal roof structure in 1835. Commercial buildings similarly made use of the benefits of iron: the Galerie d'Orléans at the Palais-Royal, completely built in cast iron by Pierre-François-Léonard Fontaine in 1829; the Bazar Montesquieu by Victor Lenoir and the Galerie de Fer in 1830; the Galeries du Commerce et de l'Industrie by Jean-Louis Victor Grisart in 1839. The first metal greenhouses were also appearing in England, starting around 1815, then in France. In the greenhouses of the Jardin des Plantes, partially built in 1834–36, the architect and Ecole Polytechnique graduate Charles Rohault de Fleury, who did research when he traveled to England in 1833, showed with great virtuosity that the combination of metal and glass allowed for new and innovative architectures.[6]

The price of cast iron had already begun to drop significantly. If England was still providing half of the world production in 1830, France was providing a quarter, or 350,000 tons. There, cast iron was mainly produced using charcoal. Out of a total of 408 working blast furnaces, only 29 were then burning coke. But by quickly substituting charcoal for coal and perfecting the techniques used, France was able to raise its production capacity. If metal frameworks remained most often hidden in the attic, the plasticity of cast iron led to the massive use of cast ornaments, which were quite visible. Static structural pieces, such as columns, could also lend themselves to decorative purposes.

The process of producing iron by refining cast iron was also improved through a series of technical developments, such as mechanizing the puddling and laminating process. But iron remained twice as expensive as cast iron, which was therefore the preferred metal until the 1840s, despite the fact that it was less resistant to tension and bending.

5. Cited by Mark K. Deming, *La Halle au blé de Paris, 1762–1813* (Brussels: Archives d'Architecture Moderne, 1984), 192.

6. See Charles Rohault de Fleury, *Muséum d'histoire naturelle. Serres chaudes, galerie de minéralogie, etc.* (Paris: n.p., 1837).

2. Henri Labrouste, Bibliothèque Sainte-Geneviève, iron floor on the upper level, plan and details, May 23, 1846, drawing, 66.5 × 102.2 cm, Archives nationales de France, Paris, Maps and Plans, VA /XLV piece 5

3. Henri Labrouste, Bibliothèque Impériale, partial plan of the floor in the central storeroom, undated, 46 × 71 cm, Bibliothèque nationale de France, Paris, Archives, 2011-001-1031

Next pages:

4. Henri Labrouste, Bibliothèque Sainte-Geneviève, study for the reading room's cast-iron trusses and iron rafters, c. November 1846, 66.4 × 101 cm, Bibliothèque Sainte-Geneviève, Paris, Ms.4273 (21)

BIBLIOTHÈQUE R
DÉTAILS RELATI
DU CO
EN FER FORGÉ
4. 25
détail des petits arcs
suivant le grand axe du batiment
15 arcs semblables
assemblage des grands arcs et des petits arcs sur le chapiteau
4. 25
Plan général.
84.55
20.75
20.60
17.30

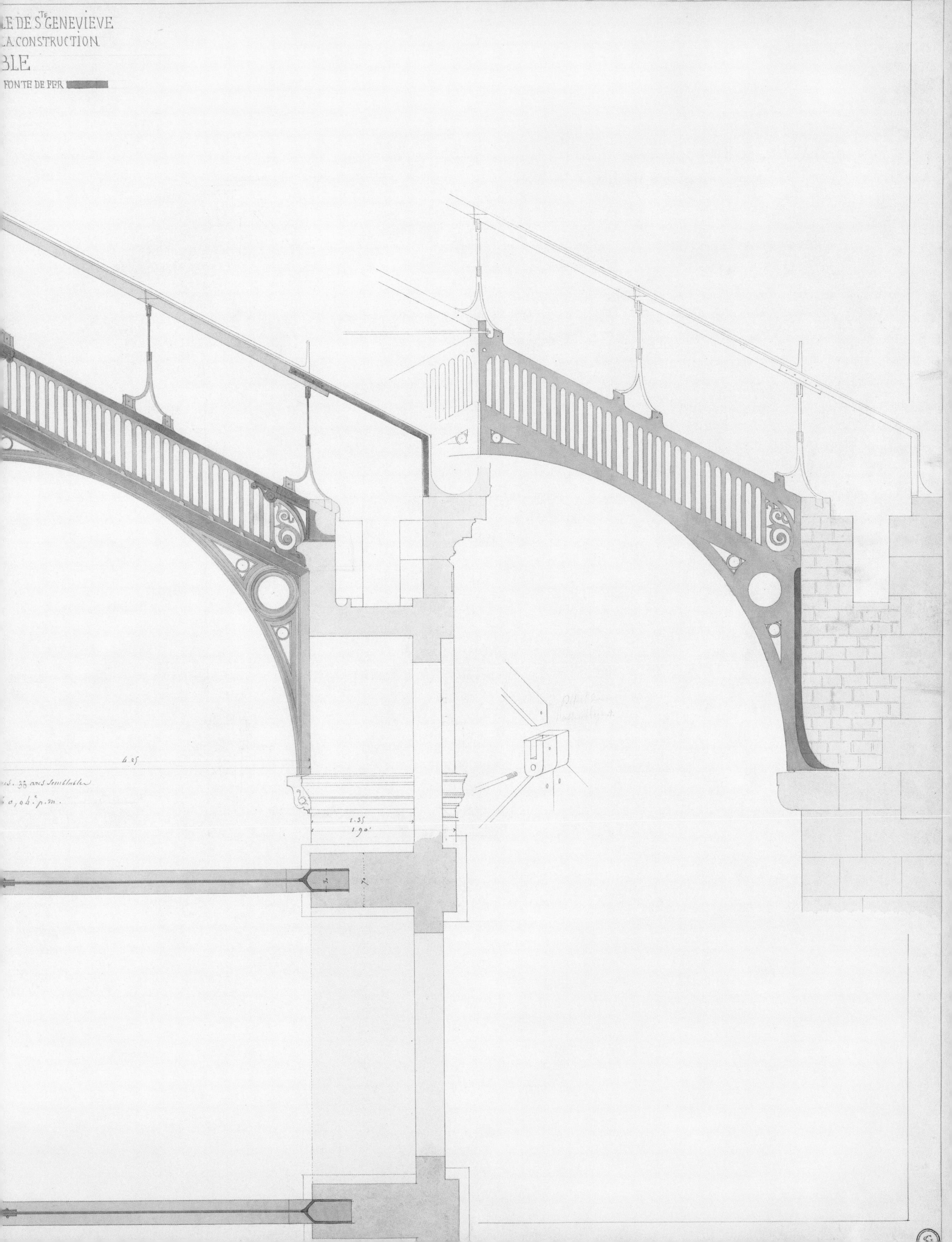

LE DE S^TE GENEVIEVE
LA CONSTRUCTION
BLE
FONTE DE FER
4 25
1.35
1.90

As for steel, which was obtained by more precisely refining cast iron in a converter, it was only used in building from the 1880s on. Drawing on ironworkers' traditional craftsmanship and skills, several businesses specializing in installing metallic roof structures would appear in the 1830s. One could cite, among others, the ironworkers Baron, Baudrit, Jacquemart, Joly, Leturc, Mignon, Rigolet, Roussel, and Travers. An ironwork examination was established in 1820, at the Ecole des Beaux-Arts, among the four school-competition exercises.

THE BIBLIOTHÈQUE SAINTE-GENEVIÈVE

So it was in a climate of intense experimentation and the rapid spread of metal construction processes that Labrouste undertook to design the Bibliothèque Sainte-Geneviève. He imagined a reading room, the building's tour de force, its cover resting on the lateral walls, pierced by high windows, and on a central line of elegant cast-iron columns, crowned by composite capitals turned 90° for better support. Two series of highly decorated arches, also in cast iron, carry a double barrel arch coated with white plaster which hides the roof's metal structure (fig. 6). The many sketches preserved show that the architect worked hard to find the right design for the arches, using a thistle flower pattern, symbolizing the spread of knowledge by the winds. Bolted together, they are molded in two parts that fit at the key joint and the base, and are set on a base. Screwed-on caps hide the joints. Technically the structure is not so different from that of other contemporary buildings, but the high quality of its design and, especially, its location within a major Paris monument helped iron acquire its architectural laurels. Labrouste thus presaged the remarks of Léonce Reynaud, who would write in 1850: "For the new material that has just been offered us, we will need new forms and new proportions, for it differs essentially from all others that have been used to this day. What is suitable for stone could not, by any means, be suitable for iron."[7]

At the Bibliothèque Nationale, completed in 1868, Labrouste once again inserted a delicate metal roof structure within a masonry casing, this time with sixteen cast-iron columns holding up iron arches. Indeed, from that point on, iron became a constant on the building scene. In 1851, at the Great Exhibition in London, the Crystal Palace showed how effective modular construction with cast iron and wood could be, yet other buildings drew even more from iron's expressive potential, such as Les Halles Centrales in Paris, whose first pavilions—all metal—were finished in 1857, or train stations, which showcased spectacular metal structures.[8] Advances in laminating sheet metal and iron sections[9] helped spread the use of iron girders in floors as of 1845, and in bridges and roof structures, where the use of lattice girders assembled with rivets quickly spread in the early 1850s. Cast iron was now used only for ornaments or columns, uses it retained until the 1890s, when riveted sheet metal supports definitively replaced cast-iron columns.

7. Reynaud 1850:448.
8. In Paris alone, the former train stations of the Gare Montparnasse, Gare de l'Est, Gare de Lyon, and Gare Saint-Lazare were fine examples of this at the time.
9. The first I-beams appeared in the construction of the Kew Gardens greenhouses in 1844.

5. Leturc and Baudet, contractors, Bibliothèque Nationale, cross section of the domes and ceiling of the reading room, undated, 63.1 × 170.5 cm, Musée d'Orsay, Paris, gift of Serge Gosset, 1986, ARO 1986 1118

The reading room in the Bibliothèque Nationale remains a masterpiece of refined elegance. There are many similarities with the Bibliothèque Sainte-Geneviève: the shape of the arches, the design of the columns and their capitals, the same breadth, the white ceramic decorations on the ceilings, the wall paintings evoking nature. The cast-iron columns, which are particularly elegant, have composite capitals at a 90° angle on which are set riveted lattice arches with cross-braced webs. The base of the arches is nevertheless cast iron, which allows for the inclusion of decorative figures. The use of paint underscores the structure's different elements, down to the rivet bolts. The domes are pierced by glazed skylights, protected on the outside by a second layer of glass, and draw in an exceptional amount of light (fig. 5). This is one of the first examples of a double glass dome, a solution that spread in the 1880s to all decorative glasswork. The work was carried out by the ironworkers Leturc and Baudet. All of the domes seem to float amid the mass of books that line the walls. The book stacks located at the back of the reading room also offers the first example of a multistory metal structure (p.184,fig.3).

If iron took hold as a construction material in its own right from the 1850s, debate about its role in creating new forms remained heated. The rationalist school, spearheaded notably by César Daly's influential *Revue générale de l'architecture et des travaux publics*, saw it as a lever for displacing the established order. Eugène-Emmanuel Viollet-le-Duc considered iron a means for revisiting the principles of Gothic architecture, a position echoed with greater creativity by his contemporary Louis-Auguste Boileau, a zealous proponent of "ironwork architecture," who designed the church of Saint-Eugène in 1855, a fine example of an all-metal neo-Gothic building. As for the architects of the

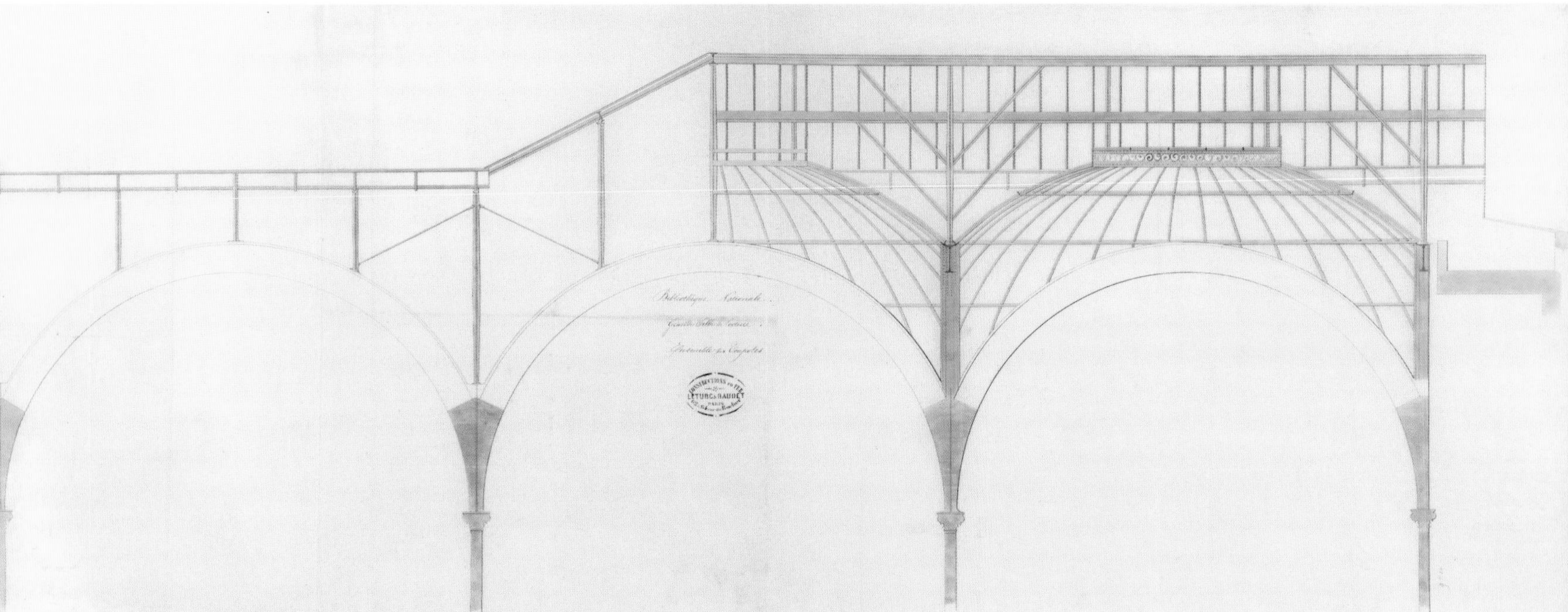

first rationalist generation, such as Jacques Ignace Hittorff, Guillaume-Abel Blouet, Émile-Jacques Gilbert, Félix Duban, Henri Labrouste, Louis Duc, and Léon Vaudoyer, they remained true to the Neoclassical tradition and employed stone as the main material for their architecture, even if metal was sometimes used, discreetly, of course, but with an unabashed affirmation of its own nature. For the eclectic architects, there was a search, as for Victor Baltard with Les Halles de Paris or the church of Saint-Augustin and its metal vaults, for a "rational application of the resources industry has put at builders' disposal."[10] In reality, the debate, however impassioned it might seem, was not polarized as claimed, as iron offered new resources to all architects who were open to using it. Nevertheless, the finesse of metal structures hardly lent itself to an imitation of forms made out of stone, aside from columns and their capitals, and iron often remained invisible, relegated to the roof or reinforcing the floor. Iron caught hold in the 1850s both as a material that could give rise to an architecture specific to certain types of programs in which the structures are necessarily exposed, such as train stations, covered markets, or exhibition halls, and as a complementary material used in eclectic architecture. From that point of view, the Bibliothèque Nationale is an unusual masterpiece, academic in some of its details and radically new in its conception because of its visible skeleton, which was championed by the moderns in the twentieth century, all while seeming to be a pure product of its time. It is a masterpiece beyond any partisan debate.

10. Victor Baltard, *Rapport au Préfet de la Seine sur la construction de l'église Saint-Augustin*, December 7, 1859.

6. Bibliothèque Sainte-Geneviève, view of the vaults in the reading room. Photograph: Jean-Claude N'Diaye

MARC LE CŒUR
Bibliothèque Nationale
de France

LABROUSTE AND HIS SCHOOL

My students, my School—that is the most useful thing I have done, my finest title, and I will always refer to it with pride.
—Letter from Henri Labrouste to his brother Théodore, 1855[1]

In July 1830, when he was approached by eight students from the Vaudoyer-Lebas workshop seeking to continue their studies under his guidance,[2] Labrouste, who had just returned from Italy, first wanted to make sure their respective opinions converged. To do so, he offered them "all of [his] thoughts on architecture," pragmatic ideas based on reason—and ones that went against the grain of official thinking:

> If the elements of architecture cannot remain immutable because of our new needs and the means that industry puts at our disposal to satisfy them, they cannot, either, respond to our whims. These elements, which are truly the organs of a whole, are modified according to the particular functions they must fulfill and by that fact require a very specific choice of materials, made according to their aptitude to make those functions possible. These materials' special aptitudes thus have the most direct influence on the form it is best to give them, and decoration is therefore intimately linked to construction. A monument's beauty lies in the harmonious balance between its needs and the means of satisfying them.[3]

Once his young would-be students had clearly accepted his profession of faith, Labrouste opened his workshop on August 1 of that year on the Rue des Beaux-Arts, a stone's throw from the Ecole. His desire to contribute to fixing the archaic way he believed architecture was being taught rang out like a new challenge to the Academy,

1. [Laure Labrouste] 1928:88.
2. The students were Dominique-Jean Dupuis (1810–1864), Adrien Carville (b. 1811), Gustave Klotz (1810–1880), Adolphe Gréterin (1806–1852), Jean-Baptiste Lassus (1807–1857), Pierre-Marie Marcel (1805–1875 [?]), Ambroise-Charles-François-Théodore Penavère (b. 1808), and Pierre-François Dumesnil (b. 1809).
3. Léon Labrouste 1902:214–15.

1. Juste Lisch, Plan for a Lighthouse, elevation, second-year competition at the Ecole des Beaux-Arts, c. 1851, 95.7 × 62.5 cm, Musée d'Orsay, Paris, ARO 2000 8

while he was still caught up in the polemic that had arisen from his submission on the temples of Paestum.

Labrouste followed a path forged by his friend Félix Duban. On returning from Rome, Duban had temporarily become head of Abel Blouet's workshop—Blouet had been sent to accompany the Peloponnese scientific expedition (March 1829–March 1830)—and from that time had also been running a second workshop with his brother-in-law François Debret, with whom he would soon have a falling-out. The two former fellow students at the Villa Medici came up against forceful resistance. In late 1829, Duban complained of the "outcry [he was] subject to,"[4] and, one year later, Labrouste in turn would bemoan "unjust persecutions from the academic aristocracy" and the "pitiless tenacity" with which their respective students were treated.[5] In 1833, the press echoed this "fanatical struggle between the new professors and the old, between the students of the latter and the students of the former ... In competitions, where the old professors are judge and plaintiff, all the honors and all the awards were and still are for their faithful apprentices—for those of Duban and Labrouste, nothing, and still nothing."[6] The conflict would never end. For twenty-six years, Labrouste "strictly and virtuously [professed] the same doctrine,"[7] and his students would continue to be vilified in the school's competitions, such that few of them would be promoted to the first class (the upper class) and none of them would obtain the Prix de Rome. That did not, however, keep the workshop from flourishing[8] and even attracting many foreigners.[9]

Labrouste founded his teaching on what he had learned from his personal exploration of Italian monuments, from which he aimed to draw permanent principles. He opposed the Academy's dogmatic approach with empirical training, combining "the very difficult art of composition" and "the art of building."[10] Indeed, Labrouste refused to consider that "architecture and construction were two different things that could be studied separately."[11] Consequently, all of his renderings from Italy became indispensable pedagogical tools. He left them at the students' disposal[12] and invited the students to reproduce them, a fact attested to by copies in other archives, which we still have today.[13] Through that copying work, the young students worked on modes of graphic representation while lastingly assimilating the model they had before their eyes.[14] An analytical view of the roof trusses of the cathedral in Messina, represented with and without its painted ornamentation,[15] thus illustrates one of the essential principles of Labrouste's teaching: harmonizing structure and decoration. It is therefore not surprising that there are several reproductions of it, for instance by Detlef Lienau (1818–1887; fig. 2), Anthony Willem van Dam (1815–1901; fig. 3), and a certain Rivaud.[16] As for Emile Boeswillwald (1815–1896), he was very likely inspired by his own copy of it when designing the ceiling trusses of the imperial chapel in Biarritz, built in 1864.[17]

His Italian drawings allowed Labrouste to display methodically the different processes used in the past and to inculcate, in the end, the solutions that seemed to him most apposite. In building an arch, for example, "the master's conclusions were always in favor of an extradosed arch, which he imposed on his students in all cases."[18] But his

4. Letter from Duban to Louis Duc, undated; see Charles Lucas, "Inauguration du monument de Félix Duban," *La Construction moderne* (November 10, 1894): 62.
5. Letter from Labrouste to Louis Duc, December 6, 1830; see Lucas 1895:254.
6. P. B., "Du mouvement en architecture," *L'Artiste*, 1st ser., vol. 6 (1833): 76.
7. Trélat [1875]:15.
8. "Les professeurs d'architecture s'en vont," *Encyclopédie d'architecture*, 6th year, no. 8 (August 1856): col. 123.
9. Among Labrouste's main foreign students, we should cite the Swiss John-Henry Foretay (b. 1825), Jean-Jacques Stehlin (1826–1894), and Jules Verrey (1822–1896); the German Christian Friedrich von Leins (1814–1892) and Albert Rosengarten (1809–1893); the Belgian Théophile Fumière (1828–1904); the Danish Niels Sigfried Nebelong (1806–1871); the Swedish Albert Törnqvist (1819–1898); the Spanish Lorenzo de la Hidalga (1810–1872); the Polish Alexandre Matuszynski (1812–1893); the Romanian Demetre Berendey [or Berindei] (1832–1884); the Turkish Nigoğos Balyan (1826–1858); and the Chilean Manuel

2. Detlef Lienau, details of the paintings decorating the roof of the cathedral in Messina, after Labrouste, c. 1842–46, 25.1 × 40.3 cm, Columbia University, New York, Avery Architectural & Fine Arts Library, LIENAU BOX 2, 19, 1936.002.00796
3. Anthony Willem van Dam, details of the paintings decorating the roof of the cathedral in Messina, after Labrouste, c. 1838–39, 25.7 × 39.3 cm, Rijksdienst voor het Cultureel Erfgoed/Cultural Heritage Agency, Amersfoort, VD-001 BOX 2-number 1

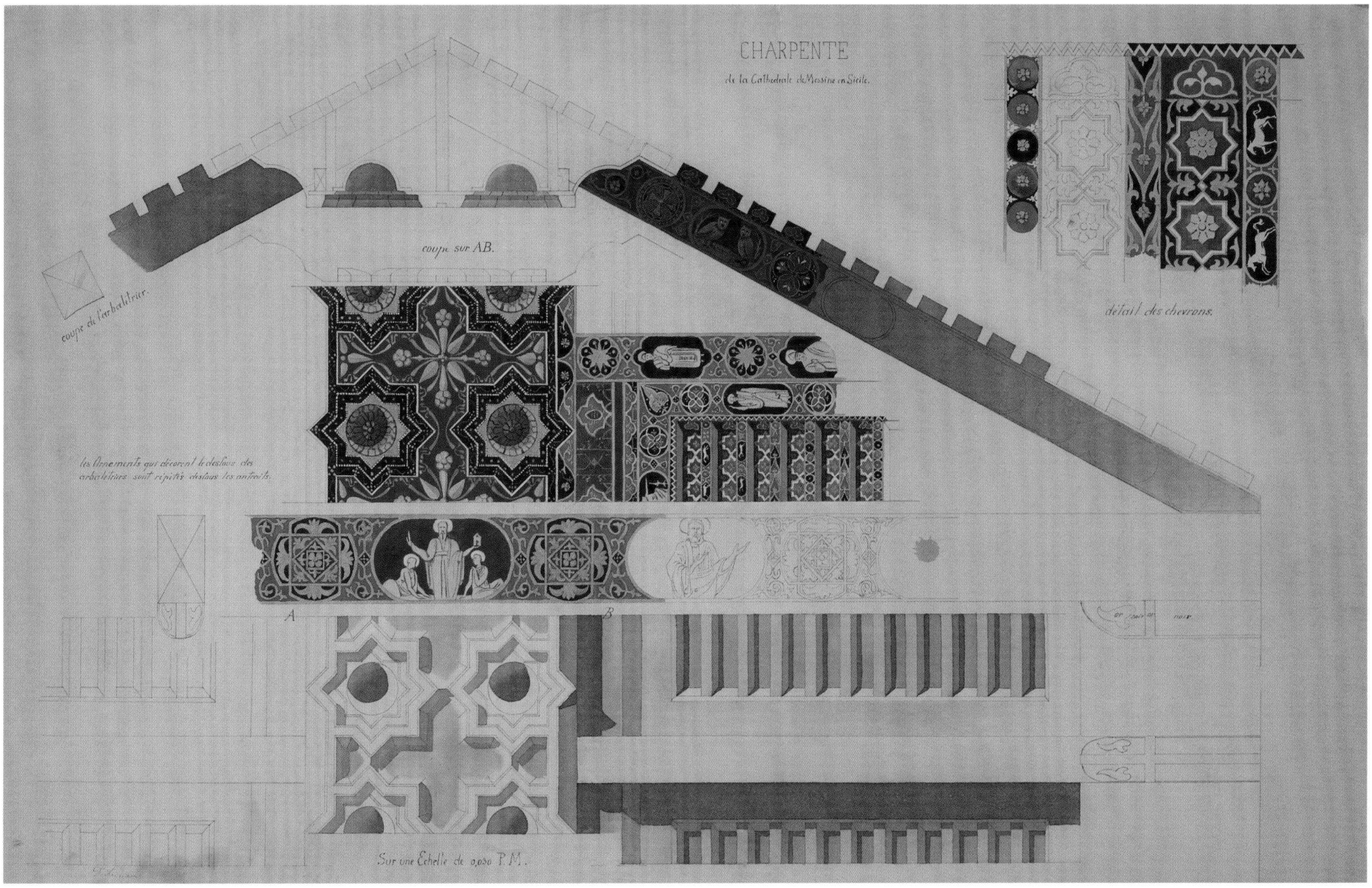

CHARPENTE

de la Cathédrale de Messine en Sicile.

coupe sur AB.

coupe de l'arbalétrier.

détail des chevrons.

Les Ornements qui décorent le dessous des arbalétriers sont répétés dessous les entraits.

A

B

Sur une Echelle de 0,050 P.M.

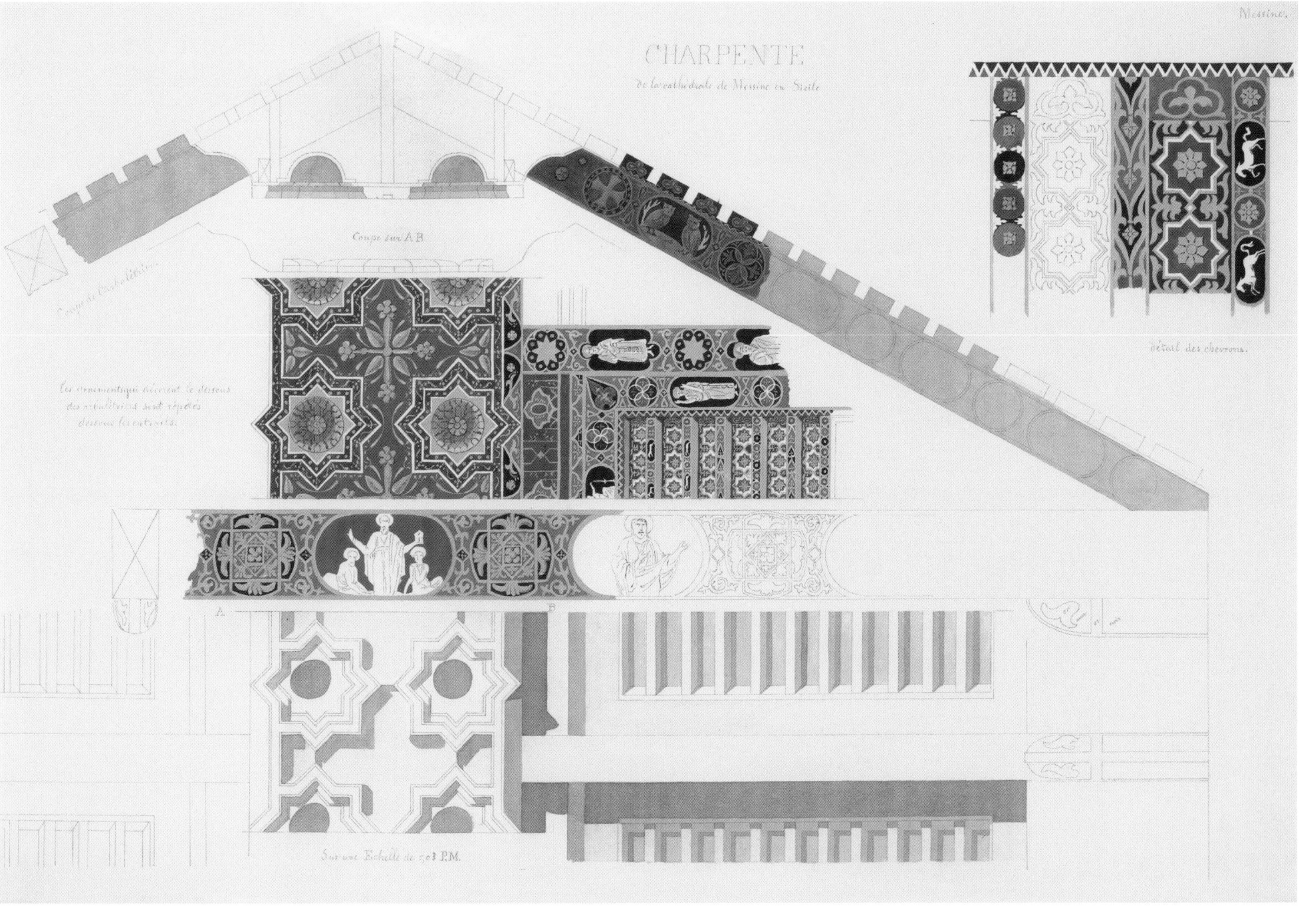

Messine.

CHARPENTE

de la cathédrale de Messine en Sicile

Coupe sur AB

Coupe de l'arbalétrier

détail des chevrons.

Les ornements qui décorent le dessous des arbalétriers sont répétés dessous les entraits.

A

B

Sur une Echelle de 0,03 P.M.

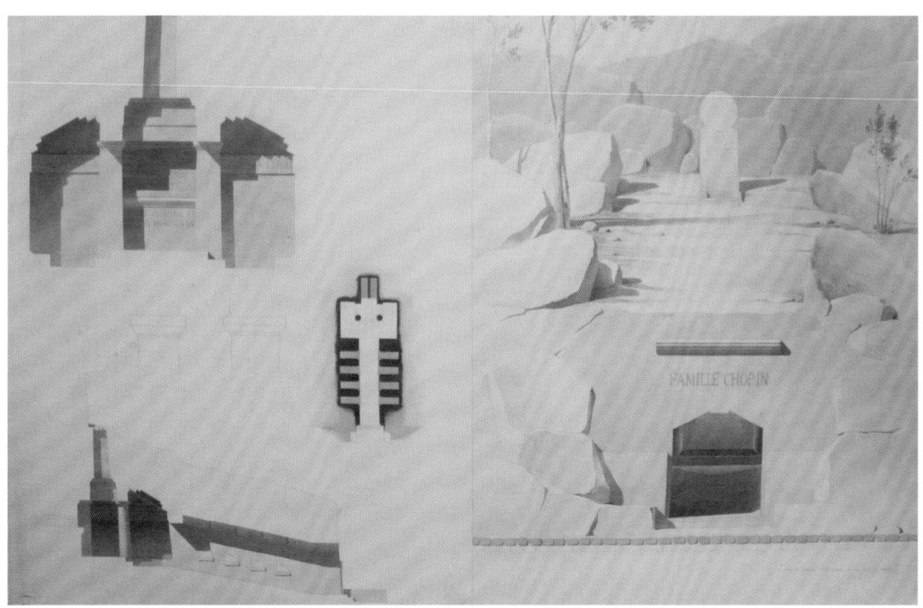

Aldunate y Avaria (1815–1904). On the Dutch Van Dam and Leliman, see, in the present work, Sigrid de Jong's essay.
10. Millet 1879–80:210.
11. Labrouste 1840: col. 59.
12. Millet 1879–80:210.
13. During the same era, as was very frequently done, several of his friends would also copy Labrouste's Italian renderings in order to round out their documentation; see notably Pierre Pinon, "Le portefeuille des voyages de Prosper Morey," *Voyages en Italie et en Grèce de Prosper Morey (1805–1886): Architecte lorrain* (Nancy: Musée des Beaux-Arts, 1990), 39–130.
14. The very day he first came to the workshop, March 12, 1831, Gabriel Toudouze recopied the detail of a capital from the Villa Poniatowski in Rome; see Georges Toudouze, "Gabriel Toudouze. Architecte et graveur," *Le Musée: Revue d'art mensuelle* (January 31, 1906): 17.
15. Bibliothèque Nationale de France, Prints, VZ-1030 (2)-FOL, MFLM P-64370.
16. Draft reproduced in *La Décoration ancienne et moderne*, 3rd year [1895], pl. 22 ("Comble en charpente décoré de peintures dans l'église cathédrale de Messine (Sicile): Dessin de Rivaud, d'après Labrouste").
17. See *Revue générale de l'architecture et des travaux publics* 36 (1879): pl. 32–35.
18. Millet 1879–80:210.
19. See Bibliothèque Nationale de France, Prints, HD-1176 (2)-BOITE FOL.
20. Anatole de Baudot, "L'Architecture Contemporaine," *L'Union des architectes et des artistes industriels* (June 16, 1902): 4.
21. Millet 1879–80:210.
22. Trélat 1875:17.
23. Ibid.
24. Labrouste 1840 (2): col. 544.

rational teaching was not based only on historical studies. His portfolios also contained many drafts of modern works, specially drawn up for the workshop: wood or iron roofs and arches; woodwork, hardware, and plumbing details; plans of railway stations; etc.[19] And when work began on his first major project, he made sure to "[support] his doctrine in the conception and construction of the Bibliothèque Sainte-Geneviève."[20]

For projects to be composed, he himself drew up programs that were "neat, precise, well-calibrated,"[21] which he then recommended be subjected to the "rules of good sense,"[22] offering his students "incessant encouragement," for "an art education is training, not violence."[23] The results could be seen in the competitions organized by the Ecole des Beaux-Arts for all of the second-class students. In 1840, in the *Revue générale de l'architecture*, Labrouste commented on one of them, whose subject was a "palace for the government in Algiers."[24] He was first surprised that "most [of the competitors], completely failing to take the designated location into account, presented projects that resembled a ministry in the Faubourg Saint-Germain rather than a palace in which the higher administration of Africa would be quartered," then he wondered: "Are they ignorant of the fact that the climate must necessarily have a certain influence on buildings' architectural forms? Are the conventions, then, for the palace of a fully military government the same in a conquered land as the conventions for a simple regional prefecture?"

Last, he singled out "[the project] of Mr. Bailly, which … draws attention because of the solid, grandiose look of its facade, as well as a well-articulated intention to take into account … the climate and the materials being used, and the needs of the program." Labrouste refrained from saying that Edmond Bailly (1815–1878) was one of his students.

Several works studied in the workshop are a testament unto themselves of the effects of his lessons. In the 1830s, Gabriel Toudouze (1811–1854) adapted the Etruscan models Labrouste held dear for a family tomb project (fig. 5) and an arena project for the South of France (fig. 4), whose entrance was topped with a modern polychromatic scene, like a monumental retail sign. In the 1840s, Eugène Millet (1819–1879) composed a concert hall whose exterior plainly expressed the parts that comprised it by playing with volume, alternating fullness and emptiness, and individualizing the types of openings (fig. 6). Finally, in the 1850s, Juste Lisch (1828–1910) designed a lighthouse that presented a powerful mass of pyramid-forming stones topped with a gallery and an iron kiosk; his project, which borrowed some details from the tomb of Dumont d'Urville, erected by Constant-Dufeux in 1844,[25] was published by César Daly as a testament to "current trends in architecture"[26] (fig. 1).

Labrouste believed in "the influence of teaching on the future of the fine arts."[27] During a banquet on June 18, 1856, organized to celebrate his retirement from the workshop, he said to all of his gathered students: "I regret nothing of what I have done and what I have said. But there is still work to be done: it will soon be you who will continue alone what we began together."[28]

Twenty years later, Viollet-le-Duc claimed that "[his] students, now masters, could never obtain in state-commissioned work, even in a minuscule role. The ostracism the master of their school was struck with extended to include them."[29] Such an allegation reinforced the dark legend of Labrouste, but it was false. From 1863, Maréchal Vaillant, then an imperial minister in charge of the fine arts, recognized that the workshop had "provided [his] administration with a breeding-ground for subjects of the first order."[30] After being discredited by the Académie, Labrouste's teaching was retrospectively validated by the state. Dispersed through France and abroad, serving ministries, regions, and towns, the workshop's former students in turn helped renovate architecture, thus granting their master's wish.

25. *Revue générale de l'architecture et des travaux publics* 8, no. 11/12 (1849–50): pl. 45–47.
26. César Daly, "Projets de phares (concours de deuxième classe. École des Beaux-Arts)," *Revue générale de l'architecture et des travaux publics* 10, no. 5/6 (1852): col. 147 and pl. IX.
27. Labrouste 1840 (1): col. 58.
28. Millet 1879–80:214.
29. Viollet-le-Duc (March 13, 1877).
30. Millet 1879–80:216.

Previous pages:
4. Gabriel Toudouze, Plan for an Arena, cross section and elevation, c. 1835, 64.9 × 100 cm, Bibliothèque nationale de France, Paris, Prints, SNR-6, TOUDOUZE

5. Gabriel Toudouze, Plan for a Tomb for the Chopin Family, transverse and longitudinal cross sections, elevation, c. 1835, 65 × 100.7 cm, Bibliothèque nationale de France, Paris, Prints, SNR-6, TOUDOUZE

6. Eugène Millet, Plan for a Concert Hall, elevation, 1839, 41 × 25.2 cm, Académie d'architecture, Paris, 392

VOORGEVEL.

SIGRID DE JONG
Leiden University

LESSONS IN ARTISTIC FREEDOM: LABROUSTE'S DUTCH PUPILS AND HIS IMPACT IN THE NETHERLANDS

"This shows you the influence of the materials *in situ* on the character of architecture in these fortunate eras of modern art, an influence that one should never be unaware of, and this influence alone is able to produce a national architecture for every country and even a local architecture for every province."[1]

Henri Labrouste captured here in one phrase his vigorous conviction on how the local conditions of a place shape building forms, decorations, and construction methods, a principal that gained new prominence in nineteenth-century thought. The passage stems from a letter to a Dutch pupil in his atelier, Anthony Willem van Dam (1815–1901). It is the same conviction that led Labrouste to write twelve years earlier in his controversial *mémoire* on the temples of Paestum how their architecture could not be transferred to France as a timeless and universal model.[2] Thus he argued that, rather than academic doctrines and universalism, artistic freedom and individual answers

1. Letter from Labrouste to Van Dam, with postal stamp January 3, 1840, Collection Rijksdienst voor het Cultureel Erfgoed (RDCE) Amersfoort, Van Dam Papers.

1. Anthony Willem van Dam, Plan for a Theater, submission to the Royal Academy of the Fine Arts in Amsterdam, 1838, NAi, Rotterdam, van Dam Collection, DAMA t 1

to contemporary issues should prevail. By the same token, architectural history as a whole should serve the architect in this anti-academic approach to designing buildings. His Bibliothèque Sainte-Geneviève gave a three-dimensional demonstration of these ideas in propagating the inventiveness of the architect through a free combination of historical forms.

It was in this climate that two Dutch architects would study at Labrouste's atelier and would be introduced to Labrouste's thoughts on a modern and free way of thinking about architecture, history, and design. Van Dam studied at the atelier in 1838–39 and Johannes Hermanus Leliman (1828–1910) in 1852–53; Labrouste's Bibliothèque, his statement in stone of his revolutionary ideas, came to light during the period in-between. The drawings, letters, articles, publications, and lectures these two Dutch students left behind enable us to reconstruct Labrouste's methods of teaching and the ideas he transmitted to his students in his atelier, foremost how these ideas could form the basis of nineteenth-century Dutch architectural thought that would shape the art of building in the Netherlands until well into the twentieth century.

INSTRUCTING VAN DAM ON THE *GENIUS LOCI*

Van Dam arrived in 1838 at Labrouste's atelier, after having won the Dutch Prix de Rome of the Royal Academy of Fine Arts at Amsterdam in 1837 (fig. 1). Paris was his first stop in a three-year-long journey through Belgium, France, Italy, and Greece. The many drawings that remain of his Parisian period demonstrate how he conspicuously depicted and copied Labrouste's drawings.[3] In Labrouste's atelier he was taught how the rendering of the building material in watercolors was an important feature, and his drawings are vivid and colorful testimonies of this focus on materiality. They make visible how Labrouste educated his students in considering the history of architecture in many different styles and periods as a source of inspiration, but also how they should study other important aspects of architecture, such as construction methods, spatiality, and the role of decoration. Following his Parisian sojourn, while traveling to Italy and Greece (1839–41), Van Dam stayed in contact with his former teacher. Labrouste advised him to thoroughly study the architecture of northern Italy, as he had done himself. He also told his student that it was important to analyze buildings from different angles to fully understand their construction, for example from the cupola of the Milan cathedral: "There is always something of interest to discover there when one wants to study buildings not only for the beauty of the forms of decoration but also for the mechanism of their construction."[4] The emphasis Labrouste consistently put on both construction and building materials is also apparent in his advice to Van Dam on Tuscan architecture. The building material used in medieval and Renaissance monuments, such

2. For the reception of Paestum and how Labrouste's ideas were rooted in but also transformed eighteenth-century thought see Sigrid de Jong, *Rediscovering Architecture: Paestum in Eighteenth-Century Architectural Experience and Thought* (Ph D diss., Leiden University, 2010; London: Yale University Press, forthcoming).
3. See on Van Dam: Coert Peter Krabbe, *Droomreis op papier: De Prix de Rome en de Nederlandse architectuur (1808–1851)* (Leiden: Primavera Pers, 2009).
4. Quoted letter from Labrouste to Van Dam. See note 1.

as the Florentine San Miniato, the Baptistry, the Duomo, and Santa Maria Novella, built with green and white marble, had fascinated Labrouste during his own travels and proved to him that architecture possesses local specificity that can be defined as the *genius loci*.

Van Dam arrived in Rome at the end of 1839. Labrouste had recommended that he stay in close contact with the French *pensionnaires*, and Van Dam continued his tutelage in a sense by copying drawings from these students at the Académie de Beaux-Arts. Then, with Naples as his base, he explored the surrounding islands and cities. At Pompeii, Van Dam made some of his most beautiful drawings in vibrant colors of the decorations, mural paintings, and floor mosaics of monuments and houses that he considered as Greek (fig. 2). He had already copied some of Labrouste's Pompeii drawings during his Parisian time and he now added many more decorations he had seen with his own eyes, both at the site and in the archaeological museum at Naples. Labrouste's interest in the urban structure and history of Pompeii were transmitted to his pupil: Van Dam drew here not only ornamentations but depicted also plans of houses and structural aspects.

During this voyage Van Dam thus often traveled in Labrouste's footsteps, but the extension of his travels to the Greek mainland meant that he realized an unfulfilled wish of his teacher. Where the French architect had to be satisfied with Greek

2. Anthony Willem van Dam, *Wall Painting, Pompeii*, c. 1839, Rijksdienst voor het Cultureel Erfgoed/Cultural Heritage Agency, Amersfoort, van Dam Collection, VD-012

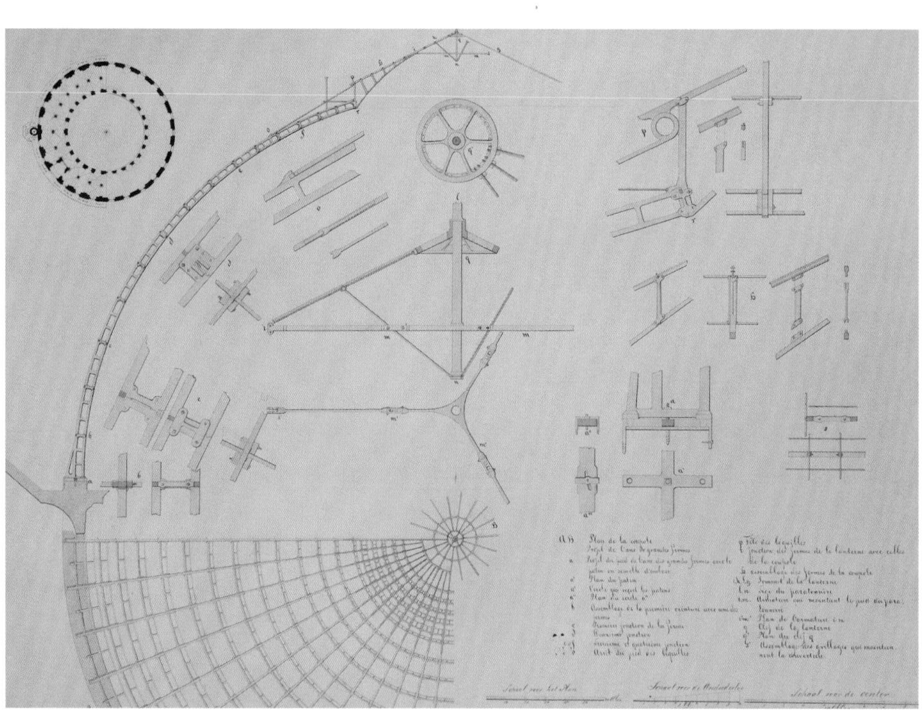

architecture in the ancient colonies of Paestum and Sicily while dreaming about Athens, his Dutch pupil was able to see Greek mainland architecture *in situ*. Van Dam stayed for almost five months in the Greek capital. Eagerly he measured and examined the monuments and he enthusiastically wrote about ancient Greek construction methods and decorations that he had witnessed nowhere else in such beauty and quality (fig. 4). Van Dam worked with Danish and German architects, including the brothers Theophilus and Christian Hansen, under whose influence he ventured upon reconstructing the polychromy of the Temple of Hephaestus. Here we can still sense the impact of his former master Labrouste, who had used polychromatic reconstructions of the temples at Paestum in his fourth-year *envoi*.

Back in the Netherlands, Van Dam would start his own architectural practice in Rotterdam and built both Neo-Gothic churches and public buildings in a Beaux-Arts fashion. Labrouste's influence is rather to be found in the educational methods Van Dam used in the architecture lessons he gave at the Academy in Rotterdam between 1851 and 1887, with a focus on the technical and constructional aspects of architecture, on letting the decoration develop from the construction, and on new building types instead of the monumental public buildings that still determined the lessons of the Royal Academy at Amsterdam.[5] Leliman admired these educational methods initiated by Van Dam because of their emphasis on architectural history and construction techniques and not on the mere copying of the architectural orders, as he himself had been educated at the Amsterdam Academy.[6]

5. Krabbe, *Droomreis op papier*, op. cit., 222, 229.
6. J.H. Leliman, *Beschouwingen over akademiën en kunstwerkplaatsen* [...] (Amsterdam: Ten Brink & De Vries,1859), 9-10; see on Leliman: Sigrid de Jong, *J.H. Leliman: Eclecticisme als ontwerpmethode voor een nieuwe bouwkunst* (Rotterdam: BONAS, 2001).

3. Johannes Hermanus Leliman, study for the construction of an iron roof, c. 1852, Rijksdienst voor het Cultureel Erfgoed/Cultural Heritage Agency, Amersfoort, Leliman Collection, LE-047

4. Anthony Willem van Dam, Tomb of Epikrates Kephisiou Ionides in Athens, detail, c. 1840–41, Rijksdienst voor het Cultureel Erfgoed/Cultural Heritage Agency, Amersfoort, van Dam Collection, VD-065

ΕΠΙΚΡΑΤΗΣ
ΚΗΦΙΣΙΟΥ
ΙΩΝΙΔΗΣ

POSTKANTOOR

Pl. XXXVII

BUREAU DE POSTES

Doorsnede over de lengte. Coupe longitudinale.

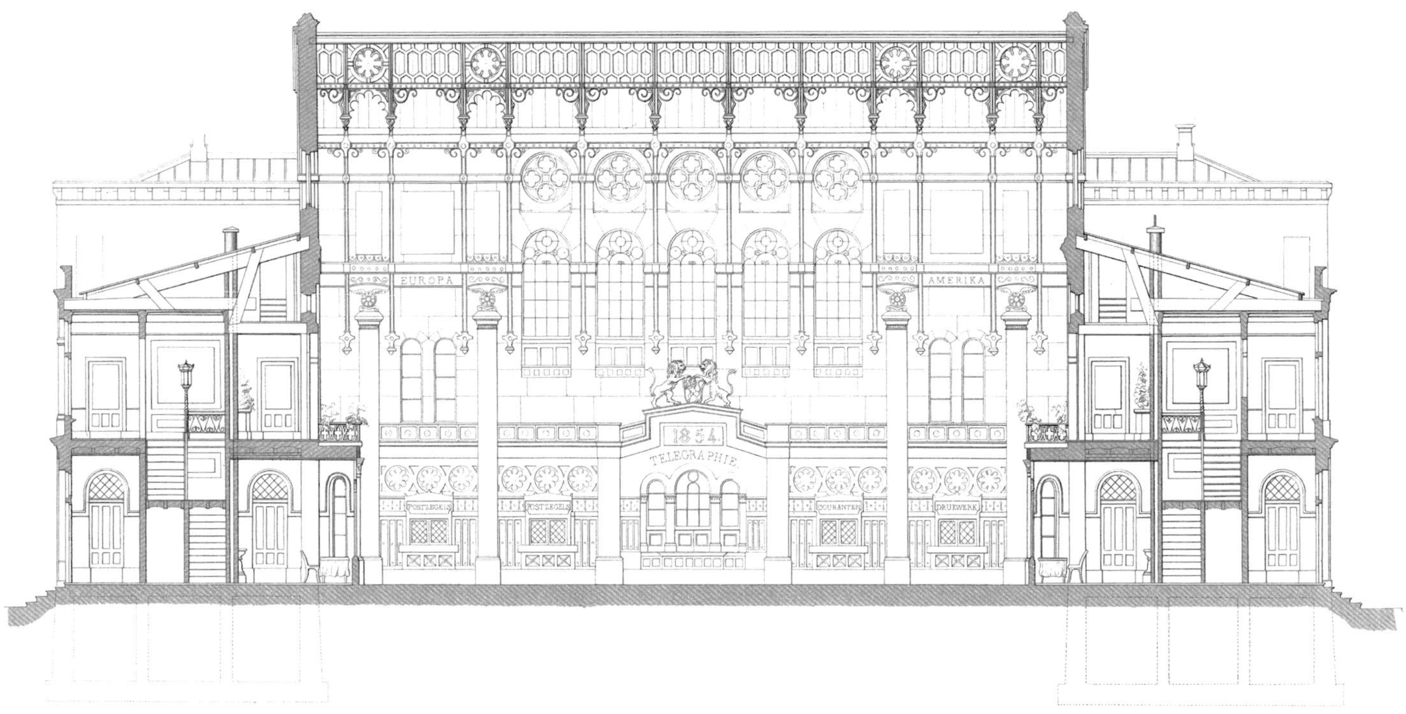

Doorsnede over de breedte Coupe transversale.

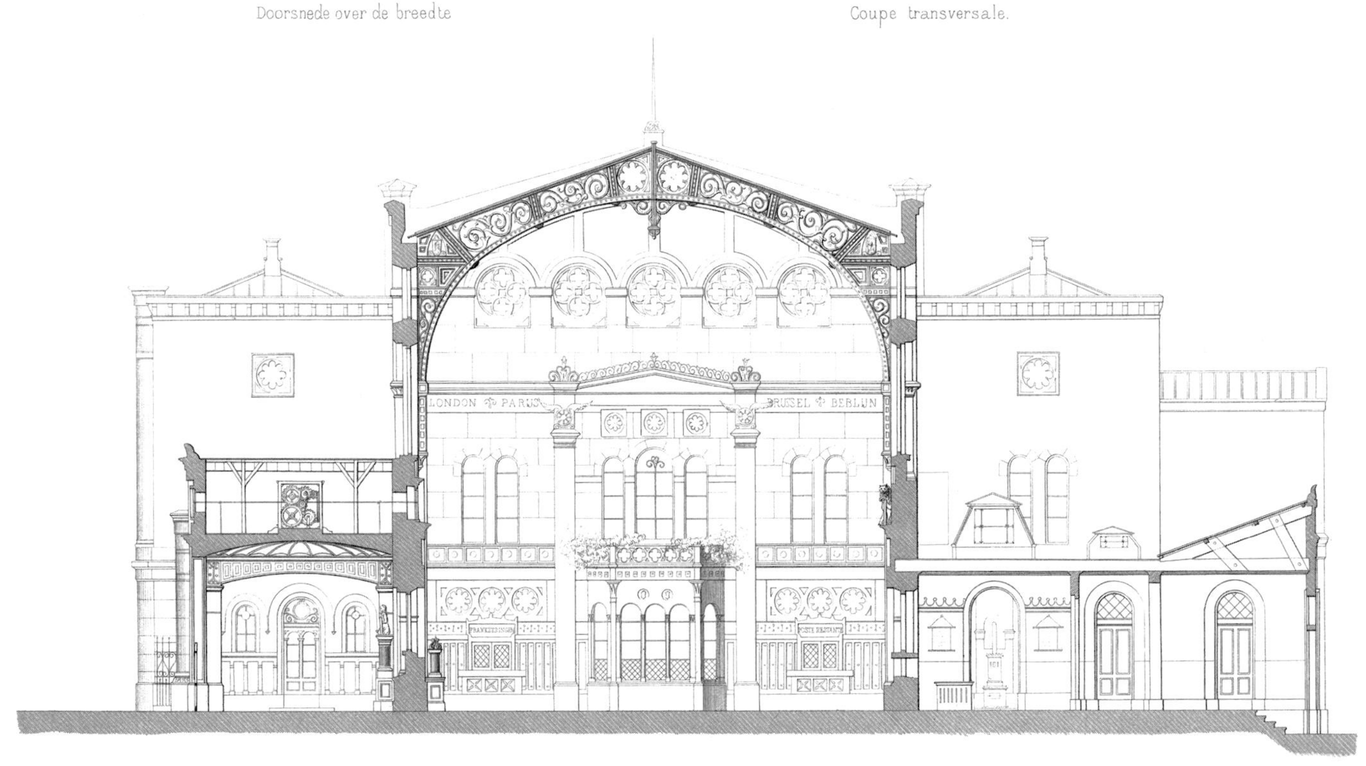

J.H. Leliman. inv.

Steendr. van R. de Vries Jr.

Schaal van 8 strepen per El.

1 2 3 4 5 6 7 8 9 10 Ellen.

EDUCATING LELIMAN ON HISTORY AS INSPIRATION

Leliman strove to change the architectural climate in the Netherlands, inspired by his time at Labrouste's atelier. He would put into clear and forceful words persuasive thoughts on architecture that he disseminated in the public realm through numerous publications and lectures, echoing his master's voice. Departing from Labrouste's design approach of drawing from a wide range of historical building forms, Leliman developed and introduced a new design method in the Netherlands that he called eclecticism.[7] His time at Labrouste's atelier, in 1852–53, cannot be so well reconstructed as Van Dam's, because far fewer drawings and no letters have been preserved (fig. 3).[8] Still, we can trace the ideas he propagated through the many texts he published in the leading Dutch periodicals and the various lectures he gave at the Dutch Society for the Promotion of Architecture and at the architectural society Architectura et Amicitia, of which he was one of the founding members, as well as in his building projects.

In a winning competition design for an unexecuted post office (1852), drawn by Leliman while in Paris, the visible use of the iron roof structure is striking, as is the deliberate absence of one single style for decoration (fig. 5). Both features displeased the jury of the competition; in an architectural climate where a distinct and pure use of one style and building materials such as wood and stone predominated, Leliman's point of view was altogether new. Following Labrouste's methods, Leliman showed the

7. See on Dutch eclecticism: Geert Palmaerts, *Eclecticisme: Over moderne architectuur in de negentiende eeuw* (Rotterdam: 010 Publishers, 2005); for the Dutch debates: Auke van der Woud, *The Art of Building: From Classicism to Modernism: The Dutch Architectural Debate 1840–1900* (Aldershot/ Burlington: Ashgate, 2001).

8. A drawing of the Arc d'Aragon at Naples, a copy after Labrouste, is held at the NAi, Collection MBBO 74. Leliman exhibited in 1852–67 drawings of his time at Labrouste's atelier. See de Jong, *J.H. Leliman*, 99–102.

5. Johannes Hermanus Leliman, winning plan in a competition for the construction of a post office for a large city (1852), cross sections, never built, *Verzameling van bouwkundige schetsen en ontwerpen [...] Collection of architectural projects [...]* (Amsterdam: L. van Bakkenes, 1856), pl. 37

6. Johannes Hermanus Leliman, Arti et Amicitiae in Amsterdam, 1854. Photograph by Carl Rensing, 1862, Amsterdam, Municipal Archives, Atlas Splitgerber Collection, inv. 10001

different functions of the building on its exterior. He let the decorations develop from the iron structure, and he designed new capitals for the columns. His design for a building for Arti et Amicitiae (1855) in Amsterdam also showed a free combination of different historical forms, thus transforming history instead of imitating or continuing it (fig. 6).[9] Most of all, the construction of the building was discernible from the exterior, with the decoration supporting instead of concealing it. With this edifice Leliman presented the architect as a free and innovative artist, like his professor had done. Even Dutch contemporaries of Leliman recognized Labrouste's influence in his designs, and we can clearly consider him as an agent for Labrouste's ideas in the Netherlands.[10] Just as Labrouste did, Leliman saw the entire history of architecture as a source of new building forms, supported the architect's originality and artistic freedom, and rejected academic traditions and doctrines.

In the decades after his time at Labrouste's atelier, Leliman traveled often to France.[11] He was well informed on the recent French debates and could thus function as an intermediary to inject French thought in the Dutch debate. Labrouste had provided him with his ideas through his teachings and buildings, and the writings of César Daly (1811–1894) and Paul Sédille (1836–1900) served to further construct his ideas. Leliman had set out the path to disseminate this design method in the Netherlands in *Bouwkundige Bijdragen*, the leading architectural periodical of the time, as the mouthpiece of the Society for the Promotion of Architecture, and in a publication of a set of three volumes entitled *Album: Verzameling van bouwkundige schetsen en ontwerpen* (1862–66), in both Dutch and French, in which his own designs, but also projects by other Dutch architects, were meant to convince the reader of the diversity of possible building forms and building typologies (fig. 7).

The importance of Labrouste to Dutch architectural culture is discernible from a letter which Leliman wrote to him twelve years after having left the Parisian atelier, in which he proposed that his French master become an honorary member of the Society for the Promotion of Architecture.[12] He reminds his "cher Professeur" that this election was made "on my proposition, unanimously," hoping that he still remembers his pupil "who has had the honor to benefit from your good teachings."[13] Through Labrouste's lessons Leliman had learned how, by studying the entire history of architecture, the architect could exercise his artistic freedom in choosing historical building forms to construct a contemporary architecture. Thus Labrouste's teachings, new in the Netherlands at the time, entered Dutch architectural culture through his former students: through Van Dam in his courses at the Rotterdam Academy and through Leliman in lectures and in books and in the leading periodicals. This would pave the way for late-nineteenth-century and twentieth-century developments in which individualism and the specific requirements of a contemporary society would be more than ever fundamental features.

9. As van der Woud has put it in his *The Art of Building*, 35.
10. "J.H. Leliman," *De Opmerker* 33, no. 26 (1898): 201.
11. Leliman returned at least in 1859, 1866, 1867, 1870, and 1889 to France. He wrote and lectured often on Parisian and French subjects, see de Jong, *J.H. Leliman*, 18–19, 145–61.
12. Letter from Leliman to Labrouste, Amsterdam, November 6, 1865, Académie d'Architecture, Paris, Fonds Labrouste, file 12, pochette 17.
13. Letter from Leliman to Labrouste, Amsterdam, December 3, 1865, Académie d'Architecture, Paris, Fonds Labrouste, file 12, pochette 18. Labrouste's answer: letter from Labrouste to Leliman, Paris, December 7, 1865, Académie d'Architecture, Paris, Fonds Labrouste, file 3, pochette 57.

7. Johannes Hermanus Leliman, competition entry for the construction of a William III museum in Amsterdam, elevations, plan, and cross sections (1865), ineligible for the competition, *Verzameling van bouwkundige schetsen en ontwerpen [...] Collection of architectural projects [...]*, vol. 3 (Amsterdam: C. L. Brinkman, 1866), pl. 29–30

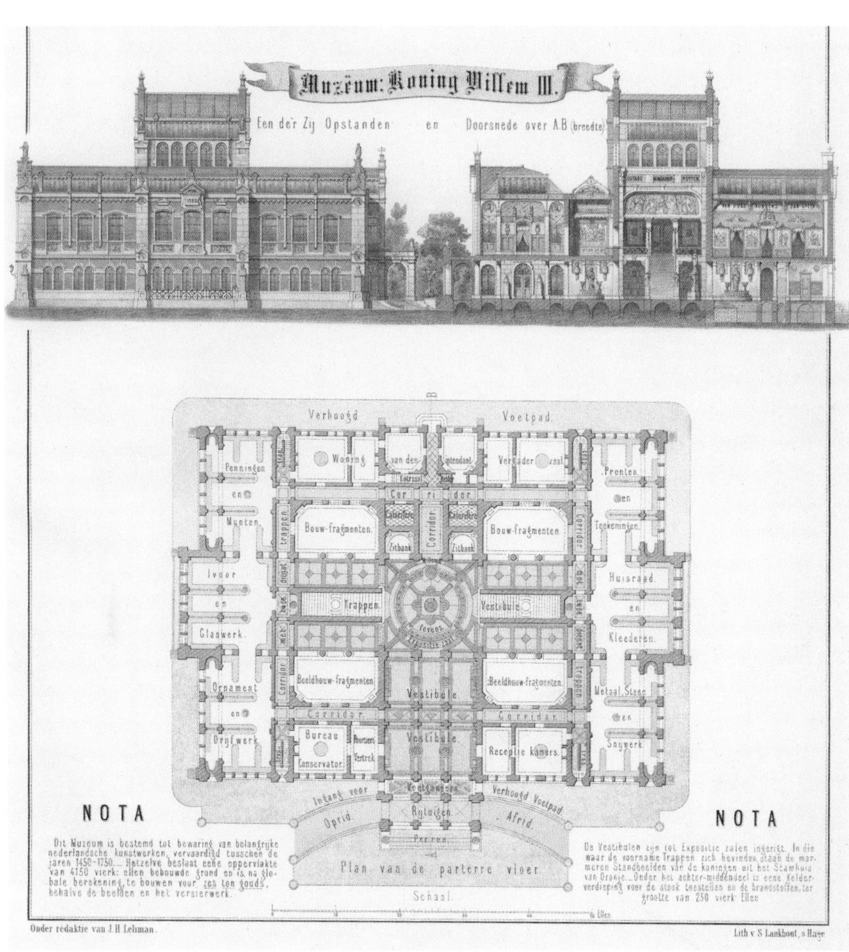
Muzeum: Koning Willem III.
Een der Zy Opstanden en Doorsnede over A.B (breedte)
Verhoogd Voetpad.
Plan van de parterre vloer.
Schaal.
NOTA
Dit Muzeum is bestemd tot bewaring van belangryke nederlandsche kunstwerken, vervaardigd tusschen de jaren 1450-1750.— Hetzelve beslaat eene oppervlakte van 4150 vierk: ellen bebouwde grond en is, na globale berekening, te bouwen voor zes ton gouds, behalve de beelden en het versierwerk.
NOTA
De Vestibulen zyn tot Expositie zalen ingerigt. In die waar de voorname Trappen zich bevinden staan de marmeren Standbeelden van de koningen uit het Stamhuis van Oranje.— Onder het achter-middendeel is eene Kelderverdieping voor de stook toestellen en de brandstoffen, ter grootte van 250 vierk: Ellen
Onder redaktie van J.H. Lehman.
Lith v S Lankhout, s Hage

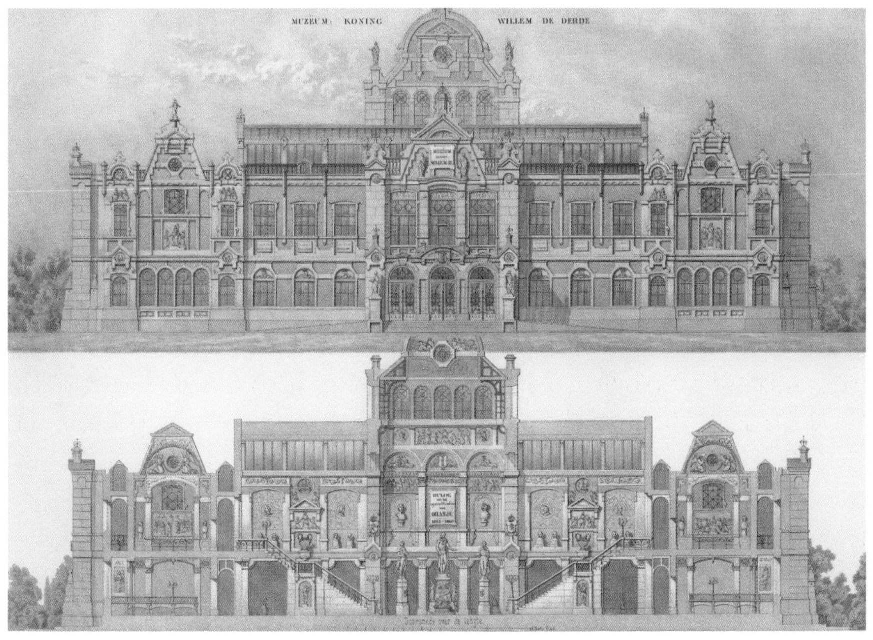
MUZEUM: KONING WILLEM DE DERDE

DAVID VAN ZANTEN
Northwestern
University

HENRI LABROUSTE AND THE AMERICAN ARCHITECTURAL IMAGINATION

Two architectural historians of an older generation, Henry-Russell Hitchcock and William Jordy, explored the observation that around 1890 there were profound formal similarities between the first works of the American architects we have come to regard as classicists, especially Charles Follen McKim, who established himself with the Boston Public Library (1887–95, figs. 2, 3), and those we call modernist, namely Louis Sullivan, then assisted by Frank Lloyd Wright, coming forward at this moment with his first definitive design, the Wainwright Building, in St. Louis (1890–91, fig. 1).[1] Both structures are four-square volumes with a flat facade plane carried to knife-sharp corners and animated by a single "motif" across their faces—a double row of windows in Boston; a square field of piers and square openings in St. Louis. Barry Bergdoll has studied Labrouste's impact on certain American library designs, especially McKim's Boston structure.[2] In light of Hitchcock's and Jordy's observations, a next step might be to explore form rather than function.

1. Henry-Russell Hitchcock, "Frank Lloyd Wright and the 'Academic Tradition' of the Early Nineties," *Warburg and Courtauld Institutes Journal* 7 (1944): 46–63; William Jordy, *American Buildings and their Architects*, vol. 3 (Garden City: Doubleday, 1972), beginning with a chapter pivoting on Sullivan's Wainwright Building and ending with the Boston library. Also: William Jordy, "The Tall Buildings," in *Louis Sullivan: The Function of Ornament*, ed. Wim de Wit, 65–157 (New York: W. W. Norton, 1986).

MCKIM AND SULLIVAN: FORM CAREFULLY DISCOVERED

It is the respect for the block in McKim's library that distinguishes it from earlier American precedents like Richard Morris Hunt's Lenox Library in New York

1. Louis Sullivan and Dankmar Adler, Wainwright Building in Saint-Louis, anonymous, photograph, undated, Library of Congress, Washingotn, D.C., HABS collection, HABS MO,96-SALU,49-1

2. Barry Bergdoll, "Sainte-Geneviève en Amérique: la fortune critique de Labrouste et sa bibliothèque aux États-Unis," in Leniaud 2002:101–11.
3. Charles Moore, *The Life and Times of Charles Follen McKim* (Boston: Houghton Mifflin, 1929), 64; Charles C. Baldwin, *Stanford White* (New York: Dodd, Mead, 1931), 185–93; Jordy, "The Tall Buildings," 314–75; Leland Roth, *McKim, Mead & White, Architects* (New York: Harper & Row, 1983), 115–30; and Mosette Broderick, *Triumvirate: McKim, Mead & White* (New York: Knopf, 2010), 266–72.
4. In his later elaboration of his thesis, "The Tall Buildings," loc. cit. Cf. Sullivan, "The Tall Building Artistically Considered," *Lippincott's Magazine*, March 1896, 403–9.
5. Cf. Jordy (1986).
6. Lauren S. Weingarden, *Louis H. Sullivan and a 19th-Century Poetics of Naturalized Architecture* (London: Ashgate, 2009).
7. His record in that capacity: Archives Nationales (AN) AJ53 129.

2. Charles Follen McKim, William Rutherford Mead, and Stanford White, Boston Public Library (1887–95), *American Architect and Building News*, vol. 23, no. 650, June 9, 1888
3. Charles Follen McKim, William Rutherford Mead, and Stanford White, Boston Public Library (1887–95). Photograph by Baldwin Coolidge, undated, Boston, Public Library

(1870–80, fig. 5).[3] The Boston building is not devolved from inner structure but instead from a suddenly intense sense of regular urban texture—all the more important at Copley Square because of the presence, confronting McKim's library, of H. H. Richardson's symphonic Trinity Church, standing like the Panthéon in Paris before Labrouste's smooth Bibliothèque Sainte-Geneviève. McKim's design overtly translates the facade of the Bibliothèque Sainte-Geneviève, complete with mini-windows a half beat above the ground floor (elaborated almost to cacophony on the side elevations). But this, in fact, is all of Labrouste that is evident. McKim transforms the Frenchman's spectacular skeletal part-iron, part-stone interior into gentle High Renaissance vaulting. His narrow windowed mass is expanded to become just one side of an elegantly arcaded Italianate courtyard. Even the Labroustian facade is modified to reflect the side elevation of Alberti's church of San Francesco at Rimini—all this making the Parisian reference a mere inflection of the familiar palazzo type.

Sullivan's Wainwright Building is a volume not defining the edge of a public space but fixed in a texture of blocks manifest as skyscrapers in a street grid (in this part of St. Louis a French 300-by-300-foot grid laid out in 1764). The result is an almost perfect cube—150 feet by 150 feet by 150 feet, not "tall and soaring" as Sullivan later said a skyscraper should be[4]—and the window pattern that constitutes its principal embellishment is a square panel let into each surface like a decorative field.[5] The unexpected emphases in the Wainwright facade—its compositional mannerism, its unexpectedness, its "modernity"—is attributable to each square facade being treated as a unit in the middle of which Sullivan has inscribed a single, huge "motif"—that tight, gridded pattern of windows and slim piers—explaining the contrasting inarticulateness of the base and edges as the "ground," a neutral surface, against which this "motif" is set. As a ten-story "motif," the building becomes a huge piece of poetry.[6] One of the first observers of the Wainwright Building wrote in the December 1891 issue of the *Engineering News*: "Toy-Block Architecture seems the most suitable name for a species of design which appears to have originated in Chicago ... It is as though a child with an assortment of toy blocks had erected such a structure as the fancy of the moment suggested."

The Wainwright cube is Sullivan's foundation for elaboration, and in each of his subsequent skyscrapers he plays variations on it, again as Jordy explored. That fundamental cube is the "principle so general that it admits of no exceptions," which he claimed to have learned in Paris from Christian-Victor Clopet, whom he presents as a mathematician rather than the Beaux-Arts-trained architect (in the atelier of Honoré Daumet) that he, in fact, was.[7] In his *Autobiography of an Idea* (1924), introducing the Wainwright Building, Sullivan acknowledges his lesson from Clopet.

Both the Boston and St. Louis projects are tensely elemental, incipient designs, McKim's to combine and balance hints, Sullivan's to leave clear an originating

IN VSVM BIBLIOTHECAE POPLICATAE AD MDCCCLII HOC AEDIFICIVM EST VRBIS BOSTONIENSIS MVNIFICENTIA MDCCCLXXXVIII

4. Richard Morris Hunt, Archive Building, main elevation, drawing from the workshop, 1852, Library of Congress, Washington, D.C.

5. Richard Morris Hunt, Lenox Library in New York, anonymous, photograph, undated, New York Public Library

declaration.[8] One notices immediately that a Labrouste design is also somehow stillborn and close to its originating geometry. He resists commitments to finish; his detailing is under-scaled and incipient; his sometimes startling polychromy can wear off to return his design to mute geometry.[9] The Bibliothèque Sainte-Geneviève had the excuse of a tightly constrained site and the need to speak softly before the stentorian Panthéon, but with his Bibliothèque Impériale of two decades later successive plans start from compressed rectangles and asymmetrical symmetries before making the jump to a quite ugly box reading room and balancing courtyard and then suddenly (and, in surviving drawings, invisibly) transforming into the Pompeiian garden shelter now so loved. Flip through the drawings in reverse chronology and this "architecture" is gone. What is fascinating is not just the hard Aurelian Wall of the Bibliothèque Sainte-Geneviève's exoskeleton or the soft white domes of the Bibliothèque Impériale, borne aloft by the fictive breezes released between the landscape lunettes, but the quietness of their evocation.

This was all evident in his Grand Prix–winning scheme for a *Cour de cassation*, designed when Labrouste was only twenty-three. The neat quartering in peristyles of the lower half dissolves in the *salle des pas perdus* thrown across the middle, then modulates to the file of three vertical courtrooms of clearly contrasted insides and

outsides across the top. This plan fits its square sheet like a flat graphic pattern rather than the projection of a building—it is mad with relationships, but they are two-dimensional.

Arrived in Rome, Labrouste spent five years in intense study documented by masses of careful, encyclopedic *relevés*, only to produce as his culminating *envoi* nothing more than a bridge between France and Italy, an exercise in symbolism rather than conventional planning compsition.[10] The academicians were shocked, but Labrouste's younger fellow *pensionnaire* Léon Vaudoyer explained to his father (one of the academicians) that he would follow suit, sending a belfry: "If I am told tomorrow that a vast project … must be produced, I will answer that I am not an architect, that my studies are not finished, and this is because the arts are not taught in France as they should be."[11]

Labrouste, McKim, and Sullivan were struggling so hard to keep from doing too much. In what follows, I would like to explore three points devolving from this focus on form: first, how McKim's and Sullivan's readings of Labrouste (and especially his Bibliothèque Sainte-Geneviève) differed from the more functional understanding demonstrated by several Americans of an earlier generation, Detlef Lienau, Hunt, and Richardson; second, how McKim and Sullivan later saw Labrouste through the lens of a broader rationalist milieu coalescing at the time of their stay in Paris during the late 1860s and early 1870s; third, how one specific aspect of those seminal experiments was especially sympathetic to another architect of the older generation, Henry Van Brunt, as well as to Sullivan himself.

8. McKim's biographer Charles Moore relates in detail the crisis he experienced designing the Boston library; Jordy discovers a very different preliminary project for Sullivan's Wainwright and surmises a crisis there as well; Frank Lloyd Wright speaks of the presentation to him of the Wainwright design as a moment of revelation: Moore, *The Life and Times of Charles Follen McKim*, chap. 7; Frank Lloyd Wright, "Louis Sullivan—His Life," *Architectural Record* 56 (1924): 29.

9. For my idea of Labrouste as an architectural composer, I am indebted to Neil Levine and the essays in Drexler 1977. Cf. Jacques Lucan, *Composition, Non-Composition: Architecture and Theory in the Nineteenth and Twentieth Centuries* (New York: Routledge/EPFL Press, 2012).

10. Neil Levine explored this in Levine 1977.

11. November 17, 1831. Institut National d'Histoire de l'Art, Paris. Cf. Bergdoll 1994: chap. 3.

HUNT, LIENAU, RICHARDSON: FUNCTION PROCLAIMED

Whichever argument one makes for a connection to Labrouste—iconographic with McKim or procedural/conceptual with Sullivan—these are tenuous links, all the more so for being filtered through the internalization of Labrouste's innovations by the generation of Parisian designers emerging between 1865 and 1880. Several other American architects stood closer to Labrouste in different ways: the emigrant New York architect (and Labrouste student) Detlef Lienau, and the first American products of the Ecole des Beaux-Arts, Richard Morris Hunt (who himself conducted an atelier in New York in 1858 and 1859[12]) and Henry Hobson Richardson.

Hunt had been a pupil at the Ecole of Hector Lefuel, but his surviving student drawings evince curiosity about Labrouste's Neo-Grec decorative experiments, and one specific project for an archive building of 1852 shows a gymnastic play on the syncopated relationships of the Bibliothèque Sainte-Geneviève in its spaces and pattern of openings (fig. 4). In 1870, Hunt got the opportunity to expand Labrouste's model with the commission for the Lenox Library on Fifth Avenue (fig. 5).[13] Here, as in

6. Detlef Lienau, Georgia Historical Society in Savannah (1876), interior view. Photograph by the author

7. Detlef Lienau, Georgia Historical Society in Savannah (1876), exterior view. Photograph by the author

1852, he reduces the Sainte-Geneviève pier, screen-wall, and lunette forms to motifs repeated in balancing blocks and superimposed stories—missing the point understood clearly by Lienau in his contemporaneous Georgia Historical Society, in Savannah (figs. 6, 7), that Labrouste's was a single, unified structural organism defining a super-space within which a series of local needs were satisfied with a peppering of contrasting, characterizing openings. Hunt's more ample Lenox budget, however, permitted him a powerfully expressive *ravalement* of broad stylized moldings in Neo-Grec profile denied Lienau working in brick and stucco.

Hunt had been followed at the Ecole by Richardson, a student of Jules André from 1861 to 1865 (André was Labrouste's assistant at the Bibliothèque Nationale and, disputably, his atelier successor in 1856) and then employee of Labrouste's brother Théodore.[14] He brought back to America both a conventional idea of composition in characteristic volumes—as we see, for example, in the Winn Memorial Library at Woburn, Massachusets of 1876–79 (figs. 9, 10)—and an explicit desire to be original. He achieved the latter gloriously in his experiments in surface—rugged if carefully calculated and cut rather than the smooth and curving surfaces of the Lenox Library—and achieved the former in mass compositions studied in extraordinary thumbnail sketches. He was a great observer and in the stack wing of the Woburn library he plays an extraordinary riff on the whole organism of Labrouste's Bibliothèque Sainte-Geneviève, the plaster double barrel vault becoming a single delicate wooden half-cylinder and the window embrasures deepening to become bookshelf alcoves. But, like Hunt a few years before, here it is a motif in a larger composition, not a consistent embracing structural organism, merely a reference communicating function.

These buildings identify themselves as libraries through their array of volumes as McKim's Boston building did *not*, and it is that refusal which it shares with the Bibliothèque Sainte-Geneviève.

WITNESSES TO A NEW DISPENSATION IN FRENCH

How would McKim and Sullivan have encountered the Bibliothèque Sainte-Geneviève, as Americans in Paris between 1867 and 1875, two generations younger than Labrouste? In the case of Sullivan we can be a bit specific, remembering that he lived on the Rue Racine behind the Ecole des Arts Décoratifs, the *Petite Ecole*, and left among his papers copies of Victor Ruprich-Robert's ornament exercises demonstrated there; that he knew the Franco-American Louis Millet, who lived with his uncle the sculptor Aimé Millet at 21, Boulevard des Batignolles, a *cénacle* of rough and ready Paris artists some linked to Labrouste[15]; that he chose to be a student of the recently established atelier of Emile Vaudremer.[16] This places him close to the center of events

12. Ellen Weill Kramer, *The Domestic Architecture of Detlef Lienau, a Conservative Victorian*, privately published, 2006; *Architecture and Society: Selected Essays of Henry Van Brunt*, ed. William A. Coles (Cambridge, Mass.: Harvard University Press, 1969).

13. See my "The Lenox Library: What Hunt Did and Did Not Learn in France," in *The Architecture of Richard Morris Hunt*, ed. Susan R. Stein, 91–106 (Chicago: University of Chicago Press, 1986).

14. Kenneth Breisch, *Henry Hobson Richardson and the Small Public Library in America: A Study in Typology*, chap. 3 (Cambridge, Mass.: MIT Press, 1997).

15. Among them, Julien and Armand Sibien, both father and son, Labrouste students, as well as Edouard Toudouze, son of Gabriel, student of Labrouste. I owe this information to Marc Le Cœur.

16. Sullivan's address and atelier are given in his brief Ecole record, AN AJ52 383; the drawings are in the Art Institute of Chicago; information about 21, Boulevard des Batignolles I owe to Marc Le Coeur and the French branch of the Millet family.

at this tense and seminal moment in the development of French architecture, after the crisis of 1870–71 and before the death of Eugène-Emmanuel Viollet-le-Duc in 1879. There had come a new dispensation in Paris architectural scholarship between 1865 and 1880, of which both McKim and Sullivan were close witnesses.[17] Three intertwined like-minded ateliers emerged just then, those of McKim's teacher Honoré Daumet (opened 1862), Sullivan's teacher Emile Vaudremer (1860), and Millet's teacher Eugène Train, being from 1853 professor of architecture at the *Petite Ecole* where Victor Ruprich-Robert had taught ornamental design (in succession to Viollet-le-Duc) since 1850.[18] These ateliers were all linked to that more democratic, experimental institution by their students, who were, records show, registered for courses there while in the three ateliers: among the Americans were McKim himself; Alfred Thorp and Robert Peabody, who were students of Daumet in 1867; and Alfred Greenough, who was Vaudremer's student in 1868.[19] Earlier, all three of these *maîtres d'atelier* had been students of the progressive Blouet-Gilbert-Questel atelier, with Daumet also working under Questel on the Sainte-Anne Asylum in the late 1860s and marrying his daughter. This development was also deeply linked to institutional construction. When a board to supervise school building was created in 1879 by Jules Ferry, Vaudremer was named a member along with Viollet-le-Duc (just before his death later that same year). In 1865, Train had been named to design the pioneering Collège Chaptal. When, in 1880, an institution project was specified in the Grand Prix competition, "Un hospice ... pour les enfants infirmes et malades," all three laureates—Louis Girault, Jacques Hermant, and Alphonse Ruy—were students of Daumet and Vaudremer.[20] But it is also clear that more than dutiful social architecture was taught here: Ruprich-Robert's course on ornamental design proceeded from the abstraction of botanical realities; Train and Vaudremer's architectural vocabulary pivoted on the juxtaposition of multiple materials in contrasting colors. Emile Trélat put it very simply in 1880, stating that the tradition emanating from the Bibliothèque Sainte-Geneviève—he names this as the source—was extended in Vaudremer's Saint-Pierre-de-Montrouge (1864–70) but broke into two branches: one functional, characterized by the use of contrasting materials to display construction; one symbolic, represented by the architect Léon Danjoy and tomb design.

The Vaudremer constructional vocabulary we know; Danjoy's poetic one is more obscure, but we find it in 1861, when Henry Van Brunt published the first American appreciation of Labrouste in an essay entitled "Greek Lines," in the *The Atlantic Monthly*.[21] He would already have known about Labrouste from Lienau and previous training in Hunt's ad hoc atelier in 1858. Van Brunt depicts Labrouste's study of historical models as the work of a *pensionnaire* in Rome devoting his explorations to the Greek temples at Paestum. Van Brunt writes:

> He perceived a remarkable freedom from the restraints of his school—a freedom which, so far from detracting from the grandeur of the architecture, gave

17. The 1870s have not been closely studied beyond François Loyer's work and Alice Thomine, *Emile Vaudremer, 1829–1914* (Paris: Picard, 2004). A telling contemporary summary of events: Emile Trélat, "L'architecture contemporaine," *Encyclopédie d'architecture*, 2nd ser., vol. 9 (1880), 40–48.
18. Ulrich Leben, Renaud d'Enfert, Rosella Froissart-Pezone, Sylvie Martin, *Histoire de l'Ecole nationale supérieure des arts décoratifs (1766–1941)* (Paris: ENSAD, 2004).
19. AN AJ 53143: foreign students enrolled at the Ecole des Arts Décoratifs, which stops in 1870.
20. Carefully reviewed by the rationalist Alphonse Simil, *Encyclopédie d'architecture*, vol. 10 (1881), 1–7.
21. Van Brunt 1861.

8. Detlef Lienau, office building located at 62-64 Cedar Street, New York, study for staircase balustrade, 1876, Columbia University, New York, Avery Architectural & Fine Arts Library, Portfolio 11, n° 20-1936.002.00284

Section C-D.
Plan of Landing on first flight
Looking up.
only.

9. Henry Hobson Richardson, Public Library, also known as Winn Memorial Library, in Woburn, Mass. (1876–79), interior view of the storeroom wing. Photograph: Ann Van Zanten

10. Henry Hobson Richardson, Public Library, also known as Winn Memorial Library, in Woburn, Mass. (1876–79), exterior view of the storeroom wing. Photograph: Ann Van Zanten

> to it a degree of life and refinement which his appreciative eye now sought for in vain among the approved models of the Academy ... Thus was founded the new Renaissance in France; and in this genial atmosphere, Greek lines began to exercise an influence far more thorough and healthy than had hitherto been experienced in the whole history of Art ... It has decorated the perfumer's shop on the Boulevards with the most delicate fancies woven out of the odor of flowers and the finest fabrics of Nature, and, in the hands of Labrouste, has built the great Bibliothèque Ste. Geneviève, the most important work with pure Greek lines, and perhaps the most exquisite, while it is one of the most serious of modern buildings.

Van Brunt's is a more expansive interpretation of Labrouste's contribution than those in the European professional journals focusing on the Bibliothèque Sainte-Geneviève itself, starting with Labrouste's Hamburg student Albrecht Rosengarten's in the *Allgemeine Bauzeitung*, in 1851,[22] and F. Barrière's journalistic presentation in the *Journal des débats*, in 1850,[23] both of which laid out the logic of the design, evidently following a text the architect himself sketched, first in his original presentation of the project in 1839 and then elaborated for definitive publication in the *Revue générale de l'architecture et des travaux publics* in 1852.[24] It is different from Labrouste's earlier declarations of his intentions as a *maître d'atelier*.[25] It is the ambitions of Labrouste's atelier that Van Brunt records. What must have been a secondary theme in Labrouste's concentrated forms here expands—perhaps through its resonance in contemporary theorists like Charles Blanc—to become an abstract language of architectural expression. With Van Brunt we see that this too crossed the Atlantic as "Labroustianism."

22. Rosengarten 1851.
23. Barrière 1850.
24. Labrouste 1852.
25. Declared in a letter to his new atelier in 1830, Léon Labrouste 1902:214–15, and again in a letter to his architect brother Théodore, November 1830 ([Laure Labrouste] 1928:43–45).

CORINNE BÉLIER
Cité de l'Architecture
& du Patrimoine

AFFINITIES AND POSTERITY: THE FRENCH HERITAGE

With Henri Labrouste and his three companions at the Villa Medici—Félix Duban, Léon Vaudoyer, and Louis Duc—on the one hand, and Eugène Viollet-le-Duc on the other, French architecture engaged fully with the demands of the nineteenth century, abandoning eighteenth-century ideals. There was not simply a break with past styles; rather, references and methods were transformed. French society was then undergoing major upheavals brought on by the Industrial Revolution. Unprecedented building techniques and architectural programs were emerging as urbanization grew.

Labrouste had a decisive influence on the architecture of his century, helping to renew it fundamentally. He laid the foundations for architectural rationalism by forgoing imitations of classical models and basing his work on reasoning and deduction, by analyzing the program and its context, and by reaffirming that an architectural composition was all the richer for being based on a consideration of the practicalities of construction. His ideas, which were adopted and developed throughout the century, would allow several generations of architects to freely undertake projects that were infinitely more complex than before. With Viollet-le-Duc, he was thus one of the few architects whose work and thought had an influence on architectural design well into the early twentieth century.

Though Labrouste published little—unlike Viollet-le-Duc, whose theories were widely disseminated because they were written down—his ideas were often shared. He taught for twenty-six years, instructing more than four hundred students, some of whom would

1. Auguste and Gustave Perret, Musée des Travaux Publics in Paris (1936–48), view of the rotunda. Photograph by the Chevojon studio, November 3, 1958, CAPA, Archives du XXe siècle, CNAM-36-01-W

1. Millet 1879–80:218.
2. Letter to Théodore Labrouste, November 1830 (Laure Labrouste 1928:24).
3. Millet, op. cit., 213.
4. Letter to Théodore Labrouste, op. cit.
5. Millet, op. cit., 210.

in turn become professors themselves. His precepts spread quickly outside his atelier as his students began to work for other major Parisian architects or established their own practices in the French provinces. The important positions he held with professional or governmental bodies also allowed him to establish his views in an influential setting. After his death, expressions of esteem and admiration came from a diverse range of architects, from Charles Garnier to the rationalists Julien Guadet and Anatole de Baudot. In 1882, Eugène Millet summed them up: "His teaching was so renowned that it is not infrequent, even today, to hear our greatest and most famous colleagues, his contemporaries, say that they benefited from the master's professorship and that they all consider themselves to some extent to be the students of Henry [sic] Labrouste."[1]

RATIONAL ARCHITECTURE

Labrouste taught how to compose well and build well. He explained to his students that an architectural project was based on an analysis of the program and must take into account cultural and geographical contexts. He wanted his students to "grasp clearly the work's purpose, to organize its various parts according to the importance they should logically have"[2]—and this, because it was the architect's duty to create a building that was perfectly suited to its function, not only in the layout of its plan but equally in its demeanor, its ornament, and finally in its attention to economy. As Millet reports, this was a new attitude in 1830: "The laws that must govern the art of composition, which are now professed by all and which have become commonplace, were not then admitted at the schools grouped under the banner of official instruction."[3]

Construction was to be an integral part of any architectural undertaking, and, unlike many atelier masters, Labrouste included it in his teaching from the outset. He asked students to adopt a well reasoned use of materials, not in order to reproduce the forms of the past but in order to develop new structural possibilities. "I explain to them that solidity depends more upon the combination of materials than on their mass, and [...] I tell them that they must derive from construction itself a reasoned, expressive approach to ornamentation."[4] The ability to foresee new forms was based on great knowledge of works of the past, studied from the perspective of construction. "We reviewed the Pelasgians' different masonry structures and the Cyclopean monuments to understand the way materials were deployed in the most beautiful walls of antiquity or the Middle Ages."[5] Fundamentally, by defending a method of study rather than a doctrine or a style, Labrouste encouraged his students to practice their trade freely and produce new works of architecture that were very different, though they were all founded on reason.

2. Eugène-Emmanuel Viollet-le-Duc, Plan for a House with Metal Framework and Ceramic Infill (1871), *Entretiens sur l'architecture*, vol. 2 (Paris: A. Morel, 1872), pl. 36

After absorbing such lessons, many of Labrouste's students went to work for the Service des Monuments Historiques, which had just been set up, or became diocesan architects serving the needs of France's cathedrals and their schools and bishops' residences. They

GRAND DÉPÔT DES
EN ETOFFES D
LA
NOUVEAUTES

helped develop the Service's doctrine and practices. This administration would become one of the bastions of architectural rationalism in France, particularly with its attention to structural analysis of buildings, which was acknowledged to be a necessary preliminary step before any restoration work. Labrouste opened his atelier in 1830, at the same time as the first Inspecteur Général des Monuments Historiques, Ludovic Vitet, was appointed. Some of the most influential architects to work in the Service des Monuments Historiques got their start in the Labrouste atelier: Jean-Baptiste Lassus (1807–1857), Emile Boeswillwald (1815–1896), François-Gustave Klotz (1810–1880), and Eugène Millet (1819–1879), who, respectively, restored the Sainte-Chapelle and Notre-Dame de Paris, Laon Cathedral, Strasbourg Cathedral, and the Château de Saint-Germain-en-Laye. Juste Lisch (1828–1910) should also be mentioned as one of Labrouste's students. Labrouste himself worked as an architect for the Service des Monuments Historiques beginning in1838. Though his admiration for ancient Greek architecture was well known, his students often became major players in the rediscovery of medieval monuments.

3. Eugène-Emmanuel Viollet-le-Duc, Vaulted Hall: Iron and Masonry, known as the Concert Hall (1864), *Entretiens sur l'architecture*, vol. 2, 12th discussion (Paris: A. Morel, 1872), fig. 18

4. Jules Saulnier, Mill at the Menier Chocolate Factory in Noisiel (1871–72), perspective view of the metal structure, *Nouvelles Annales de la construction*, vol. 18, March 1872, pl. 11–12

VIOLLET-LE-DUC AND LABROUSTE

In the 1840s, Viollet-le-Duc, thirteen years younger than Labrouste, began developing his influential theories. His standing as an authority became indisputable in the 1850s, when he published his *Dictionnaire raisonné de l'architecture française*. A key figure in the Service des Monuments Historiques, Viollet-le-Duc would—through his restorations, writings, and drawings—come to embody the French rationalism of the nineteenthcentury.[6] Doubtless more indebted to Labrouste than he admitted, Viollet-le-Duc held him in high esteem and saw him as someone who had, like him, opposed the Académie and its prejudices. He admired Labrouste's methods, and explained that he "had brought to his work a spirit of examination and observation, which is the foundation for any modern scientific study,"[7] because for Viollet-le-Duc only a scientific approach could allow architects to remain at the helm of a construction site in the face of its engineers and builders.

Viollet-le-Duc thus shared a certain number of key ideas with Labrouste. "In architecture, there are, if I may put it thus, two necessary ways of being true. One must be true to the program and true in the construction processes. Being true to the program means exactly, scrupulously meeting the necessary conditions for a given need. Being true in the construction processes means using materials according to their qualities and properties."[8] Nevertheless, he privileged a structure-based approach. "Indeed, any architecture proceeds from a structure, and the first condition it must meet is making its visible form match its structure."[9] In his *Entretiens sur l'architecture*, published between 1863 and 1872, Viollet-le-Duc spends little time on issues involving plans, circulation, lighting, and technical installations, preferring to concentrate on construction and the possibilities afforded by new materials.

For Viollet-le-Duc, architectural thinking must be founded on historical analysis, but he differed from Labrouste in the choice of his references and in what could be learned from them. With his Paestum studies Labrouste was one of the first to develop a rational approach to this site and to abandon the picturesque vision of the ruins conveyed by Piranesi's drawings. In a similar manner, Viollet-le-Duc refused to see the Middle Ages as picturesque in any way and was one of the staunchest defenders of Gothic architecture as a rational system of construction. Moreover, he would reproach Labrouste for the "antique touches thrown into the modern room" at the Bibliothèque Sainte-Geneviève. According to him, the library echoed the large double-naved medieval assembly hall; the "antique touches" added nothing to the prestige of the design and, instead, broke up its unity by presenting a combination "of forms derived from two opposing principles."[10]

Viollet-le-Duc considered the statics of Gothic architecture—based on equilibrium—to be much more useful in thinking about modern buildings than the passive statics of ancient buildings. It seemed particularly fitting for developing architecture made from metal. In the second volume of his *Entretiens*, published in 1872, he developed striking propositions about it. His contemporaries' work, including the Bibliothèque Nationale, doubtless did not seem to follow through completely the logic of using that material. He much admired the mill at the Menier chocolate factory in Noisiel

6. See Jean-Michel Leniaud, *Viollet-le-Duc ou les délires du système* (Paris: Éditons Mengès, 1994).
7. Viollet-le-Duc 1877: letter, March 5, 1877. (This quote refers to the restoration of Paestum, but can be understood to carry a broader sense.)
8. Viollet-le Duc, 10th Entretien, *Entretiens sur l'architecture*, (repr., Bruxelles: Mardaga, 1986), 451.
9. Ibid., 11th Entretien, 3.
10. Ibid., 10th Entretien, 465.

11. Young architects were named inspectors to help confirmed architects manage the worksites they were in charge of.
12. Anatole de Baudot, *L'Architecture: Le passé, le présent* (Paris: Librairie Renouard/H. Laurens, 1916), 132–33.
13. "Discours de M. de Baudot," *Union syndicale des architectes français: Bulletin*, no. 14 (February 1898):478.
14. Baudot, *L'Architecture*, op. cit., 197.
15. Julien Guadet, *Éléments et théorie de l'architecture*, vol. 1, 5th ed. (Paris: Librairie de la Construction moderne, 1915), 135.
16. Ibid., 134.

(fig. 4), built by Jules Saulnier in 1871–72, and wrote in favor of perfecting mixed structures that combined metal and stone or brick and benefited from the advantages of each material. In the twelfth *Entretien*, in an engraving dated 1864, he presented his project for a 3,000-seat concert hall, a theoretic proposition which has since become a major reference point (fig. 3). A network of iron bars resting on cast-iron columns and obliquely angled struts supports the room's masonry vaults. The proposal fully illustrates the differences in approach of Labrouste versus Viollet-le-Duc. Labrouste, in his two libraries, pragmatically separates the metal and masonry structures, while Viollet-le-Duc combines these into a single system of construction. Labrouste works with vertical load distribution, while Viollet-le-Duc uses oblique forces to express a dynamic balance. Finally, Labrouste draws upon a classical ornamental repertoire, while Viollet-le-Duc designs a "skeleton-building" whose joints are like powerful knee sockets, using an anatomical metaphor that would gain currency in later nineteenth-century architectural thought and design.

STRUCTURAL LOGIC, COMPOSITIONAL LOGIC

In 1856, when Labrouste closed his atelier, his students were divided: some followed Anatole de Baudot (1834–1915) and asked Viollet-le-Duc to open an atelier, while others, led by Julien Guadet (1834–1908), sought out Jules André (1819–1890), who had been Labrouste's inspector on the Bibliothèque Impériale construction site,[11] and who would be the official heir to Labrouste's atelier. Two tendencies took shape: one privileged a structural approach; the latter, well reasoned composition.

De Baudot thus became a strident defender of Viollet-le-Duc's theories and structural rationalism. For him, construction was the architect's foremost source of inspiration.[12] As for the shift of his connection from Labrouste to Viollet-le-Duc over his student career, de Baudot viewed this as a logical progression down the path of rationalism. "To the former, I owe the birth of my convictions; it is the latter who fed them, who helped them bear fruit."[13] Labrouste's teaching was, he felt, indispensable to be sure, but it was insufficient "because [his] knowledge was limited to antiquity."[14] Convinced that architects must be good practitioners, de Baudot virulently criticized the Ecole des Beaux-Arts' pedagogy and argued in favor of establishing solid instruction in medieval architecture. In 1887 he succeeded in having a chair of French Architecture of the Middle Ages and Renaissance created, not at the Ecole des Beaux-Arts, but at the Musée de Sculpture Comparée at the Trocadéro. His lectures would be published in 1916 as *L'Architecture: Le passé, le présent.*

On the opposing side, André, then Guadet, were proponents of a classical rationalism based on the lessons of antiquity. They also worked to reconcile Labrouste's instruction with that of the Ecole des Beaux-Arts: in 1867, André took over one of the school's

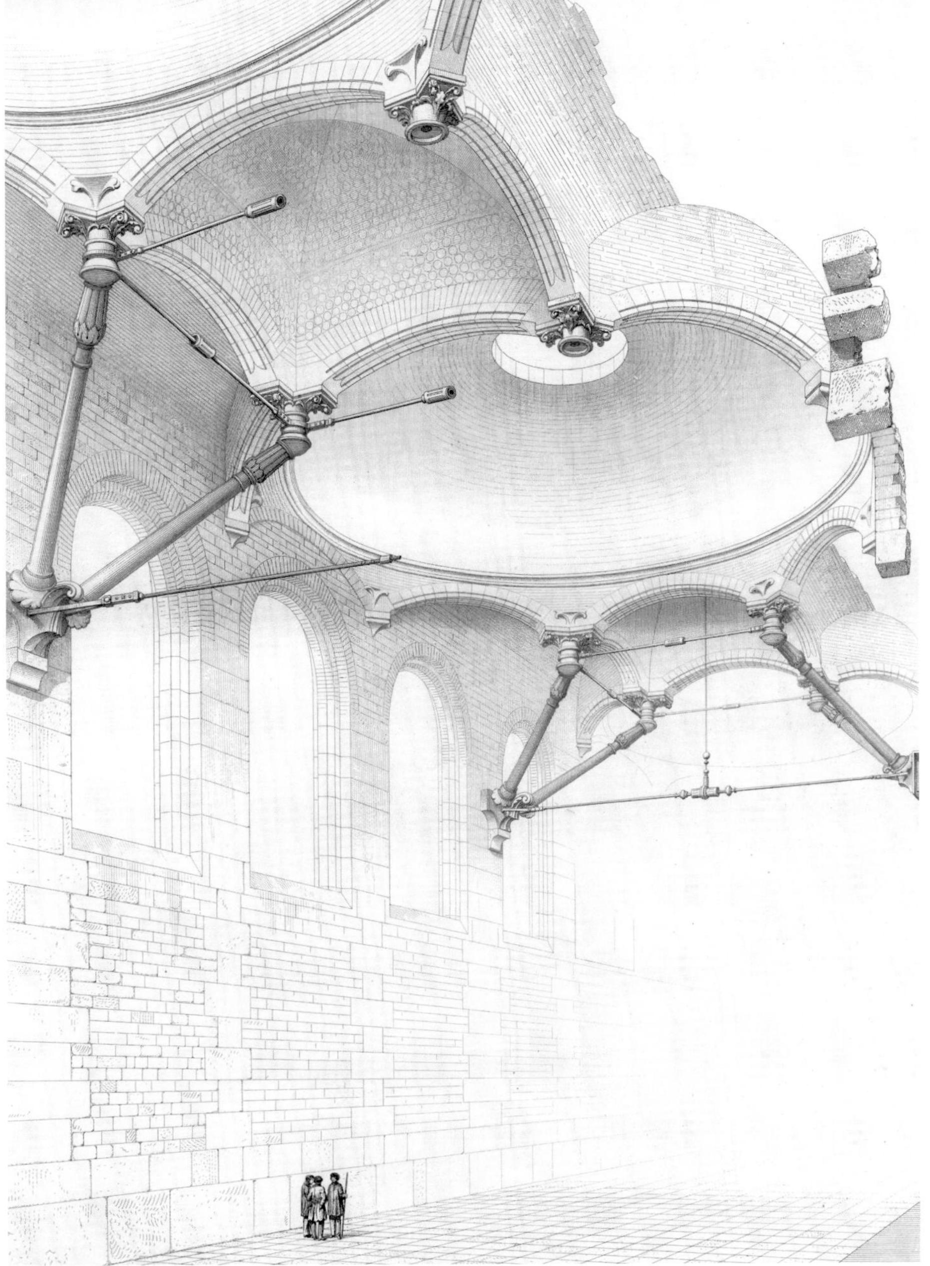

three official ateliers, and, in 1894, Guadet would begin teaching theory courses. He devoted his course to the art of composition and professed that such an art "proceeds by necessary sacrifices"[15] in order to reconcile the contradictory constraints of the program and project and attain architectural unity. Like Labrouste, Guadet maintained that only architecture that can be built is worth consideration. Nevertheless, unlike Labrouste, he accepted that composition and construction classes should be separate because the important technological developments of the late nineteenth century were forcing architects to call more often upon specialists. Even more than Labrouste, Guadet emphasized the importance of analyzing the program. "You must be true to the program, immerse yourself in it, and also see to what extent it should really be taken into account."[16] He characterizes "a good program" as one that creates a hierarchy of needs from the essential to the incidental without shackling the architect to a predetermined solution, then adds, "The program, as I have often told you, does not fall to the architect, who must—or, rather, should—receive it fully prepared. And yet, to create a program, one requires good intuition into the possibilities, such ability to foresee what is impracticable and such a sense of general proportion, that only the architect may

5. Eugène-Emmanuel Viollet-le-Duc, Vaulted Room: Masonry, *Entretiens sur l'architecture*, vol. 2 (Paris: A. Morel, 1872), pl. 22

Dessiné par T. Royal

make a workable program."[17] Guadet provided his students with an exceptional compendium of architectural references, reviewing all the programs of his day: secondary schools, hospitals, apartment buildings, museums, banks, etc. Taken together, they are the portrait of a culture. His course, published in 1901 as *Éléments et théorie de l'architecture*, is a weighty work in four volumes, reprinted many times over the years.

Guadet would remain staunchly hostile to the theories of Viollet-le-Duc and Anatole de Baudot. Like Labrouste, he valued the lessons of antiquity and was resistant to those of the Middle Ages, which he largely omitted from his classes: "I am firmly convinced that, in all things, and especially in architecture, the first subjects of study must be essentially classical."[18] Nevertheless, Labrouste, Viollet-le-Duc, Baudot, and Guadet would all be important teachers, convinced of the relevance of architecture based on reasoning and attentive to the architect's social responsibility.

17. Ibid., vol. 2, 408.
18. Ibid., vol. 1, 82.
19. Bernard Marrey, *La Querelle du fer, Eugène Viollet-le-Duc contre Louis-Auguste Boileau* (Paris: Éditions du Linteau, 2002), 47–48.
20. Académie d'Architecture, Labrouste collection, no. 166.

IRON IN ARCHITECTURAL COMPOSITION

In 1850, the Bibliothèque Sainte-Geneviève was an architecture that elicited astonishment: here metal had taken on a truly architectural role in a public building. In 1868, the new reading room at the Bibliothèque Nationale was immediately hailed as a masterpiece. It revealed what was possible to achieve with the new material, not in terms of technical prowess, but rather as art. Metal then began to interest the entire profession and became the subject of heated debates. Such discussions were not about its advantages for construction, but rather about its architectural value, which was highly contested. And in the background lingered an essential question: how could architecture be freed from imitating historical styles and be given its own distinct character for the nineteenth century?

By the time of the Bibliothèque Sainte-Geneviève, and well before the construction in the 1850s of Les Halles Centrales (Central Wholesale Markets) in Paris by Victor Baltard (1805–1874), numerous plans—some ingenious, others purely visionary—were drawn up, veritable manifestos of the new material. In 1849, Louis-Auguste Boileau (1812–1896) had designed an iron building system that allowed for the erection of large-scale structures, such as cathedrals and exhibition centers. His use of what he called "synthetic compositions" provided spectacular images (fig. 6). In hopes of convincing the government, he intensely promoted his work and won the support of Albert Lenoir and personalities like Labrouste.[19] Hector Horeau (1801–1872) would also go on to draw up imaginary projects in metal architecture, notably designs for Les Halles Centrales (of which Labrouste owned a photographic reproduction of the drawings[20]), for world's fairs, for fireproof portable houses, etc. In 1866, his studies for roofing over the boulevards of Paris with giant glass greenhouses were particularly interesting for the way metal was taken out into public space and became part of urban décor. Delicate spirals of iron decorated with flowering garlands were displayed on a large scale (fig. 7).

6. Louis-Auguste Boileau, Plan for a Building with a System of Interlocking Arches, interior perspective, drawn by Tiburce-Sylvain Royol, undated, 62.6 × 72.5 cm, École nationale supérieure des beaux-arts, Paris, EBA 3297

21. Marrey, op. cit., 83.
22. Ibid., 105.
23. Charles Garnier, *À travers les arts: Causeries et mélanges* (1869; repr. Paris: Picard, 1985), 95–96.
24. Laure Labrouste, op. cit., 74.
25. Cited in Laure Labrouste, op. cit., 78.
26. See Bertrand Lemoine, *L'Architecture du fer: France: XIXe siècle* (Seyssel: Champ Vallon, 1986).

In 1855, Boileau built the first church to use exposed metal: the church of Saint-Eugène in Paris. A heated argument ensued between Boileau and Viollet-le-Duc, who accused Boileau of imitating Gothic forms too literally. More fundamentally, Viollet-le-Duc accused him of not making architecture: "a system whose whole solidity lies in the extreme precision of its combinations is more like the work of a mechanic than the art of an architect."[21] And, he went on, "For what reason does he believe that I have put his work on the same level as Monsieur H. Labrouste's? That was not at all my intent."[22] In 1869, Charles Garnier (1825–1898), likewise no enthusiast of Boileau's work, developed a similar view about metal: "So, if, as construction in the true sense of the word, iron has innumerable resources and lends itself to unsuspected boldness, as art, its only future is as a support or a covering."[23] For Garnier, the material with its thin forms was not in and of itself a catalyst for architectural creation. He admired "the elegant rooms at the Bibliothèques Sainte-Geneviève and Impériale," because there "the (artist's) personal feelings can be felt." In other words, iron had not transformed art but had instead been transformed by art.

Indeed, Labrouste achieved something rare in architecture: he invented a new type of composition, a new way of joining structure, building envelope, and ornamentation, a system which creates a great sense of unity. Without overtly polemicizing for the use of iron and cast iron, he was the first to give these materials a monumental form. "It is often repeated that iron cannot be used in our edifices in a visible way, because that material does not lend itself to monumental forms; it would be more reflective of the reality and reason to say that the monumental forms adopted, being the consequence of materials possessing other qualities than those of iron, cannot adapt to that material. Therefore we should not retain the forms, but find ones that are suggested by the properties of metal."[24]

What proportions were to be used for metal supports that could reach considerable heights with unprecedented thinness? The columns are one of the least successful aspects of Boileau's synthetic cathedral, with their connections between the individual sections of the shaft being overly expressed. Labrouste worked on a continuous structure from the floor to the ceiling: the columns in the reading room were extended into posts supporting the roof structure. To resolve the composition, he drew on classical sources, whether using domes that closed the space or columns scaled in relation to human proportions. Much later, in the United States, Louis Sullivan, who knew Labrouste's work well, would be confronted with the same problem in designing the first skyscrapers: what proportions should be used for metal-frame buildings that could, in theory, be extended infinitely? Sullivan would successfully develop an approach that was imitated often, an analogy with the column—base, shaft, and entablature—with the base operating as the transition between the human scale and that of the new tall building (p. 210, fig. 1).

The unity between construction and ornamentation also caught the eye of Labrouste's contemporaries. Boileau did not mask his admiration: "Everything, down to the last bolt and rivet, becomes an *objet d'art* of fresh design. There is no deception, no hidden piece to the structure; everywhere, there is the decoration naturally provided by the

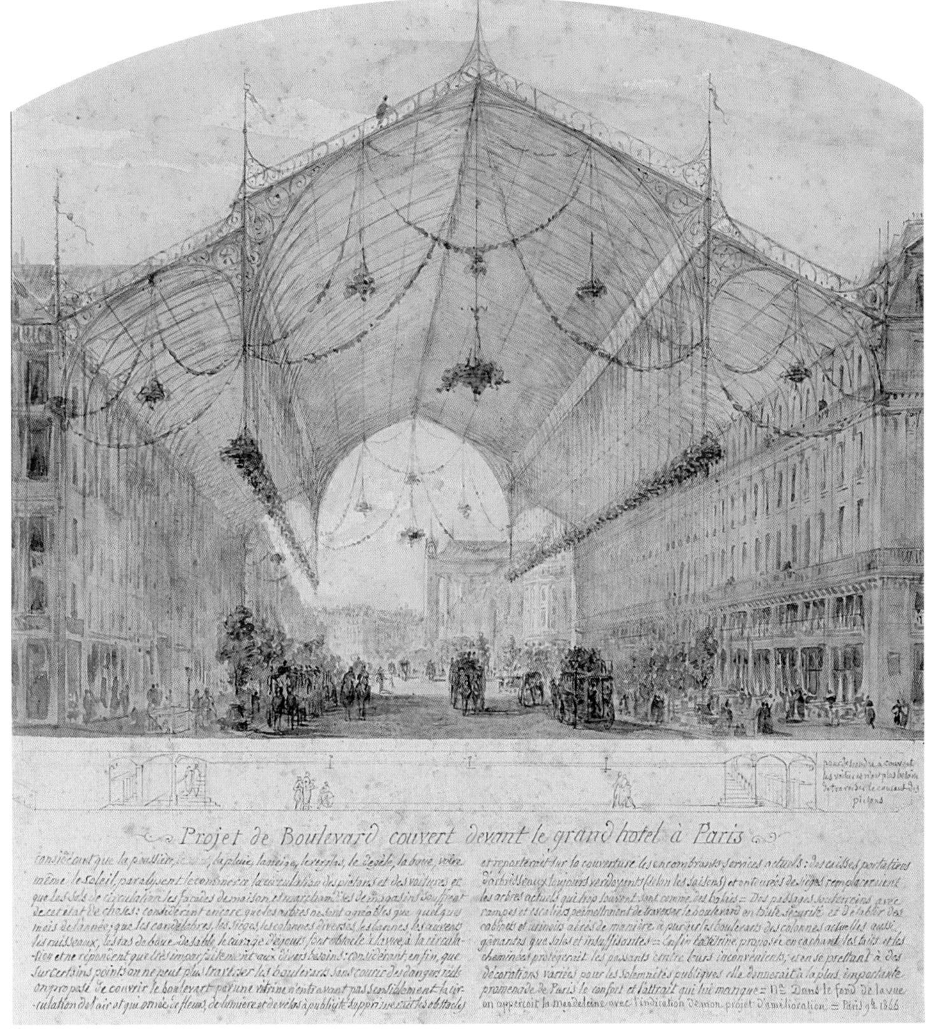

7. Hector Horeau, Plan for Covering the Boulevards in Front of the Grand Hôtel in Paris, perspective view, longitudinal cross section, elevation, and plan, November 1866, 62.4 × 46.9 cm, Académie d'architecture, Paris, 202

Next pages:
8. Central aisle of the Grand Gallery of Evoluation (formerly zoology gallery) at the Muséum National d'Histoire Naturelle, detail of structure. Photograph: Laurent Bessol
9. Hector Guimard, Le Castel Béranger, Rue La Fontaine in Paris (1894–98), *L'Art dans l'habitation moderne: Le Castel Béranger* (Paris: Librairie Rouam, 1898), pl. 11

construction."[25] The correlation between ornamentation and construction would be sought out by rationalist architects and would resonate with the proponents of Art Nouveau and the modern movement. De Baudot set off the ribs of the vaults of the church of Saint-Jean de Montmartre (1904) with ceramic inlay; Auguste Perret "quoted" the underlying framework on the facade in his apartment building on the Rue Franklin (1903); Hector Guimard magnified the metal tie rods of the facade and detailed them as seahorses at the Castel Béranger (1898) (fig. 9).

THE GREAT PUBLIC HALL

Metal architecture underwent its most important and productive evolution between the 1850s and the 1880s, when new types and models were designed.[26] The large public hall had become the archetype of a space for modern times. In this regard,

Viollet-le-Duc noted that, if the mission of a democracy was to raise buildings for all, the "places where the public goes for its business, needs, or pleasures are never large enough."[27] Labrouste's students or disciples would contribute to such developments with some remarkable projects, using metal and later concrete, in which their master's influence was combined with that of Viollet-le-Duc and inspiration drawn from other buildings of their times.

Jules André, the architect of the Muséum d'Histoire Naturelle in Paris, built between 1877 and 1889 a building for the zoology collections so that it could show all of its collections, including very large specimens, such as the skeleton of a whale. The museum, a vast quadrangle of masonry buildings facing the Jardin des Plantes (botanical gardens), came rapidly to be viewed as an important work of architecture. The sobriety of its facade was praised by critics and judged to serve well the building's "character,"[28] as did the décor: engraved on the frieze were the names of scholarly men, a homage to the history of zoology also evoked in portrait medallions. The culmination was, without doubt, the large central hall (figs. 11, 12). Covered by a large glass roof and ringed by two levels of balconies, it is the luminous heart of the museum. Its iron structure is, like that of the Bibliothèque Nationale, contained within the building envelope of masonry. Rich ornamentation highlights the different elements, contrasting with the rest of the building (fig. 13). The metal supports are in scale with the grandeur of the main vessel, extending visually from the floor to the lofty glass ceiling, even while they are detailed to retain a human scale by being broken down into individual story components. The other parts of the building—the galleries, the vestibules, and the monumental staircases—are all very different in character, combining stone, cast iron, and plaster rendering. The unselfconscious embrace of metal construction, the attention to constructional

27. Viollet-le-Duc, 13th Entretien, op. cit., 111.

28. See *Revue générale de l'architecture et des travaux publics*, vol. 40 (1883): col. 16–22, col. 250–51; 41 (1884): col. 163–67; 42 (1885): col. 248–51; and *La Construction moderne*, no. 38 (1889): 591–93; and no. 42: 16–18.

10. Auguste and Gustave Perret, apartment building, 25 bis Rue Franklin in Paris (1903–4). Photograph: Marc Le Cœur

11. Jules André, New Zoology Galleries at the Muséum d'Histoire Naturelle in Paris (1877–89), interior perspective view, *Revue générale de l'architecture et des travaux publics*, vol. 40, 1883, pl. 59

12. Jules André, New Zoology Galleries at the Muséum d'Histoire Naturelle in Paris (1877–89), general view of the grand gallery. Photograph: Pierre Petit, undated, 21.6 × 27 cm, Paris, MNHN, Bibliothèque centrale, IC 97

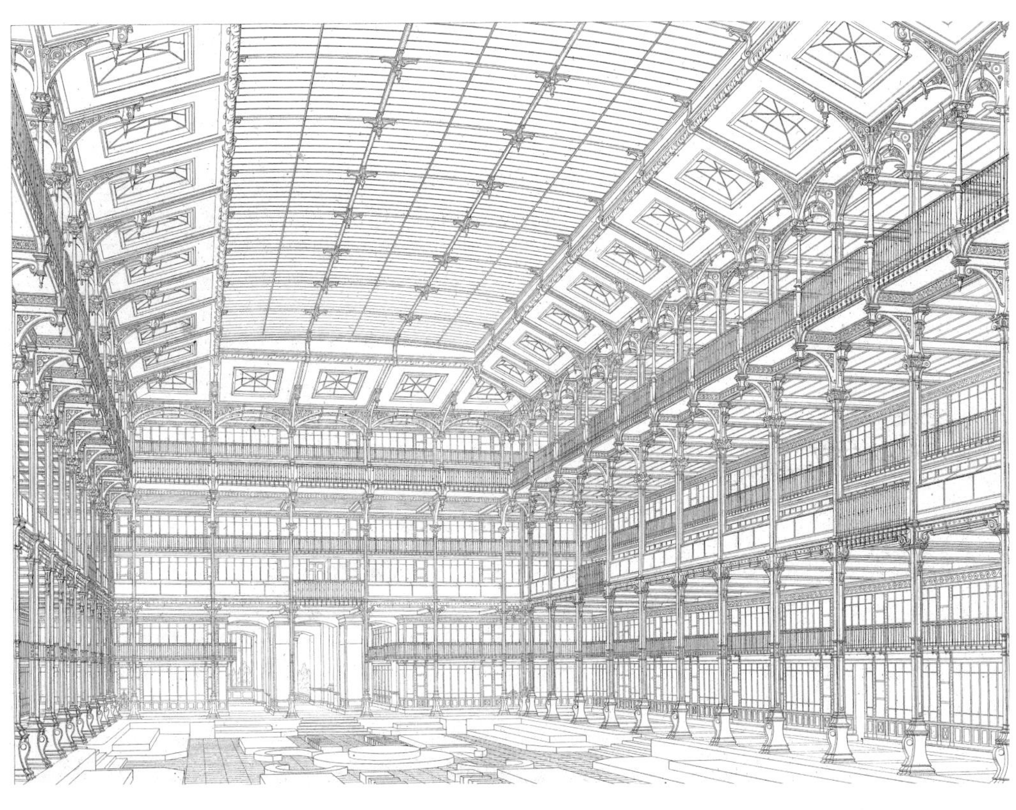

Collet du plafond vitré
D
Coupe de la Colonne C
2e Etage
Bagues des Colonnes
(Rez-de-Chaussée)
D
Plan
de la base A.
1er Etage
Base des Colonnes
A
Coupe E.F.
E
Colonnes et planchers
des différents étages
Face
F
Colonnes et planchers
des différents étages
Profil
Echelle de 0m 05c pr metre

finesse, the firm proportions, the ornament, and the luminosity, as well as the great unity of the facade, all evoke the art of Labrouste.

The innovative technical installations at the Bibliothèque Nationale, from the skylighting system to the use of open iron grates in the stacks, which allowed light to reach far down, offered solutions that could be applied to an array of building tasks, in particular government buildings, office buildings, and banks. William Bouwens van der Boijen (1834–1907), who had studied with both Labrouste and Léon Vaudoyer, designed the landmark bank headquarters for the Crédit Lyonnais in Paris.[29] The program was unprecedented; a new type of building needed to be invented. It was built in several phases from 1876 to 1913, under the supervision of Bouwens van der Boijen, and later of his successors. The design's modernity is affirmed in the suite of large glass-roof-covered banking halls. The great glazed central hall is particularly striking (fig. 14). Here again was a metal structure embedded in a masonry structure which creates a noble street facade. Guadet felt that, in office buildings, public reception areas "always retain somewhat the look of a market or a shelter,"[30] all the more as this arrangement lent

29. *Revue générale de l'architecture* 38 (1881): col.12–16; 41 (1884): col. 17, 152–56, 202–7.
30. Guadet, op. cit., vol. 2, 415.

13. Jules André , New Zoology Galleries at the Muséum d'Histoire Naturelle in Paris (1877–89), details of iron structures and ornaments, *Revue générale de l'architecture et des travaux publics*, vol. 40, 1883, pl. 60–61

14. William Bouwens van der Boijen then André Narjoux and Victor Laloux, Headquarters of Crédit Lyonnais in Paris (1876–1913), securities hall and new rotunda, anonymous photograph, undated, Commission du Vieux Paris

itself easily to subsequent modifications. The building's technical systems—heating, gas, electricity, and fire safety—were much noted, as were the glass-tile floors which allowed light to pass through the two levels of basements to the areas housing the safe deposit boxes.
At the end of the century, de Baudot offered a new vision of the grand public hall type, this time using a technique known as "reinforced cement," a material he turned to after meeting the engineer Paul Cottencin in 1891. He was convinced that the material, which was solid, supple, and economical, fulfilled the aspirations of a democratic society, because "as democratic trends develop, luxury constructions will increasingly give way to material and economic demands."[31] And he began to study its possible applications, first for the church of Saint-Jean de Montmartre, from 1894 to 1904, then in a series of projects for large assembly halls, designed from 1905 to the end of his life. Unlike the metal halls discussed here, de Baudot's designs have a sense of continuity in their structure: the reinforced cement is both the building's skeleton and its envelope. In 1914, the architect, whose quest was to cover very large spaces, proposed plans for a "large covered space lit from above," one hundred meters long on each side, and designed in two variants, of which "the tangency solution," with nine large skylights and four central pillars was clearly inspired by the composition of the Bibliothèque Nationale's reading room (figs. 15, 16).[32]

31. Baudot, *L'Architecture . . .*, op. cit., 171.
32. Ibid., 173–80.
33. Guadet, op. cit., vol. 2, 382.
34. See Leniaud 2002.

THE LIBRARIES

The Bibliothèque Sainte-Geneviève and the Bibliothèque Nationale became de rigueur models for building libraries. In 1894, Guadet was still recommending they be studied, because: "There are basically two ideas, two principles, which can govern the composition of a library: either the readers are in the same room that houses the books, which is the case at the Bibliothèque Sainte-Geneviève and all specialized libraries; or, on the contrary, the readers are in a reading room while the large book stacks are nearby. That is the "Department of Printed Matter" (main reading room) at the Bibliothèque Nationale."[33] He also praised their lighting, compactness, book delivery, reader surveillance, comfortable temperature, and organization of the book stacks.
The second half of the century saw the construction of many public libraries in France and elsewhere.[34] Some were directly inspired by the plans and technical systems perfected by Labrouste; others paid tribute primarily to his architecture. The Lenox Library (1870–80) by Richard Morris Hunt (1827–1895), in New York, elegantly evoked the facade of the Bibliothèque Sainte-Geneviève without, however, adopting its plan (p. 215, fig. 5). The same is true of the Boston Public Library (1887–95) by the architects McKim, Mead, and White (p.213, figs. 2, 3). For the New York State Education Building (1912) in Albany, Henry Hornbostel (1867–1961) repeated the pattern of the Bibliothèque Nationale's domes, in this case using the Guastavino system of terra-cotta tile construction. In Stockholm the architect Gustaf Dahl (1835–1927) completed the National Library, from 1871 to 1877, in which metal's shining role can be read as an interpretation of the work of Labrouste (p.24, fig. 1).

15. Anatole de Baudot, Plan for a Large Covered Space Lit from Above, plan, March 1914, 52.7 × 52.6 cm, Charenton-le-Pont, Médiathèque de l'architecture et du patrimoine, 26815
16. Anatole de Baudot, Plan for a Large Covered Space Lit from Above, interior perspective, March 1914, 37.4 × 61, 3 cm, Charenton-le-Pont, Médiathèque de l'architecture et du patrimoine, 26817

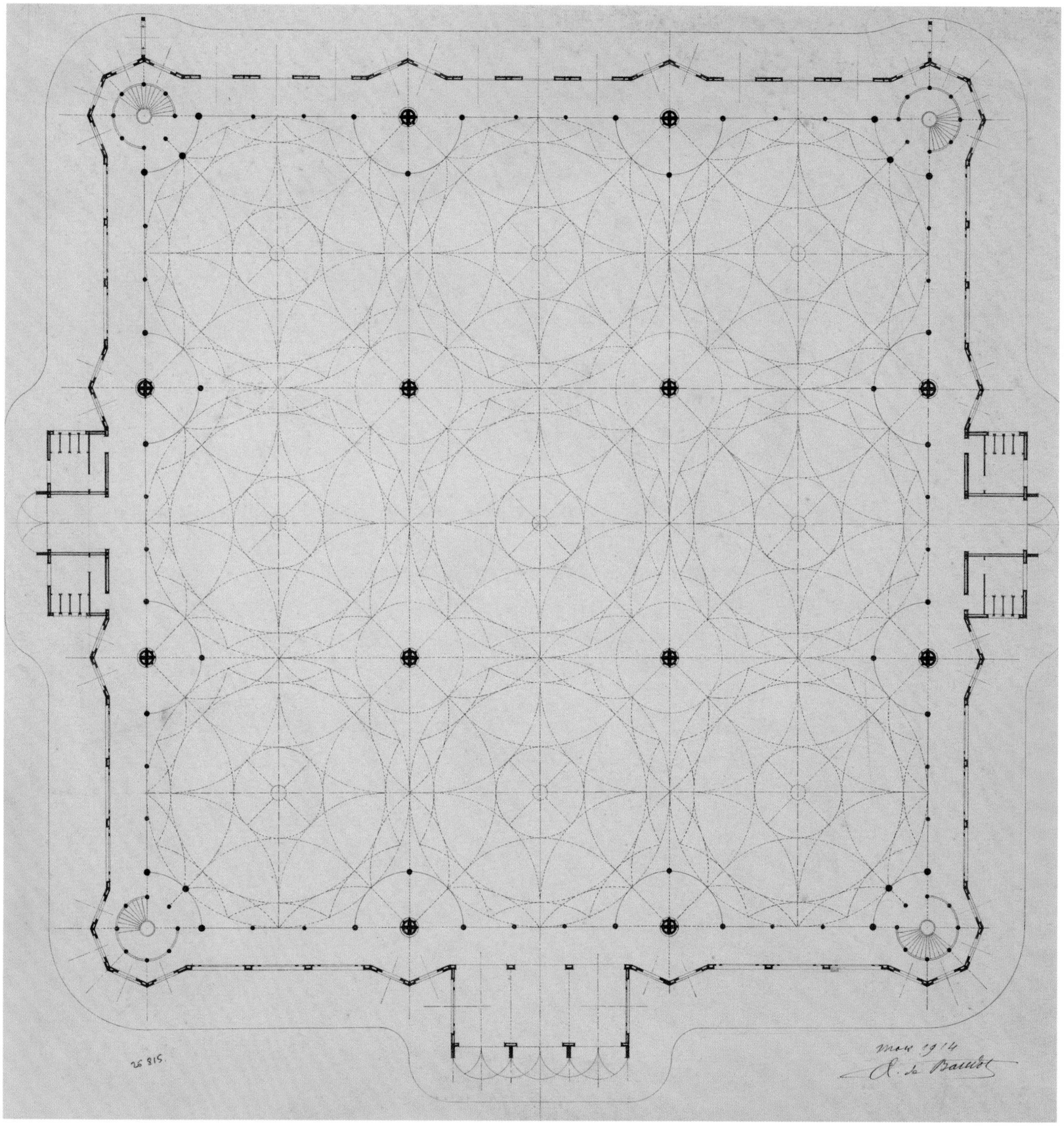
26 815.
Mars 1914
A. de Baudot

Mars 1914
A. de Baudot

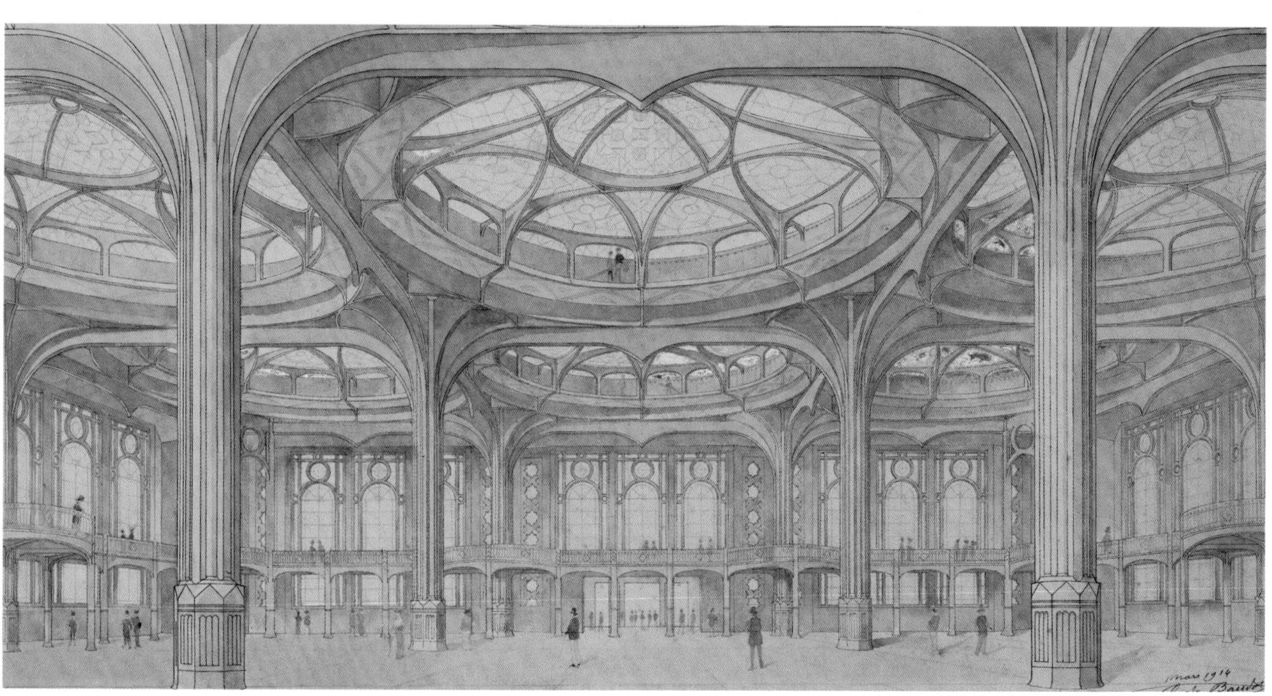

In France, the Hôtel des Archives Départementales de la Gironde (1859–66), in Bordeaux, by Pierre-Auguste Labbé (1825–1881), and the Musée-Bibliothèque de Grenoble (1862–72), by Charles Questel (1807–1888), also attest to the influence of the Bibliothèque Sainte-Geneviève. However, the building for which the connection remains the most direct and fullest is the Bibliothèque de l'Ecole de Droit (Law School Library), built between 1876 and1878 by Louis-Ernest Lheureux (1827–1898), a student of Labrouste.

The Bibliothèque de l'Ecole de Droit was his major work. A specialized library, with the books arranged around the perimeter of the reading room, it had seats for seventy-six readers. Although much smaller than the nearby Bibliothèque Sainte-Geneviève, it shared its spirit. The facade on the Rue Cujas was very sober and drew its aesthetic effects from a sheer unadorned wall, accented by three great round arch windows (fig. 18). Inside, three arches separating the two reading rooms echoed them. Each of the reading rooms was covered with a central glass roof, supported on metal trusses projecting from the four corners of the rooms (fig. 17). The skylights were set into glazed brick vaults sprung from the unadorned masonry walls. If the constructional system and combination of materials were tributes to Viollet-le-Duc, the atmosphere and general harmony of the space attest to Labrouste's influence: a dual lighting system—zenithal from skylights

17. Louis-Ernest Lheureux, Library at the Ecole de Droit in Paris, first reading room (1876–78, demolished c. 1969), F. Narjoux, *Paris, Monuments élevés par la ville, 1850–1880*, vol. 2 (Paris: Vve A. Morel, 1883)

18. Louis-Ernest Lheureux, Library at the Ecole de Droit in Paris, elevation of the main facade (1876–78, demolished c. 1969), F. Narjoux, *Paris, Monuments élevés par la ville, 1850–1880*, vol. 2 (Paris: Vve A. Morel, 1883)

19. Louis-Ernest Lheureux, Library at the Ecole de Droit in Paris, second reading room (1893–98, demolished c. 1969). Photograph: A. Cary, undated, CAPA, Archives du XXe siècle, Paris, FD-25-10-11-01

and lateral from the great glazed bays—the rich decoration of the upper reaches of the walls, the polychromy of the iron painted dark blue-gray with gold highlights are all to be noted.[35]

Lheureux built a second reading room for the law school, with 230 seats, between 1893 and 1898 (fig. 19). The interior now was closer to the Bibliothèque Nationale, particularly in its proportions. The principle behind its construction was similar to the first reading room's, although it was more complex. The glazed skylight was still carried on arches at the corners of the room, but these now held aloft four large and particularly spectacular iron trusses spanning the great width of the room. Many ornamental details recalled Labrouste's work: the open-work metal trusses had palmettes similar to those of the Bibliothèque Sainte-Geneviève; the detailing of the railings evoked the aesthetic of the great lamp standards on the Pont de la Concorde; the draped motif on the brick vaults was often used by Labrouste, as in the entrance hall of the Bibliothèque Nationale. The Bibliothèque de l'École de Droit's two reading rooms were demolished in 1969.

THE RATIONAL EXPRESSION OF THE PROGRAM

The Crédit Lyonnais headquarters illustrates the complexity of the new programs architects confronted in the second half of the nineteenth century. In that time of innovation, Labrouste's students excelled at organizing plans and were sought out by the government and large businesses.

35. *Encyclopédie d'architecture*, vol. 10 (1881), 91; and vol. 1 (1888–89), 179–80.
36. Similarities in program also cited by Guadet in *Éléments et théorie de l'architecture*.
37. Marc Le Coeur, *Charles Le Coeur (1830–1906): Architecte et premier amateur de Renoir* (Paris: Réunion des musées nationaux, 1996), 61.

Throughout his career, Charles Le Coeur (1830–1906) applied the principles he had learned from his master: a rational composition based on an analysis of the program, a choice of appropriate materials and facade design, and the accommodation of occupants and users. In 1869, Le Coeur was commissioned to provide a design for the Lycée at Bayonne, where construction would last from 1874 to 1879. There, the architect would perfect one of the very first models for the expanding system of French secondary schools. Labrouste's seminary at Rennes, then nearing completion, inspired the plans and in part the decoration: Le Coeur's school was organized like a monastery around a large courtyard, with a chapel on the axis of entry. The courtyard was ringed with arcades whose round arches are picked out in alternating white and gray key voussoirs (fig. 20).[36] Le Coeur's attention to the needs of the students added to the project's success—the Lycée at Bayonne looked neither like a barracks, nor like a monument, but rather like a "house for learning."[37]

In 1879, when he was named Minister of Public Instruction, Jules Ferry set out to reform French primary and secondary education, which included an ambitious architectural policy. Several of Labrouste's students—de Baudot, Boeswillwald, Le Coeur—were on

20. Charles Le Cœur, Lycée de Bayonne (1869, 1874–79), perspective of a gallery in the courtyard and perspective of the north facade with the chapel, undated, CAPA, Archives du XXe siècle, Paris, FD-14-12-07-19

21. Charles Le Cœur, Petit Lycée Condorcet in Paris (1881–82), view of the entrance, anonymous, photograph, undated, 38.7 × 28.4 cm, Musée d'Orsay, Paris

38. Ibid., 62–64.
39. This quote and the following ones: Julien Guadet, "Le Nouvel hôtel des Postes à Paris," *Encyclopédie d'architecture*, no. 12 (June 1887): 83–95.
40. Jacques Lucan, "La tradition rationaliste," "Eugène Viollet-le-Duc," and "Julien Guadet," in *Encyclopédie Perret*, eds. Jean-Louis Cohen, Joseph Abram, Guy Lambert (Paris: Monum/Éditions du Patrimoine, Éditions du Moniteur, 2002).

the board of the new Commission des Bâtiments des Lycées et Collèges (Commission of Secondary School Buildings).[38] De Baudot would build the remarkable Lycée Lakanal in Sceaux and Le Coeur no fewer than seven secondary schools, including the Lycée Montaigne and the new Lycée Louis-le-Grand in Paris. The new school architecture was stamped with a spirit of rationalism and can be understood as "a lesson in things," or more specifically, as a lesson in construction. The interplay of materials, the distinction between structure and non-load-bearing elements, acted as decoration. Le Coeur also added more precise references to the universe of Labrouste's style. The main entrance to the Petit Lycée Condorcet (1881–82), with its severely detailed round arched portal adorned with three antique-style heads and above a series of openings cut into the wall, has the same type of Etruscan austerity that Labrouste valued (fig. 21).

The new main post office (Hôtel des Postes) in Paris, built by Guadet from 1880 to 1886, is another example of a complex, unprecedented building (fig. 22). It must be understood, as the architect explained, as both a factory—handling all the mail received in and sent from the nation's capital—and as a monument set in the very heart of the city. In order to superimpose on different floors vast open spaces able to support considerable loads, the architect conceived an extremely modern building, both structurally speaking and in its technical systems: a metal frame construction that would resist any structural deformation and whose masonry facades "support only their own weight and are nothing but enclosures"[39] (fig. 23). The building is thus well suited for "potential changes from the initial layout that might be frequent or even sweeping." Answering his critics, Guadet affirmed that he attached great importance to giving the building an appearance in harmony with its function. He explained that the Hôtel des Postes was not a palace and should not pretend to be one, and underscored that rich effects were easy to create, where as nothing was more difficult than producing an artistic impression with sobriety. As a result, the building's facades are the exact transcription of its construction, with their protruding buttresses, and of its plan, through the dimensions of the spans and openings. Guadet derived his architecture also from the building's need to fill out its site to the street-line on the Rue du Louvre—which meant that it could only be seen obliquely. So Guadet developed a rhythm of wall buttresses which provided rich effects seen from the side: "The rational expression of the construction thus offered me effects which worked well in the building's particular setting."

22. Julien Guadet, New Hôtel des Postes (Central Post Office) in Paris (1880–86), cross section, *Encyclopédie d'Architecture*, no. 12, June 1887, pl. 1124
23. Julien Guadet, New Hôtel des Postes in Paris (1880–86), elevation of the main facade, July 13, 1880, 58.6 × 91.3 cm, Paris, CAPA, Archives du XXe siècle, FC-01-02-02-09

"THE ART OF MAKING STRUCTURAL JOINTS SING"

Auguste Perret (1874–1954) was without doubt the last French architect with an explicit connection to Labrouste. A student of Guadet at the Ecole des Beaux-Arts and an attentive reader of Viollet-le-Duc, he offered a synthesis of rationalist viewpoints, not without complexities and ambiguities.[40] His work is grounded in structural

COUPE TRANSVERSALE
Echelle de 0 10 20 Mètres

Dressé par l'Architecte soussigné
Paris le 13 Juillet 1880

41. Auguste Perret, Sébastien Voirol, *Le Style sans ornement* (1914), in *Auguste Perret: Anthologie des écrits, conférences et entretiens* (Paris: Éditions du Moniteur, 2006), 82.
42. Auguste Perret, "L'Architecture," *Revue d'art et d'esthétique*, nos. 1–2 (June 1935): 41–50 and plate.
43. Interview with Oscar Nitzchke (1983), published in Joseph Abram, "Perret et l'école du classicisme structurel (1910–1960)," vol. 2 (research report, SRA-EAN, Nancy, 1985), 68.
44. Auguste Perret, "L' Architecture," op. cit., 49.

thinking, apparent in all of his designs, given the prominence of an expressed structural frame which orders the construction, layout, and aesthetic of the buildings. His thinking was a continuation of the teachings of the Ecole des Beaux-Arts since the nineteenth century. For Perret, the design process should be governed by a rational composition and a principle of unity, even though such an approach was considered false thinking by the architects in the modern movement. In that respect, Perret occupied a somewhat anachronistic place in his period. He was, like Labrouste, someone who transmitted a font of historical knowledge.

Furthermore, Perret never hid his admiration for Labrouste, whom he recognized as a precursor and, above all, a great architect. In 1914, he wrote: "We have a first modern architecture; it belongs to those who had the courage to use iron. Labrouste designed the great reading room at the Bibliothèque Nationale using a modern principle that offered up the most elegant of results."[41] He would repeat this idea in numerous lectures. Labrouste's work for him was an essential milestone in the history of architecture. This can be seen in the four photographs he chose in 1935 to illustrate the publication of his lecture "L'Architecture": the Parthenon, Chartres Cathedral, the reading room at

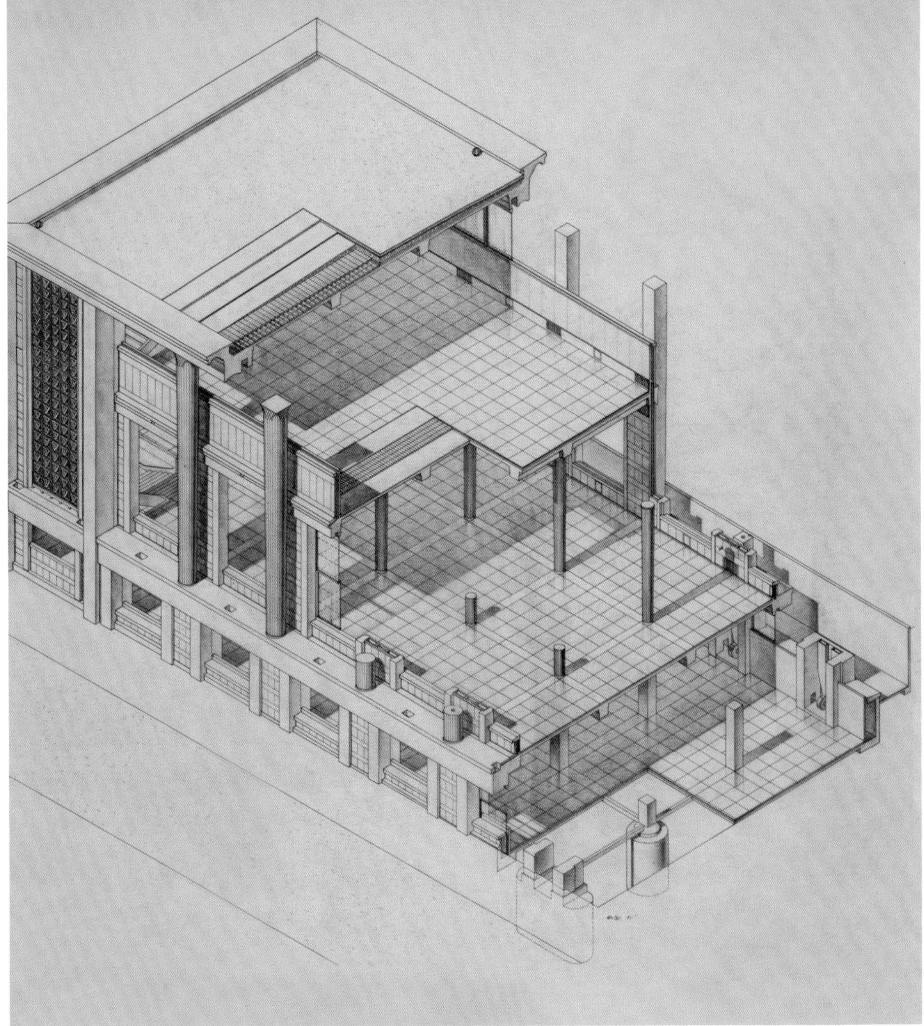

the Bibliothèque Nationale, and finally his own Théâtre des Champs-Elysées—that is, an ancient temple, a Gothic cathedral, iron architecture, and modern concrete architecture.[42] The acknowledged connection did not escape Perret's students, as Oscar Nitzchke noted: "He was very proud of the projects he had undertaken at the Ecole des Beaux-Arts and sent us to the library to admire the Grand Prix de Rome designs of architects such as Labrouste ... It's true, they were great! He considered himself to be something of a successor to Labrouste and told us to go see Sainte-Geneviève and the reading room at the Bibliothèque Nationale."[43]

Confronted, like Labrouste, with the search for a form to give a new material, Perret would give reinforced concrete its place among noble materials. Guadet had instilled in him the conviction that classical architecture was the best source of inspiration for designing contemporary buildings. Indeed, concrete's "true" structure, provided by wooden formwork, is that of a skeleton made up of posts and lintels; it was thus the natural descendant of the ancient temple, the column, and the flat arch beam. Like Labrouste, Perret would favor strictly vertical distribution of loads. Architecture, according to Perret, was essentially a "noble shelter." Like the reading room at the Bibliothèque Nationale, the large naves he built seem to be "composed from the top": a vault, a protecting ceiling set upon lightweight supports. "Architecture is the art of making structural joints sing,"[44] he wrote—a definition that applies perfectly to Labrouste's work. Perret would thus undertake a continuous search to define the reinforced concrete column. At the church of Notre-Dame du Raincy (1923), the extremely pared down columns, with neither base nor capital, are the expression of a

Previous pages:
24. Musée des Travaux Publics in Paris, view of the hypostyle hall. Photograph: Benoit Fougeirol

25. Auguste and Gustave Perret, Musée des Travaux Publics in Paris (1936–48), view of the hypostyle hall. Photograph: Chevojon studio, undated, 22.8 × 28.9 cm, Paris, CAPA, Archives du XXe siècle, CNAM-36-01-FF

26. Auguste and Gustave Perret, Musée des Travaux Publics in Paris, (1936–48), uncovered axonometric projection, undated, 66.5 × 99.2 cm, Paris, CAPA, Archives du XXe siècle, CNAM-36-01-0343

45. Auguste Perret, "Contribution à une théorie de l'architecture," *Techniques et architecture* (January 1945).

continuous material (fig. 27); at the Musée des Travaux Publics (1936–48), they grow progressively wider and flare at the top into extraordinary capitals that unite post and lintel (fig. 25). Furthermore, Perret employed a process of interlocking structures that are revealed by the building's axonometrics (fig. 26): the exterior columns support the roof-terrace and form the "shelter," while a double row of interior columns supports an intermediary floor, creating a hypostyle room that is just as remarkable as Labrouste's reading rooms in its coherency, elegance, and luminosity. "The architect is a poet who thinks and speaks in construction."[45]

Henri Labrouste had a profound influence on architectural design, on his fellow artists at the Villa Medici, on his pupils, on his contemporaries, and on later generations. It can be seen in the developments of architectural rationalism and its ramifications, structural rationalism or reasoned composition, with references to Gothic architecture or classical models. The great diversity of his students' works is a testament to the richness of his teachings. Labrouste invented a new architecture. For the first time in centuries, a material with properties radically different from those of stone, brick, or wood was available and opened up new horizons for construction, aesthetics, and composition. Labrouste masterfully teased out its possibilities and left as his legacy a vision of construction and form that could further develop in diverse directions. His art in handling structural joints, ornamentation, and light, in designing large public halls that were elegant and engaging, inspired generations of architects. However, World War I was a time of transition. If Perret still claimed a direct connection to Labrouste, the rise of the modern movement signaled the decline of the latter's influence on architectural production and, along with it, the growing importance of his place in historiography. The work of this exceptional architect has thus entered the history of architecture, becoming an indispensable reference point that is reinterpreted by each generation.

27. Auguste and Gustave Perret, Eglise Notre-Dame-de-la-Consolation in Raincy (1922–23), interior view facing the gallery. Photograph: Chevojon studio, undated, CAPA, Archives du XXe siècle, CNAM-22-01-L

APPENDICES

LABROUSTE'S PRINCIPLE PROJECTS AND CONSTRUCTIONS

Marc Le Cœur

AT THE ECOLE DES BEAUX-ARTS, 1818–24

1821 – Competition entry for the Grand Prix de Rome: "A courthouse" (2nd grand prize)
1824 – Competition entry for the Grand Prix de Rome: "A royal court of appeals" (1st grand prize)

SUBMISSIONS FROM ROME, 1825–30

1825–26 (1st year)
("Studies of details from the most beautiful ancient monuments: One quarter scale") Temple of Antoninus and Faustina in Rome
1826–27 (2nd year)
(same guidelines as for the 1st year submission) Trajan's Column in Rome, Arch of Trajan in Benevento, and the Arch of Titus in Rome
1827–28 (3rd year)
("Studies of details from the most beautiful ancient monuments, as well as a portion of the building from which these details are taken, indicating its proportions and construction") A parallel drawing of the Flavian Amphitheater (Colosseum) and the Theater of Marcellus in Rome
1828–29 (4th year)
("The restoration of an ancient monument in Italy and a historical synopsis of its antiquity and construction, etc.") "Plan for the restoration of the ancient city of Poseidonia (Paestum)"
1829–30 (5th year)
("A project for a public monument of his own composition in keeping with French conventions")
1st study plan (not sent): "Monument designed to house the wreckage of a famous shipwreck" (Cenotaph of La Pérouse and his crew)
2nd study project: "Plan for a monument to be situated on the border of France and Italy" (border bridge)

1830 – Studies for the tomb of Victor de Lanneau (1758–1830), re-founder then head of the Collège Sainte-Barbe in Paris

---

1831 – Organization of celebrations for the first anniversary of the July 1830 Revolution and laying of the July column's cornerstone, Place de la Bastille, Paris, July 27, 1831 (Jean-Antoine Alavoine, managing architect; Labrouste and Félix Duban, assistant architects)

C. 1831 – Studies for a commemorative monument for the July 1830 revolution

---

1832–38 – Enlargement of the Ecole des Beaux-Arts (Labrouste, Félix Duban's inspector)
Paris, 14 Rue Bonaparte (today Ecole Nationale Supérieure des Beaux-Arts)

1835–36 – Competition entry for the construction of the Eglise Saint-Paul in Nîmes, Gard (submitted?)

1836–37 – Competition entry for the construction of a cantonal asylum for the insane in Lausanne, Switzerland (1st prize)

1836–40 – Project for the decoration and lighting of the Pont de la Concorde (bridge) in Paris (with architect Théodore Labrouste)

1837 – Tomb of Baron André de Ridèle (Andreas von Riedel; 1748–1837)
Paris, Cimetière de Montparnasse, 8th division (tomb demolished in April 1988)

1838 – Preliminary plans for a cantonal asylum for the insane in Lausanne, Switzerland, "on a flat site" and "on a sloped site"

1838–48 – Restoration studies of several historic monuments in the Paris region: the Collégiale Notre-Dame de Mantes (now Mantes-la-Jolie; 1838–43), Tour de Montlhéry (1842–47), churches in Triel (Triel-sur-Seine; 1842), Deuil (Deuil-la-Barre; 1842), Saint-Leu-Taverny (Taverny; 1842–48), and Villiers-le-Bel (1844–47)

1838–50 – Reconstruction of the Bibliothèque Sainte-Geneviève
Paris, 10 Place du Panthéon (library) and 8 Place du Panthéon (administration building: currently university buildings and the Jacques-Doucet literary library)

1838–71 – Maintenance of the Dépôt des Marbres
Paris, 182 then 216 Rue de l'Université (all demolished in 1936)

1839–40 – Competition entry for the construction of a prison in Alessandria, near Turin, Piedmont (1st prize)

1840 – Streetlights for the Pont de la Concorde
Paris, Pont de la Concorde (candelabras removed when the bridge was enlarged in 1930–32; one relocated to a private residence, Fontainebleau)

1840 – Title page and introductory frontispiece of the *Revue générale de l'architecture et des travaux publics*, newly founded by César Daly, with the engravers John Andrew, Adolphe-Jean Best, and Isidore Leloir (title page), and A. Thiebault (frontispiece)
The two images appear as an opening to the first thirty volumes of the review (1840–73)

1840 – Project for the construction of public slaughterhouses in Provins, Seine-et-Marne (honorable mention)

1840 – Organization of the ceremony for the return of the remains of Napoléon in Courbevoie and Paris on December 15, 1840 (with architect Louis Visconti)

1840–41 – Tomb of François Brunet (1733–1818), architect-engineer, and his family, Paris, Père-Lachaise cemetery, 28th division

1840–54 – Reconstruction of the Collège Sainte-Barbe (with architect Théodore Labrouste)
Paris, 2 Rue Cujas (buildings demolished in 1942, except the entry building, constructed by Théodore Labrouste alone, today the Cujas Library)

1841 – Project for the construction of the tomb of Napoléon I beneath the dome of the Eglise des Invalides in Paris (gold medal)

1843 – Construction of a building with wood panels in the courtyard of a house
Paris, formerly 10 Rue des Beaux-Arts (building demolished?)

1843–63 – Upkeep and development of Gabriel Dutillet's mansion
Paris, 20 Rue de l'Université

1843–44 – Theater project for the city of Bucharest, Romania

1844 – Medal commemorating the laying of the first cornerstone for the new Bibliothèque Sainte-Geneviève (with sculptor Jean-Baptiste-Jules Klagmann and engraver D. Fournera)

1844 – Competition entry for the construction of the church of Saint-Aubin in Toulouse, Haute-Garonne

1844 – Project for a cast-iron staircase for the home of Prince Barbu Stirbei (1799–1869), Minister of the Interior, in Bucharest, Romania

1844 – "Project for a building to house a trial furnace for steam engine machines,"
Paris, Dépôt des Marbres, Rue de l'Université (all demolished in 1936)

1845 – Project for the home of Charles de Chollet in Fribourg, Switzerland

C. 1845 – Project for the home of M. Frémy

C. 1845 – Project for a home in Bilbao, Spain

C. 1845 – Studies for framing a portrait of Rachel Félix, called Rachel (1821–1858), a dramatic actress

1845–48 – Works for the Mesnil-Saint-Firmin agricultural colony, essentially expanding the building for colonists and building a stable for cattle
Rouvroy-les-Merles, Oise (the buildings, later expanded, would until 2009 house a Center for Agricultural Training).

1846–47 – Attendance token for the Société Centrale des Architectes (with the sculptor and engraver Eugène-André Oudiné)

1848 – Organized a national funeral for the victims of the June 1848 insurrections on July 6, 1848 (with the architect Louis-Joseph Duc)

1850 – "Project for storehouses and warehouses ... intended to store orange trees and equipment for the Tuileries garden, furniture for public holidays and ceremonies, and the different services related to them"
Paris, Dépôt des Marbres, Rue de l'Université (all demolished in 1936)

1851–52 – Project for rebuilding the Marché du Temple in Paris

1851–70 – Upkeep of several Paris residential buildings belonging to Armand Marchand (1803–1870), Councillor of State: 16 (later 108) Rue Lafayette, 288 Rue Saint-Honoré, 37 Rue de l'Arbre-Sec and 1 Rue Bailleul, 18 Rue de Paradis-Poissonnière

1852 – Tomb of Antoine Albouse (1795-1852), head joiner on the Bibliothèque Sainte-Geneviève worksite in Paris, Cimetière de Montparnasse, 6th division (tomb demolished in May 1953)

1852–53 – Transformation of Alexandre Labrouste's Fontenay house ("Le Petit-Bard")
Fontenay-aux-Roses, Hauts-de-Seine (house demolished)

1852–60 – New buildings for the annex of the Collège Sainte-Barbe ("Sainte-Barbe-des-Champs")
Fontenay-aux-Roses, Hauts-de-Seine, 6 to 10 Place du Château-Sainte-Barbe and 4 to 6 Avenue du Parc (buildings modified in 1928 by architect Georges Boiret to house different municipal departments and a school; only the facade of the former entrance to the school remains unchanged)

C. 1852? – Project for framing a portrait of Victor de Lanneau (see 1830), most likely for the Collège Sainte-Barbe in Paris

1854–75 – Restoration and enlargement of the Bibliothèque Impériale, later Nationale
Paris, 58 Rue de Richelieu (currently the Bibliothèque Nationale de France, Richelieu site; in 2014, the main reading room and former central print storehouse will be allocated to the INHA, and part of the lateral storehouses to the Ecole Nationale des Chartes)

1854–75 – Upkeep of the old seminary, the cathedral, and the bishop's (later archbishop's) residence in Rennes, Ille-et-Vilaine

1854–75 – Reconstruction of the seminary in Rennes
Rennes, Ille-et-Vilaine, 7 Place Hoche (currently the Université de Rennes-1, Department of Economics)

1855–56 – Medal commemorating the reconstruction of the seminary in Rennes (with the sculptor and engraver Eugène-André Oudiné)

1856–58 – Mansion of Louis Fould (1794–1858), banker and collector
Paris, 29 and 31 Rue de Berri (mansion demolished c. 1929)

C. 1856–60 – "Project for a general livestock market" in Paris (two distinct plans, including one for the La Villette site)

1857 – Preliminary plans of a home for Armand Marchand (see 1851), Rue de Paradis-Poissonnière in Paris

1857 – Iron greenhouse in the garden of the bishop's residence in Rennes, Ille-et-Vilaine

1857–58 – Tomb of Charles-Marie Magnin-Cugny (1809–1857), subprefect of studies at the Collège Sainte-Barbe-des-Champs
Fontenay-aux-Roses, Hauts-de-Seine, municipal cemetery, 1st division

1857–58 – Project for the restoration of the Banque de France's Gilded Gallery, Paris (with architect Gabriel Crétin)

1857–59 – Covering for one or two sets of front steps with a cast-iron veranda at the château of Henri-Louis Thuret (1811–1871), Louis Fould's son-in-law
Château de Lévy, by Lurcy-Lévis, Allier; Château de Lévis, formerly Lévy (the verandas are no longer extant)

1857–61 – Repair work on the château of Baron André-Hélène Roger (1804-1880), banker
Saint-Martin-du-Tertre, Val-d'Oise, Château de Franconville-aux-Bois (rebuilt in 1876–82 by architect Gabriel-Hippolyte Destailleur)

1857–67 – Diverse works for the mansion of Baron André-Hélène Roger (Hôtel de Massa), notably: decoration and furniture for a living room (1860), and the construction of a photography workshop in the garden for Alfred Régnier de Gronau, Duc de Massa (1837–1913), the owner's stepson (1864–65)
Paris, 6 Rue d'Angoulême-Saint-Honoré, later 2 Rue de Morny (mansion transported to 38 Rue du Faubourg-Saint-Jacques in 1927–28, where it has since housed the headquarters of the Société des Gens de Lettres)

1858–59 – Project for a reconstruction of the Ecole Polytechnique on Chaillot hill in Paris

1858–59 – Diverse works for the château of Ernestan-Charles-Adrien, Baron Fayau de Vilgruy (1799–1879), businessman, in Perray
Saint-Pierre-du-Perray, Essonne (château destroyed by fire in 1993)

1860 – Monument to Abbé Charles-François Lhomond (1727–1794), grammarian (with sculptor Eugène-Louis Lequesne)
Chaulnes, Somme, Place de la Mairie (monument destroyed in World War I; a replica of the statue by sculptor Albert Roze was erected on the same site around 1930)

1860 – Preliminary plans for the construction of a protestant church in Munster, Haut-Rhin

1860–C. 1862 – Villa of François-Armand Thouret (c. 1814–1889), goldsmith
Neuilly-sur-Seine, Hauts-de-Seine, 68 Boulevard Bourdon

1860–1862 – Alteration and decoration works on the mansion of Thomas-Philippe-Antoine Riera et Roses, Marquis de Casa Riera (1790–1881); former Hôtel Fould
Paris, 29 and 31 Rue de Berri (mansion demolished in 1929)

1860–1863 – Diverse works for the Congrégation des Dames de la Retraite
Paris, formerly 15 Rue du Regard

1860–1863 – Headquarters of the Compagnie des Chemins de Fer de Paris à Lyon et à la Méditerranée
Paris, formerly 44 Rue Neuve-des-Mathurins (the large covered courtyard and part of the buildings were destroyed in the late 1860s, when the Boulevard Haussmann was cut through; it seems, however, that facades designed by Labrouste remain at the corner of the Rue de Provence and the Rue Charras)

C. 1861–C. 1863 – Villa of François-Pierre-Léon Rouvenat (1809–1874), jeweler
Neuilly-sur-Seine, Hauts-de-Seine (villa demolished?)

1863–C. 1866 – Mansion of Ernestan-Charles-Adrien, Baron Fayau de Vilgruy (1799–1879), businessman (Hôtel de Vilgruy)
Paris, 9 Rue François-Ier and 16 Rue Jean-Goujon

1865 – Tomb of Bernard Zolla (1797–1864), architect
Chalon-sur-Saône, Saône-et-Loire, Cimetière de l'Est (tomb demolished c. 1971)

1867–1868 – Project for a villa for [Adolphe?] de Lanneau in Cannes, Alpes-Maritimes

---

1868 – Competition entry for the construction of a protestant church in Lille, Nord (submitted?)

1868–1875 – Reconstruction of the stables and sheds at the archbishop's residence in Rennes, Ille-et-Vilaine

---

C. 1868 – Project for a tomb for the Meritorrem family

C. 1871 – Project for a storehouse for the Hachette bookstore, no doubt on the Rue Pierre-Sarrazin in Paris

---

1872 – Project for the tomb of Félix Duban (1798–1870), architect, in Paris

---

1872 – Competition entry for the erection of "commemorative stones on various battlefields in the Seine and Seine-et-Oise departments, in honor of Paris's defenders"

1872–1873 – Tomb of Louise Thouret (1843–1858), her brother Auguste (1842–1843), and their mother, née Esther Rouvenat (c. 1815–1869), with the sculptor Pierre-Jules Cavelier
Paris, Cimetière de Montmartre, 5th division

1874 – Monument to Ulrich Gering, creator of the first printing house in France, in 1470 (with the sculptor Louis-Joseph Daumas)
Paris, at the Bibliothèque Sainte-Geneviève (monument moved to its current location in Puteaux, Fonds National d'Art Contemporain)

1875 – Competition entry for the construction of a "Funeral monument commemorating the battle fought by the French against the Prussian army in Coulmiers on November 9, 1870"

1875 – Project for a monument to Augustin Cochin (1823–1872), the prefect of Seine-et-Oise, member of the Institut de France (carried out after Labrouste's death by the architect Paul Abadie, with "some slight modifications")
Paris, garden of the Hôpital Cochin, 27 Rue du Faubourg-Saint-Jacques (monument demolished?)

SELECTED BIBLIOGRAPHY

Compiled by Marc Le Cœur

Alaux, Jean-Paul. "Labrouste. 1801–1875." In *Académie de France à Rome. Ses directeurs. Ses pensionnaires*. Vol. 2. Paris: Duchartre, 1933.

Anonymous. "Le pont de la Concorde. Exécution du Projet de M. Labrouste." *L'Artiste*, 2nd ser., vol. 7, no. 3 (1841): 35–37, ill.

Anonymous. "Translation des cendres de Napoléon." *Le Magasin pittoresque* 9 (February 1841): 41–48, ill.

Anonymous. "Bibliothèque de Sainte-Geneviève. Translation et établissement provisoire. Construction définitive projetée." *Revue générale de l'architecture et des travaux publics* 3 (July 1842): col. 332–35.

Anonymous. "Colonie agricole du Mesnil-Saint-Firmin." *L'Illustration. Journal universel* 9, no. 218 (May 1, 1847): 133–34, ill.

Anonymous. "Histoire de la semaine," *L'Illustration. Journal universel* 9, no. 281 (July 15, 1848): 295–97, ill.

Anonymous. "Funeral of the 'Victims of June.'" *The Illustrated London News* 13, no. 326 (July 15, 1848): 19–20, ill.

Anonymous. "Jeton et médaille de la Société centrale des architects." *Revue générale de l'architecture et des travaux publics* 8, no. 4/5 (1849–50): col. 151, pl. 17.

Anonymous. "The New Building of the Library, Saint Genevieve, place du Pantheon, Paris." *The Builder* 9, no. 417 (February 1, 1851): 72–73.

Anonymous. "Bibliotheque Sainte Genevieve, at Paris. M. Labrousse [sic], Architect." *The Architect: In Cooperation with the Civil Engineer and Architect's Journal* 14, no. 181 (May 3, 1851): 258–59, ill.; no. 207 (November 1, 1851): 561, pl. 20.

Anonymous. "Die Bibliothek St. Geneviève in Paris." *Allgemeine Bauzeitung*, 17th year (1852): 139–42, pl. 469–75.

Anonymous. "[Histoire] Monographie de la Bibliothèque Impériale." *Le Moniteur des Architectes*, 2nd ser., vol. 7, no. 1 (January 15, 1857): col. 5–8, pl. 457–62; no. 2 (March 1857): col. 37–38, pl. 480; no. 6 (November 1857): col. 116–19.

Anonymous. "Restauration des bâtiments de la Bibliothèque impériale." *Encyclopédie d'architecture* 8, no. 2 (February 1858): col. 25–26; no. 3 (March 1858): pl. 28; no. 4 (April 1858): pl. 38–40; no. 10 (October 1858): pl. 99, 100; no. 12 (December 1858): pl. 116, 117; vol. 10, no. 10 (October 1860): pl. 97, 98.

Anonymous. "The New Reading-Room at the Imperial Library of Paris." *The Illustrated London News* 53, no. 1508 (October 24, 1868): 409–10, ill.

Anonymous. "The Imperial Library of Paris." *The Westminster and Foreign Quarterly Review* 37, no. 2 (April 1, 1870): 429–60.

Anonymous. "La Bibliothèque nationale." *Paris nouveau illustré*, no. 19 (1872): 290–98, ill.

Anonymous. "Bibliothèque nationale, rue de Richelieu, à Paris, par M. Henri Labrouste, architecte." *Revue générale de l'architecture et des travaux publics* 30 (1873): col. 245, pl. 56–58.

Anonymous. "Porte et tambour d'entrée de la grande salle de travail des imprimés de la Bibliothèque nationale, à Paris." *Revue générale de l'architecture et des travaux publics* 36 (1879): col. 153, pl. 40, 41.

Anonymous. *Décorations intérieures et extérieures de la Bibliothèque Nationale. Ancien Palais Mazarin*. 2 vols. Paris: Armand Guérinet, n.d. [c. 1900].

Arrechea Miguel, Julio. "Modelos para una síntesis. L'Ecole des Beaux-Arts y la biblioteca Sainte Geneviève." *Anales de arquitectura*, 2nd year, no. 2 (1990): 25–35.

Avakian, Gr. "Rilievi inediti di monumenti etruschi e romani." *Ephemeris Dacoromana. Annuario della Scuola romena di Roma* 6 (1935): 129–203.

Bacha, Myriam, and **Christian Hottin**, eds. *Les Bibliothèques parisiennes. Architecture et décor*. Paris: Action artistique de la Ville de Paris, 2002.

Bailly, Antoine-Nicolas. [*Institut de France, Académie des beaux-arts*] *Notice sur M. Henri Labrouste. Lue dans la séance du 16 décembre 1876*. Paris: Firmin-Didot, 1876.

Banti, Luisa. "Disegni di tombe e monumenti etruschi fra il 1825 e il 1830: l'architetto Henri Labrouste." *Studi Etruschi* 35, 2nd ser. (1967): 575–93, pl. 108–20.

Banville, Théodore de. "Le quartier Latin et la bibliothèque Sainte-Geneviève." In *Paris-Guide*. Vol. 2, *La Cie*. Paris: A. Lacroix, Verboeckhoven, 1867.

Barone, Maria Chiara. "Piliers cruciformes et colonnes en fonte: Le cas de la Bibliothèque Sainte-Geneviève de Labrouste." In *La Colonne. Nouvelle histoire de la construction*, edited by Roberto Gargiani. Lausanne: Presses polytechniques et universitaires romandes, 2008.

Barrière, François. "[Feuilleton du Journal des débats] Embellissements de Paris." *Journal des débats politiques et littéraires* (December 31, 1850): n.p.

Baudot, Anatole de. "Bibliothèque impériale de Paris. Nouvelle salle de lecture." *Gazette des architectes et du bâtiment*, 3rd year, no. 7 (1865): 107–8.

Bellenger, Sylvain, and **Françoise Hamon,** eds. *Félix Duban. 1798–1870. Les couleurs de l'architecte*. Paris: Gallimard/Electa, 1996.

Benoît, Jérémie, Agnès Delannoy, and **Alain Pougetoux.** *Napoléon. Le Retour des Cendres (1840–1990)*. Courbevoie: Musée Roybet-Fould, 1990.

Béraldi, Henri. *Voyage d'un livre à travers la Bibliothèque nationale*. Paris: G. Masson, 1893.

Bergdoll, Barry. *Léon Vaudoyer: Historicism in the Age of Industry*. New York: Architectural History Foundation; Cambridge, Mass.: MIT Press, 1994.

———. "'. . . en général de très honnêtes rebelles': Fragmentary Notes on a Newly Discovered Album of French Romantic Architectural Compositions." In *Fragments: Architecture and the Unfinished: Essays Presented to Robin Middleton*, edited by Barry Bergdoll and Werner Oechslin. London: Thames & Hudson, 2006.

Bernard, Léo de. "La nouvelle salle de lecture de la Bibliothèque impériale inaugurée le 15 juin." *Le Monde illustré*, 12th year, no. 585 (June 27, 1868): 408, 410, ill.

Beutler, Christian. "Saint-Eugène und die Bibliothèque Nationale. Zwei Eisenkonstruktionen und ihr Ideengehalt." In *Miscellanea Pro Arte. Festschrift für Hermann Schnitzler*. Düsseldorf: Verlag L. Schwann, 1965.

Blasselle, Bruno, and **Jacqueline Melet-Sanson.** *La Bibliothèque nationale. Mémoire de l'avenir*. Paris: Gallimard, 1990.

Bougy, Alfred de. *Histoire de la bibliothèque Sainte-Geneviève*. Paris: Comptoir des Imprimeurs-Unis, 1847.

Bouquillard, Jocelyn. *La Résurrection de Pompéi. Dessins d'archéologues des XVIIIe et XIXe siècles*. Arcueil: Anthèse, 2000.

Bresler, Henri. "Henri Labrouste. Les leçons de l'élève et du maître." In *L'Architecture et la ville. Mélanges offerts à Bernard Huet*, edited by Emmanuelle Sarrazin. Paris: École d'architecture de Paris-Belleville/Éditions du Linteau, 2000.

Bressani, Martin. "Projet de Labrouste pour le tombeau de l'empereur Napoléon. Essai d'interprétation symbolique de l'architecture romantique." *Revue de l'art*, no. 125 (1999): 54–63.

———. "Le discours sur le mythe dans la pensée architecturale romantique en France." In *L'Architecture, les sciences et la culture de l'histoire au XIXe siècle*. Saint-Étienne: Publications de l'université de Saint-Étienne, 2001.

———. "The Hybrid: Labrouste's Paestum." In *Chora. Intervals in the Philosophy of Architecture*, edited by Alberto Pérez-Gómez et Stephen Parcell. Vol. 7. Montréal and Kingston: McGill-Queen's University Press, 2007.

Bressani, Martin, and **Marc Grignon.** "Henri Labrouste and the Lure of the Real: Romanticism, Rationalism and the Bibliothèque Sainte-Geneviève." *Art History* 28, no. 5 (November 2005): 712–51.

———. "Les fantasmagories du gaz d'éclairage à Paris au xixe siècle." In *Spielraum. Walter Benjamin et l'architecture*, edited by Libero Andreotti. Paris: Éditions de La Villette, 2011.

Cain, Julien, Jean Vallery-Radot, and **Roger-Armand Weigert.** *Labrouste. Architecte de la Biblothèque [sic] Nationale de 1854 à 1875*. Paris: Bibliothèque Nationale, 1953.

Caisse Nationale des Monuments Historiques. "Henri Labrouste." Special issue, *Les Monuments historiques de la France* 6 (1975).

Calonne, Alphonse de. "[Beaux-Arts. Études sur l'art contemporain. I. L'architecture dans Paris] Bibliothèque Sainte-Geneviève." *Revue contemporaine*, 2nd year, vol. 7 (April–May 1853): 462–70.

Celada, Gianni. *Documentazione sul l'architetto Henri Labrouste e la sua opera*. Unpublished manuscript, n.d. [c. 1959].

Chabat, Pierre. *Fragments d'architecture*. Paris, A. Morel, 1868 [–1871].

Chaine, Henri. "La Bibliothèque Sainte-Geneviève à Paris." *L'Union des architectes et des artistes industriels. Journal bi-mensuel de l'Union syndicale des architectes français*, 2nd ser., 11th year, no. 1 (May 15, 1902): 4–5.

Cifarelli, Francesco Mari, and **Carla Ciccozzi**. "Henry Labrouste a Segni." In *Lazio e Sabina. 6 ("Atti del Convegno : Sesto Incontro di Studi sul Lazio e la Sabina, Roma, 4-6 marzo 2009")*, edited by Giuseppina Ghini. Rome: Edizioni Quasar, 2010.

Cockerell, Fred. P. "Biographical Notices of Deceased Foreign Members." In *Sessional Papers Read at the Royal Institute of British Architects: 1875–76*. London: Royal Institute of British Architects, 1876.

Cozic, Henri. "Nouvelle salle de lecture de la Bibliothèque impériale." *L'Illustration. Journal universel*, 26th year, vol. 51, no. 1318 (May 30, 1868): 341, 343–46, ill.

Craig, Robert M. "Medieval Historicism Amidst Pioneer Modernism: Works by Labrouste and Perret." *Southeastern College Art Conference Review* 10, no. 2 (Spring 1982): 75–79.

Daly, César. "Cérémonie de la Translation des Cendres de l'Empereur Napoléon." *Revue générale de l'architecture et des travaux publics* 2 (January 1841): col. 46–48.

———. [C. D.]. "Candélabres du pont de la Concorde." *Revue générale de l'architecture et des travaux publics* 2 (July 1841): col. 377–79, pl. 16.

———. "Exposition des projets de tombeau pour Napoléon." *Revue générale de l'architecture et des travaux publics* 2 (October 1841): col. 521–28; (November 1841): col. 571–81; (December 1841): col. 593–629, pl. 32.

———. "Des bibliothèques publiques." *Revue générale de l'architecture et des travaux publics* 8, no. 11/12 (1849–50): col. 415–37, pl. 38–42.

———. "Bibliothèque Sainte-Geneviève." *Revue générale de l'architecture et des travaux publics* 10, no. 11/12 (1852): col. 379–81, pl. 21–27.

———. "Bibliothèque Sainte-Geneviève. (Paris. M. H. Labrouste, arch.)." *Revue générale de l'architecture et des travaux publics* 11, no. 11 (1853): col. 392–93, pl. 30–32.

———. "Vue intérieure d'un tombeau étrusque (Corneto)." *Revue générale de l'architecture et des travaux publics* 20, no.1–2 (1862): col. 3–8, pl. 1–3.

———. "Henri Labrouste, Architecte, Membre de l'Institut." *Revue générale de l'architecture et des travaux publics* 34 (1877): col. 60–63, pl. 21.

———. "[Vieux souvenirs] Une causerie avec Henri Labrouste à propos de l'école de 'la vérité dans l'art.'" *La Semaine des Constructeurs*, 2nd ser., 1st year, no. 52 (June 25, 1887): 613–14.

Dassy, Léon [pseudonyme de Laure Labrouste]. *Protestation contre l'épithète de Bertrand donnée à un maître*. Paris: n.p., 1878.

———. *Compte rendu sur la restauration de Paestum exécutée en 1829 par Henri Labrouste, grand prix d'architecture en 1824, membre de l'Institut*. Paris: J. Baur, 1879.

Dauban. "Restauration extérieure du palais Mazarin (Bibliothèque impériale)", *L'Illustration. Journal universel* 28, no. 699 (July 19, 1856): 37–38, ill.

Delaborde, vicomte Henri. [*Institut de France, Académie des beaux-arts*] *Notice sur la vie et les ouvrages de M. Henri Labrouste. Lue dans la séance publique annuelle du 19 octobre 1878*. Paris: Firmin-Didot, 1878. Also in *Journal officiel de la République française*, 10th year, no. 287 (October 21, 1878): 9874–77, and *Encyclopédie d'architecture. Revue mensuelle des travaux publics et particuliers*, 2nd ser., vol. 7 (1878): 82–88.

Drexler, Arthur, ed. *The Architecture of the Ecole des Beaux-Arts*. New York: The Museum of Modern Art, 1977.

Driskel, Michael Paul. "By Competition or administrative Decree? The Contest for the Tomb of Napoleon in 1841." *Art Journal* vol. 48, no. 1 (Spring 1989): 46–52.

———. *As Befits a Legend: Building a Tomb for Napoleon, 1840–1861*. Kent, Ohio: The Kent State University Press, 1993.

Dubbini, Renzo. *Architettura delle prigioni. I luoghi e il tempo della punizione (1700–1880)*. Milan: Franco Angeli, 1986.

———. "Le parole e il monumento. La Bibliothèque Sainte-Geneviève commentata da Henri Labrouste." *Annali della Scuola Normale Superiore di Pisa. Classe di Lettere e Filosofia*, 5th ser., no. 1 (2009): 105–19, ill.

Dubbini, Renzo, ed. *Henri Labrouste, 1801–1875*. Milan: Electa, 2002.

Dufournet, Paul, Claudine de Vaulchier, and **Gilbert Dumas**. *Académie d'Architecture. Catalogue des collections*. Vol. 1. Paris: Académie d'architecture, 1987.

Duplessis, Georges [G. D.]. "Correspondance de M. Lassus avec M. Ingres au sujet du portrait de M. Labrouste (1852)." In *Nouvelles Archives de l'art français. Année 1873*. Paris: J. Baur, 1873.

[Envois de Rome]. *Pompéi. Travaux et envois des architectes français au XIXe siècle*. Paris: École nationale supérieure des beaux-arts/École française de Rome, 1981.

[Envois de Rome]. *Paris-Rome-Athènes. Le voyage en Grèce des architectes français aux XIXe et XXe siècles*. Paris: École nationale supérieure des beaux-arts, 1982.

[Envois de Rome]. *Roma Antiqua. Forum. Colisée. Palatin*. Rome: École française de Rome; Paris: École nationale supérieure des beaux-arts, 1985.

[Envois de Rome]. *Italia Antiqua. Envois de Rome des architectes français en Italie et dans le monde méditerranéen aux XIXe et XXe siècles*. Paris: École nationale supérieure des beaux-arts, 2002.

d'Espouy, Hector. *Fragments d'architecture antique d'après les relevés & restaurations des anciens pensionnaires de l'Académie de France à Rome*. Vols. 1 and 2. Paris: Charles Schmid, n.d.

Étievant, Camille. "La Bibliothèque Impériale." *Le Monde illustré*, 12th year, no. 568 (February 29, 1868): 133, ill.

Fortier, Bruno. *La Métropole imaginaire. Un atlas de Paris*. Liège and Bruxelles: Pierre Mardaga, 1989.

Fossier, François, Isabelle Chave, and **Jacques Kuhnmunch**, eds. *Horace Vernet. 1829–1834*. Saint-Haon-le-Vieux: Le Puits aux Livres, 2010.

Foucart, Bruno. "Henri Labrouste par-delà les doctrines." In *Académie d'architecture. Écrits et conférences*. Paris: Académie d'architecture, 1978.

Foucaud, Jean-François. "Extensions et travaux de la Bibliothèque nationale." In *Histoire des bibliothèques françaises*, edited by Dominique Varry, vol. 3, *Les bibliothèques de la Révolution et du XIXe siècle. 1789–1914*. Paris: Promodis-Éditions du Cercle de la Librairie, 1991.

Fussinger, Catherine, and **Deodaat Tevaearai**. *Lieux de folie. Monuments de raison. Architecture et psychiatrie en Suisse romande, 1830–1930*. Lausanne: Presses polytechniques et universitaires romandes, 1998.

Gaiani, Marco. "Il Voyage d'Italie di Henri Labrouste." *Casabella*, 55th year, no. 581 (July–August 1991): 29-30.

———. "Henri Labrouste e il progetto della citta antica, Voyage d'Italie 1824–1830." *Parametro*, no. 206 (January–February 1995): 14–69.

Gargiani, Roberto. "Ornamento e costruzione nella biblioteca Sainte-Genevieve, Parigi, 1839–1850." *Casabella*, 61st year, no. 645 (May 1997): 60–73.

Giedion, Sigfried. *Bauen in Frankreich. Bauen in Eisen. Bauen in Eisenbeton*. Leipzig and Berlin: Klinkhardt & Biermann, 1928. (English-language edition: *Building in France, Building in Iron, Building in Ferroconcrete*. Santa Monica, Calif.: Getty Center for the History of Art and the Humanities, 1995; French-language edition: *Construire en France. Construire en fer. Construire en béton*. Paris: Éditions de La Villette, 2000.)

———. *Space, Time, and Architecture: The Growth of a New Tradition*. Cambridge, Mass.: Harvard University Press, 1941. (French-language edition: *Espace, temps, architecture. La naissance d'une nouvelle tradition*. Bruxelles: La Connaissance, 1968.)

Giedion, Siegfried [sic]. "Labrouste. 1801–1875." In *Les Architectes célèbres*, edited by Pierre Francastel. Vol. 2. Paris: Éditions d'art Lucien Mazenod, 1959.

Gosset, Alphonse. *Les Coupoles d'orient et d'occident. Étude historique, théorique et pratique*. Paris: A. Lévy, 1889.

Gourlier, Charles, Jean-Marie-Dieudonné Biet, Edme-Jean-Louis Grillon, and **Jean-Jacques Tardieu**.

"Édifices d'instruction publique." In *Choix d'édifices publics projetés et construits en France depuis le commencement du XIXe siècle*. Vol. 3. Paris: Louis Colas, 1845–50.

Grieder, Josephine. "The Search for the Néo-Grec in Second Empire Paris." *Journal of the Society of Architectural Historians* 70, no. 2 (June 2011): 175–89.

Guadet, Julien. "Un souvenir d'Henri Labrouste." *L'Architecture. Journal hebdomadaire de la Société centrale des architectes français*, 3rd year, no. 39 (September 27, 1890): 465–66.

Haumesser, Laurent. "Les architectes français et les relevés de tombes étrusques: Félix Duban et Albert Lenoir." *Studi Etruschi*, vol. 72, 3rd ser. (2006/2007): 3–46, pl. 1–12.

Hautecœur, Louis. *Histoire de l'architecture classique en France*. Vol. 6, *La Restauration et le gouvernement de Juillet. 1815–1848*. Paris: A. et J. Picard, 1955.

———. *Histoire de l'architecture classique en France*. Vol. 7, *La Fin de l'architecture classique. 1848–1900*. Paris: A. et J. Picard, 1955.

Hermant, Achille. "La Bibliothèque Sainte-Geneviève." *L'Artiste*, 5th ser., vol. 7 (December 1, 1851): 129–31.

———. "[Architecture] La nouvelle salle de la Bibliothèque Impériale." *Revue internationale de l'art et de la curiosité* (March 15, 1869): 217–31.

Heurgon, Jacques. "La découverte des Étrusques au début du XIXe siècle." *Comptes-rendus des séances de l'Académie des inscriptions et belles-lettres*, 117th year, no. 4 (1973): 591–600.

Huard, Étienne. "Concours pour le monument de Napoléon." *Journal des Artistes*, 15th year, vol. 2, no. 18 (October 31, 1841): 273–75; no. 19 (November 7, 1841): 289–93; no. 20 (November 14, 1841): 308–9.

Humbert, Jean-Marcel, ed. *Napoléon aux Invalides. 1840, Le Retour des Cendres*. Thonon-les-Bains: Éditions de l'Albaron; Paris: Musée de l'Armée, 1990.

Jannot, Jean-René. "La tombe de la Mercareccia à Tarquinia." *Revue belge de philologie et d'histoire* 60, no. 1 (1982): 101–35.

Jong, Sigrid de. "Staging Ruins: Paestum and Theatricality." *Art History* 33, no. 2 (April 2010): 334–51.

Laborde, comte Léon de. *De l'organisation des bibliothèques dans Paris*. Eighth letter, "Étude sur la construction des Bibliothèques." Paris: A. Franck, April 1845.

———. *De l'organisation des bibliothèques dans Paris*. Fourth letter, "Le Palais Mazarin et les Habitations de ville et de campagne au dix-septième siècle." Paris: A. Franck, December 1845.

Labrouste, Henri. "[Mélanges] Travaux des Élèves de l'École d'Architecture de Paris, pendant l'année 1839." *Revue générale de l'architecture et des travaux publics* 1 (January 1840): col. 58–60.

———. "[École des Beaux-Arts] Travaux des Élèves de l'École d'Architecture de Paris et de l'Académie de France à Rome." *Revue générale de l'architecture et des travaux publics* 1 (September 1840): col. 543–47.

——— [H. L.], "[École des Beaux-Arts] Concours pour le Grand Prix d'Architecture." *Revue générale de l'architecture et des travaux publics* 1 (September 1840): col. 547–48.

———. "A M. le Directeur de la *Revue d'Architecture*." *Revue générale de l'architecture et des travaux publics* 10, no. 11/12 (1852): col. 381–84.

———. "Tombeau d'Albouse." A M. le Directeur de la *Revue d'Architecture*. *Revue générale de l'architecture et des travaux publics* 11, no. 1 (1853): col. 43–44, pl. 6.

———. *[Institut de France, Académie des beaux-arts] Notice sur M. Hittorff. Lue dans la séance ordinaire du 29 août 1868*. Paris: Firmin-Didot, [1868].

———. *Restaurations des monuments antiques par les architectes pensionnaires de l'Académie de France à Rome depuis 1788 jusqu'à nos jours: Temples de Paestum par Labrouste*. Paris: Firmin-Didot, 1877.

[Labrouste, Laure]. *Souvenirs d'Henri Labrouste. Architecte. Membre de l'Institut. Notes recueillies et classées par ses Enfants*. Fontainebleau: n.p., 1928 (n'a pas été mis en vente).

Labrouste, Laure, see also Dassy, Léon.

Labrouste, Léon. "Bibliothèque nationale, rue de Richelieu, à Paris, par M. H. Labrouste, membre de l'Institut."

Revue générale de l'architecture et des travaux publics 35 (1878): col. 144–52, pl. 40–42.

———. "Bibliothèque nationale, à Paris. Bâtiments sur la cour d'honneur (XVIIIe siècle)." *Revue générale de l'architecture et des travaux publics* 36 (1879): col. 3–4, pl. 1–3.

———. *La Bibliothèque Nationale. Ses bâtiments et ses constructions*. Paris: H. Lutier, 1885 (n'a pas été mis en vente).

———. *Esthétique monumentale*. Paris: Charles Schmid, 1902.

Lamathière, **Théophile**. *Panthéon de la Légion d'honneur [Les Labrouste]*. Paris: n.d. [c. 1911], unpaginated plate.

Laviron, **Gabriel**. "Translation des restes mortels de l'empereur Napoléon." *L'Artiste*, 2nd ser., vol. 6, no. 25 (1840): 390–97.

Lebarbé, **Annabelle**. "Le collège Sainte-Barbe de Paris: Des frères Labrouste à Ernest Lheureux." *Livraisons d'histoire de l'architecture*, no. 13 (2007): 137–48.

Le Cœur, **Marc**. "Le fonds d'archives de l'architecte Henri Labrouste." *Revue de la Bibliothèque nationale de France*, no. 30 (2008): 21–29.

Leliman, **Johannes Hermanus W**. "Henri Labrouste. 1801–1875." *Bouwkundig Weekblad*, 21st year, no. 2 (January 12, 1901): 9–12; no. 3 (January 19, 1901): 18–21, ill.

Leniaud, **Jean-Michel**. "La cité utopie ou l'asile dans la première moitié du XIXe siècle." *Conférences de l'Institut d'histoire de la médecine de Lyon. Cycle 1982–1983*. Lyon: Institut d'histoire de la médecine, 1983.

———. *Les Cathédrales au XIXe siècle. Étude du service des édifices diocésains*. Paris: Economica/Caisse nationale des monuments historiques et des sites, 1993.

———, ed. *Des palais pour les livres. Labrouste, Sainte-Geneviève et les bibliothèques*. Paris: Bibliothèque Sainte-Geneviève/Maisonneuve & Larose, 2002.

Leniaud, **Jean-Michel**, **Béatrice Bouvier**, and **François Fossier**, eds. *Procès-verbaux de l'Académie des beaux-arts*. Vol. 3. Paris: École des chartes, 2003.

Leniaud, **Jean-Michel**, dir., and **François Naud**, eds. *Procès-verbaux de l'Académie des beaux-arts*. Vol. 5. Paris: École des chartes, 2004.

Leniaud, **Jean-Michel**, dir., **Béatrice Bouvier**, and **François Fossier**, eds. *Procès-verbaux de l'Académie des beaux-arts*. Vol. 4. Paris: École des chartes, 2005.

Le Normand-Romain, **Antoinette**, **François Fossier**, and **Mehdi Korchane**. *Pierre-Narcisse Guérin. 1823–1828*. Troyes: Le Trait d'Union, 2005.

Lesage, **Claire**. "Henri Labrouste et le département des Imprimés." In *Mélanges autour de l'histoire des livres imprimés et périodiques*, edited by Bruno Blasselle and Laurent Portes. Paris: Bibliothèque nationale de France, 1998.

Levine, **Neil**. "Architectural Reasoning in the Age of Positivism: The Néo-Grec Idea of Henri Labrouste's Bibliothèque Sainte-Geneviève." PhD diss., Yale University, 1975.

———. "The Romantic Idea of Architectural Legibility: Henri Labrouste and the Néo-Grec." In *The Architecture of the Ecole des Beaux-Arts*, edited by Arthur Drexler, 325–416. New York: The Museum of Modern Art, 1977.

———. "The Competition for the Grand Prix in 1824: A Case Study in Architectural Education at the Ecole des Beaux-Arts." In *The Beaux-Arts and Nineteenth-Century French Architecture*, edited by Robin Middleton, 67–123. Cambridge, Mass.: MIT Press, 1982.

———. "The Book and the Building: Hugo's Theory of Architecture and Labrouste's Bibliothèque Ste-Geneviève." In *The Beaux-Arts and Nineteenth-Century French Architecture*, edited by Robin Middleton, 139–73. Cambridge, Mass.: MIT Press, 1982.

———. *Modern Architecture: Representation & Reality*. New Haven: Yale University Press, 2009.

———. "The Template of Photography in Nineteenth-Century Architectural Representation." *Journal of the Society of Architectural Historians* 71, no. 3 (September 2012): 308–33.

Loach, **Judi**. "On Words and Walls." In *An Interregnum of the Sign. The Emblematic Age in France. Essays in Honour of Daniel S. Russell*, edited by David Graham, 149–70. Glasgow: University of Glasgow, 2001.

Loyer, François. "(Pierre-François-)Henri Labrouste." In *The Dictionary of Art*, edited by Jane Turner, 581–84. Vol. 18. New York: Grove, 1996.

Lubtchansky, Natacha. "I fratelli Labrouste e la scoperta della pittura etrusca." *Bollettino d'Arte*, 89th year, 6th ser., no. 130 (October–December 2004): 11–24.

———. "Voyageurs français à Corneto 1825–1850." In *Du voyage savant aux territoires de l'archéologie. Voyageurs, amateurs et savants à l'origine de l'archéologue moderne*, edited by Manuel Royo, Martine Denoyelle, Emmanuelle Hindy-Champion, and David Louyot, 187–216. Paris: De Boccard, 2011.

Lucas, Charles [Ch. L.]. "Henri Labrouste. Lettres inédites sur l'enseignement de l'architecture (Paris, 1830–1831)." *La Construction moderne*, 10th year, no. 22 (March 2, 1895): 253–55; no. 23 (March 9, 1895): 268–69.

Malcotte, Léon. "La jeunesse d'Henri Labrouste." *La Construction moderne*, 69th year, no. 9 (September 1953): 326–29.

Margherita, Daria. *Au sud de l'Italie. Interazioni tra Francia e Italia Meridionale nella cultura architettonica tra i secoli XVIII e XIX*. Naples: Grimaldi & C., 2008.

Maytham, Thomas N. *Henri Labrouste, Architect: A Bibliography*. Charlottesville, Va.: American Association of Architectural Bibliographers, 1955.

Mertens, Dieter. "I templi di Paestum paradigmi per lo studio dell'architettura classica." In *Architettura pubblica e privata nell'Italia antica*, edited by Lorenzo Quilici and Stefania Quilici Gigli, 143–61. Rome: L'Erma di Bretschneider, 2007.

Middleton, Robin. "Henri Labrouste." *International Architect* 1, no. 3 (1980): 40–46.

———, ed. *The Beaux-Arts and Nineteenth-Century French Architecture*. Cambridge, Mass.: MIT Press, 1982.

———. "The Iron Structure of the Bibliothèque Sainte-Geneviève as the Basis of a Civic Décor." *AA Files*, no. 40 (winter 1999): 33–52. (Italian-language publication: "La struttura in ferro della Bibliothèque Sainte-Geneviève come base di un decoro civico." In *Henri Labrouste, 1801–1875*, edited by Renzo Dubbini, 121–42. Milan: Electa, 2002.)

Millet, Eugène. "Notice sur la vie et les travaux de Pierre-François-Henry [sic] Labrouste. Membre de l'Institut, Président de la Société centrale des Architectes." *Bulletin mensuel de la Société centrale des architectes*, 5th ser., vol. 3 (1879–80): 203–19.

Normand, Louis-Marie. *Paris modern*. Vol. 4. Paris: Normand, 1857.

Oppermann, Charles-Alfred. "[Notes et documents] La nouvelle Salle de lecture de la Bibliothèque Impériale de Paris." *Nouvelles Annales de la construction*, 15th year, no. 169 (January 1869): col. 1–3, pl. 1–2.

———. "[Notes et documents] Nouvelle Salle de lecture de la Bibliothèque Impériale." *Nouvelles Annales de la construction*, 15th year, no. 173 (May 1869): col. 42, pl. 21.

Peyré, Yves. *La Bibliothèque Sainte-Geneviève à travers les siècles*. Paris: Gallimard, 2011.

———. *Le Rétablissement d'une architecture. Honneur à Labrouste*. Paris: Bibliothèque Sainte-Geneviève, 2011.

Piland, Sherry. "A Positivist Reading of Labrouste's Bibliothèque Sainte-Geneviève," *Athanor*, no. 10 (1991): 45–51.

Pinon, Pierre, and François-Xavier Amprimoz. *Les Envois de Rome (1778–1968). Architecture et archéologie*. Rome: École française de Rome, 1988.

Plouin, Renée. *Henry Labrouste, sa vie, son œuvre (1801–1875)*. 5 vols. Paris: Faculté des lettres et sciences humaines, 1965.

———. "Les grandes bibliothèques parisiennes au XIXe siècle." *Médecine de France*, no. 181 (1967).

Pocquet du Haut-Jussé, Barthélémy-Amédée. "Préliminaire de la construction du séminaire de Rennes (faculté des lettres) par Henri Labrouste." *Annales de Bretagne* 61, no. 1 (1954): 96–110.

———. *Visites et excursions à Rennes et aux alentours*. Mayenne: Joseph Floc, 1974.

Quicherat, Jules. *Histoire de Sainte-Barbe. Collège, communauté, institution*. Paris: Hachette, 1864.

Rapetti, Silvia. "La nascita dei 'penitenziari' nel Regno Sardo: la riforma carlo-albertina e le carceri di Alessandria e di Oneglia." *Bollettino della Società Piemontese di Archeologia e Belle Arti*, no. 48, 1996 (1998): 323–43, ill. 1–11.

Reynaud, Léonce. *Traité d'architecture*, 1st part ("Éléments des édifices"). Paris: Carilian-Gœury et Victor Dalmont, 1850; 2nd part ("Édifices"). Paris: Victor Dalmont, 1858 (2nd ed.: Paris: Dalmont et Dunod, puis Dunod, 1860–63; 3rd ed.: Paris: Dunod, 1867–70).

Rosengarten, Albrecht/Albert. "Die Bibliothek Ste. Geneviève in Paris." *Allgemeine Bauzeitung*, 16th year (1851).

Roux-Spitz, Michel. "La Bibliothèque nationale de Paris." *L'Architecture d'aujourd'hui*, 9th year, no. 3 (March 1938): 30–45.

———. "Bibliothèque nationale. Campagne de transformations effectuées suivant un plan d'ensemble de 1932 à 1939." In *Réalisations*, 13–40, pl. 22–42. Vol. 2. Paris: Vincent, Fréal & Cie, 1951.

———. "Surélévation du grand Magasin Central des Imprimés à la Bibliothèque Nationale [1955]." In *Réalisations*, 37–42. Vol. 3. Paris: Vincent, Fréal & Cie, 1959.

Roze, Jean-Pierre. "Henri Labrouste et les bibliothèques." *Revue de la Bibliothèque nationale de France*, no. 8 (2001).

Saboya, Marc. *Presse et architecture au XIXe siècle. César Daly et la Revue générale de l'architecture et des travaux publics*. Paris: Picard, 1991.

Saddy, Pierre. "Labrouste: un hospice d'aliénés." *AMC. Architecture Mouvement Continuité*, no. 38 (1976): 40–41.

———. *Henri Labrouste. Architecte. 1801–1875*. Paris: Caisse nationale des monuments historiques et des sites, 1977.

Semper, Gottfried. "Der Wintergarten zu Paris." *Zeitschrift für praktische Baukunst* 9 (1849): 516–28; reprinted as "Ueber Wintergärten" in Gottfried Semper, *Kleine Schriften*. Berlin and Stuttgart: W. Spemann, 1884.

Tampieri, Maria Grazia. "La Bibliothèque Impériale a Parigi di Henri Labrouste, 1854–1875." PhD diss., Università degli Studi di Firenze, 1996.

———. "La Bibliothèque Impériale di Henri Labrouste (1854–1875)." Special issue, *Parametro. Rivista internazionale di Architettura e Urbanistica*, no. 218 (March–April 1997).

Texier, Edmond. *Tableau de Paris*. Vol. 2. Paris: Paulin et Le Chevalier, 1853.

Trélat, Émile. Untitled speech, *École spéciale d'architecture. Séance d'ouverture. 9 novembre 1875. Présidence de M. Bardoux*. Paris: Siège de l'École, 1875.

Trianon, Henry. "Nouvelle bibliothèque Sainte-Geneviève." *L'Illustration. Journal universel* 17, no. 411 (January 11, 1851): 29–30, ill.

[Van Brunt, Henry]. "Greek Lines." *The Atlantic Monthly* 7, no. 44 (June 1861): 654–67; vol. 7, no. 45 (July 1861): 76–88; reprinted as Henry Van Brunt, *Greek Lines, and Other Architectural Essays*. Boston: Houghton, Mifflin, 1893.

Van Eck, Caroline. "What was Revolutionary about the Romantic Pensionnaires: The Role of Biology in the Work of Labrouste, Vaudoyer and Reynaud." In *L'Architecture, les sciences et la culture de l'histoire au XIXe siècle*. Saint-Étienne: Publications de l'université de Saint-Étienne, 2001.

Van Zanten, David. "Architectural Ornament: On, In, and Through the Wall." In *Ornament*, edited by Stephen Kieran, 49–56. Philadelphia: The Graduate School of Fine Arts, University of Pennsylvania, 1977.

———. "Architecture" and "Pierre-François-Henri Labrouste." In *L'Art en France sous le Second Empire*, 57–65 and 81–83. Paris: Réunion des musées nationaux, 1979. (American edition: *The Second Empire, 1852–1870: Art in France under Napoleon III*. Philadelphia and Detroit: Philadelphia Museum of Art/The Detroit Institute of Arts, 1978.)

———. "Labrouste, Henri." In *Macmillan Encyclopedia of Architects*, edited by Adolf K. Placzek, 592–96. Vol. 2. New York: Free Press; London: Collier Macmillan, 1982.

———. *Designing Paris: The Architecture of Duban, Labrouste, Duc, and Vaudoyer*. Cambridge, Mass.: MIT Press, 1987.

———. *Building Paris: Architectural Institutions and the Transformation of the French Capital, 1830–1870*. Cambridge, Mass.: Cambridge University Press, 1994.

Vaudoyer, Antoine-Laurent-Thomas, and **Louis-Pierre Baltard**. *Grands Prix d'architecture. Projets couronnés par l'Académie royale des beaux-arts de France*. Vol. 2, *Grands Prix de 1816 à 1831 inclusivement*. Paris: n.p., 1834.

Veillard, Jean-Yves. *Rennes au XIXe siècle. Architectes, urbanisme et architecture*. Rennes: Éditions du Thabor, 1978.

Vendredi-Auzanneau, Christine, and **Alain Colas**. *Visions. Bibliothèque Sainte-Geneviève*. Paris: Bibliothèque Sainte-Geneviève, 2002.

Vernoy, Henri. "La Bibliothèque nationale. Nouvelle façade sur la rue de Richelieu." *L'Univers illustré*, 16th year, no. 934 (February 15, 1873): 97, 102, ill.

Viollet-le-Duc, Eugène-Emmanuel. "Lettres extra-parlementaires." *Le XIXe siècle*, 7th year, no. 1909 (March 5, 1877 [letter VII]); no 1917 (March 13, 1877 [letter VIII]); no. 1925 (March 21, 1877 [letter IX]).

Watteville, Adolphe de. "La colonie agricole de Saint-Firmin." *Revue des Deux Mondes*, 14th year, vol. 12 (December 15, 1845): 1082–90.

LABROUSTE AND HIS ARCHIVES

In the last years of his life, Henri Labrouste became concerned with the fate of his archives, notably his drawings, which he had long left "available to all"[1]: they were, to him, "the best thing [he had done]" and "the best part of [his] legacy."[2] In 1866, he considered bequeathing them to Julien Thobois, one of his former students who had become his chief collaborator, "requiring him to give them after his death or when he sees fit to a young architect of his choice, on condition that that man should himself hand them on to another young architect without changing anything about the categorization of the drawings and engravings." He would change his mind three years later and limit himself to giving "full ownership, unconditionally ... ten large or small drawings of [their] choice" to four architects trained in his workshop, "as a testament to [his] memory of and affection for [his] former students": along with the loyal Thobois, the legatees this time were Emile Boeswillwald (1815–1896), Charles-Jules Simonet (1826–1896), and Maximilien Mimey (1826–1888). Finally, once again rethinking his choice, he abandoned the idea of handing down all or part of his archives to his young colleagues. In March 1872, he said that "[his] office and what it contains—books, engravings, drawings, etc." would go to his daughter Laure. Then, in May of that year, he extended his bequest to his son Léon, himself an architect. After their father's death on June 24, 1875, Laure and Léon Labrouste would thus share his collection. Thanks to the generosity of their own heirs, the totality of the architect's archives is now divided between several Paris institutions. The Bibliothèque Nationale de France, the Académie d'Architecture, and the Bibliothèque Sainte-Geneviève have a majority of the holdings.

THE LABROUSTE COLLECTION AT THE BNF

Held in the department of Prints and Photography, this collection of around four thousand documents is partly drawn from archives donated by the descendants of Henri Labrouste in 1952,[3] and in 2009–11.[4] It is made up of three distinct groups.

The hundreds of renderings of ancient monuments the architect produced during his stay at the Villa Medici (1825–30) were first considered of interest for their purely documentary value: in 1953, Jean Vallery-Radot, then head curator of the Prints Department, saw them as "a particularly precious addition to our already rich collections of Italian topography."[5] This exceptional collection was thus long interspersed among the volumes in the topographical series rather than kept together as a whole. It was reconstituted as a monographic collection nearly sixty years later and now consists of ten specific volumes, which should facilitate work on it in the future.[6]

A second series of documents, now categorized and inventoried, sheds light on Labrouste's career itself, his projects and works, as well as his diverse other activities: for building maintenance, advisory roles, competition juries. First, there are many sketches and manuscripts (letters, reports, accounts, etc.) relating to over sixty individual matters, rounded out by different printed materials as well as family papers (personal correspondence of the architect's father and his children, photographic portraits, cards, etc.)[7]; then there are the major drawings (preliminary studies, finished plans, or details for scale models), photographs, and prints related to his principal works.[8]

The third set is entirely comprised of documents on the Bibliothèque Nationale.[9] These 721 drawings are the ones Sigfried Giedion thought lost, having looked for them in vain in the 1930s[10]; although they had never left the library, they were only much later returned to the Prints Department. Other drawings by Labrouste and several notes in his own hand are also held in a touching album, acquired from a merchant in 1891 and very likely put together by Félix Perin (1836–1891), Labrouste's last deputy on the Bibliothèque construction site.[11]

Finally, several personal objects of highly symbolic interest have recently joined the archives. Along with several fine medals, a crown of artificial laurel leaves that was awarded him when he won the Grand Prix de Rome for architecture (1824) as well as his Académicien uniform, with cocked hat and sword (1867), are now in the collections.

For this exhibition, all of Labrouste's drawings from Italy as well as all of the documents regarding his work on the Bibliothèque Nationale, restored and digitized, have been put online at http://gallica.bnf.fr. The architect's other drawings and other projects will soon receive the same treatment.

Marc Le Cœur

THE HENRI LABROUSTE COLLECTION AT THE ACADÉMIE D'ARCHITECTURE

The Académie d'Architecture was founded in 1840 as the Société Centrale des Architectes. A cultural institution, its purpose is to promote quality in architecture, work on developing urban space, teaching, and research. The Société Centrale originally housed a library that included periodicals and reviews, medals, engravings, and photographs, to which were added architects' drawings. The purpose of these collections was pedagogical and for publication. It also ensured that documents in danger of dispersion or destruction remained together and were preserved. The Académie d'Architecture pursued that goal and established a first catalogue in 1987 for collections from 1750 to 1900. The catalogue of twentieth-century holdings followed a few years later.

For an exhibition on Labrouste organized in 1976 to commemorate the centenary of his death, Labrouste's heirs gave the Académie many items, which became the Labrouste Collection. Yvonne Labrouste, whose husband was Henri's grandson, made a first donation to the Académie, which she later enlarged. Her donation included Labrouste's *envois* from Rome, renderings of ancient monuments, plans for the Bibliothèque Sainte-Geneviève, and handwritten manuscripts. Around the same time, Léon Malcotte, Henri's great-grandson, gave the Académie many documents as a loan that was later changed to a donation, thus reuniting documents that had remained separated since Labrouste's time. The collection was digitized by the Académie in 2003 and 2004 with support from the French Ministry of Culture and Communication.

The Labrouste collection is made up of different types of documents. It includes around five hundred drawings, sketches, and notebooks; medals; three portraits; two busts; decorations and some personal items; and over a thousand textual documents, both handwritten and printed. The large drawings, often watercolors (from T0 to B3), 414 in number, are the best known. They include submissions from Rome and renderings of ancient monuments, such as the Arch of Septimius Severus in Rome (1829), the Pantheon in Rome (1828), and many others. The collection also includes plans for competitions and buildings. The sixty-two small or very small format sketches, often on precarious materials, were saved by his family. Thirty-one notebooks round out the collection, mostly dating from Labrouste's student years and his stay in Italy. The collection also includes the "Drawings by Friends" album, with work by Jean-Baptiste Lassus, Hippolyte Lebas, and Achille Leclerc.

If the large-format drawings were well known, exhibited and presented to Labrouste's fellow architects and students, the handwritten documents were unknown. There are around a thousand of them.

The correspondence deals with his family life; his professional life; his teaching, which spanned twenty-five years; and his relations with the Société Centrale and with his friends. It is accompanied by reports and letters related to his work as part of the Service des Édifices Diocésains, the Conseil Général des Bâtiments Civils, and the Commission des Monuments Historiques.

These documents shed light on the quality of his consulting work, and those that relate to his teaching show the lasting ties that formed between Labrouste and his students. The rich nature of this additional part of the architect's legacy, which was rediscovered in 2002, mixing as it does private and public topics, as well as being a historic fresco that sheds light on the life of an era, allows us to witness the birth of a new architecture. Gérard Uniack

THE LABROUSTE COLLECTION AT THE BIBLIOTHÈQUE SAINTE-GENEVIÈVE

"As soon as the building was finished, with great satisfaction I burned a huge quantity of papers that filled my boxes—briefs, bills, progress reports, studies, drawings, details—just as after finishing a building, you cart away the rubble."[12]

Henri Labrouste's plans and drawings for the construction of the Bibliothèque Sainte-Geneviève (BSG: MS 4273) make up a collection of nearly 170 documents. Donated by Yvonne Labrouste in 1952, they spent some time in the Bibliothèque Nationale de France before reaching their initially intended destination in 1999. This body of graphic work is a precious source of documentation on the architect's thought process over time and the gestation of his first major building. A protean set of materials, it includes preliminary plans, building diagrams, masonry or metalwork attachments, studies for the décor—all in different stages of completion. If some drawings have a simple structure and subject, others are more complex and allow us to see, along with the initial drawing, a profusion of sketches, notes, and manuscripts in different stages of completion and in varying levels of engagement with the drawing's main theme. A final set offers a number of small drawings, some on tracing paper, mounted in a haphazardly overlapping way on thicker supports, with a pedagogical aim, as part of Labrouste's teaching throughout his career as an architect. One set traces the development of the monument to Ulrich Gering in 1873.

Most of the textual sources (MSS 3910-3939) were given directly to the Bibliothèque Sainte-Geneviève in 1953 by Yvonne Labrouste and Léon Malcotte. In addition to the *Construction Site Journal* (1843–51), there are twenty-nine files concerning the construction and upkeep of the building, which Labrouste would remain responsible for until his death: contractors' memos, furniture inventories, administrative correspondence, etc. In recent years, the collection has at times been enriched by acquisitions from specialized booksellers.

The celebrations in 2001 saw the launch of a program at the library for promoting these sources, whose descriptions were expanded and completed. The graphic works, restored and inventoried item by item,[13] are now available online[14] and will soon be newly digitized to replicate the original works more closely. A restoration of the south facade in 2008 offered a chance to exhibit drawings relating to the structure and decoration of that part of the building on picture rails in the book stacks,[15] and large-scale photographs (by Michel Nguyen) of details of the facade as it was being restored were displayed on the balusters in the reading room's central walkway.[16] Those beginnings are now converging into the development of a "virtual Henri Labrouste library" centered on a critical edition of the *Construction Site Journal*: the presentation of a facsimile with a parallel transcription and critical apparatus to shed light on the text (an index of proper names, a technical glossary compiled from architecture dictionaries and building manuals contemporary with the building's construction aimed at offering, beyond simple definitions, a kind of "Guide to the Art of Building" in the nineteenth century). Marie-Hélène de La Mure

---

1. Millet 1879–80:217.
2. For more detail on this topic, see Le Cœur 2008.
3. Donation by Yvonne Labrouste and Geneviève-Caroline Labrouste, Labrouste's daughter-in-law and daughter, respectively.
4. Donation by Monique Malcotte, widow of the architect Léon Malcotte, himself a great-grandson of Henri Labrouste. These archives had belonged to Laure Labrouste.
5. Cain, Vallery-Radot, and Weigert 1953: no pagination.
6. BNF, Prints, VZ-1030 (1-10)-FOL.
7. BNF, Prints, HZ-465 (1-9)-PET FOL.
8. BNF, Prints, HD-1176 (1-2)-BOITE FOL and HD-1018 (1-2)-FT 6.
9. BNF, Prints, HD-1019 (1-10)-FT 6.
10. Giedion 1941.
11. BNF, Prints, HC-15 (B)-FT 4 ("Plans for the Bibliothèque Nationale").
12. Henri Labrouste to César Daly, "Note de présentation de la Bibliothèque Sainte-Geneviève," *Revue générale de l'architecture et des travaux publics*, vol. X (1852).
13. http://www.calames.abes.fr/pub/ms/Calames-20092241123614O1.
14. http://www.bsg.e-corpus.org/fre/ref/88159/Ms._4273/.
15. http://www-bsg.univ-paris1.fr/www/ExposVirtuelles/expofacade/expo_facade_accueil.html.
16. These images, as well as Labrouste's drafts concerning the facade, make up the iconography in Yves Peyré's album published in 2011, *Le Rétablissement d'une architecture: honneur à Labrouste* (Paris: Bibliothèque Sainte-Geneviève, 2011).

PHOTOGRAPHY CREDITS

© Académie d'architecture, Paris : p. 54, pp. 57–60, p. 67, p. 72, pp. 77–78, p. 81, p. 84 (bottom), p. 100, p. 105 (top), p. 147 (right), p. 163 (left), p. 199, p. 233; © Académie de France, Rome: p. 45; © American Institute of Architects, Washington, D.C.: p. 214; © Archives Nationales de France, Paris (VA/LVI, pièce 11): p. 76; Archives Nationales de France, Paris (N III Seine 1138): p. 171 (left); Archives Nationales de France, Paris (VA/XLV pièce 5): p. 184 (top); © Artedia/Leemage: pp. 102–3; © Avery Architectural & Fine Arts Library, Columbia University, New York: p. 70 (right), p. 195 (top), p. 219; © Jean-Christophe Ballot: p. 147 (left); © Laurent Bessol/MNHN: p. 234; © Bibliothèque centrale, MNHN, Paris: pp. 237–38; © Bibliothèque Sainte-Geneviève/Michel Nguyen: pp. 108–9, p. 128; © Bibliothèque Sainte-Geneviève, Paris: p. 106, p. 107 (right), pp. 110–11, pp. 114–15, pp. 120–21, p. 127, pp. 186–87; © Artedia/Leemage/Luc Boegly: pp. 138–39; © CAPA/MMF: p. 50 (top), p. 105 (bottom), p. 159, p. 225, p. 226 (left), p. 229, p. 235, p. 242, p. 243 (left); © David Paul Carr: p. 149; © CESE/Benoit Fougeirol: pp. 248–49; © Cliché Bibliothèque nationale de France: p. 46 (top), p. 49, p. 50 (bottom), p. 51, p. 52 (right), p. 56 (left), pp. 62–66, p. 68, p. 70 (left), p. 71, p. 84 (top), pp. 86–87, p. 99, p. 104, p. 107 (left), p. 117, pp. 136, 142, p. 146, p. 148, p. 150, pp. 156–58, p. 160 (right), p. 162, p. 163 (right), pp. 173–78, p. 184 (bottom), pp. 196–98, p. 254; © CNAM/SIAF/CAPA/Archives du xxe siècle: p. 243 (right), p. 244, p. 247; © Collection particulière, Paris: p. 242, p. 243 (left); © Commission du Vieux Paris, Paris: p. 239; DIGITAL IMAGE © 2012, The Museum of Modern Art, New York/Scala, Florence: pp. 32–33; Coolidge Baldwin © Courtesy of the Boston Public Library, Print Department: p. 213 (bottom); © École nationale supérieure des beaux-arts, Paris: p. 56 (right), p. 88, pp. 91–93, p. 169, p. 226 (right), p. 230; © Georges Fessy: p. 134, pp. 144–45, p. 161; © Fonds Perret, CNAM/SIAF/CAPA/Archives du xxe siècle/UFSE/SAIF/2012: p. 222, pp. 250–51, p. 253; © Harvard College Library, Houghton Library, Printing and Graphic Arts: p. 168; © Candida Höfer/VG Bild-Kunst, Bonn 1998: pp. 12–13, p. 255; © Institut National d'Histoire de l'Art, Bibliothèque, collections Jacques Doucet: p. 80; Charles Lansiaux © Musée Carnavalet/Roger-Viollet: p. 97, p. 112; © Marc Le Cœur: p. 46 (bottom), p. 137, p. 140, pp. 154–55, p. 167, p. 236; © Alain Le Toquin: p. 21, p. 160 (left); © Neil Levine: p. 172; © Library of Congress, HABS collection, HABS MO, 96–SALU, 49-1: p. 210; © Lindman Photography: p. 24; © Bérangère Lomont: p. 4; © National Gallery of Art, Washington, D.C.: p. 52 (left); © Jean-Claude N'Diaye/LA COLLECTION: p. 42, p. 94, p. 98, p. 113, pp. 123–24, pp. 130–31, p. 180, p. 190; © Nederlands Architectuurinstituut, Rotterdam, Nederlands: p. 200, p. 206, p. 209; © Photononstop/Karl Johaentges: p. 152; © Rijksdienst voor het Cultureel Erfgoed/Cultural Heritage Agency, Amersfoort, Nederlands: p. 195 (bottom), pp. 203–5; © RMN-GP (Musée d'Orsay)/Droits réservés: p. 119; © RMN-GP (Musée d'Orsay)/Hervé Lewandowski: pp. 74–75, pp. 82–83, p. 153, p. 189, p. 192; © RMN-GP (Musée d'Orsay)/Patrice Schmidt: p. 245; © RMN-GP (Médiathèque de l'architecture et du patrimoine): p. 241; © Stadsarchief of Amsterdam/Collection RDCE: p. 207; © The Museum of Modern Art, New York: p. 28, p. 37; © The New York Public Library: p. 215; © The Picture Desk/Collection Dagli-Orti/Pier Luigi Nervi: pp. 38–39; © Ann Van Zanten: pp. 220–21; © David Van Zanten: p. 216.

•••••••••••••••••••

Published in conjunction with the exhibition *Henri Labrouste: Structure Brought to Light*, at The Museum of Modern Art, New York, March 10–June 24, 2013.

The exhibition is supported by The International Council of The Museum of Modern Art.

Produced by the Department of Publications, The Museum of Modern Art, New York

Edited by Ron Broadhurst
Designed by Astrid de l'Aulnoit
Production by Marc Sapir
Printed and bound by CS Graphics Sdn Bhd, Melaka, Malaysia

This book is typeset in Weiss. The paper is 157 gsm Goldeast Matte.

The essays by Corinne Bélier, Martin Bressani, Marie-Hélène de La Mure, François de Mazières, Marc Grignon, Marc Le Cœur, Bertrand Lemoine, Bruno Racine, and Gérard Uniack were translated from the French by Sharon Bowman.

Published by The Museum of Modern Art, New York, 11 West 53 Street, New York, New York, 10019-5497

Library of Congress Control Number: 2012953335
ISBN: 978-0-87070-839-8

Distributed in the United States and Canada by ARTBOOK | D.A.P., New York
155 Sixth Avenue, 2nd floor, New York, NY 10013
www.artbook.com

Distributed outside the United States and Canada by Thames & Hudson Ltd
181A High Holborn, London WC1V 7QX
www.thamesandhudson.com

Page 4: Bibliothèque Nationale, view of the reading room domes from below. Photograph: Bérangère Lomont
Pages 12–13: Candida Höfer, *Bibliothèque Nationale de France Paris XXIII*, 1998
Pages 254–55: Candida Höfer, *Bibliothèque Nationale de France Paris XV*, 1998

Printed in Malaysia